THE LAST SALUTE:
CIVIL AND MILITARY FUNERALS
1921-1969

by
B. C. Mossman
and
M. W. Stark

DEPARTMENT OF THE ARMY
WASHINGTON, D.C., 1971

Library of Congress Catalog Card Number: 77–606843

First Printing

For sale by the Superintendent of Documents, U.S. Government Printing Office
Washington, D.C. 20402 - Price $5.75
Stock Number 0829–0086

Foreword

Our national tradition of honoring prominent officials is never more in evidence than following the death of an American dignitary. The ceremonies of the public funeral salute his accomplishments in life and demonstrate the Nation's recognition of a debt owed for his services.

Long-standing military customs and the wishes of the next of kin are the foundations of these ceremonies. The military departments consequently have important roles in performing last rites, although many other agencies of the Federal Government participate in varying degrees. Collectively, these agencies conduct several types of funerals, ranging from the modest to the elaborate. This gradation permits the Nation to recognize properly the wishes of the next of kin and the rank or public station held by an official prior to or at the time of his demise.

This book presents accounts of funerals conducted for civil and military officials, active and retired, and for the unknown servicemen of three wars between 1921 and 1969. Also described are farewell ceremonies honoring foreign dignitaries who died while on duty in the United States. Since the pattern for present-day public funerals has evolved from these ceremonies, this volume, in addition to being a valuable historical record, contains guidance for arranging final honors.

Washington, D.C.   STANLEY R. RESOR
1 April 1971   Secretary of the Army

The Authors

A graduate of Wayne State (Nebraska), B. C. Mossman is the author of studies and monographs on U.S. Army operations in the Korean War and of two chapters, "Peace Becomes Cold War, 1945–1950," and "The Korean War, 1950–1953," in *American Military History*, a volume in the Army Historical Series. He also contributed to *Origins, History, and Accomplishments of the U.S. Army Reserve*, published by the Historical Evaluation and Research Organization, and to *Challenge and Response in Internal Conflict*, published by the Center for Research on Social Systems, American University.

During World War II Mr. Mossman served as a platoon leader with the 381st Infantry, 96th Infantry Division, and participated in the Leyte and Okinawa campaigns in the Pacific theater. In the Korean War he was a military historian with the Eighth Army, Army Forces, Far East, and the United Nations Command Military Armistice Commission.

Joining the Office of the Chief of Military History as an Army officer in 1954, he became a civilian staff member in 1957. Deputy Chief of the Staff Support Branch, he is presently at work on a volume in the Korean War series.

Warner Stark received the B.A. and M.A. degrees from San José State College. He attended a special one-year program in Military History at the University of California at Davis, where he began working toward his Ph.D. He served in the 49th Infantry Brigade of the California Army National Guard and later with the 820th Engineers and the 199th Signal Group, U.S. Army Reserve. In 1967 he joined the Office of the Chief of Military History where he is working on a volume in the Army's official history of the Vietnam War.

Preface

On 14 December 1799, General George Washington died at Mount Vernon after an illness of only a few hours. The funeral for the nation's first President was held at his home on Wednesday, 18 December.

About 11 o'clk numbers of persons began to assemble to attend the funeral, which was intended to have been at twelve o'clk; but as a great part of the Troops expected could not get down in time it did not take place till 3.—Eleven pieces of Artillery were brought down [from Alexandria].—And a Schooner belonging to Mr. R. Hamilton came down and lay off Mt. Vernon to fire minute guns.—The Pall holders were as follows—Colonels Little, (Charles) Simms, Payne, Gilpin, Ramsay, & Marsteller—and Colo. Blackburne walked before the Corps. [Col. Deneal marched with the military.]

[About three o'clock the procession began to move.] Col. Little, Simms & Deneal and Dr. Dick formed the arrangements of the Procession—[The procession moved out through the gate at the left wing of the house, and proceeded round in front of the lawn, and down to the vault on the right wing of the house.] which was as follows—The Troops—Horse & foot—Music playing a Solemn dirge with muffled Drums.—The Clergy—viz The Revd. Mr. Davis—Mr. (James) Muir, Mr. Moffatt, & Mr. Addison—[The General's horse, with his saddle, holsters, and pistols, led by two grooms, Cyrus and Wilson, in black.] The Body borne by officers & masons who insisted upon carrying it to the grave.—The Principal Mourners—viz. Mrs. Stuart & Mrs. Law—Misses Nancy & Sally Stuart—Miss Fairfax & Miss Dennison—Mr. Law & Mr. Peter—Doctor Craik & T. Lear—Lord Fairfax & Ferdinando Fairfax—Lodge No. 23.—Corporation of Alexandria.—All other persons, preceded by Mr. Anderson, Mr. Rawlins, the Overseers, &c., &c.—

The Rev. Mr. Davis read the service & made a short extemporary speech—The Masons performed their ceremonies—and the Body was deposited in the Vault—All then returned to the House & partook of some refreshment—and dispersed with the greatest good order & regularity . . . .[1]

Since the time of this ceremony in the infancy of the United States, citizens who have held high offices in the federal government and in the military establishment have been honored by public funerals. The military customs observed, many of which are rooted so deeply and distantly in the past as to defeat any tracing of their exact origin, have changed little over the years. The ceremonies themselves have changed with the times.

Contingency plans for several types of funeral ceremonies were published for the first time in 1949. These were revised and refined in 1958, and again in 1965. By no means rigid, the plans have often been altered to conform to the known wishes of an American dignitary and those of his family.

---

[1] The above account was written by Tobias Lear, General Washington's secretary, who participated in the funeral ceremony. Quoted in Worthington Chauncey Ford, ed., *The Writings of George Washington,* vol. 14 (New York: G. P. Putnam's Sons, 1893), pp. 254–55.

The policies and plans governing public funerals are largely based on past experience. This volume presents chapters of that experience covering ceremonies conducted between 1921 and 1969 for twenty-six eminent American officials, four foreign diplomats on assignment in the United States, and the unknown American servicemen killed in World War I, World War II, and the Korean War. The Office of the Chief of Military History, Department of the Army, undertook the preparation of the book in 1968 at the direction of General Harold K. Johnson, Chief of Staff, U.S. Army. The ceremonies to be described were selected in the Office of the Chief of Staff. The volume is intended primarily for use as a reference work by agencies of government involved in arranging and conducting public funerals. As a historical record, it may also serve the interests of a wider government audience and of the general public.

In preparing the manuscript, the authors received considerable help both in and out of the Office of the Chief of Military History. They appreciate the assistance of Dr. David C. Skaggs, associate professor of history at Bowling Green State University, who during a tour of active duty training completed the research and prepared the initial draft of the chapter covering the ceremony for General Hoyt S. Vandenberg, U.S. Air Force. They are especially grateful to Dr. Emma J. Eaton, a former member of the Office of the Chief of Military History, who contributed to the drafts of several chapters, polished others, and located many much-needed photographs.

The authors are deeply indebted to Mr. Paul C. Miller, Chief, Ceremonies and Special Events, Headquarters, Military District of Washington. Besides giving valuable aid to the authors in their search for documentary materials, Mr. Miller contributed the firsthand information so essential to rounding out many of the chapters.

The main editing of the volume was in the experienced and capable hands of Loretto C. Stevens. She was ably assisted by Barbara J. Harris and Christine A. Otten. With highest competence, Mary E. Howard and Dorothy B. Speight typed the initial draft and revisions of the manuscript. The many diagrams were prepared by Mr. Marlin E. Fenical and the draftsmen under his supervision in the office of The Adjutant General.

Notwithstanding the substantial assistance given by many individuals and organizations, the authors alone are responsible for the content of the volume, including any errors of omission or commission.

Washington, D.C.   B. C. MOSSMAN
1 April 1971   M. W. STARK

Contents

Appendixes

Tables

Chart

Diagrams

THE UNKNOWN SOLDIERS OF WORLD WAR II
AND THE KOREAN WAR

DONALD A. QUARLES

JOHN FOSTER DULLES

WILLIAM D. LEAHY

WILLIAM F. HALSEY, JR.

George C. Marshall

Walter Bedell Smith

Edward Drozniak

John F. Kennedy

Douglas MacArthur

Illustrations

THE UNKNOWN SOLDIER OF WORLD WAR I

Stephen T. Early

Robert P. Patterson

Hoyt S. Vandenberg

Peyton C. March

Richard E. Byrd

The Unknown Soldiers of World War II and the Korean War

DONALD A. QUARLES

JOHN FOSTER DULLES

GEORGE C. MARSHALL

FOREIGN AMBASSADORS

JOHN F. KENNEDY

Douglas MacArthur

Herbert C. Hoover

All pictures in this volume are from Department of Defense files.

THE LAST SALUTE:
CIVIL AND MILITARY FUNERALS
1921-1969

CHAPTER I

The Unknown Soldier of World War I
State Funeral
23 October-11 November 1921

The idea of honoring the unknown dead of World War I originated in Europe. France and England first paid such honors on 11 November 1920, and Italy and other European nations soon followed.

The commanding general of American forces in France, Brig. Gen. William D. Connor, learned of the French project while it was still in the planning stage. Favorably impressed, he proposed a similar project for the United States to the Army Chief of Staff, General Peyton C. March, on 29 October 1919.

That General March disapproved General Connor's proposal is suggested by the Chief of Staff's later reply to Mrs. M. M. Melony, editor of the *Delineator*, who made a similar suggestion. General March explained to Mrs. Melony that while the French and English had many unknown dead, it appeared possible that the Army Graves Registration Service eventually would identify all American dead. Furthermore, the United States had no burial place for a fallen hero similar to Westminster Abbey or the *Arc de Triomphe*. In any case, March pointed out, the matter was one for Congress to decide.

On 21 December 1920, Congressman Hamilton Fish, Jr., of New York introduced a resolution calling for the return to the United States of an unknown American soldier killed in France and his burial with appropriate ceremonies in a tomb to be constructed at the Memorial Amphitheater in Arlington National Cemetery. The measure was approved on 4 March 1921 as Public Resolution 67 of the 66th Congress. It included a provision for the construction of the tomb of the unknown soldier at Arlington National Cemetery. As then established, the tomb was to be a simple structure that eventually would serve as the base for an appropriate monument. (It was not until 3 July 1926 that Congress appropriated $50,000 to complete the tomb. The design and a further appropriation were approved on 21 December 1929 and a contract for the work was entered upon. Meanwhile, on 29 February 1929, Congress had granted money for improving the landscape and approaches to the tomb.)

Congressman Fish wanted the burial ceremony for the unknown soldier to be held on Memorial Day, 1921, but on 12 February, while the bill was still before the Senate Committee on Military Affairs, Secretary of War Newton D. Baker informed the committee that the date was premature. He had been advised by the Quartermaster General, who would be in charge of selecting and preparing the body of the unknown soldier, that only 1,237 American dead were still unidentified and that the cases of almost all of these were being investigated. Haste, the Quartermaster General had pointed out, could result in the burial of a body which might later be identified.

Congressman Fish tried again through the new Secretary of War, John W. Weeks, who replaced Baker on 4 March 1921 when President Warren G. Harding took office, to arrange the ceremony, this time for 31 May. But Secretary Weeks upheld Baker's earlier view for the same reasons and chose Armistice Day, 1921, the third anniversary of the war's end, as the appropriate time to conduct the services. In response to this choice, Congress, on 20 October 1921, declared 11 November 1921 a legal holiday to honor all those who participated in World War I; an elaborate ceremony in Washington would pay tribute to the symbolic unknown soldier.

The War Department had charge of ceremonies both overseas and in the United States. Plans for overseas included ceremonies attending the choice of an unknown soldier and the transfer of his body to the Navy for transportation to the United States. In the United States, arrangements were made for receiving the unknown soldier from the Navy at Washington, D.C., for a lying in state ceremony in the Capitol, and for funeral and burial services at Arlington National Cemetery.

On 9 September 1921 the Quartermaster General received orders from the War Department to select an unknown soldier from those buried in France. Following the selection ceremony, he was to deliver the body to Le Havre, where the Navy would receive it for transportation to the United States. The necessary arrangements were completed by the Quartermaster Corps in France in co-operation with French and U.S. Navy authorities. According to plans, the selection ceremony was to take place at Châlons-sur-Marne, ninety miles east of Paris, on 23 October 1921.

After a final search of the records of unknown dead for any evidence of identity, special Quartermaster Corps teams chose four bodies to be exhumed as possible recipients of the honors. Four others were selected as alternates should the exhumation of any of the first four reveal evidence of identity.

The body of an unidentified American was exhumed from each of four American cemeteries—Aisne-Maine, Meuse-Argonne, Somme, and St. Mihiel—on 22 October 1921. Each was examined to ensure that the person had been a member of the American Expeditionary Forces, that he had died of wounds received in combat, and that there were no clues to his identity whatsoever. After mortuary preparation, the bodies were placed in identical caskets and shipping cases. The next day they were carried by truck to Châlons-sur-Marne for the selection ceremony.

At 1500 on 23 October all four caskets arrived by truck at the city hall of Châlons-sur-Marne. Awaiting them was a large delegation of French and American officials. The American group was headed by the Quartermaster General, Maj. Gen. Harry L. Rogers, and included Col. Harry F. Rethers, the chief of the American Graves Registration Service in Europe; Lt. Col. William G. Ball, Quartermaster Corps; Maj. Robert P. Harbold, also of the Quartermaster Corps, who was the officer in charge and controlled all ceremonies; Capt. E. Le Roch, a liaison officer from the French Army; Mr. Keating, the chief supervising embalmer; and representatives of the press. The chief French representatives were General Duport, commanding the French 6th Army Corps; M. Brisac, *Préfet de la Marne*; and M. Servas, *Maire de Châlons-sur-Marne*.

Members of the American Quartermaster Corps and town officials had prepared the city hall for the selection ceremony. The outside of the building was decorated with French and American flags; inside, the aisles and corridors were ornamented with palms, potted trees, and flags, and a catafalque had been constructed and set up in the main hall. Another room was decorated for the reception of the four unknown soldiers and a third was prepared for the ceremony in which the chosen unknown soldier was to be transferred to a different casket. (*Diagram 1*)

French troops carried the shipping cases from the trucks into the reception room of the city hall. The caskets were then removed, set on top of the cases, and draped with American flags. A French guard of honor stood watch until 2200 when six American pallbearers arrived from Headquarters, American Forces in Germany, at Coblenz. From this time on, a combined American-French guard maintained constant vigil.

Early on the morning of 24 October Major Harbold, aided by French and American soldiers, rearranged the caskets so that each rested on a shipping case other than the one in which it had arrived. There was now little chance that someone would know even the cemetery from which an unidentified body came. Major Harbold then chose Sgt. Edward F. Younger of Headquarters Company, 2d Battalion, 50th Infantry, American Forces in Germany, to select the unknown soldier. Originally, a commissioned officer was to do the choosing, but General Rogers changed the plans after learning that the French had designated an enlisted man to choose their unknown soldier. The choice was delegated to Major Harbold, who then appointed Sergeant Younger.

Before the selection a French military band formed in the city hall courtyard adjoining the reception room. The ceremony began as General Duport led French and American officers and French civil officials to the entrance of the reception room, where they rendered honors to the dead. They then lined the hallway leading to the room.

After General Duport and General Rogers made brief speeches Sergeant Younger led the way from the main hall, carrying a spray of white roses presented by a Frenchman who had lost two sons in the war. As the French band in the

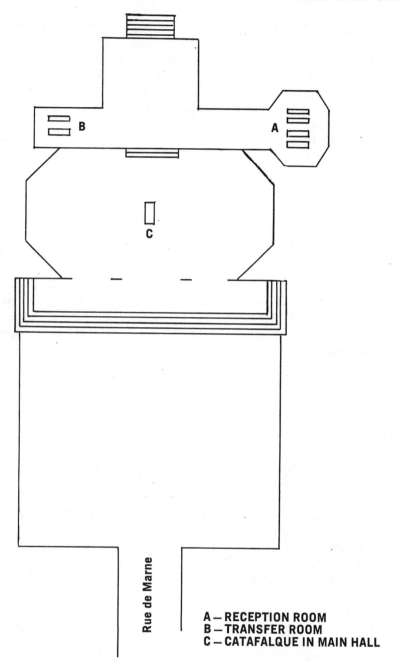

Diagram 1.   City Hall, Châlons-sur-Marne, France, site of the selection
ceremony.

courtyard played a hymn, Younger walked around the caskets several times before placing the roses on one to indicate his selection. He then saluted the chosen unknown American, after which the officials in the hallway, led by General Duport, came forward to present their respects. (The roses that had been placed on the casket remained there and were buried with the unknown American in Arlington.)

Following this ceremony the pallbearers, all Army noncommissioned officers from American units in Germany, moved the casket to the second room where Mr. Keating, in the presence of General Rogers, Colonel Rethers, Colonel Ball, and Major Harbold, transferred the body to a special casket brought from the United States. This casket was then sealed. The empty casket was returned to the reception room, where one of the three remaining bodies was placed in it so that the casket could not be identified. The caskets of the three remaining unknown Americans were then placed in shipping cases and at 1100 were put aboard trucks

CASKET IS CARRIED FROM CITY HALL, CHÂLONS-SUR-MARNE, FRANCE

that took them to Romagne Cemetery, 152 miles east of Paris, for immediate burial.

The casket of the nameless American who was to be honored in the United States as the Unknown Soldier of World War I was draped with an American flag and carried in procession to the catafalque in the main hall. The spray of roses lay on top of the casket and floral tributes were banked around it. An honor guard of six French and five American soldiers and a uniformed representative of the American Legion took post. After the press had been admitted to photograph the catafalque, the room was opened to the public.

According to plans, the Unknown Soldier was to be carried in procession through Châlons-sur-Marne to the railroad station. The casket was then to be put aboard a special funeral train provided by the French government and taken via Paris to Le Havre. The procession through Châlons-sur-Marne was to follow the Rue de Marne, which stretched for almost a mile directly from the city hall entrance to the railroad station. An honor cordon of dismounted French cavalry lined both sides of the route. The military escort of French Army units included a band, a regiment of dragoons, a regiment of infantry, two field artillery battalions, and a motor transportation company. The single American Army unit was from the Quartermaster Corps. Also in the escort were French Boy Scouts, firemen, war veterans, representatives of local societies, and students.

The departure ceremony opened late in the afternoon of 24 October with speeches by the mayor of Châlons-sur-Marne and by Maj. Gen. Henry T. Allen, who came especially for the occasion from Germany where he commanded American forces. The American body bearers then carried the casket of the Unknown Soldier out of the city hall. While the French military band played "Aux Champs" and the escort troops presented arms, the body bearers placed the casket on a caisson. Boy Scouts picked up the flowers that had surrounded the catafalque and took positions near the caisson. After General Allen, General Rogers, Colonel Rethers, General Duport, and other officials joined the cortege, the procession moved to the railroad station at the slow cadence of funeral marches played by the band.

At the station the band played the American national anthem while the body bearers transferred the Unknown Soldier from the caisson to the funeral car of the special train. The train left Châlons-sur-Marne at 1810 and arrived in Paris three hours later, where it remained overnight. Posted as a guard of honor during the night were three American soldiers and a uniformed representative of the American Legion.

On 25 October, after French officials and representatives of patriotic societies had paid their respects and left tributes to the Unknown Soldier, the special train left Paris at midmorning and reached Le Havre about 1300. On hand to escort the Unknown Soldier to the docks were representatives of the French and American governments, an American Army honor guard, a large contingent of French Army troops, a French Army band, a detachment of French sailors, representatives of various French societies and associations, and mounted gendarmes. Thirty French soldiers removed the floral pieces from the train and took position in the column for the procession to the docks. The American body bearers then carried the casket from the funeral car and placed it on a waiting caisson while the band played "Aux Champs" and French school children showered the caisson with flowers. The procession then started for the Pier d'Escale where the cruiser USS *Olympia*, Admiral Dewey's old flagship, waited to take the Unknown Soldier to the United States. En route via the Boulevard Strassbourg, the procession stopped briefly at the city hall where members of the city council presented a wreath to the Unknown Soldier.

At the pier, after speeches by American and French officials and the presentation of the Croix de chevalier de la Légion d'honneur to the Unknown Soldier by M. Maginot, the Minister of Pensions who later inspired the Maginot Line, the body bearers carried the casket to the *Olympia*. A group of American marines on the dock presented arms, and the cruiser's band played the French and American national anthems and Chopin's "Funeral March" as six sailors and two marines relieved the Army body bearers and carried the casket aboard ship. Rear Adm. Lloyd H. Chandler, commanding the *Olympia*, members of his staff, and French and American officials marched behind the casket as it was taken to the stern, which had been decorated. Tributes of flowers, some brought aboard by French school children, were placed around the casket.

The *Olympia*, escorted by the American destroyer *Rueben James* (DD–245 —later the first American warship to be sunk in World War II) and eight French naval vessels, put out to sea at 1520. She received a 17-gun salute as she cleared harbor and another as the French ships dropped astern just outside French territory.

Brig. Gen. Harry H. Bandholtz, commanding the Military District of Washington, was responsible for planning the ceremonies in the United States. On 19 October he published plans for the reception of the Unknown Soldier's body from the Navy at the Washington Navy Yard; its movement in procession to the Capitol on 9 November; the lying in state period in the rotunda, ending 10 November; and the procession to Arlington National Cemetery, funeral service in the Memorial Amphitheater, and burial service at the newly constructed tomb on 11 November.

On a rainy 9 November the *Olympia* sailed up the Potomac River, receiving and returning salutes from military posts along the way, and docked at the Washington Navy Yard about 1600. On hand to receive the body of the Unknown Soldier were General Bandholtz, who was the escort commander; the 3d Cavalry and its mounted band from Fort Myer, Virginia; and military and civil officials, including the Army Chief of Staff, General of the Armies John J. Pershing, Chief of

CEREMONY AT THE PIER, LE HAVRE, FRANCE

Naval Operations, Admiral Robert E. Coontz, Commandant of the Marine
Corps, Maj. Gen. John A. Lejeune, Secretary of War John Weeks, and Secretary
of Navy Edwin Denby.

When the *Olympia* docked, the two squadrons of the 3d Cavalry were already
in line facing the cruiser from the far side of the dock area. To the left of these
squadrons, at a right angle to their line, was the mounted band. After members of
the ship's crew installed the gangplank, the ship's complement of marines and the
band marched off and formed a line at the near edge of the pier facing the cavalry
squadrons. The military and civil dignitaries next aligned themselves at the right
of the cavalrymen and opposite the mounted band, thus completing a box formation.

After Navy buglers aboard the *Olympia* sounded attention, a body bearer detail of marines and sailors from the ship's company carried the casket to the gangplank. Simultaneously, the cruiser commenced firing minute guns and the ship's
band began to play Chopin's "Funeral March."

As the casket was carried through the railings, the boatswain piped the Unknown Soldier ashore in the fashion accorded a full admiral. Admiral Chandler

and his staff in full dress, bareheaded and hats held against their chests, followed the casket. On the dock the civil dignitaries removed their hats as the troops saluted. When the Navy procession cleared the foot of the gangplank, it halted and the boatswain sounded his pipe to signify that the party had left the ship. The ship's band then ceased playing the funeral march, a marine bugler sounded four flourishes, and the ship's band played the national anthem.

At the close of the anthem, the *Olympia*'s band resumed the funeral march while the procession moved through the box formation to a draped caisson standing between the two squadrons of cavalry at the far side. The reception ceremony ended as eight Army body bearers from the 3d Cavalry took the casket from the ship's detail and placed it on the caisson.

The cavalry band, playing "Onward Christian Soldiers," led the procession to the Capitol. Following in order were a squadron of cavalry, the caisson, the remaining cavalry squadron, and the military and civil dignitaries in their automobiles. The route taken by the column through the Washington Navy Yard to the gate was lined on both sides by marines at present arms. Once outside the yard, the procession moved via M Street and New Jersey Avenue to the East Plaza of the Capitol.

At the Capitol the 3d Cavalry formed a line facing the building with a squadron on either side of the plaza driveway at the foot of the east steps. Along each side of the driveway and the steps was an honor cordon of troops from the 13th Engineers, commanded by Maj. Charles P. Gross from Camp Humphreys (later Fort Belvoir), Virginia. Inside the rotunda four honor guards, also from the 13th Engineers, were already posted at the corners of the Lincoln catafalque on which the casket of the Unknown Soldier would rest. In addition to the members of the 13th Engineers who served as honor guards through the night of 9 November, Major Gross had under his command details of one noncommissioned officer and four men each from Army aviation, field artillery, coast artillery, and infantry, and from the Navy, Marine Corps, and District of Columbia National Guard. These details acted as reliefs for the guards at the bier on 10 November. Some 250 marines also joined Major Gross on 10 November for duty outside the building to help control the movement of the public into the Capitol to pay respect.

The horse-drawn caisson stopped before the Capitol steps and the Army body bearers removed the casket, carried it past the honor cordon and into the rotunda, and placed it on the Lincoln catafalque, with the foot of the casket to the west. Walking behind the casket were the military and civil officials who had accompanied the body from the Navy Yard.

Shortly thereafter, President Warren G. Harding and Mrs. Harding walked up the east steps through the honor cordon and entered the rotunda. Mrs. Harding placed a wide white band of ribbon, which she had made herself, on the casket. President Harding then stepped forward, pinned a silver National Shield with forty-eight gold stars to the ribbon, and placed a great wreath of crimson

CASKET IS CARRIED DOWN EAST STEPS OF THE CAPITOL

roses on the casket. Vice President Calvin Coolidge and Speaker of the House Frederick H. Gillette next advanced together followed by Chief Justice William H. Taft, Secretary Weeks, and Secretary Denby, in that order, and placed wreaths for the Congress, Supreme Court, Army, and Navy, respectively. After these presentations other officials, including General Pershing, made floral offerings. The assembled dignitaries then filed out of the rotunda leaving the guard of honor to maintain a vigil through the night.

In preparation for receiving the public on 10 November, Capitol employees on the evening of the 9th roped off areas in the rotunda which would channel the crowds as they entered from the east, moved past the bier, and continued out the west door. Also at that time the casket was turned around so that its foot was to the east. With this change the body bearers would not have to maneuver for correct position when taking the Unknown Soldier from the rotunda on 11 November but could carry the casket straight out the east door.

The public was admitted to the rotunda at 0800 on 10 November. Delegations of various patriotic and fraternal organizations were among the lines of people passing the bier four abreast. Having received permission to conduct brief services, some organizations assembled on the steps of the Senate wing, entered the rotunda through the north entrance, and, after placing wreaths and conducting their rites, filed out with the public through the west door. Many foreign diplomatic delegations also arrived to offer their respects and leave floral tributes. Because the lines were still long at 2200, the scheduled hour of closing, the rotunda was kept open until midnight. By that hour some 90,000 persons had passed the bier.

The funeral procession was scheduled to leave the Capitol at 0830 on 11 November. Well before that time the military escort and the dignitaries who would march in the procession formed on the East Plaza. All other participating groups assembled on side streets near either the Capitol grounds or Pennsylvania Avenue where they could join the cortege at the proper point. Army and Navy troops meanwhile formed an honor cordon on the east steps of the Capitol.

Of eight body bearers selected to handle the casket, five were Army noncommissioned officers, two were Navy petty officers, and one was a Marine Corps noncommissioned officer. Nine general officers and three flag officers, all of whom had served in World War I, had been appointed as honorary pallbearers. At 0800 the body bearers, followed by the honorary pallbearers, carried the casket of the Unknown Soldier from the rotunda and down the east steps to the caisson. While the U.S. Army Band on the plaza played a dirge, the military units stood at present arms. At the same time a field artillery battery brought in from Camp Meade, Maryland, and positioned on the Capitol Mall near the Washington Monument began firing minute guns. Except for a scheduled pause at noon to observe a two-minute period of silence during the funeral service, the battery continued to fire a round each minute until the end of all ceremonies. At the foot of the east steps of the Capitol four body bearers, flanked on the outside by six honorary pallbearers, took station on each side of the caisson as General Bandholtz, the escort commander, led the way toward Pennsylvania Avenue for the march to Arlington National Cemetery.

Behind General Bandholtz and his staff of three, all mounted, were a band, a drum corps, a composite foot regiment (in a column of battalions), a mounted field artillery battalion, and a squadron of cavalry, in that order. (*Table 1*)

Leading the long cortege behind the military escort were four clergymen, two of them active chaplains and two retired. At their head was the Right Reverend Charles H. Brent, who had been the Senior Chaplain of the American Expeditionary Forces during World War I and who was in charge of the religious rites of the funeral ceremony. The clergy and all other members of the cortege were on foot except former President Woodrow Wilson who was ill and rode in a carriage.

The caisson was next in column followed by the President with the Army Chief of Staff at his left, the Vice President with the Chief of Naval Operations at his left, and the Chief Justice of the United States with the Commandant of the Coast Guard at his left. Originally, former President Wilson was to have followed the Chief Justice, but he entered the procession late and therefore joined the

TABLE 1—MILITARY ESCORT, MAIN PROCESSION FOR THE
UNKNOWN SOLDIER OF WORLD WAR I

Composition	Organization
1 Band.............................	U.S. Army Band, Washington Barracks (later Fort McNair), D.C.
1 Drum corps........................	Army Drum Corps, Washington Barracks, D.C.
1 Composite foot regiment..............	3d Battalion, 64th Infantry, Fort Washington, Maryland Combined battalion, bluejackets and marines, Washington Navy Yard and Quantico, Virginia Engineer battalion, District of Columbia National Guard
1 Artillery battalion...................	2d Battalion, 3d Field Artillery, Fort Myer, Virginia
1 Cavalry squadron....................	2d Squadron, 3d Cavalry, Fort Myer, Virginia

column farther back. Instead, the remaining members of the Supreme Court came after the Chief Justice and were followed by members of the cabinet, state governors, and members of the Senate and House of Representatives, in that order.

To help maintain the quick-time cadence at which the procession was to move, a section of the Army Drum Corps was next in column. Behind the drums marched soldiers who had received the Medal of Honor. All holders of this highest military award had been invited to participate, but only those who had won it in World War I were invited at government expense. The medal of honor winners marched eight abreast, ranging from front to rear according to the dates of their medals, those holding the oldest medals leading. It was behind this honored group that the carriage bearing former President Wilson joined the procession.

A group composed of an officer and an enlisted man from each arm and service of the Army, Navy, Marine Corps, and Coast Guard followed the former President, also marching eight abreast, according to rank from front to rear. Behind this formation were 132 state and territorial representatives of the troops who had served in World War I. Each state and territory had been invited to send not more than three men, to be selected by the governor. Those participating marched eight abreast, arranged alphabetically according to state from front to rear.

The remaining contingents consisted of representative groups of forty-four patriotic, fraternal, and welfare organizations. Following one another in no particular order, each group marched in a column of eight with one representative leading. (*Table 2*)

The procession moved along Pennsylvania Avenue to 15th Street, on 15th Street to Pennsylvania Avenue again, past the White House to M Street, then on M Street to Aqueduct Bridge, which was slightly upstream from the present Francis Scott Key Bridge. When the column reached the White House, it stopped briefly while President Harding, Vice President Coolidge, Chief Justice Taft and the other justices of the Supreme Court, and members of the cabinet, Senate, and

TABLE 2—PARTICIPATING PATRIOTIC, FRATERNAL, AND WELFARE
ORGANIZATIONS, MAIN PROCESSION FOR THE UNKNOWN
SOLDIER OF WORLD WAR I

The Grand Army of the Republic
Confederate Veterans
Distinguished Service Order
The American Legion
National War Mothers (including Gold Star Mothers)
Veterans of Foreign Wars
Military Order of Foreign Wars
Military Order of the World War
Indian War Veterans Association
Military Order of the Loyal Legion of the U.S.A.
Spanish-American War Veterans
Naval and Military Order of the Spanish-American War
Imperial Order of the Dragon
Navy League of the U.S.
National Association of Naval Veterans
Society of World War Veterans, Inc.
Jewish Veterans of the World War
Military Training Camps Association
World War Veterans (Northwest)
Colored Veterans of the War
Grand Army of Americans
Divisional Societies (in numerical order of divisions)
Red Cross
Salvation Army
Young Men's Christian Association
Knights of Columbus
Jewish Welfare Board
American Library Association
Overseas Service League
Red Cross Overseas Service League
Overseas League, Young Men's Christian Association Women Workers
National Catholic War Council
American Women's Legion
American Defense Society, Inc.
Rotary Club
Society of Cincinnati
Daughters of Cincinnati
Sons of the Revolution
Daughters of the American Revolution
Sons of American Revolution
Children of the American Revolution
Daughters of 1812
Ladies Auxiliary, Veterans of Foreign Wars
Georgetown Cadets

PRESIDENT HARDING SPEAKS AT MEMORIAL AMPHITHEATER SERVICE

House of Representatives left the procession to travel by car to Arlington National Cemetery. They took a separate route via Highway Bridge at 14th Street and entered the cemetery through Treasury Gate. President Harding was almost late for the cemetery ceremonies; his car was caught in a tight traffic jam, and only by cutting across an open field was he able to arrive on time.

The main procession marched to Aqueduct Bridge, where the clergy dropped out and continued by car to the cemetery. The U.S. Army Band also left the procession at the bridge and was replaced for the remainder of the march by the U.S. Marine Band. Upon reaching the cemetery's Arlington (Fort Myer) Gate, the cavalry squadron, field artillery battalion (less one firing battery), and machine gun company of the infantry battalion left the column and paraded on a drill ground facing the cemetery. As the Marine Band played a funeral march, the rest of the procession moved through the cemetery to the west entrance of the Memorial Amphitheater, reaching it about 1140, three hours after leaving the Capitol.

The military escort, except for the artillery battery, drew up on line facing the amphitheater, presented arms, and held the salute while the caisson was brought to the entrance and the casket was carried to the apse inside the amphitheater.

The band, which had played while the casket was borne to the apse, then entered the amphitheater and was seated in the right colonnade. The artillery unit, Battery E of the 3d Field Artillery, meanwhile moved to a position north of the amphitheater in preparation for firing the gun salutes. After the entrance ceremony, the other units of the escort re-formed in preparation for leaving the cemetery via the McClellan Gate at the conclusion of the burial service. The escort was to depart immediately after President Harding left the cemetery.

Over 5,000 tickets had been distributed by the office of The Adjutant General for admission to the Memorial Amphitheater. (Since the number of tickets exceeded the seating capacity of the amphitheater, it is apparent that not all persons invited were expected to attend.) All participating in the procession were given tickets except the patriotic, fraternal, and welfare organizations, which received tickets only for selected delegates. Participants who held tickets entered the amphitheater after the body of the Unknown Soldier had been taken to the apse; the remainder joined the public standing behind ropes outside.

All others attending were seated when the President arrived about 1155, and the ceremony began as soon as he had taken his place in the apse. The Marine Band opened the ceremony with the national anthem which was followed by the invocation, delivered by the Army Chief of Chaplains, Col. John T. Axton. After a bugler sounded attention three times, the assemblage observed a two-minute period of silence.

At the conclusion of the period of silence the audience, accompanied by the band, sang "America." President Harding then delivered an address, paying tribute to the Unknown Soldier and pleading for an end to war. After a hymn sung by a quartet from the Metropolitan Opera Company, the President placed upon the casket of the Unknown Soldier the Medal of Honor and the Distinguished Service Cross. High-ranking representatives of other countries also presented decorations of high order, some of which never before had been given to a foreigner. Hymns and scriptural readings followed, and to conclude the service the audience sang "Nearer My God to Thee."

In preparation for the burial service, the Marine Band moved out of the amphitheater to a position near the tomb. The band played "Our Honored Dead" as the casket, preceded by the clergy, was moved in procession from the apse and placed in the tomb. During this transfer the Army body bearers again were flanked by the honorary pallbearers. Following the casket were President and Mrs. Harding; Vice President and Mrs. Coolidge; Mrs. R. Emmett Digney, who was the president of the American National War Mothers, and who had lost a son in the war; and Mrs. Julia McCudden, who represented the British War Mothers, and who had lost three sons. Heads of foreign delegations were next in procession; behind them were the Secretaries of State, War, and Navy, and military officials, both American and foreign. The band played "Lead Kindly Light" as the rest of the audience moved from the amphitheater to the area around the tomb.

BURIAL IN ARLINGTON CEMETERY

Bishop Brent read the burial service. Congressman Fish, who had introduced the legislation leading to the honors being paid the Unknown Soldier, next came forward and laid a wreath at the tomb. Among the many others who then offered tribute was Chief Plenty Coups, Chief of the Crow Nation. Representing all American Indians, he laid his war bonnet and coup stick at the tomb.

The saluting battery then fired three salvos as the casket was lowered into the crypt, the bottom of which had been covered with a layer of soil from France. The bugler sounded taps, and after the last note the battery fired twenty-one guns in final salute to the Unknown Soldier of World War I.

CHAPTER II

Former President William Howard Taft
State Funeral
8-11 March 1930

After a long illness William Howard Taft, at the age of seventy-two, died at his home in Washington, D.C., late in the afternoon of 8 March 1930. Mr. Taft, the only man to have held both the office of President and of Chief Justice of the United States, was accorded a State Funeral in Washington with full military honors.

The responsibility for arranging and conducting the funeral was assigned to the Commanding General, 16th Brigade, stationed at Fort Hunt, Virginia. President Herbert Hoover meanwhile appointed his own aide, Col. Campbell B. Hodges, to assist the Taft family and help co-ordinate funeral arrangements. According to plans the ceremonies, all scheduled for 11 March, were to begin at 0900 when Mr. Taft's body was to be escorted from his residence to the Capitol to lie in state on the Lincoln catafalque in the rotunda until noon. A procession would then form to accompany the body to All Souls' Unitarian Church for the funeral service. President Hoover had offered the East Room of the White House for the service, but Mrs. Taft declined since her husband had asked that it be held in the church of which he was a communicant. Dr. Ulysses G. B. Pierce, pastor of the church and long-time friend of Mr. Taft, was to conduct both the funeral and the graveside service. The members of the Supreme Court were to be honorary pallbearers.

At the request of the family, burial was to be in Arlington National Cemetery. Mr. Taft would be the first President buried there. Following the funeral service, a motor procession without military escort was to accompany the body to the Fort Myer Gate of the cemetery. There a military escort was to meet the motorcade and conduct it to the gravesite, a 2,500-square-foot plot in the northeastern area which held few graves but was well landscaped. Mrs. Taft and her two sons and daughter, accompanied by Colonel Hodges and Col. Charles G. Mortimer, the officer in charge at Arlington, had visited the cemetery on 9 March and selected the site.

Extensive military honors were scheduled after President Hoover on 8 March proclaimed a thirty-day period of national mourning and formally directed the Secretary of War and Secretary of the Navy to render "suitable military and naval honors" on the day of the funeral. As prescribed in existing regulations, all Army posts possessing the necessary equipment prepared to fire thirteen guns at reveille, one each half hour thereafter until retreat, and then a 48-gun salute to the Union on Monday, 10 March. This was the salute customarily fired upon receipt of news of the death of a President or ex-President except, as in the case of Mr. Taft, when the notice was received on a Sunday.

Also by established custom, and as specifically directed by Secretary of War Patrick J. Hurley through Army Chief of Staff General Charles P. Summerall, Army posts were to fire twenty-one minute guns at 1430 on 11 March, the time scheduled for the end of the funeral service. Flags were to be displayed at half-staff, colors and standards were to be draped in mourning, and all officers were to wear "the usual badge of military mourning around the left sleeve of the uniform coat and overcoat and on the saber" for thirty days. Similarly, Navy instructions prescribed that on the day of the funeral "the ensign at each naval station and on board each vessel in commission be displayed at half mast and that a gun be fired at half-hour intervals from sunrise to sunset at each naval station and on board flagships and all saluting ships acting singly." Officers of the Navy and Marine Corps also were to wear mourning badges for thirty days.

Although existing regulations established the military honors to be rendered during the ceremonies in Washington, the size of the military escorts in the funeral of a former President was left to the Secretary of War. A squadron of cavalry (two troops), it was decided, would escort Mr. Taft's body from the Taft home to the Capitol. The main procession from the Capitol to the church was to include two service bands, a battalion of infantry, a battalion of field artillery, a battalion of marines, and a company of bluejackets. The escort commander, another choice left to the Secretary of War, was to be Maj. Gen. Fred W. Sladen, the commanding general of the Third Corps Area, with headquarters in Baltimore, Maryland.

At the cemetery, a squadron of cavalry and a mounted band were to escort the motorcade from the gate to the gravesite. A service band, a cavalry regiment, less one squadron, a battalion of engineers, and a company of marines were to stand in formation at the graveside service.

Almost all the ceremonies involved the 3d Cavalry Regiment, the "President's Own," stationed at Fort Myer, Virginia, after World War I and consistently called upon to render funeral honors. Besides furnishing the cavalry contingents of the escorts, the regiment was to supply the caisson and caisson detachment, four of eight body bearers (four from the Army, two from the Navy, two from the Marine Corps), half the guard of honor at the Capitol (twenty from the Army, ten from the Navy, ten from the Marine Corps), and the saluting battery, firing party, and bugler at the cemetery.

The 3d Cavalry alone was to provide the escort from the Taft residence to the Capitol and from the cemetery gate to the grave. In the main procession from the

CASKET IS PLACED ON CAISSON OUTSIDE THE TAFT HOME, *above. Procession to the Capitol, below.*

Capitol to All Souls' Unitarian Church, the escort commanded by General Sladen
was to include the U.S. Army Band and the 1st Battalion, 16th Field Artillery,
from Fort Myer, Virginia; the 3d Battalion, 12th Infantry, from Fort Washington, Maryland; the U.S. Marine Band and a battalion of marines from the Marine Barracks, Washington; and a company of bluejackets from the Naval District
Washington, in that order of march. At the grave, the U.S. Navy Band; the 3d
Cavalry Regiment, less one squadron; a battalion of the 13th Engineers from Fort
Humphreys (later Fort Belvoir), Virginia; and a company of marines were to
form a hollow square around the perimeter of the large gravesite as a guard of
honor during the graveside service.

In a misty rain, the 2d Squadron, 3d Cavalry, caisson detachment, and body
bearers reached the Taft home at 2215 Wyoming Avenue, N.W., shortly before
0900 on 11 March. Facing the residence from the opposite side of the street, the
mounted troops formed a front as the body bearers brought the casket from the
house and secured it on the caisson.

Neither officials nor members of the family rode in the procession to the Capitol. With Metropolitan Police leading the way and the caisson between Troop E
in front and Troop F to the rear, the procession made its way to the Capitol via
Connecticut Avenue, Massachusetts Avenue, 16th Street, H Street, Madison
Place, East Executive Avenue, Treasury Place, and Pennsylvania Avenue. Rain
fell heavily as it moved over the northeast Capitol driveway to the East Plaza.

After the casket was carried into the rotunda and an honor guard, commanded by Capt. Frank Goettge, a White House aide, was posted, an hour and a
half remained of the scheduled period of lying in state. Some 7,000 persons in two
lines filed by during that time, despite interruptions each fifteen minutes when a
new honor guard relief took post.

At noon the casket was taken from the rotunda to the caisson on the East
Plaza, where the entire escort had formed for the procession to the church. The
Army Band led off, followed by the caisson and the remainder of the escort. As in
the morning ceremony, officials and members of the family did not ride with the
procession. As the column retraced its morning route as far as 16th Street, then
turned north to All Souls' Unitarian Church at Harvard Street, a heavy down-
pour of rain with strong winds made it difficult for the escort troops to maintain a
precise step and formation. Despite the weather, the public lined the entire route
as the procession, marching to the slow tempo of Chopin's "Funeral March,"
spent almost two hours in reaching the church.

Considerably before the arrival of the cortege and escort from the Capitol,
some 900 people had filled All Souls' Unitarian Church. Orderly seating was as-
sured by Army officers acting as ushers under the direction of Charles Lee Cooke,
the ceremonial officer of the State Department. Among those in attendance were
President and Mrs. Hoover, Vice President Charles Curtis, cabinet members, committees of the Senate and House of Representatives, the Chief Justice of the

Casket Is Carried Up East Steps of the Capitol, *above. Body of President Taft lies in state in the rotunda, below.*

United States and associate justices of the Supreme Court (the honorary pall-bearers), state governors, Army and Navy officials, and many members of the diplomatic corps.

Mrs. Taft and her family entered the church shortly before 1400, just ahead of the arrival of the procession. As the cortege reached the canopied entrance to the church a historic bell in the church steeple, made at the Paul Revere Foundry and presented to the church in 1822,tolled the message of Mr. Taft's passing, just as it had tolled the death of every President since 1822.

Doctor Pierce, as Mr. Taft had requested, omitted any eulogies from the funeral service. The half-hour program included a processional, prayers, hymns, and readings from the poems of Wordsworth and Tennyson. Network radio systems broadcast the service over nearly a hundred stations throughout the nation, including some with short-wave transmitters that were monitored regularly in foreign countries.

At the conclusion of the service, Mr. Taft's casket was borne from the church and placed in a hearse for the motor procession to Arlington National Cemetery. The military units of the escort from the Capitol, which had remained in formation outside the church during the funeral service, stood as a guard of honor while the motorcade formed and departed. The procession, escorted only by motorcycle police, included a hundred cars. The leading car carried Doctor Pierce and the second the honorary pallbearers. The hearse came next, and was followed by cars bearing the Taft family, President Hoover's car, and the cars of high government officials. In some thirty minutes, the motorcade moved south on 16th Street and New Hampshire Avenue, west on Pennsylvania Avenue and M Street to Key Bridge (Memorial Bridge and Memorial Drive were under construction at the time), then to Fort Myer and through it to the cemetery's Fort Myer Gate.

The rain had stopped by the time the motor procession reached the gate. The 3d Cavalry's saluting battery, positioned near the roadway in the cemetery, signaled the arrival by firing the first of twenty-one minute guns. Over the twenty minutes in which this salute was fired, the 3d Cavalry's mounted band, at reduced cadence, and the 1st Squadron, which had formed at the gate, escorted the motor procession to the gravesite.

At the grave the remainder of the 3d Cavalry (dismounted), the Engineer battalion, and the Marine company, all together about a thousand men, already were in the hollow square guard of honor formation. The honor guard presented arms, ruffles and flourishes were sounded, and the Navy Band played a hymn as the casket, followed by the Taft family and dignitaries, was borne to the canopied grave. When Dr. Pierce concluded the brief service, a 3d Cavalry firing party of sixteen men delivered the traditional three volleys. The battery meanwhile had begun the final 21-gun salute. At the end of the salute, taps was sounded for the twenty-seventh President and tenth Chief Justice of the United States.

CASKET IS CARRIED FROM THE CAPITOL, *above. Procession to All Souls'*
Unitarian Church, below.

CHAPTER III

Former Army Chief of Staff
General Malin Craig
Funeral Without Formal Classification
26-30 July 1945

After a year's illness General Malin Craig, who had been Chief of Staff of the Army from 1935 to 1939, died at Walter Reed General Hospital in Washington, D.C., on 25 July 1945. He had retired from the Army in 1939, but returned to active duty in September 1941 to head the War Department Personnel Board and was still on active duty at the time of his death. He would have been seventy years old on 5 August.

General Craig was entitled under Army regulations to a funeral with military honors and ceremonies befitting his rank as former Chief of Staff of the Army. These included a 17-gun salute and a funeral procession with a military escort composed of a regiment of infantry, a squadron of cavalry, and a battalion of field artillery.

Had usual procedures been followed, orders announcing the death of General Craig would have directed that these and other honors be rendered, but the general during his fatal illness had asked that his funeral be kept entirely private. Acting Secretary of War Robert P. Patterson acknowledged this request in announcing the death of the former Chief of Staff to the Army on 25 July. The "funeral will be private," the secretary informed all major commands, "and all ceremonies and honors omitted." Deference to General Craig's wish was repeated in War Department General Order 61 formally announcing the general's death on 26 July. In this order, issued in the name of the Army Chief of Staff, General of the Army George C. Marshall, who was in Europe at the time, it was announced that General Craig would be buried in Arlington National Cemetery on 30 July.

Surviving General Craig were his son, Col. Malin Craig, Jr., and a brother, General Louis A. Craig. Colonel Craig, at the time of his father's death, was stationed in Europe; the Army arranged to have him flown to Washington, where he arrived during the evening of 28 July. Lt. Col. H. M. Pasco, Acting Secretary of the General Staff, meanwhile offered the full assistance of the Chief of Staff's office to the Craig family. "General Marshall," he told the former Chief of Staff's brother, "wanted me to put every facility at your disposal that was needed."

Col. F. Granville Munson, an Army officer assigned to the Chief of Staff's office, met with Mrs. Malin Craig, Jr., to offer help in arranging the private funeral; together they drew up a list of twenty-seven honorary pallbearers. Although it was known that General Marshall, General Arnold, General Somervell, and Colonel Lee were out of the country and could not attend, their names were placed on the list. On 27 July the names were turned over to The Adjutant General, who dispatched a formal invitation to each of the following honorary pallbearers:

General of the Army George C. Marshall
General of the Army Henry H. Arnold
Lt. Gen. Brehon B. Somervell
Lt. Gen. Thomas T. Handy
Maj. Gen. Emory S. Adams
Lt. Gen. Stanley D. Embick
Lt. Gen. Ben Lear
Maj. Gen. Guy V. Henry
Col. Charles W. Exton
Maj. Gen. Amos A. Fries
Brig. Gen. Edwin D. Bricker
Maj. Gen. William E. Cole
Brig. Gen. Jacob C. Johnson
Brig. Gen. William P. Wooten

Brig. Gen. Walter J. Reed
Brig. Gen. William G. Grant
Maj. Gen. Everett S. Hughes
Lt. Gen. Charles D. Herron
Brig. Gen. Raymond F. Metcalfe
Maj. Gen. Joseph A. Green
Maj. Gen. Kenneth T. Blood
Brig. Gen. Charles H. White
Maj. Gen. William Bryden
Maj. Gen. Oley Danielson
Maj. Gen. Lorenzo D. Gasser
Lt. Gen. John L. DeWitt
Col. Carnes Lee

The members of the Craig family, accepting support from the Army as needed, but adhering strictly to General Craig's desire to have a private funeral, held the service in the Fort Myer Chapel at 1400 on 30 July. Following the service, final rites were conducted in Arlington National Cemetery at a gravesite in Section 2, on the slope below the Custis-Lee Mansion.

CHAPTER IV

General of the Armies John J. Pershing
State Funeral
15-19 July 1948

General of the Armies John J. Pershing, then the nation's highest ranking military official, died on 15 July 1948, at the age of eighty-seven, at the Army's Walter Reed General Hospital, Washington, D.C. He had been a patient there since 6 May 1941, residing in a small wing set aside for him.

A plan to honor General Pershing with a State Funeral had been written ten years earlier when he seemed near death. After his recovery, the plan was closely guarded and over the decade following was substantially revised to incorporate changes directed by the Army Chief of Staff with the consent of F. Warren Pershing, the general's son. The version finally used was prepared in 1945 (and classified Top Secret), but it included some changes made later.

The plan met the preferences of General Pershing. Years before his death he had expressed a wish to be buried in Arlington National Cemetery and had selected a small hill in a southeastern section of the cemetery as his gravesite. The ground sloped away from this site to a level plot containing the graves of hundreds of men whom he had commanded in World War I. A military man for sixty-six years, General Pershing had insisted upon a purely military funeral. Accordingly, the plan restricted organizational participation in the ceremonies to the active Army, Navy, Marine Corps, and Air Force. The National Guard, the Organized Reserve Corps, and patriotic organizations were to be represented only in the audience invited to attend the funeral service.

The ceremonies were scheduled for 17–19 July. For twenty-four hours the general's body was to lie in the chapel at Walter Reed General Hospital, to be visited only by relatives, close friends, members of the hospital staff, and long-time fellow patients. For another twenty-four hours the body was to lie in state in the rotunda of the Capitol, where the public would be admitted. During the afternoon of the third day, General Pershing's body was to be escorted by a procession from the Capitol to Arlington National Cemetery for honors at the Tomb of the Unknown Soldier, funeral service in the Memorial Amphitheater, and last rites at the gravesite.

Following protocol established in the funeral plan, the commanding general of Walter Reed General Hospital, Maj. Gen. George C. Beach, was to announce

General Pershing's death first to President Harry S. Truman who would make the public proclamation. When General Pershing died at 0350 on 15 July, President Truman was en route by train to Washington from Philadelphia. General Beach was at Washington's Union Station when the President's train arrived at 0515 and notified the President's secretary.

At 0830 President Truman announced General Pershing's death from the White House in a statement paying tribute to the general. The Department of State later in the day issued the President's proclamation of a period of national mourning in which it was ordered that the national flag be displayed at half-staff "upon all public buildings and at all forts and military posts and naval stations, and on all vessels of the United States" until funeral services had been held.

According to the order of notification, General Beach meanwhile sent word of General Pershing's death to the Army Chief of Staff, General Omar N. Bradley. Word, in turn, reached Headquarters, Military District of Washington, the executive agency designated to conduct the funeral, and the agencies of the Department of the Army staff responsible for specific details of the arrangements. (*Table 3*)

The commander of the Military District of Washington, Maj. Gen. Hobart R. Gay, acting as the direct representative of the President, co-ordinated arrangements for the ceremonies from an operations center established in the Pentagon early on 15 July. One of General Gay's first acts was to request the use of the rotunda of the Capitol for the lying in state ceremony. Such a request ordinarily results in an act of Congress, but in this instance, since Congress was in adjournment, the Speaker of the House, Joseph W. Martin, Jr., and the president pro tempore of the Senate, Arthur H. Vandenberg, gave joint consent. In an early administrative step, General Gay downgraded the highly classified funeral plan after

TABLE 3—RESPONSIBLE ARMY AGENCIES, CEREMONIES FOR GENERAL
OF THE ARMIES JOHN J. PERSHING

Agency	Responsibility
Headquarters, Military District of Washington.	Executive handling of all funeral arrangements and ceremonies.
Secretary of the General Staff.........	Assistance to the Pershing family, General Staff heads, Chief of Staff, Secretary of the Army, Secretary of Defense, members of Congress, and the President in their participation in the ceremonies.
Director of Personnel and Administration (delegated to The Adjutant General).	Processing of all invitations, announcements, and orders pertaining to General Pershing's death and the funeral ceremonies.
Director of Organization and Training. .	Selection and movement of ceremonial troop units stationed outside the Washington area.
Chief of Chaplains....................	Arrangement of religious services.

TABLE 4—PARTICIPATING UNITS, CEREMONIES FOR GENERAL
OF THE ARMIES JOHN J. PERSHING

Unit	Station
1st Battalion, 504th Airborne Infantry Regiment, 82d Airborne Division.	Fort Bragg, North Carolina
3d Infantry Regiment.................	Fort Myer, Virginia
3d Mechanized Cavalry Reconnaissance Squadron.	Fort Meade, Maryland
410th Engineer Construction Battalion..	Fort Belvoir, Virginia
456th Field Artillery Battalion, 82d Airborne Division.	Fort Bragg, North Carolina
1 Battalion, cadets..................	U.S. Military Academy, West Point, New York
2 Squadrons, Air Force troops.........	Bolling Field, Washington, D.C.
1 Company, bluejackets..............	Potomac River Naval Command, Washington, D.C.
1 Company, marines.................	Marine Barracks, Washington, D.C.
U.S. Army Band....................	Fort Myer, Virginia
U.S. Army Ground Forces Band.......	Fort Meade, Maryland
356th Army Band...................	Fort Belvoir, Virginia
1 Squadron, Air Force planes.........	....

the President announced General Pershing's death and authorized the extraction of information from it for release to the press.

All military units that were to participate in the funeral were alerted by noon on 15 July; through the afternoon, officers representing units that were to act as escort in the funeral procession joined Military District of Washington officials in conference on details and procedures. Of the units with distant home stations, two battalions from Fort Bragg, North Carolina, were scheduled to move in convoy on 17 and 18 July into temporary quarters at Fort Belvoir, Virginia; a battalion of cadets of the U.S. Military Academy, coming directly from summer field maneuvers, was to proceed by train from West Point to Washington early on 19 July, the day of the funeral. (*Table 4*)

Alongside the Military District of Washington operations center in the Pentagon, The Adjutant General opened a center on 15 July to process invitations, announcements, and orders, all of which already existed in draft form. He issued general orders announcing General Pershing's death to the Army and specifying that the flag be displayed at half-staff for thirty days "at the headquarters of all military commands and vessels" under the control of the Department of the Army. Later, because special arrangements to accommodate the Army's longer period of mourning were lacking, the flags at several buildings in the Washington, D.C., area occupied by the Army but administered by the Public Buildings Administration were raised to full staff immediately after General Pershing's funeral, as prescribed for government buildings in the Presidential proclamation.

By evening of 15 July, The Adjutant General's center had dispatched all necessary telegrams and letters of notification of death and had forwarded credentials to some 3,000 persons invited to attend the funeral. (Since the number of guests approximated the seating capacity of the Memorial Amphitheater, the public could not be admitted to the funeral service.) Among those who received invitations were the honorary pallbearers (officers and dignitaries) and honorary body

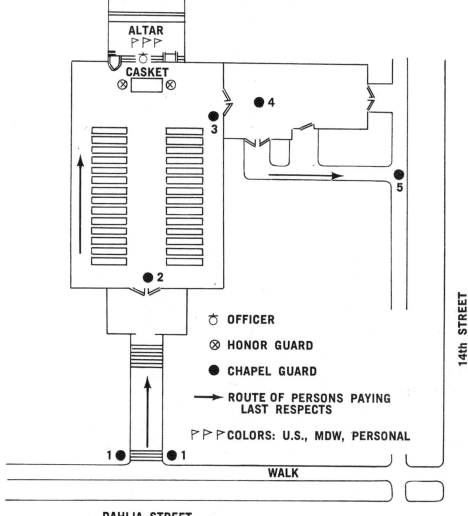

Diagram 2.   Guard of honor, Walter Reed General Hospital Chapel, Washington, D.C.

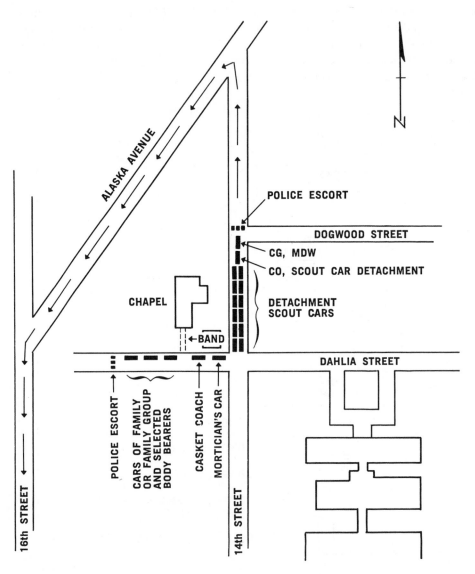

Diagram 3.   Departure ceremony, Walter Reed General Hospital Chapel.

bearers (enlisted men), among them Sgt. Alvin C. York of World War I fame. The center's staff over the next three days was fully occupied in handling the responses to these communications.

Virtually all other preliminary arrangements, administrative and ceremonial, were completed on 16 July. Among changes to the basic funeral plan that had to be considered, some of them made near the last moment, was President Truman's decision not to deliver a eulogy previously scheduled for the funeral service. He also canceled the 21-gun salute that otherwise would have accompanied his arrival at and departure from Arlington National Cemetery. The honor in this instance, he considered, would constitute an interruption of the funeral rites.

Secretary of Defense James V. Forrestal changed his plans to participate in the ceremonies, electing to attend only the funeral service in the Memorial Amphitheater. He delegated his role in the ceremonies to Secretary of the Army Kenneth C. Royall.

A proposal that a six-star insignia be affixed to General Pershing's uniform was dropped in favor of the four stars the general had always worn. Finally, at the request of the Pershing family, a plan to display the general's medals during the lying in state period at the Capitol was canceled.

General Pershing's body was placed in the Walter Reed General Hospital chapel at noon on 17 July. The Ceremonial Company, 3d Infantry Regiment, furnished an honor guard, as well as a chapel guard to guide persons paying their respects. (*Diagram 2*) Hospital staff members and patients were admitted to the chapel from 1300 to 1900. All other hours of the period, ending at 1300 on 18 July, were reserved for the Pershing family and close friends.

At the closing hour General Gay, as escort commander, took charge of General Pershing's body at the chapel for movement in the procession to the Capitol for the formal lying in state. (*Diagram 3*) The 356th Army Band from Fort Belvoir, Virginia, played a hymn as body bearers (four Army, two Air Force, one Navy, one Marine Corps) moved the casket to a coach. The cortege of coach and family cars escorted by a scout car detachment from the 3d Armored Cavalry Reconnaissance Squadron, Fort Meade, Maryland, and Metropolitan Police proceeded at normal speed via 16th Street, Massachusetts Avenue, and New Jersey Avenue, reaching the East Plaza about 1330.

In formation to receive General Pershing's casket at the Capitol were the three service secretaries, the Army Chief of Staff and Deputy Chief of Staff, the vice chairman of the American Battle Monuments Commission, and a joint committee from Congress. (*Diagram 4*) This group joined the Pershing family and General Gay in escorting General Pershing's casket into the rotunda. The Army Band, attired for the occasion in gray uniforms which had been chosen for the band by General Pershing when he was Chief of Staff, played as the procession moved up the Capitol steps through a cordon of troops from the Ceremonial Company, 3d Infantry Regiment.

The casket was placed on the Lincoln catafalque in the exact center of the rotunda, the foot of the casket toward the east door through which the public would enter. The first relief of an honor guard from the Ceremonial Company took post

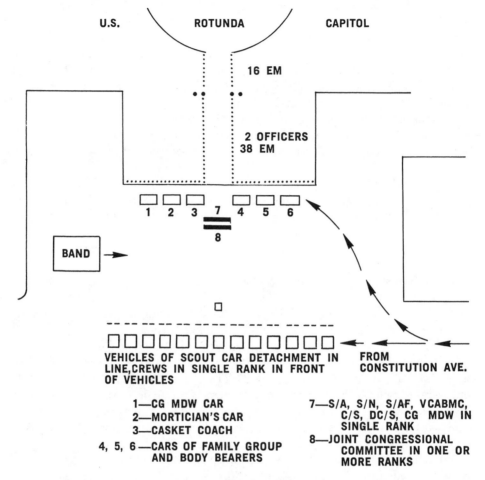

Diagram 4.   Reception ceremony at the Capitol.

immediately. Thereafter a succession of reliefs, each composed of one officer and four men, took post at half-hour intervals to maintain constant vigil throughout the lying in state period. From 1500 until 1900 on 18 July and again from 0900 until noon on 19 July, the public passed by the open casket in single file and left by the entrance on the west side of the rotunda. Hundreds of persons had to be turned away at the closing hour, as preparations began for the procession to Arlington National Cemetery.

Troop units and other participating groups assembled by 1250 to form the procession; a receiving formation took position on the East Plaza, the remainder formed in march order on Constitution Avenue. (*Diagram 5*) The Army Band

CASKET ARRIVES AT EAST STEPS OF THE CAPITOL, *above. Honor guard keeps vigil in the rotunda, below.*

CASKET IS CARRIED FROM THE CAPITOL *through the cordon of honorary pallbearers, above. Procession to Arlington National Cemetery, below.*

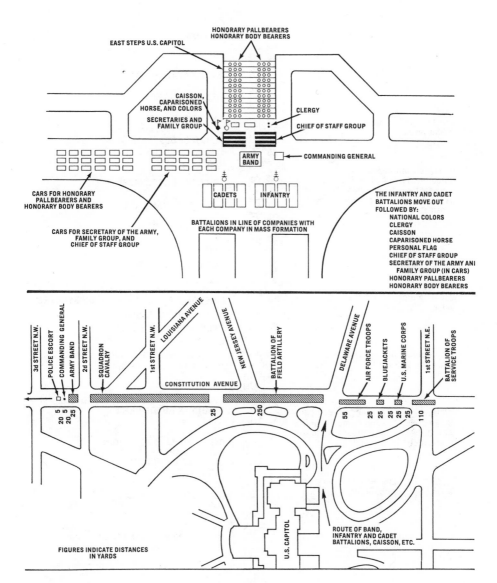

Diagram 5. Formation of procession at the Capitol and on Constitution
Avenue.

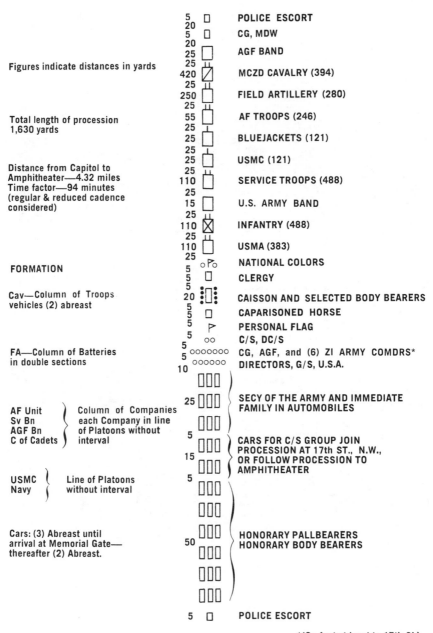

Figures indicate distances in yards

5	POLICE ESCORT
20	
5	CG, MDW
20	
25	AGF BAND
25	
420	MCZD CAVALRY (394)
25	
250	FIELD ARTILLERY (280)
25	
55	AF TROOPS (246)
25	
25	BLUEJACKETS (121)
25	
25	USMC (121)
25	
110	SERVICE TROOPS (488)
25	
15	U.S. ARMY BAND
25	
110	INFANTRY (488)
25	
110	USMA (383)
25	
5	NATIONAL COLORS
5	CLERGY
5	
20	CAISSON AND SELECTED BODY BEARERS
5	
5	CAPARISONED HORSE
5	PERSONAL FLAG
5	C/S, DC/S
5	CG, AGF, and (6) ZI ARMY COMDRS*
5	DIRECTORS, G/S, U.S.A.
10	

Total length of procession
1,630 yards

Distance from Capitol to
Amphitheater—4.32 miles
Time factor—94 minutes
(regular & reduced cadence
considered)

FORMATION

Cav—Column of Troops
vehicles (2) abreast

FA—Column of Batteries
in double sections

25	SECY OF THE ARMY AND IMMEDIATE FAMILY IN AUTOMOBILES	
5		
15	CARS FOR C/S GROUP JOIN PROCESSION AT 17th ST., N.W., OR FOLLOW PROCESSION TO AMPHITHEATER	
5		
50	HONORARY PALLBEARERS HONORARY BODY BEARERS	

AF Unit ⎫
Sv Bn ⎬ Column of Companies
AGF Bn ⎬ each Company in line
C of Cadets ⎭ of Platoons without
                interval

USMC ⎫ Line of Platoons
Navy ⎭ without interval

Cars: (3) Abreast until
arrival at Memorial Gate—
thereafter (2) Abreast.

5	POLICE ESCORT

*(On foot at least to 17th St.)

Diagram 6.   Order of march, full procession, Capitol to Arlington National
Cemetery.

Procession Approaches the Cemetery, *above. Ceremony at the Tomb of the Unknown Soldier, below.*

SERVICE IN MEMORIAL AMPHITHEATER, *above. Firing party delivers three volleys, below.*

rendered honors as General Pershing's casket was borne from the rotunda at 1300 through a cordon of honorary pallbearers and honorary body bearers to a caisson at the foot of the east steps.

At the close of the plaza ceremony, the march units on Constitution Avenue moved forward at a reduced cadence until the cortege and other formations on the plaza had joined the column. (*Diagram 6*) The mile-long procession then moved at normal cadence toward Arlington National Cemetery via Constitution Avenue, 23d Street, Memorial Bridge, and Memorial Drive. A squadron of Air Force planes appeared overhead and 300,000 spectators lined the route of march despite a heavy shower of rain that fell soon after the procession started.

On reaching Memorial Gate of the cemetery, troop units not scheduled for further participation in the ceremonies kept near the head of the column; those scheduled for further participation only at the gravesite, who were next in column, left the procession and proceeded to their assigned dismissal point or next station. (*Diagram 7*) The remainder of the procession moved into the cemetery via Roosevelt and Wilson Avenues to the Tomb of the Unknown Soldier. As the procession moved, the saluting battery of the Ceremonial Company, 3d Infantry, in position nearby the route of march, fired nineteen minute guns.

The ceremony at the Tomb of the Unknown Soldier was brief. (*Diagram 8*) Salutes and musical honors were rendered as the casket was moved from the caisson to a catafalque on the plaza. A silence of one minute was observed. General

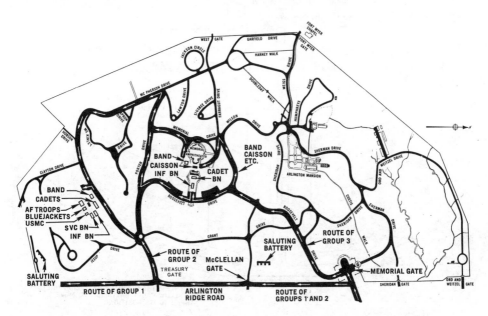

Diagram 7.   Procedure upon arrival of procession at Memorial Gate.

Pershing's casket was then borne into the apse of the Memorial Amphitheater for the funeral service. Maj. Gen. Luther D. Miller, the Army Chief of Chaplains, assisted by the Very Reverend John W. Suter, D.D., dean of Washington Cathedral, conducted an Episcopal funeral service. At its conclusion, the procession reformed on and below the plaza of the Tomb of the Unknown Soldier for the march to the gravesite. President Truman then left the cemetery.

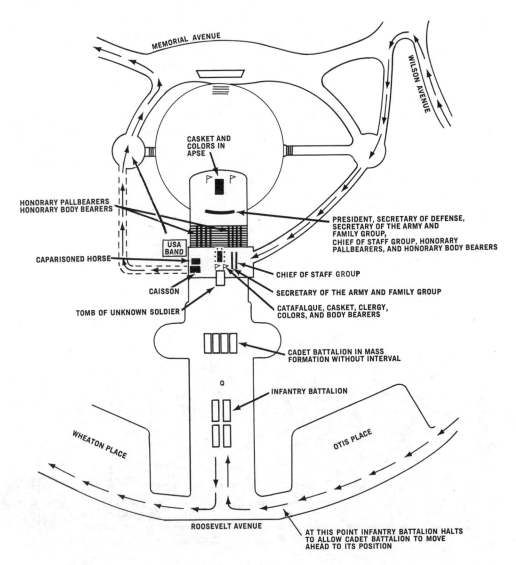

Diagram 8.   Formation at the Tomb of the Unknown Soldier

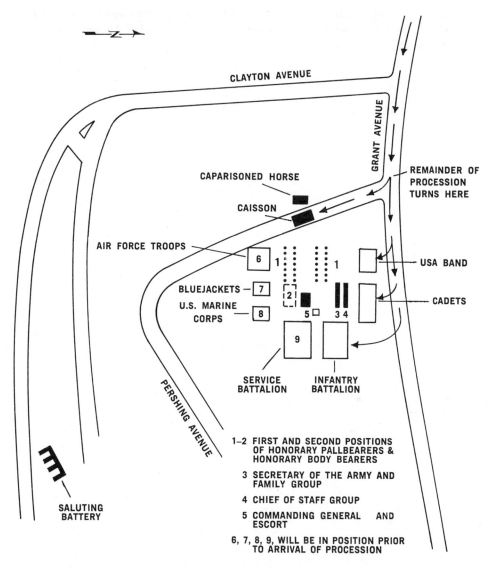

CLAYTON AVENUE

GRANT AVENUE

CAPARISONED HORSE

CAISSON

REMAINDER OF
PROCESSION
TURNS HERE

AIR FORCE TROOPS

6   1   1

USA BAND

BLUEJACKETS — 7   2

U.S. MARINE
CORPS   8   5   3 4

CADETS

9

PERSHING AVENUE

SERVICE   INFANTRY
BATTALION   BATTALION

**1–2 FIRST AND SECOND POSITIONS
OF HONORARY PALLBEARERS &
HONORARY BODY BEARERS**

**3 SECRETARY OF THE ARMY AND
FAMILY GROUP**

4 CHIEF OF STAFF GROUP

**5 COMMANDING GENERAL   AND
ESCORT**

**6, 7, 8, 9, WILL BE IN POSITION PRIOR
TO ARRIVAL OF PROCESSION**

SALUTING
BATTERY

Diagram 9.   Formation for the burial service.

The procession moved to the grave via Roosevelt, Porter, McPherson, and Grant Avenues, a large part of the audience from the amphitheater following. (*See Diagram 7.*) At the graveside Chaplain Miller and the Reverend Dr. Suter offered brief prayers. The 3d Infantry battery, having repositioned its cannon near the gravesite during the ceremony at the amphitheater, fired a 19-gun salute.

(*Diagram 9*) The traditional three volleys by a firing party and the sounding of taps ended the final honors for the general at the rise of ground soon to be known as Pershing Hill.

CHAPTER V

Former Secretary of Defense James V. Forrestal
Official Funeral
22-25 May 1949

On 22 May 1949 former Secretary of Defense James V. Forrestal, the first man to hold that cabinet post, took his own life while undergoing psychiatric treatment at the U.S. Naval Hospital in Bethesda, Maryland. He was fifty-seven years old.

At the time of his death, Mrs. Forrestal and one of her two sons were in France to find a place where the former Secretary could recuperate from the depression that had overtaken him. Secretary of State Dean Acheson was also in France, having flown to Paris in President Truman's plane, the Independence, for a meeting of the Council of Foreign Ministers. The President's plane was put at the disposal of Mrs. Forrestal who, with her son, flew back to the United States, arriving at National Airport in Washington, D.C., early on 23 May. She was accompanied on the plane by Brig. Gen. Robert B. Landry, Air Force Aide to the President, and Col. Louis Renfrow, Assistant to the Secretary of Defense. Among those on hand to meet her were the incumbent Secretary of Defense, Louis Johnson, Secretary of the Navy John L. Sullivan, former Secretary of the Army and Mrs. Kenneth C. Royall, former Under Secretary of the Army William R. Draper, her other son, and several personal friends.

Mr. Forrestal was to be given an Official Funeral, although the term was not formally used until later in 1949. Secretary of Defense Johnson designated Maj. Gen. Hobart R. Gay, commander of the Military District of Washington, as his representative, responsible for planning the funeral ceremonies. This planning, accomplished on 23 and 24 May, was as simple as possible, in keeping with the wishes of the Forrestal family and those of Mr. Forrestal.

Services and burial were to take place in Arlington National Cemetery; Mr. Forrestal had served in the Navy during World War I and as Secretary of the Navy from March 1944 until he became Secretary of Defense in September 1947. The gravesite selected was in Section 30, not far from the grave of William Howard Taft.

Originally, only a simple graveside service was planned, but it quickly became apparent that even though attendance was to be limited to relatives, personal friends, and the official government family, the number of persons expected could not be accommodated at the gravesite. The final plan, therefore, called for a modest funeral service in the Memorial Amphitheater and a private burial service. The Right Reverend Wallace R. Conkling, bishop of the Episcopal Diocese of Chicago and an intimate friend of the Forrestal family, was to officiate both in the amphitheater and at the grave.

In accordance with Mrs. Forrestal's wishes, there was to be no procession through the streets of Washington, only a cortege from the Memorial Gate of the cemetery to the amphitheater. Mr. Forrestal's body was to be borne by hearse from the hospital in Bethesda to the gate, where the casket was to be transferred to a caisson, and accompanied to the amphitheater by a military escort.

The U.S. Navy Band, a battalion of midshipmen from the U.S. Naval Academy, and a composite battalion made up of a company each from the Army, Marine Corps, Navy, and Air Force were to constitute the escort. Because of Mr. Forrestal's service and close association with the Navy, a naval escort commander, Rear Adm. John W. Roper of the Naval Bureau of Personnel, was appointed. Body bearers, who were to flank the caisson as the procession moved from Memorial Gate to the amphitheater, included two men each from the Army, Marine Corps, Navy, and Air Force.

Other military formations scheduled to participate in the ceremonies included the 3d Infantry battery, which was to fire a 19-gun salute during the procession through the cemetery and a second nineteen guns during the graveside service. The U.S. Army Band was to play during the funeral service in the amphitheater, and the U.S. Marine Band, at the request of the Forrestal family, was to play during the graveside service and to furnish two buglers.

Twenty-two men, all friends of Mr. Forrestal, were invited to serve as honorary pallbearers; they were not scheduled to march in the procession or to participate in the graveside service, but they were to be present at the service in the amphiteater:

Herbert C. Hoover, former President of the United States

Fred M. Vinson, Chief Justice of the United States

General of the Army George C. Marshall, former Secretary of State and former Chief of Staff, U.S. Army

James F. Byrnes, former Secretary of State

John J. McCloy, former Assistant Secretary of War

Kenneth C. Royall, former Secretary of the Army

Artemus L. Gates, former Assistant Secretary of the Navy for Air

Cornelius V. Whitney, Under Secretary of Commerce and former Assistant Secretary of the Air Force

James A. Farley, former Postmaster General

General of the Army Dwight D. Eisenhower

Fleet Admiral William D. Leahy, former Chief of Staff to the Commander in Chief

Bernard M. Baruch

Robert P. Patterson, former Secretary
of War
John L. Sullivan, Secretary of the Navy
Robert A. Lovett, former Under
Secretary of State and former
Assistant Secretary of War

Clarence Dillon
Nicholas S. Ludington
Thomas G. Corcoran
Edward L. Shea
Ferdinand Eberstadt
Dean Mathey
Paul V. Shields

At midmorning on 25 May, Rear Adm. John E. Gingrich, a long-time friend and aide to Mr. Forrestal, accompanied the former Secretary's casket in the hearse from the Naval Hospital to the Memorial Gate of the cemetery. The military escort already was in position at the gate when the hearse arrived about 1050. In one change of plans, made when it was discovered that the U.S. Navy Band was on tour, the U.S. Naval Academy Band was substituted to lead the procession. After the body bearers transferred the casket to the caisson, the procession moved into the cemetery in the following order of march: U.S. Naval Academy Band; two companies of midshipmen; national and U.S. Naval Academy colors; two companies of midshipmen; U.S. Army company; U.S. Marine Corps company; service colors; U.S. Navy company; U.S. Air Force company; caisson and body bearers. The Forrestal family, clergy, and honorary pallbearers did not accompany the cortege, but awaited the procession at the amphitheater. As the column proceeded at the slow cadence of funeral marches played by the band, the 3d Infantry saluting battery fired nineteen guns, spacing the rounds so that the last one was fired as the caisson reached the west entrance of the amphitheater at 1115.

All persons attending the service in the amphitheater had been seated before the procession arrived. The 2,500 guests, among whom were President and Mrs. Harry S. Truman and their daughter, Margaret, Vice President Alben W. Barkley, members of the cabinet, Congress, and Supreme Court, the highest military officials of all the armed forces, and representatives of the diplomatic corps, were seated by 1100. At that time members of the public were permitted to fill unoccupied seats. Outside the amphitheater some 4,000 additional onlookers stood behind ropes to watch the arrival of the procession.

After the body bearers lifted Mr. Forrestal's casket from the caisson, Bishop Conkling and Rear Adm. William N. Thomas, the Navy Chief of Chaplains, led the way into the amphitheater. As the Army Band played the hymn "Lead Kindly Light," the clergy and body bearers escorted Mr. Forrestal's casket around the colonnade to the apse. In the apse, which was shielded from the sun by a green canopy, waited the Forrestal family, President Truman, Vice President Barkley, and the honorary pallbearers.

Bishop Conkling conducted a twenty-minute service, reading from two psalms, the New Testament, and the Episcopal Book of Common Prayer. After the benediction the Army Band played a hymn, "God of Our Fathers," while the body bearers took the casket out the west entrance and secured it to the caisson. As the

CASKET IS CARRIED INTO MEMORIAL AMPHITHEATER, *above. Service in Memorial Amphitheater, below.*

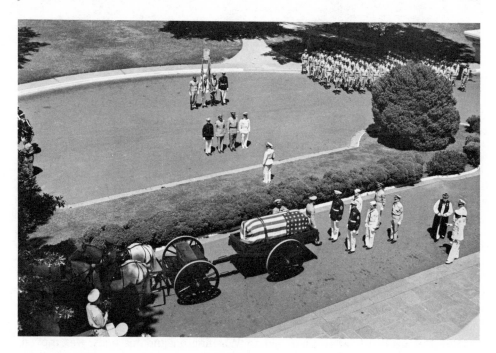

CASKET IS SECURED TO CAISSON FOR PROCESSION TO THE GRAVESITE

procession formed and moved toward the gravesite for the private service, the
Army Band played "Onward Christian Soldiers." The amphitheater audience remained inside until the cortege had departed and President Truman had left.

Besides the Forrestal family at the graveside were the former Secretary's aide,
Admiral Gingrich, and Capt. George N. Raines, the naval hospital physician who
had attended Mr. Forrestal. At the request of the family, the Marine Band played
two of Mr. Forrestal's favorite selections during the rites: Handel's "Largo" and
Rimsky-Korsakoff's "Hymn to the Sun." Bishop Conkling then read the Episcopal
service, the 3d Infantry battery fired a 19-gun salute, and the Marine firing squad
delivered three volleys. The ceremony was concluded by having one bugler blow
taps and a second bugler sound the notes as an echo.

CHAPTER VI

Chief of Naval Operations
Admiral Forrest P. Sherman
Special Military Funeral
22-27 July 1951

Admiral Forrest P. Sherman, the youngest officer to hold the post of Chief of Naval Operations, died unexpectedly on 22 July 1951 in Naples, Italy, at the age of fifty-four. He had been touring the North Atlantic Treaty Organization defense area and was visiting Admiral Robert B. Carney, commander of the North Atlantic Treaty Organization forces in southern Europe, as his last stop before he returned to the United States. Admiral Sherman suffered a heart attack early in the morning and a second and fatal attack just after noon.

Word of his death was dispatched to Washington and his body was moved from the hotel to the *Mount Olympus*, Admiral Carney's flagship, in Naples Harbor. A brief funeral service was held aboard the *Mount Olympus* on the morning of 24 July, while four United States destroyers formed a floating guard of honor around the flagship.

After the ceremony the admiral's casket, draped with an American flag, was taken ashore, placed in an Italian hearse, and escorted by Italian motor police to Naples' Capodichino Airport, where it was put aboard a Navy transport plane for return to the United States. An Italian armed forces guard and band rendered honors a few minutes before the plane departed.

When the Navy transport arrived at Washington National Airport on the afternoon of 25 July, the following prominent civil and military officials were there to honor Admiral Sherman: Secretary of Defense George C. Marshall; Secretary of State Dean G. Acheson; Secretary of the Army Frank Pace, Jr.; Secretary of the Navy Francis P. Matthews; Secretary of the Air Force Thomas K. Finletter; Deputy Secretary of Defense Robert A. Lovett; Under Secretary of the Navy Dan A. Kimball; Assistant Secretary of the Navy John T. Koehler; Assistant Secretary of the Navy for Air John F. Floberg; Chairman, Joint Chiefs of Staff, General of the Army Omar N. Bradley; Army Chief of Staff General J. Lawton Collins; Acting Chief of Naval Operations Admiral Lynde D. McCormick; Air Force Chief of Staff General Hoyt S. Vandenberg; Commandant of the Marine Corps General Clifton B. Cates; Assistant Commandant of the Marine Corps Lt. Gen.

Merwin H. Silverthorn; and Fleet Admiral Chester W. Nimitz. No planes were permitted to land or take off during a brief ceremony in which the U.S. Navy Band played ruffles and flourishes while three members of the clergy and a seaman bearing the admiral's colors escorted the casket past the officials to a hearse. The casket was then taken to the U.S. Naval Hospital in Bethesda, Maryland.

Under Department of Defense policies and plans published in 1949, Admiral Sherman was to be given a Special Military Funeral by virtue of his position as Chief of Naval Operations. Policy also prescribed that the officer in charge of funeral arrangements, acting as the representative of the Secretary of Defense, should be from the same service; in this instance the responsibility for arranging the funeral was given to the commandant of the Potomac River Naval Command, Rear Adm. George H. Fort.

According to the plan drawn up by Admiral Fort in close consultation with the Sherman family, the body of Admiral Sherman was to lie in the Bethlehem Chapel of the Washington National Cathedral for twenty-four hours, beginning 26 July. On the afternoon of the 27th, the body was to be moved in a hearse from the cathedral to Constitution Avenue at 15th Street, where a procession was to form for the march to Arlington National Cemetery. The funeral service was to be held in the Memorial Amphitheater, and burial was to be in Section 30 of the cemetery, the same northeastern section which contained the graves of William Howard Taft and James V. Forrestal. Graveside rites were to be attended only by members of the family.

On 26 July Admiral Sherman's body was moved from the Naval Hospital to the Washington National Cathedral, where it remained in the Bethlehem Chapel from the afternoon of the 26th to the afternoon of the 27th. An honor guard of members from all services maintained a constant vigil at the casket, but the chapel was not open to the public.

Early in the afternoon of 27 July, Admiral Sherman's casket was taken by hearse from the cathedral to Constitution Avenue at 15th Street, where it was transferred to a caisson for movement in procession to the cemetery. The military escort of the procession included units of the active Army, Navy, Marine Corps, and Air Force. As prescribed for Special Military Funerals, a military escort was to comprise two bands, a battalion of cadets from the appropriate academy, a company or comparable unit from each of the combat arms of the Army, and a company from each of the other armed forces. But this prescription was not rigid and in the arrangements for Admiral Sherman's funeral it was modified by adding to the escort a third band, a second battalion of cadets, and a composite company of servicewomen — a platoon each from the Women Accepted for Volunteer Emergency Service, Women's Army Corps, Women in the Air Force, and Women Marines. Admiral Fort, the escort commander, thus led approximately 1,500 troops, constituting three marching groups, each of about the same strength and each including a band. Scheduled to fly over the procession were 137 Navy and

HONOR GUARD KEEPS VIGIL IN BETHLEHEM CHAPEL

Marine Corps planes, including 44 jets, 48 Corsairs, 36 Skyraiders, and 9 Merca-
tor patrol bombers. A special honor guard was to march in the cortege directly
behind the caisson. The twelve members were Fleet Admiral William D. Leahy;
General of the Army Omar N. Bradley, Chairman, Joint Chiefs of Staff; General
J. Lawton Collins, Chief of Staff, U.S. Army; Admiral Lynde D. McCormick,
Acting Chief of Naval Operations; General Hoyt S. Vandenberg, Chief of Staff,
U.S. Air Force; General Clifton B. Cates, Commandant, U.S. Marine Corps;
Vice Adm. Merlin O'Neill, Commandant, U.S. Coast Guard; General Wade H.
Haislip, Vice Chief of Staff, U.S. Army; Vice Adm. Donald B. Duncan, Deputy
Chief of Naval Operations; General Nathan F. Twining, Vice Chief of Staff, U.S.
Air Force; Lt. Gen. Merwin H. Silverthorn, Assistant Commandant, U.S. Marine
Corps; and Rear Adm. Alfred C. Richmond, Assistant Commandant, U.S. Coast
Guard. Next in the procession were the following thirty-six honorary pallbearers,
chiefly from the Navy, all of them either flag or general officers:

Admiral Arthur W. Radford	Vice Adm. Oscar C. Badger
Admiral William M. Fechteler	Vice Adm. John L. McCrea
Admiral Robert B. Carney	Vice Adm. Arthur D. Struble
Admiral Russell S. Berkey (retired)	Vice Adm. Thomas L. Sprague

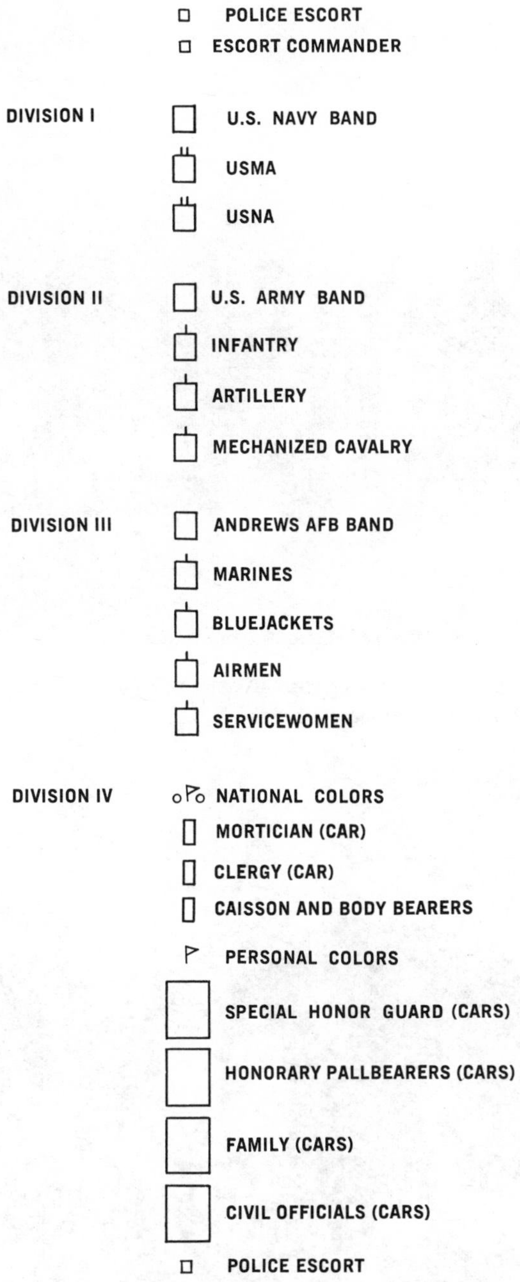

POLICE ESCORT

ESCORT COMMANDER

DIVISION I U.S. NAVY BAND

USMA

USNA

DIVISION II U.S. ARMY BAND

INFANTRY

ARTILLERY

MECHANIZED CAVALRY

DIVISION III ANDREWS AFB BAND

MARINES

BLUEJACKETS

AIRMEN

SERVICEWOMEN

DIVISION IV NATIONAL COLORS

MORTICIAN (CAR)

CLERGY (CAR)

CAISSON AND BODY BEARERS

PERSONAL COLORS

SPECIAL HONOR GUARD (CARS)

HONORARY PALLBEARERS (CARS)

FAMILY (CARS)

CIVIL OFFICIALS (CARS)

POLICE ESCORT

Diagram 10. Order of march, procession from Washington National Cathedral to Arlington National Cemetery.

CORTEGE MOVES ALONG CONSTITUTION AVENUE, *above. Cortege enters Memorial Gate of Arlington National Cemetery, below.*

SERVICE IN MEMORIAL AMPHITHEATER

Admiral Raymond A. Spruance (retired)
Admiral John H. Towers (retired)
Admiral Thomas C. Kinkaid (retired)
Admiral Dewitt C. Ramsey (retired)
Admiral Louis E. Denfeld (retired)
Admiral William H. P. Blandy (retired)
Admiral Claude C. Bloch (retired)
Vice Adm. Arthur C. Davis
Vice Adm. John J. Ballentine
Vice Adm. Felix B. Stump
Vice Adm. Charles P. Mason (retired)
Vice Adm. Arthur C. Miles (retired)
Vice Adm. Edward L. Cochrane
  (retired)
Vice Adm. Harry W. Hill
Vice Adm. Richard L. Conolly
Vice Adm. John D. Price

Vice Adm. Laurance T. DuBose
Vice Adm. Francis S. Low
Vice Adm. John H. Cassady
Vice Adm. Jerauld Wright
Rear Adm. Charles C. Hartman
Rear Adm. Henry S. Kendall
Rear Adm. William K. Harrill (retired)
Rear Adm. Richard E. Byrd (retired)
Lt. Gen. Franklin A. Hart,
  U.S. Marine Corps
Lt. Gen. Graves B. Erskine,
  U.S. Marine Corps
Maj. Gen. Field Harris,
  U.S. Marine Corps
Brig. Gen. Clayton C. Jerome,
  U.S. Marine Corps

Immediately behind the honorary pallbearers was the Sherman family group and bringing up the rear of the cortege were a number of civil dignitaries. These included the Secretary of Defense, Deputy Secretary of Defense, Secretary of the

Treasury, the Secretaries of the Army, Navy, and Air Force, the Secretary of State, and representatives of the diplomatic corps. (*Diagram 10*)

The procession moved to the cemetery via Constitution Avenue, 23d Street, Memorial Bridge, and Memorial Drive. Squadrons of planes in diamond formation passed over the column when it approached the Memorial Gate of the cemetery. As Admiral Fort led the column through the gate, the 3d Infantry battery opened a 17-gun salute. The firing was timed to match the movement of the procession at slow cadence from the gate to the Memorial Amphitheater.

Attendance at the funeral service in the amphitheater, which was scheduled for 1500, was by invitation from the Secretary of the Navy; invitations and responses to them were administered by the Office of the Chief of Naval Personnel. President Harry S. Truman attended and, as was his custom, dispensed with the honors and gun salute that usually signaled the arrival and departure of the President. Among other distinguished civilians invited were members of the cabinet, Supreme Court, Congress, Department of Defense, and diplomatic corps. Representatives of patriotic groups whose organizations had received government approval also were asked. From the armed forces, active and retired flag officers of the Navy and Coast Guard and active and retired general officers of the Marine Corps were invited. Only active general officers of the Army and Air Force received invitations.

The funeral service was conducted by the Very Reverend F. Merritt Williams, dean of St. Paul's Episcopal Cathedral in Springfield, Massachusetts, and the Reverend C. Leslie Glenn, rector of St. John's Episcopal Church in Washington, D.C., both commanders in the Navy Reserve. The Reverend Dr. Williams had been aboard the carrier *Wasp*, commanded then by Captain Sherman, when the ship was sunk east of Guadalcanal on 15 September 1942. The service, which lasted about fifteen minutes, included hymns, prayers, and scriptural readings. At its conclusion, the U.S. Marine Band played what is known as the Navy hymn, "Eternal Father, Strong to Save."

The graveside service, restricted to members of the Sherman family, also was brief. The 3d Infantry battery fired a second 17-gun salute as the rites began. Following a reading of the service, prayers, and the benediction, the traditional three volleys and the sounding of taps closed the ceremonies.

CHAPTER VII

Former Deputy Secretary of Defense Stephen T. Early
Combined Services Full Honor Funeral
11-14 August 1951

Stephen T. Early, former Deputy Secretary of Defense, died at George Washington University Hospital in Washington, D.C., on 11 August 1951. His death, at the age of sixty-one, followed a six-day illness caused by a heart ailment.

Robert A. Lovett, acting for George C. Marshall as Secretary of Defense, issued a formal memorandum announcing Mr. Early's death to the Secretaries of the Army, Navy, and Air Force on 13 August. At that time, Mr. Lovett directed that "every appropriate military honor be rendered" to Mr. Early. Under plans and policies placed in effect in late 1949, the "appropriate military honor" was a Combined Services Full Honor Funeral.

Responsibility for arranging Mr. Early's funeral rested with the Commanding General, Military District of Washington, Maj. Gen. Thomas W. Herren. General Herren, working closely with the Early family, arranged for a funeral service at the Washington National Cathedral at 1000 on 14 August. Since Mr. Early had served in the Army in World War I, burial was to take place in Arlington National Cemetery. A motorized cortege was to take Mr. Early's body from the cathedral to the Memorial Gate of Arlington National Cemetery, where, before the military escort formation, the casket was to be transferred to a caisson. The body was then to be escorted to the gravesite in Section 6, below the Memorial Amphitheater, for the final service.

After the former Deputy Secretary's death on 11 August, the body was taken to Gawler's funeral establishment where it remained until midmorning on the 14th, when it was taken by hearse to the Washington National Cathedral. Met by General Herren as escort commander, members of the clergy, the national color detail, the personal flag bearer, and a joint body bearer team of eight, the casket was taken in procession into the cathedral for the funeral service.

At 1000 Canon G. Gardiner Monks conducted the rites at the cathedral. Among those attending the service with the Early family was President Harry S. Truman. He was accompanied by Fleet Admiral William D. Leahy, who had been President Roosevelt's chief of staff during World War II, and who had been closely associated with Mr. Early when the latter had served as President Roosevelt's press secretary. Also in attendance were Mrs. Eleanor Roosevelt, government

HONORARY PALLBEARERS FOLLOW THE CASKET TO THE GRAVE

CANON MONKS PRESENTS FLAG TO MRS. EARLY AT THE GRAVESIDE

officials, and hundreds of Mr. Early's friends. Present also were dignitaries whom the Early family had asked to serve as honorary pallbearers, among them Vice President Alben W. Barkley, Chief Justice Fred M. Vinson, Secretary of Defense George C. Marshall, Secretary of the Army Frank Pace, Jr., Secretary of the Air Force Thomas K. Finletter, Mr. Sam Rayburn, General of the Army Omar N. Bradley, and Mr. Bernard M. Baruch.

At the close of the funeral service, Mr. Early's casket was taken in procession out of the cathedral and placed in a hearse. The motorized cortege then formed and proceeded to Arlington National Cemetery.

The military escort previously had formed on the lawn at the cemetery's Memorial Gate, facing on line toward Memorial Drive over which the cortege would approach. On the left of the formation was the U.S. Army Band. To the band's right, in order of seniority of service, were four ninety-man companies, one each from the Army, Marine Corps, Navy, and Air Force. Waiting on Memorial Drive directly in front of the escort troops was the caisson, and nearby stood the national color detail, personal flag bearer, and joint body bearer team.

When the cortege arrived, the hearse stopped beside the caisson. In a brief ceremony, the escort units saluted as Mr. Early's casket was transferred from the hearse to the caisson. General Herren then led the way through the cemetery to the gravesite. Following the escort commander was the band, which played Chopin's "Funeral March" as the procession moved. Next came the four troop companies. Behind them were the national color detail, an Army chaplain, the caisson flanked by the body bearers, the personal flag bearer, members of the Early family, and other mourners. As the funeral procession moved to the grave, the 3d Infantry battery, from a position in the cemetery, fired a 19-gun salute, spacing the rounds so that the last was fired as the procession reached the grave.

The graveside service was conducted by the Army chaplain, assisted by the Reverend William Kepler, pastor of Northminster Presbyterian Church. Following the benediction, a second 19-gun salute was fired, a rifle squad delivered the traditional three volleys, and an Army bugler sounded taps. At the conclusion of the rites, Canon Monks presented the flag that had draped the casket of the former Deputy Secretary of Defense to Mrs. Early.

CHAPTER VIII

Former Secretary of War Robert P. Patterson
Combined Services Full Honor Funeral
22-25 January 1952

On 22 January 1952 an American Airlines plane crashed at Elizabeth, New Jersey, as it approached a landing through fog and rain; six persons on the ground and all aboard the aircraft were killed. Among the plane's passengers was Robert P. Patterson, former Secretary of War. He was sixty years old.

By current regulations the former Secretary of War would receive a Combined Services Full Honor Funeral. Maj. Gen. Thomas W. Herren, commander of the Military District of Washington, was responsible for making the funeral arrangements in consultation with the Secretary's widow, Margaret Winchester Patterson. Ceremonies were to take place in both New York City and Washington, D.C.; General Herren was in charge of the Washington ceremonies and the co-ordination of procedures for the entire funeral. Responsibility for conducting the ceremonies in New York City rested with the Commanding General, First U.S. Army, Lt. Gen. Willis D. Crittenberger.

By virtue of his Army service in World War I, during which he received the Distinguished Service Cross, Mr. Patterson was to be buried in Arlington National Cemetery. The gravesite selected was in Section 30, near the graves of William Howard Taft, James V. Forrestal, and Admiral Forrest P. Sherman.

Mr. Patterson's body was brought to New York City from New Jersey shortly before noon on 24 January and placed in the Clark Room of the 7th Regiment Armory, where it was to lie until 2300. Massed behind the casket were four national colors, the personal flag of the Secretary of War, and the colors and standards of the parent units of two honor guards who took post at the casket. One of the guards was a member of the 306th Infantry, 77th Infantry Division (an Army Reserve unit), with which Mr. Patterson had served in France during World War I. The other was from the Army National Guard 107th Regiment. In 1916 Mr. Patterson had served with the 7th Regiment, later redesignated the 107th, on the Mexican border. All honor guards were furnished by the 107th and 306th Regiments and each two-man relief stood a half-hour watch. The honor guard members from the 306th were in battle dress, those from the 107th in dress gray uniforms specially designed for their regiment.

Beginning at noon on the 24th the armory was opened to the public for eleven hours while a steady procession of friends, associates, and admirers of Mr. Patterson filed by the bier to pay their last respects. Mrs. Patterson, her son, and her three daughters visited the Clark Room in the early afternoon. During the night of the 24th, Mr. Patterson's body was taken by train to Washington and placed in the Washington National Cathedral to await the funeral service at 1500 on the 25th.

Retired Maj. Gen. Luther D. Miller, canon of the cathedral and former Army Chief of Chaplains, conducted the midafternoon funeral service. He was assisted by the Reverend Lockett Ballard, rector of St. Phillip's Church in Garrison, New York, and minister of the Patterson family, and by the Right Reverend Angus Dun, Protestant Episcopal bishop of Washington. Hymns were played before and after the service by the U.S. Air Force Band.

Among those attending the service with the Patterson family were President Harry S. Truman and his family. Also present was a large group of dignitaries invited by the Patterson family to participate as honorary pallbearers. Those asked included:

Secretary of State Dean G. Acheson	Thomas B. McCabe
Maj. Gen. Julius Ochs Adler	General of the Army George C. Marshall
Montgomery B. Angell	Henry Morgenthau, Jr.
Warren R. Austin	William L. Marbury
Bernard M. Baruch	Admiral Ben Moreell
Chuncey Belknap	Basil O'Connor
General of the Army Omar N. Bradley	Floyd H. Odium
Dr. Ralph J. Bunche	Frederick H. Osborn
General Lucius D. Clay	Howard C. Petersen
Bradley Dewey	Samuel Pruyn
General J. Lawton Collins	Sam Rayburn
Dr. James B. Conant	John Duff Reed
Robert Cutler	Kenneth C. Royall
General James H. Doolittle	Elihu Root, Jr.
Ferdinand Eberstadt	Coolidge Sherman
Peter Finucane	General Brehon B. Somervell
Edward S. Greenbaum	Herbert Bayard Swope
Former Judge Augustus N. Hand	Dr. Dwight Sawyer
Former Judge Learned Hand	Dr. Charles Sawyer
George L. Harrison	Maj. Gen. Maxwell D. Taylor
Col. Donald R. Hyde	John W. Waters
Maj. Gen. John E. Hull	Thomas J. Watson
Judge John C. Knox	Vanderbilt Webb
Robert A. Lovett	Raymond Wilkins
M. J. Madigan	Boykin C. Wright
W. G. Maguire	

Following the simple Episcopal service led by Canon Miller, Mr. Patterson's

CASKET IS TRANSFERRED TO THE CAISSON AT MEMORIAL GATE

casket was taken in procession from the cathedral and placed in a hearse. A motorized cortege escorted by two armored cars then proceeded to the Memorial Gate of Arlington National Cemetery.

A military escort meanwhile had formed on line on the green at the gate. The units included the U.S. Army Band; Company A, 3d Infantry; the Navy Ceremonial Guard; the Marine Corps Ceremonial Company; and the 1100th Ceremonial Detachment from Bolling Air Force Base. On Memorial Drive directly in front of the military escort was the caisson, to which the casket would be transferred immediately after the cortege reached the Memorial Gate. Also on hand were a national color detail, a personal flag bearer, and a joint team of body bearers from three of the armed services: the Army, Navy, and Air Force.

When the cortege reached the Memorial Gate, the military escort presented arms and the Army Band played as the body bearers transferred the casket from the hearse to the horse-drawn caisson. Following the transfer, General Herren, as escort commander, led the way into the cemetery, entering on Roosevelt Drive. Behind him were the band, escort troop units, national color detail, Canon Miller, the caisson flanked by the body bearers, the personal flag bearer, the honorary pallbearers, the Patterson family, and other mourners, in that order. As the procession moved, the 3d Infantry battery, in position in the cemetery, fired a 19-gun salute, spacing the rounds so that the last one was fired as the procession arrived at the gravesite.

Canon Miller read the service at the grave. When he had finished, the battery from the 3d Infantry fired a second 19-gun salute. A rifle squad then delivered three volleys and an Army bugler sounded taps. The body bearers folded the flag that had draped Mr. Patterson's casket and handed it to Canon Miller, who then gave it to the Patterson family minister, the Reverend Lockett Ballard, who presented the flag to Mrs. Patterson.

CHAPTER IX

Senator Robert A. Taft
Funeral Without Formal Classification
31 July-4 August 1953

Robert A. Taft, son of former President William Howard Taft and renowned Republican senator from Ohio, died of cancer in a New York City hospital on 31 July 1953. The Senate, promptly adopting a resolution offered by Senator William F. Knowland of California, the acting Republican floor leader, ordered a State Funeral to be held for Mr. Taft on 3 August.

Under funeral plans and policies published in 1949 and then in force, a State Funeral was conducted only for a President, former President, President-elect, or "other persons when specifically designated by the President of the United States." The Senate resolution hence was extraordinary. But since the U.S. Congress controls the use of the Capitol itself and a State Funeral is distinguished by the period of lying in state in the Capitol rotunda, there was authority for the Senate action.

Nor was established procedure followed in delegating the responsibility for arranging the funeral of Senator Taft. According to current directives, the Commanding General, Military District of Washington, was "the designated representative of the President of the United States for the purpose of making all arrangements including participation of all Armed Forces and coordination with the State Department for participation of all branches of the Government and Diplomatic Corps" for a State Funeral. But in arranging the ceremonies for Senator Taft, the Senate assumed responsibility and the Military District of Washington handled only armed forces participation.

Except for the lying in state period at the Capitol, the ceremonies planned by Senate officials, working closely with the Taft family, were decidedly different from the current prescriptions for a State Funeral. On 2 August Senator Taft's body was to be brought from New York to Washington and taken to the Capitol to lie in state in the rotunda, which was to be open to the public from 1500 to 2100. At noon on 3 August a memorial service was to be held in the rotunda, attended by the Taft family, invited civil and military officials, and members of the diplomatic corps. Immediately after this service the Senator's body was to be flown to Cincinnati, home of the Taft family, where, as the family wished, a private funeral service and burial were to take place on 4 August. In none of the movements was there to be the large military escort and cortege described in the existing concept of a State Funeral.

Early on 2 August Air Force officers from Mitchel Field, Long Island, arrived by sedan at the Frank E. Campbell Funeral Home in New York, where Senator Taft's body had been taken on 31 July, to escort the body to the airfield from which it would be flown to Washington. The hearse bearing the casket and the sedan carrying the escorts left the funeral establishment about 0900. At Mitchel Field the casket was put aboard a plane furnished by the Military Air Transport Service. Two of Senator Taft's four sons, Robert A. Taft, Jr., and Lloyd B. Taft, and their wives had come from Cincinnati to accompany the body on the flight to Washington. Another son and his wife met the plane at Washington National Airport. Body bearers and a guard of honor representing all of the armed forces except the Coast Guard handled the casket and acted as escort to the Capitol.

At the Capitol the Lincoln catafalque, which in 1930 had held the casket of Senator Taft's father, stood in the center of the rotunda, with several floral pieces nearby. (The Taft family had requested that no flowers be sent, preferring that any offerings be made in the form of gifts to charities.) When the small procession from the airport reached the Capitol, the casket was borne into the rotunda and placed on the catafalque and an honor guard, representing the Army, Navy, Marine Corps, and Air Force and organized into reliefs by service, immediately took post at the bier.

From 1500 until 2100 on 2 August, the rotunda was open to the public. Persons paying their respects entered the west door of the rotunda, filed by the closed casket in two lines, one on either side of the bier, and left by the east door. By 2100 between 30,000 and 35,000 people had passed through the hall.

During the morning of 3 August, in preparation for the noontime memorial service, the casket and catafalque were moved from the center of the rotunda to a position near the west entrance, and the floral pieces were rearranged around the bier. Some 900 chairs, which fairly filled the chamber, were set up. No facilities for photographic, radio, or televised coverage of the ceremony were allowed.

In the Senate resolution ordering the State Funeral for Senator Taft, invitations to the memorial service were extended to President Dwight D. Eisenhower and his cabinet, the entire House of Representatives, all justices of the Supreme Court, the military chiefs of all the uniformed services, including the chairman of the Joint Chiefs of Staff, and representatives of the diplomatic corps. General of the Army Douglas MacArthur, a friend of Mr. Taft's for many years, received Mrs. Taft's personal invitation to attend. An invitation from the Senate also had gone to former President Harry S. Truman, but he was not able to attend.

Within the hour before the scheduled beginning of the service, the U.S. Marine Band took seats in the rotunda to play during the arrival of the invited audience. At 1140, as the band began "America the Beautiful," the members of the Senate entered the rotunda by the north door, marching two abreast but in no special order of seniority. Next to enter were the Chief Justice of the United States and associate justices of the Supreme Court. Then, through the south door, came the members of the House of Representatives. General and Mrs. MacArthur, and the general's aide, Maj. Gen. Courtney Whitney, and Mrs. Whitney entered about the same time, followed by invited military dignitaries. The diplomatic corps representatives were next to arrive. Mrs. Taft, who was an invalid, then entered in a wheelchair, escorted by two of her sons. Her other two sons followed. About five minutes before noon the last of the guests—President and Mrs. Eisenhower and the members of the cabinet—came into the rotunda.

Upon the arrival of the President and his party, the Marine honor guard on duty at the bier was replaced by a relief that included a soldier, a sailor, an airman, and a marine. After two minutes of silence had been observed, the Reverend Frederick Brown Harris, the Senate Chaplain, stood before the casket and offered the invocation. Senator John W. Bricker, Mr. Taft's Republican colleague from Ohio, then rose and delivered a eulogy. When Senator Bricker had finished, the Reverend Bernard Braskamp, Chaplain of the House of Representatives, gave the benediction, and the Marine Band concluded the service by playing the national anthem.

Shortly after the memorial service, Senator Taft's casket was taken from the rotunda and, under escort, returned to Washington National Airport, where it was placed aboard a plane of the Military Air Transport Service for the flight to Cincinnati. Two of the Senator's sons, their wives, and I. Jack Martin, who had been an administrative assistant to Mr. Taft, accompanied the body on the flight. Mrs. Taft and the remaining members of her family took a later plane for Lunken Airport in Cincinnati.

The plane bearing Senator Taft's body landed at the Greater Cincinnati Airport in Boone County, Kentucky. Morticians of the Schaefer and Busby funeral establishment of Cincinnati met the plane. Kentucky state highway patrolmen and Cincinnati motorcycle police escorted the hearse bearing the casket from the airport to the funeral establishment, where the body was to remain until the funeral service on 4 August.

Actually, two funeral services were conducted for Senator Taft on 4 August, both at noon. The private service was held in Indian Hill Church, a Protestant Episcopal-Presbyterian Church which the Tafts attended in the suburb where they had lived for many years. A public service was held in downtown Cincinnati in the Christ Protestant Episcopal Church to accommodate the many friends of Senator Taft who would be unable to attend the private service. Arranged by Mayor Carl W. Rich of Cincinnati, it was conducted jointly by the Right Reverend Henry Wise Hobson, bishop of the Episcopal Diocese of Southern Ohio, and the Reverend Morris F. Arnold, rector of Christ Church.

The private service was conducted by the Reverend Luther M. Tucker, rector of Indian Hill Church. Following the funeral service, Senator Taft was buried in

Indian Hill Church Cemetery; he was the first person to be buried there. It was Mrs. Taft's wish that her husband's grave be close to the Taft home.

CHAPTER X

Former Air Force Chief of Staff
General Hoyt S. Vandenberg
Special Military Funeral
2-5 April 1954

General Hoyt S. Vandenberg, Chief of Staff of the Air Force from 1948 to 1953, died at Walter Reed General Hospital on 2 April 1954 at the age of fifty-five. He had been ill of cancer for several years and hospitalized since 7 October 1953.

When it became known that death was imminent, Headquarters, Department of the Air Force, began to draw up plans for a Special Military Funeral for the general. Under current Department of Defense policies, General Vandenberg's status as a retired former Chief of Staff entitled him to a "combined services full honor ceremony." Authority for according the greater ceremony of a Special Military Funeral rested with the Secretary of Defense; in this case it would come from Secretary Charles E. Wilson.

Several months before the general's death, the Air Force Chief of Chaplains, Maj. Gen. Charles I. Carpenter, discussed funeral arrangements for the general with his wife, Gladys Rose Vandenberg. At that time, she preferred a family service in St. Joseph's Chapel at the Washington National Cathedral and at Arlington National Cemetery.

Wishing to hold a more elaborate ceremony for the distinguished Air Force official, Air Force Chief of Staff General Nathan D. Twining, in January 1954, directed Brig. Gen. Monro MacCloskey, who had been a member of the same U.S. Military Academy company as General Vandenberg and who was a long-time friend of the Vandenberg family, to take up the matter again with Mrs. Vandenberg. General MacCloskey and Mrs. Vandenberg reached agreement on a larger ceremony. General Vandenberg's body was to lie in St. Joseph's Chapel at the Washington National Cathedral until the funeral service, which was to be held in the cathedral nave and was to be conducted according to rites of the Episcopal Church, of which the Vandenbergs were communicants. The body was then to be moved in procession to the entrance of Arlington National Cemetery. From there a military escort was to accompany the cortege to the gravesite in Section 30, near the graves of William Howard Taft and James V. Forrestal.

On 2 April General Twining formally assigned primary responsibility for arranging the funeral to Headquarters Command, U.S. Air Force, at Bolling Air Force Base, Washington, D.C. Brig. Gen. Stoyte O. Ross, who headed the command, immediately established a liaison office in the Pentagon which was manned around the clock through 5 April, the day of the funeral. General Ross's headquarters meanwhile issued a 44-page "Special Military Funeral Plan" with ten annexes, a document based on the plan worked out by General MacCloskey and Mrs. Vandenberg.

The Air Adjutant General, Col. Kenneth E. Thiebaud, was in charge of sending out announcements of the funeral (in effect, invitations to attend) to family, friends, and dignitaries. Colonel Thiebaud also handled seating plans for the cathedral and other matters of protocol, including details covering the attendance of the family, honorary pallbearers, and special honor guard. Lt. Gen. Emmett O'Donnell, Jr., the Air Force Deputy Chief of Staff for Personnel, was responsible for conducting necessary "negotiations with the Secretary of Defense, appropriate overseas commanders, and next of kin."

At 0815 on 3 April General Vandenberg's body, which had been taken from the hospital to the Rinaldi Funeral Home, was moved in procession to the Washington National Cathedral. Eight body bearers, two each from the Air Force, Army, and Navy and one each from the Marine Corps and Coast Guard, led by an Air Force officer, handled the casket. Heading the procession to the cathedral was a police escort, and following, with intervals of twenty-five yards between, were the escort commander, the clergy, the hearse, the body bearers, and a second police escort.

Awaiting the procession at the Bethlehem Chapel entrance to the cathedral were a cordon of sixteen airmen and an officer, the general's personal flag bearer, and an Air Force ceremonial band. The band sounded four ruffles and flourishes and played the "General's March" and the honor cordon presented arms as the body bearers took the casket from the hearse. Following the clergy, the body bearers carried the casket through the Bethlehem Chapel entrance to St. Joseph's Chapel. In column behind the casket were two representatives of the mortuary, the flag bearer, and (according to the recollection of the cathedral verger) the family and honorary pallbearers. The casket was placed on a bier and an honor guard took post immediately.

The honor guard consisted of one officer and five noncommissioned officers; sixteen men from the enlisted ranks, four from each of the four armed forces; and one officer, two petty officers, and two other enlisted men from the Coast Guard. These troops were provided by the 1100th Air Base Group, the 3d Infantry, and the Potomac River Naval Command (which arranged all Navy, Marine, and Coast Guard participation in the ceremonies). Mess, housing, transportation, and other administrative support for the honor guard at the chapel were responsibil-

HONOR GUARD STANDS AT THE BIER IN ST. JOSEPH'S CHAPEL

ities of the commander of the 1100th Air Base Group, stationed at Bolling Air Force Base.

The honor guard stood watch from the morning of 3 April until noon on 5 April, performing its vigil in half-hour reliefs. Each daytime relief comprised one officer and four noncommissioned officers. A night relief consisted of one noncommissioned officer and four enlisted men. The reliefs were posted by service, not in combined formations. (It appears that the Coast Guard sentinels served in the naval watch rotation.) As is customary in the Protestant Episcopal Church, the casket remained closed during this period and during the funeral service as well.

The commander of the 1401st Air Base Wing, a Military Transport Service unit stationed at Bolling Air Force Base, provided a floral detail whose members received each flower offering at the cathedral and recorded the name of the sender. The detail worked around the clock in three shifts, an officer, three noncommissioned officers, and seven enlisted men in each shift. Although the actual arranging of flowers was done by personal friends of the Vandenberg family, in particular, by Mrs. William Pope Anderson of Washington, D.C., the detail from the Military Transport Service assisted the family friends later in the nave of the cathedral and at the gravesite.

The Air Adjutant General's office had meanwhile issued announcements of the funeral service to Washington officials as required by protocol and to individuals selected by Mrs. Vandenberg in consultation with General MacCloskey. These included retired Air Force general officers; West Point classmates of General Vandenberg; representatives of the Air Force Officers' Wives Club, Air Force Association, Air Force Arlington Committee, Civil Air Patrol, Air Force Aid Society, Air Force Historical Foundation, and other associations; and members of the aircraft and airline industries. Former President Harry S. Truman was invited but was not able to attend.

Among those invited to the funeral were twenty-four men who were asked to serve as honorary pallbearers. Some of these were the general's personal friends, others were associates from the military services, the Central Intelligence Agency, the diplomatic corps, and the aircraft industry. Seventeen were able to participate and officer guides were detailed to assist them during the ceremonies.

The funeral service announcements, along with tickets for seats in the cathedral, were delivered by courier to residents of the Washington area. Others were notified by telegraph and given seating information. Fifty ushers, all officers from Bolling Air Force Base and Andrews Air Force Base, were appointed and given detailed instructions on directing the seating in the various sections of the cathedral nave. (*Diagram 11*)

A minor ceremonial arrangement peculiar to the services for General Vandenberg concerned the special honor guard. This formation traditionally consists of the chairman of the Joint Chiefs of Staff, the chiefs and vice chiefs of staffs of the three military departments, and the commandants and assistant commandants of the Marine Corps and Coast Guard. Out of a decision to make this group an even number, General J. Lawton Collins, formerly Army Chief of Staff and now U.S. Military Representative to the North Atlantic Treaty Organization, was added. Later, when it turned out that the assistant commandant of the Coast Guard could not attend, the chief of the office of operations of that service was substituted.

At noon on 5 April the body bearers moved General Vandenberg's casket from St. Joseph's Chapel to a bier in the nave. The floral pieces were brought into the nave and arranged around the pulpit and lectern, and the honor guard again was posted. This time, in contrast to the posting of reliefs by service during the vigil in St. Joseph's Chapel, a joint service relief took post in the nave, a system followed until the beginning of the funeral service at 1400.

Dignitaries attending the funeral included President Dwight D. Eisenhower, the Secretary of Defense, the three service secretaries, the Secretary of State, and the Secretary of the Treasury. The service was conducted by the Very Reverend Francis B. Sayre, dean of the Washington National Cathedral, who was assisted

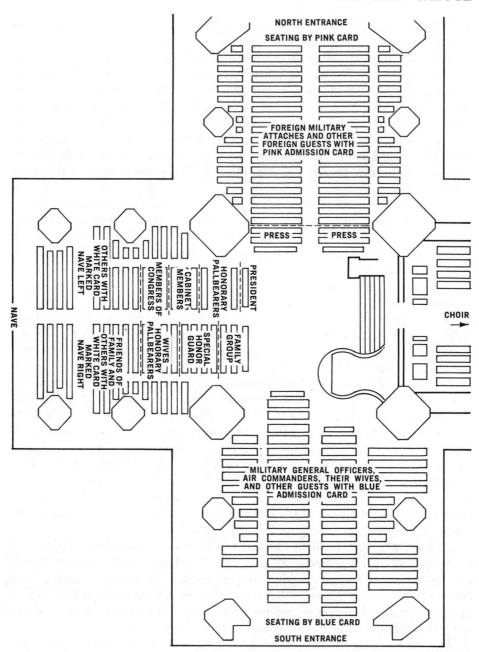

Diagram 11.   Washington National Cathedral seating plan.

CASKET IS CARRIED OUT OF THE CATHEDRAL

by the Reverend Frank E. Pulley, Chaplain of the U.S. Military Academy. In the course of a simple ceremony read from the Book of Common Prayer, the West Point Cadet Choir sang the academy hymn, "The Corps." No eulogy was delivered.

At the conclusion of the service, President Eisenhower left the cathedral and returned to the White House. After his departure the cathedral verger and the clergy led the way from the nave of the cathedral, followed by the honorary pallbearers who formed a cordon along the north transept aisle. Two body bearers then wheeled the casket on its movable bier through the cordon of pallbearers to the north entrance, where the remaining body bearers waited. Here the full contingent of body bearers took the casket and, followed by the personal flag bearer, family group, special honor guard, and other mourners, carried it through a cordon of sixteen airmen stationed on the entrance steps. The Air Force ceremonial band, across the street from the cortege vehicles, played while the casket was carried out and placed in the hearse. Those who were to travel in the cortege entered their automobiles and the motorcade departed. (*Diagram 12*) The body

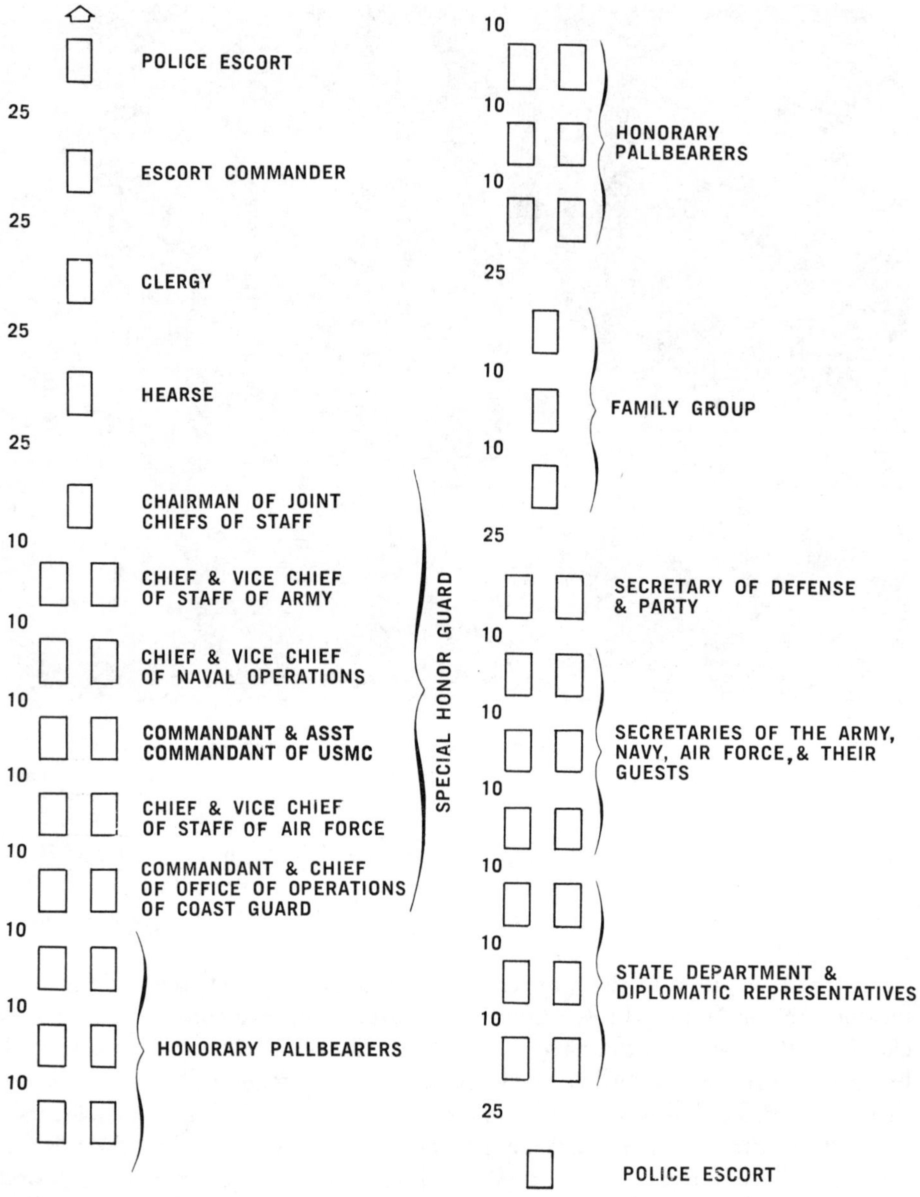

POLICE ESCORT

25

ESCORT COMMANDER

25

CLERGY

25

HEARSE

25

CHAIRMAN OF JOINT
CHIEFS OF STAFF

10

CHIEF & VICE CHIEF
OF STAFF OF ARMY

10

CHIEF & VICE CHIEF
OF NAVAL OPERATIONS

10

COMMANDANT & ASST
COMMANDANT OF USMC

10

CHIEF & VICE CHIEF
OF STAFF OF AIR FORCE

10

COMMANDANT & CHIEF
OF OFFICE OF OPERATIONS
OF COAST GUARD

10

10

HONORARY PALLBEARERS

10

SPECIAL HONOR GUARD

10

10

HONORARY
PALLBEARERS

10

25

10

FAMILY GROUP

10

25

SECRETARY OF DEFENSE
& PARTY

10

SECRETARIES OF THE ARMY,
NAVY, AIR FORCE, & THEIR
GUESTS

10

10

10

STATE DEPARTMENT &
DIPLOMATIC REPRESENTATIVES

10

25

POLICE ESCORT

Diagram 12.   Order of march, Washington National Cathedral to
Arlington National Cemetery.

bearers and flag bearer proceeded by a separate route in order to reach Memorial Gate of the cemetery ahead of the procession.

The cortege moved to Arlington National Cemetery via Woodley Road, Cathedral Avenue, Rock Creek Parkway, Memorial Bridge, and Memorial Drive. Waiting in column on Memorial Drive was the military escort, whose units included the U.S. Air Force Band, the U.S. Army Band, a battalion of cadets from the U.S. Military Academy, a battalion of midshipmen from the U.S. Naval Academy, a battalion of air cadets from Lackland Air Force Base, and a combined services battalion. This last battalion, commanded by a lieutenant colonel from the 3d Infantry with a staff of three company grade officers from the Marine Corps, Navy, and Air Force, contained a reduced company (one officer and forty-one men) each from the Army, Marine Corps, Navy, and Air Force. It was massed on an eight-man front, whereas the other battalions were massed on a nine-man front. Only the cadets and midshipmen carried arms. Also waiting were the body bearers, personal flag bearer, and a combined services national color detail.

When the cortege arrived it proceeded to the rear escort unit, where it halted while the color detail took position at the head of the procession, with the body bearers on either side of the hearse and the personal flag bearer immediately behind the hearse. The escort commander (an Air Force major general) and his staff of field grade Army, Marine Corps, and Navy officers then moved to the head of the military escort and led the full procession into the cemetery. (*Diagram 13*)

The column proceeded on Roosevelt Drive, Weeks Drive, and Sheridan Drive toward the gravesite in Section 30. Along the route was a cordon of airmen from Bolling and Andrews Air Force Bases posted at intervals of about fifteen feet. When the hearse entered Memorial Gate, the 3d Infantry battery, in position along Weitzel Drive at the north end of the cemetery, began a 17-gun salute, firing the rounds at fifteen-second intervals. Before the procession reached the gravesite, six B–47 Stratojets flew over in V-formation with the second position on the right empty as a salute to a fallen comrade. The bombers were followed by a flight of sixteen F–84 Thunderjets and sixteen F–86 Sabrejets.

When the procession reached the intersection of Sheridan Drive with Sherman Drive just above the gravesite, the escort commander and all escort units except the U.S. Air Force Band and U.S. Military Academy Cadet Company A–1 (General Vandenberg's company when he was a cadet) turned west on Sherman away from the gravesite. These units, not scheduled for further participation in the ceremonies, continued west on Sherman to the cemetery's administrative area parking lot and boarded buses to return to their respective duty stations.

Already in position at the graveside were an Army company, Marine Corps company, Navy company, and an Air Force squadron, each consisting of three officers and sixty-six men. These units were headed by an Air Force colonel (with a

MILITARY UNITS OF THE PROCESSION ENTER THE CEMETERY, *above. Cortege nears the gravesite, below.*

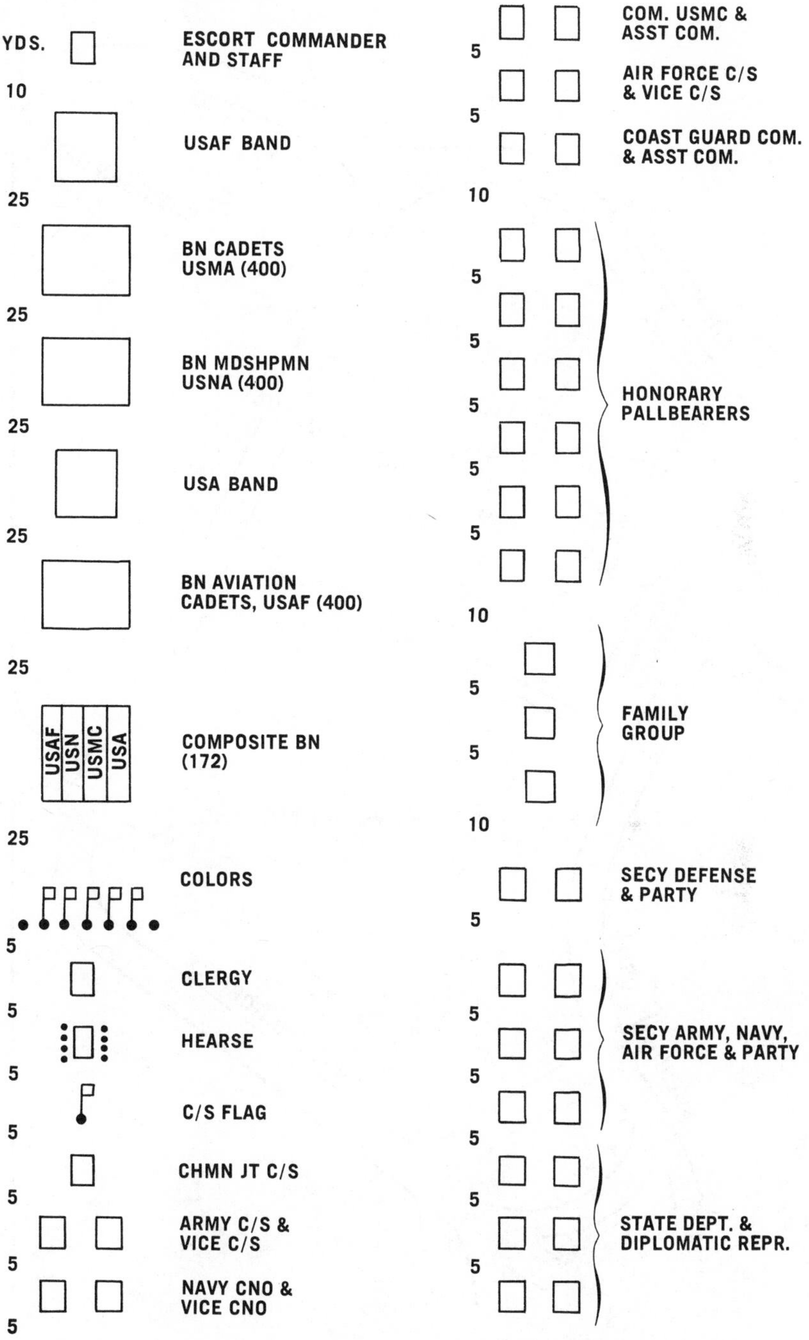

YDS. ☐ ESCORT COMMANDER AND STAFF

10

☐ USAF BAND

25

☐ BN CADETS USMA (400)

25

☐ BN MDSHPMN USNA (400)

25

☐ USA BAND

25

☐ BN AVIATION CADETS, USAF (400)

25

USAF USN USMC USA COMPOSITE BN (172)

25

COLORS

5

☐ CLERGY

5

HEARSE

5

C/S FLAG

5

☐ CHMN JT C/S

5

☐ ☐ ARMY C/S & VICE C/S

5

☐ ☐ NAVY CNO & VICE CNO

5

☐ ☐ COM. USMC & ASST COM.

5

☐ ☐ AIR FORCE C/S & VICE C/S

5

☐ ☐ COAST GUARD COM. & ASST COM.

10

☐ ☐
5
☐ ☐
5
☐ ☐
5 HONORARY PALLBEARERS
☐ ☐
5
☐ ☐
5
☐ ☐

10

☐
5
☐ FAMILY GROUP
5
☐

10

☐ ☐ SECY DEFENSE & PARTY

5

☐ ☐
5
☐ ☐ SECY ARMY, NAVY, AIR FORCE & PARTY
5
☐ ☐
5
☐ ☐

5

☐ ☐ STATE DEPT. & DIPLOMATIC REPR.

5

☐ ☐

Diagram 13.   Order of march, Memorial Gate to gravesite.

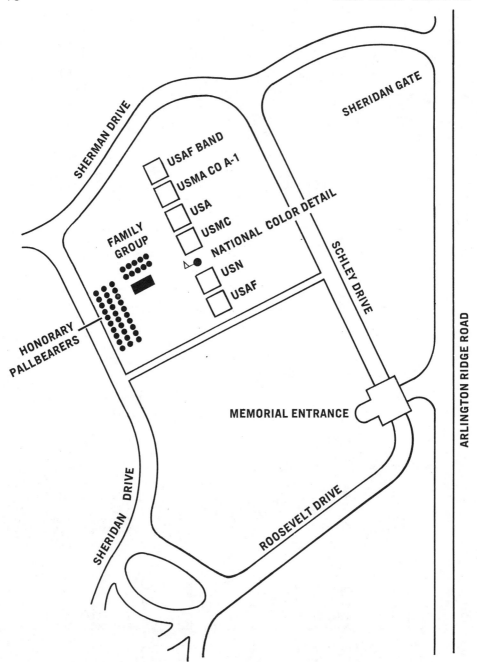

Diagram 14.   Formation at the graveside.

combined services staff of field grade officers) who would serve as escort commander during the graveside rites. Upon reaching the graveside the Air Force Band, Cadet Company A–1, and the national color detail joined the formation, in which each company was massed on a six-man front at close interval.

After the cortege halted on Sheridan Drive opposite the gravesite, the honorary pallbearers dismounted and formed a cordon along a pathway leading to the grave. The special honor guard and the Vandenberg family moved directly to positions at the grave. (*Diagram 14*) The body bearers then removed the casket from the hearse and, preceded by the clergy and followed by the personal flag bearer, carried General Vandenberg's casket to the grave. When the casket cleared the honorary pallbearers, they followed in a column of two to their graveside positions. As the casket was moved, the escort troops saluted and the band played four ruffles and flourishes and the "General's March."

Dean Sayre and Chaplain Pulley performed the graveside service. At its conclusion, the escort units saluted and the 3d Infantry battery fired seventeen guns. A bugler then sounded taps, which was echoed by a second bugler. At the last

LAST RITES AT THE GRAVESIDE

note the escort troops ordered arms. The body bearers then folded the flag that had draped the casket and handed it to Dean Sayre. He in turn presented it to the general's son, Lt. Hoyt S. Vandenberg, Jr., who received it for his mother.

The ceremonies for General Vandenberg had been marked by several departures from the prescribed Special Military Funeral, notably by the absence of the horse-drawn caisson, the omission of three volleys by a firing squad at the graveside, and the addition of a flyover of jet aircraft with one plane missing from the formation.

CHAPTER XI

Former Army Chief of Staff General Peyton C. March
Special Military Funeral
13-18 April 1955

General Peyton C. March, Chief of Staff of the Army during World War I, died at the age of ninety in Walter Reed General Hospital, Washington, D.C., on 13 April 1955. The Department of the Army immediately published General Order 26 announcing General March's death and Secretary of the Army Robert T. Stevens directed all installations under the control of the department to display the national flag at half-staff until sunset on the day of burial, 18 April. Secretary Stevens also ordered the commanding general of the Military District of Washington, Maj. Gen. John H. Stokes, Jr., to render appropriate honors. General March was entitled to a Combined Services Full Honor Funeral, but the Secretary of Defense could direct a more elaborate ceremony for one of his rank. As in the case of General Vandenberg, who had died the previous year, Secretary Charles E. Wilson authorized a Special Military Funeral.

The arrangements made by General Stokes, who took into account the preferences of the March family, involved no church or chapel service. There was to be only a procession through Washington to Arlington National Cemetery with last rites at the graveside. The burial plot was in Section 30, the northeastern section of the cemetery that contained the graves of William Howard Taft, James V. Forrestal, and Hoyt S. Vandenberg.

The procession was to form in Washington on Constitution Avenue at 15th Street, N.W. General March's casket was to be brought to this point by hearse from the funeral establishment then transferred to a caisson for the move to the cemetery.

The military escort in the procession was to consist of the escort commander and his staff; the U.S. Army Band; one battalion of cadets from the U.S. Military Academy; one company of infantry; one battery of field artillery; one company of armor; the U.S. Marine Band; one company of marines; one company of bluejackets; one squadron of airmen; and one composite company of servicewomen. The company of servicewomen had been added to the conventional plan by General Stokes, who followed the precedent set by the Navy for the funeral of Admiral Sherman in 1951. All together the strength of the military escort for the funeral of General March was to be approximately 1,200.

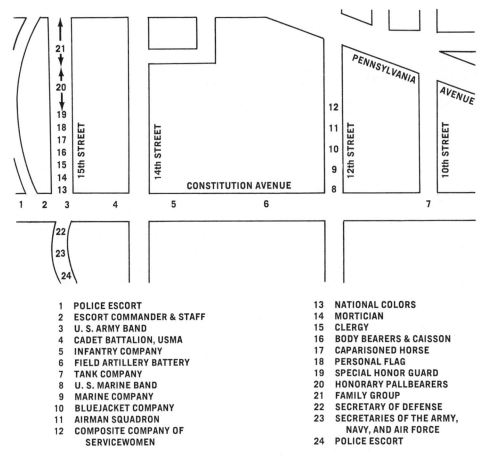

1	POLICE ESCORT	13	NATIONAL COLORS
2	ESCORT COMMANDER & STAFF	14	MORTICIAN
3	U. S. ARMY BAND	15	CLERGY
4	CADET BATTALION, USMA	16	BODY BEARERS & CAISSON
5	INFANTRY COMPANY	17	CAPARISONED HORSE
6	FIELD ARTILLERY BATTERY	18	PERSONAL FLAG
7	TANK COMPANY	19	SPECIAL HONOR GUARD
8	U. S. MARINE BAND	20	HONORARY PALLBEARERS
9	MARINE COMPANY	21	FAMILY GROUP
10	BLUEJACKET COMPANY	22	SECRETARY OF DEFENSE
11	AIRMAN SQUADRON	23	SECRETARIES OF THE ARMY,
12	COMPOSITE COMPANY OF		NAVY, AND AIR FORCE
	SERVICEWOMEN	24	POLICE ESCORT

Diagram 15.   Assembly and order of march, procession to Arlington National
Cemetery.

Scheduled to march as part of the cortege was a special honor guard composed of the Army Chief of Staff and Vice Chief of Staff, the Commandant and Assistant Commandant of the Marine Corps, the Chief of Naval Operations and his Vice Chief, the Air Force Chief of Staff and Vice Chief of Staff, and the Commandant and Assistant Commandant of the Coast Guard. Unable to be present, General Matthew B. Ridgway, the Army Chief of Staff, later appointed General John E. Hull, then temporarily assigned to General Ridgway's office before retirement, to represent him. Also to march in the cortege were the Secretary of Defense and the Secretaries of the Army, Navy, and Air Force.

On 18 April all march units assembled in the vicinity of Constitution Avenue and 15th Street by 1100, the starting hour of the procession. Each group had been

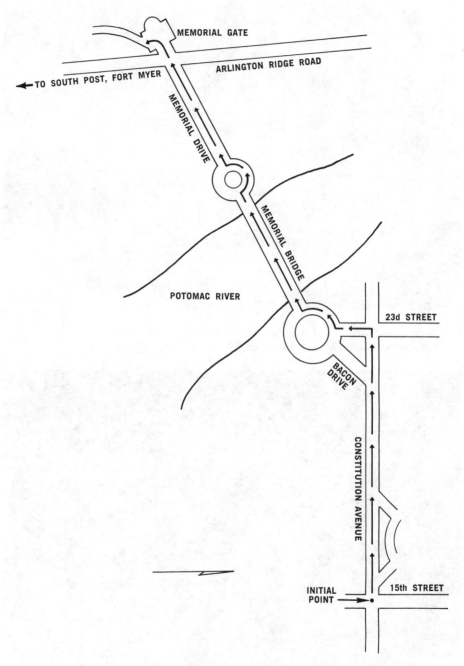

Diagram 16.   Route of march to Arlington National Cemetery.

CAISSON FOLLOWED BY CAPARISONED HORSE ENTERS THE CEMETERY, *above.*
Caisson moves through the cemetery, below.

assigned a point of assembly on the avenue or on intersecting numbered streets in a design that would allow each to join the column in proper march order. (*Diagram 15*) All segments of the cortege were on 15th Street, above and below Constitution Avenue. The caisson itself was sited north of the avenue for the ceremony of transferring General March's casket from the hearse.

The hearse arrived from the funeral establishment shortly before 1100. As the casket was shifted from the hearse to the caisson, the military escort, commanded by General Stokes, presented arms, and the U.S. Army Band, located in the intersection of Constitution Avenue and 15th Street, sounded four ruffles and flourishes and played a hymn. The procession then moved off in quick-time cadence, proceeding west along Constitution Avenue, south on 23d Street, and across Memorial Bridge toward the Memorial Gate of the cemetery. (*Diagram 16*) A flight of jet aircraft had been scheduled to pass overhead as the mile-long column crossed Memorial Bridge, but poor flying conditions forced a cancellation.

Not all of the escort entered the cemetery. General Stokes had designated the intersection of Memorial Drive and Arlington Ridge Road, just outside Memorial Gate, as a regulating point where the artillery battery, the company of armor, the U.S. Marine Band, the company of servicewomen, and accompanying police were to leave the procession and march south and north on Arlington Ridge Road. After these units left and the remaining units closed intervals, the procession moved toward the grave at reduced cadence via Roosevelt, Weeks, and Sheridan Drives.

Waiting at the grave was a large group of military, civilian, and foreign dignitaries headed by Vice President Richard M. Nixon. Also in attendance were representatives of the Society of the Cincinnati, the Descendants of the Signers of the Declaration of Independence, and the Delta Kappa Epsilon Fraternity, to all of which General March had belonged.

When they reached the grave, the U.S. Military Academy cadets, who had been marching in a column of companies, massed as a battalion, while the company of infantry, company of marines, company of bluejackets, and squadron of airmen formed a composite armed forces battalion. The Army Band also posted itself at the grave. Already present were the superintendent of Arlington National Cemetery, Mr. John C. Metzler, and the ceremonial officer and a firing party of the 3d Infantry from nearby Fort Myer. In position at a distance to render a gun salute was the 3d Infantry battery; other troops of the 3d Infantry were on station to control traffic and parking.

While the military escort units were taking their positions at the graveside, the honorary pallbearers lined both sides of a cocomat leading from the roadway to the grave. The rest of the funeral party meanwhile left the cars and assembled near the caisson. At a signal from the ceremonial officer, the escort presented arms and the body bearers removed the casket from the caisson. The Army Band sounded ruffles and flourishes and began to play a hymn.

U.S. MILITARY ACADEMY CADETS MARCH IN PROCESSION *to Arlington National Cemetery.*

Brig. Gen. Frank A. Tobey, the Army Deputy Chief of Chaplains, then led the way to the grave and the body bearers followed, carrying General March's casket through the cordon of honorary pallbearers. As the casket cleared the cordon, the honorary pallbearers fell in behind in column, two abreast. The March family and others of the funeral party followed the pallbearers and were guided to graveside positions by Superintendent Metzler.

As the casket was placed above the grave, the Army Band stopped playing and the escort units ordered arms. Chaplain Tobey then conducted a brief service. At its conclusion the military escort presented arms and the battery fired a 17-gun salute. The 3d Infantry delivered three volleys, and immediately after the bugler sounded taps. The body bearers folded the flag that had draped the casket and handed it to Superintendent Metzler, who presented it to the next of kin, the general's widow, who was accompanied by her two sons-in-law, Lt. Gen. Joseph M. Swing and Maj. Gen. John Millikin. This presentation concluded the services for General March.

CHAPTER XII

Former Army Chief of Staff
General Charles P. Summerall
Combined Services Full Honor Funeral
14-17 May 1955

General Charles P. Summerall, former Chief of Staff of the Army, died at Walter Reed General Hospital in Washington, D.C., on 14 May 1955 at the age of eighty-eight.

In Department of the Army General Order 33 announcing General Summerall's death, General Matthew B. Ridgway, Army Chief of Staff, instructed Maj. Gen. John H. Stokes, Jr., Commanding General, Military District of Washington, to render appropriate funeral honors. In the same order, General Ridgway directed that the national flag at all installations under the control of the department be lowered to half-staff until sunset on the day of General Summerall's burial.

General Stokes supervised arrangements for a Combined Services Full Honor Funeral, the ceremony authorized for a former Chief of Staff, to take place on 17 May. The funeral service was to be held in the chapel at Fort Myer, and burial was to take place in Arlington National Cemetery following a full procession from the chapel to the gravesite. The gravesite selected was in Section 30, near the graves of William Howard Taft, James V. Forrestal, Admiral Forrest P. Sherman, General Hoyt S. Vandenberg, and General Peyton C. March.

The funeral service was held at 1430 on the 17th. Before that hour, the band and troop units that would later form the escort in the procession to the grave took position outside the Fort Myer Chapel entrance as an honor guard. In the formation were the U.S. Army Band and a company each of Army, Marine Corps, Navy, and Air Force troops. Also included were ten cadets from the military academy in Charleston, South Carolina, The Citadel, some of whom acted as a color guard. General Summerall, after his retirement from the Army in 1931, had served for twenty-two years as president of The Citadel.

When the hearse bearing the casket arrived at the chapel, the honor guard troop presented arms as the band sounded four ruffles and flourishes and played the "General's March." The casket was then lifted from the hearse and borne into the chapel by the body bearers from the 3d Infantry, while the band played "Lead Kindly Light."

Former Army Chief of Chaplains Luther D. Miller, canon of the Washington National Cathedral, conducted the funeral service. With General Summerall's son, Col. Charles P. Summerall, Jr., were General of the Army George C. Marshall, General Ridgway, and General Mark W. Clark, who had succeeded General Summerall as president of The Citadel.

At the conclusion of the service, General Summerall's casket was taken out of the chapel in procession. As the body bearers with the casket reached the chapel doorway, the honor guard presented arms and the band again sounded ruffles and flourishes and played the "General's March." While the band played "Nearer My God to Thee," the casket was borne to the caisson that had been drawn up in front of the chapel and the procession formed.

General Stokes, as escort commander, led the way into the cemetery through the gate adjoining the chapel grounds. The Army Band followed, playing Chopin's "Funeral March." Behind the band marched the escort units in a column of companies. Next, in order, were the national color detail, Canon Miller, the caisson flanked by the body bearers, a personal flag bearer, a groom leading a caparisoned horse, the next of kin, and other mourners. As the procession moved, the 3d Infantry battery, from a position in the cemetery, fired a 17-gun salute in slow cadence, timed so that the last round was fired as the procession reached the grave.

After the band, escort troops, and mourners were in position for the graveside rites, the band sounded ruffles and flourishes, played the "General's March," and then began the hymn "Safe in the Arms of Jesus." While the hymn was played, the body bearers, preceded by Canon Miller, carried the casket to the grave. Canon Miller then read the burial service. Following the benediction, the battery fired a second 17-gun salute, this time spacing the rounds at five-second intervals. A firing squad then delivered three volleys, and a bugler sounded taps to conclude the final rites for General Summerall.

CHAPTER XIII

Rear Admiral Richard E. Byrd
Full Honor (Company) Funeral
11-14 March 1957

Rear Adm. Richard E. Byrd, American explorer of the polar regions, died of a heart ailment at his home in Boston, Massachusetts, 11 March 1957, at the age of sixty-eight. He was accorded a Full Honor (Company) Funeral, to take place on 14 March. By executive order of President Dwight D. Eisenhower the flags on all government buildings, except the Capitol, and on all ships and at all naval stations were to be flown at half-staff until the final rites were concluded.

The Bureau of Naval Personnel, Department of the Navy, made the arrangements for the funeral, incorporating the requests of the Byrd family. On 14 March Rear Adm. Michael F. D. Flaherty was to escort the body of Admiral Byrd by train from Boston to Washington, D.C., where a Navy honor guard was to be present in Union Station. The body was then to be escorted to the chapel at Fort Myer, Virginia, for the funeral service and to Arlington National Cemetery for burial. The Army was to provide the caisson to carry the casket, and the saluting battery from the 3d Infantry; all other troops participating in the ceremonies were to come from the Navy and the Marine Corps.

At 0830 on 14 March, the body of Admiral Byrd arrived in Washington and was taken to the Fort Myer Chapel, with Rear Adm. Charles B. Martell of the Navy acting as escort commander. Admiral Byrd's widow, son, and three daughters meanwhile had arrived from Boston and had been escorted to the chapel.

Fourteen distinguished officials, former associates, and friends served as honorary pallbearers during the ceremonies: Sherman Adams, Assistant to the President; Charles S. Thomas, Secretary of the Navy; Admiral Arleigh A. Burke, Chief of Naval Operations; Admiral Harold R. Stark, U.S. Navy (retired); Admiral Louis E. Denfeld, U.S. Navy (retired); Admiral Donald B. Duncan, U.S. Navy (retired); Vice Adm. Thomas S. Combs, U.S. Navy; Congressman Carl Vinson, Chairman, House Armed Services Committee; Admiral Arthur W. Radford, Chairman, Joint Chiefs of Staff; General Thomas D. White, Vice Chief of Staff, U.S. Air Force; Admiral Dewitt C. Ramsey, U.S. Navy (retired); Admiral William M. Fechteler, U.S. Navy (retired); Vice Adm. James L. Holloway, Jr., Chief of Naval Personnel; and Dr. Melville B. Grosvenor, President, National Geographic Society. At the chapel the pallbearers formed a cordon before the en-

CAISSON ARRIVES AT FORT MYER CHAPEL

trance. In position across the street and facing the chapel stood a military escort composed of the U.S. Navy Band, a national color detail, and a company of sailors and marines. The funeral cortege reached the chapel shortly before 1000. When the caisson halted at the entrance, Capt. John D. Zimmerman, the Navy chaplain who was to conduct the funeral service, and eight Navy enlisted men who were the body bearers moved to the rear of the caisson. As the Navy Band sounded ruffles and flourishes and the company of troops saluted, the sailors removed the casket from the caisson and, with the chaplain leading, bore it through the cordon of honorary pallbearers and into the chapel.

After the casket had been taken to the front of the chapel, the honorary pallbearers entered and were ushered to their seats. One of the pallbearers, Mr. Sherman Adams, was the representative of President Eisenhower. Other persons invited to attend the service had been seated before the cortege arrived at the chapel. Members of the family attending included the admiral's brothers, Thomas Byrd and Senator Harry F. Byrd, of Virginia.

At the conclusion of the funeral service the honorary pallbearers were the first to be ushered from the chapel so that they could re-form the honor cordon at the

PROCESSION MOVES THROUGH THE CEMETERY, *above. Last rites at the graveside, below.*

entrance. With Chaplain Zimmerman leading, Admiral Byrd's casket was then borne from the chapel. The escort units had remained in formation. As the casket was placed on the caisson, the band played a hymn and the units saluted.

After the Byrd family and others in the cortege entered their automobiles, Admiral Martell, the escort commander, led the procession into Arlington National Cemetery. As the military escort and cortege proceeded slowly toward the gravesite in Section 2, northeast of the Memorial Amphitheater and not far below the Custis-Lee Mansion, the 3d Infantry battery fired a slow-paced 13-gun salute.

At the grave the honorary pallbearers formed a cordon through which Admiral Byrd's casket was carried, the chaplain leading, a seaman bearing the two-star flag of a rear admiral following it. As the casket passed, the honorary pallbearers fell in behind and proceeded to their graveside position. The Byrd family was then escorted to the grave.

Chaplain Zimmerman read the brief graveside service. At its close, the 3d Infantry battery fired a second 13-gun salute. A Navy firing squad then delivered three volleys and a Navy bugler sounded taps. The body bearers folded the flag that had draped the casket, and in traditional fashion the flag was presented to the next of kin, thus concluding the final rites for Admiral Byrd.

CHAPTER XIV

The Unknown Soldiers of World War II
and the Korean War
State Funeral
12-30 May 1958

In June 1946 the 79th Congress passed a bill which became Public Law 429, sponsored by Congressman Charles M. Price, Democrat of Illinois, authorizing the burial in Arlington National Cemetery of the body of an unknown serviceman killed in World War II. Not until 23 July 1948, however, did the Department of the Army issue orders calling for the selection of the unknown serviceman. By 15 March 1951, the body of one unidentified serviceman was to be chosen from each of the following: the European area, the Far East area, the Mediterranean zone, the Pacific area, and the former Africa–Middle East zone, now part of the Mediterranean zone. The bodies were to be brought to Washington, D.C., by 28 May 1951, when the President was to choose the unknown serviceman to be honored.

Changes were made in the orders over the next two years. It was decided that an unknown serviceman would also be brought from the Alaska Command. The unknown serviceman was not to be chosen in Washington, but at Independence Hall in Philadelphia. The selection was to be made, not by the President, but by one of five representatives of the Army, Navy, Air Force, Marine Corps, and Coast Guard, each of whom had received the highest award of his service during World War II. The method of choosing the selector was to be decided by the five services and the selection ceremony was now scheduled for 26 May 1951. After the selection, the body of the chosen unknown serviceman was to be taken to Washington on 27 May, to lie in state in the Capitol through 29 May, and to be buried in Arlington National Cemetery on the morning of 30 May. All these plans were canceled upon the outbreak of hostilities in Korea in June 1950.

Interest in the project was revived after the Korean War. In August 1955, largely at the urging of various veterans' organizations, Secretary of Defense Charles E. Wilson asked the Department of the Army to proceed with plans to select an unknown serviceman of World War II. A year later, on 3 August 1956, the 84th Congress enacted Public Law 975, a measure also sponsored by Congressman Price of Illinois, authorizing the burial of an unknown serviceman of the Korean War in Arlington National Cemetery.

The Department of the Army drafted new, simplified plans for selecting the unknown servicemen of World War II and the Korean War. All services would participate. The Air Force was to choose one of the unknown war dead to represent the transpacific phase of World War II, and the Army was to choose one to represent the transatlantic phase. The Navy was to select one of these two and transport the body to Washington for burial. At the same time, the Navy was to bring one of the unknown dead of the Korean War, who was to be selected by the Army in Hawaii.

Secretary of Defense Wilson approved the Department of the Army plan on 31 December 1956 and directed that two of the unknown dead of World War II buried overseas be selected with appropriate ceremonies by 15 May 1958. The Commander in Chief, U.S. Army, Europe, was to select one from the European theater; the Commanding General, Far East Air Forces, one from the Pacific theater. A naval officer, to be designated by the Chief of Naval Operations, was to choose the World War II unknown serviceman from the two. All selections were to be made outside the United States, the Navy's part in the proceedings to take place at sea.

The Commanding General, U.S. Army, Pacific, was meanwhile to select in Hawaii an unknown serviceman of the Korean War. The Navy was to transport both of the dead servicemen to Washington by 27 May 1958. There the two were to lie in state until 30 May, when, after a joint funeral, both were to be buried in Arlington National Cemetery next to the Unknown Soldier of World War I.

The Quartermaster General of the Army, Maj. Gen. Andrew T. McNamara, was designated co-ordinator and on 18 September 1957 he directed the commands involved to prepare detailed plans for selecting the unknown dead. Representatives of all the armed forces were to participate and ceremonies were to be simple and dignified.

The Commanding General, Military District of Washington, Maj. Gen. John G. Van Houten, was charged with arranging the ceremonies in Washington. General Van Houten began his planning on 17 January 1957 for the ceremonies attending the arrival of the dead, the lying in state at the Capitol, the funeral procession and service, and burial at the Tomb of the Unknown Soldier. He was assisted by a planning staff, eventually organized as the Interment of the Unknowns Working Group, which consisted of a liaison officer from each service including the Coast Guard in addition to officers of his own command. (*Chart 1*)

By 15 August 1957 all sites for the various ceremonies had been chosen. One result of the planning was a determination that two crypts, rather than new tombs, would be prepared for the unknown dead. Construction of the crypts was to begin on 12 November 1957 and to be completed by 5 May 1958.

On 7 November 1957 a full draft plan had been completed and was circulating among the services for comment and concurrence. The plan was returned with a few comments from the Air Force; the other services approved without com-

CHART 1—ORGANIZATIONAL RESPONSIBILITY FOR BURIAL CEREMONIES OF THE
UNKNOWN SOLDIERS OF WORLD WAR II AND THE KOREAN WAR

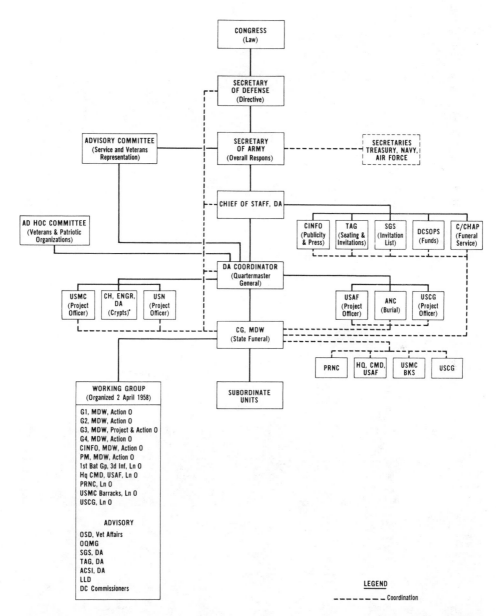

ment. By 16 January 1958 a second draft of the plan was published and sent to the White House, to all services, and to pertinent commands and staffs for final review and concurrence. This draft was approved with only minor modifications and on 12 May 1958 the final version was published.

Opening of the Selection Ceremony at Epinal, France, *above. General O'Neill places a wreath to designate his choice, below.*

FLAG-DRAPED CASKETS OF UNKNOWN DEAD LIE AT HICKAM AIR FORCE BASE, *above. Colonel Eggleston designates choice by placing lei on one casket, below.*

SELECTION CEREMONY FOR THE UNKNOWN SOLDIER OF THE KOREAN WAR

While planning went on in Washington, the selection process began overseas. The bodies of thirteen unknown American servicemen who had fought in the transatlantic phase of World War II were exhumed at cemeteries in Europe and Africa and shipped in identical caskets to the U.S. cemetery at Epinal, France. On 12 May Maj. Gen. Edward J. O'Neill, representing the Commander in Chief, U.S. Army, Europe, chose one of these; the others were reburied. The casket selected was flown to Naples, Italy, where it was transferred to the USS *Blandy* (DD–943), an Atlantic Fleet destroyer. The *Blandy* then left Naples to rendezvous with the missile cruiser USS *Canberra* (CAG–2) off the Virginia capes where the final choice of the unknown soldier of World War II was to be made.

In the selection of the serviceman from the Pacific theater, the bodies of two unknown Americans were taken from the National Cemetery of the Pacific in Hawaii and four were taken from the Fort McKinley American Cemetery and Memorial in the Philippines. The six caskets were then moved to Hickam Air Force Base, Hawaii, where on 16 May 1958 Col. Glenn T. Eagleston, an Air Force officer, chose one. A day earlier, on 15 May, the bodies of four unknown Americans killed in the Korean War were removed from the National Cemetery of the

Pacific, and M. Sgt. Ned Lyle of the Army chose the one to be honored as the unknown soldier of the Korean War. The two caskets selected were flown to Guantánamo Bay, Cuba; the others were buried in Hawaii. In Cuba the caskets were placed aboard the USS *Boston* (CAG–1), which then sailed for the waters off the Virginia capes for the selection of the unknown soldier of World War II.

The *Blandy, Canberra,* and *Boston* rendezvoused off the Virginia capes on 26 May. First the casket of the unknown serviceman from the European theater of World War II was transferred from the *Blandy* to the *Boston*. The two World War II dead and the Korean War dead then were transferred from the *Boston* to the *Canberra* and taken to the *Canberra*'s missile-handling room. Three morticians from Washington, D.C., removed the steel caskets from their shipping cases, took turns changing the positions of the caskets bearing the two World War II dead, and transferred the bodies of all three soldiers to bronze caskets in preparation for the selection ceremony.

To open the ceremony, the *Canberra*'s band played Chopin's "Funeral March" as white-clad sailors wearing black armbands brought the caskets on deck. The Korean War serviceman was placed directly in front of Hospital Corpsman 1st Class William R. Charette, who had won the Medal of Honor during the Korean War, and who was to choose the unknown soldier of World War II. The caskets bearing the World War II dead were placed on either side of the casket of the Korean War soldier. After brief speeches by Navy officials, Charette marched to his left around the row of caskets, saluted, then lifted a floral wreath from a nearby stand, and marched back to face the caskets astern. After glancing left, he stepped to the right, placed the wreath at the casket to denote his selection, and saluted.

Following the selection ceremony, the caskets of the Korean War and World War II servicemen were transferred to the *Blandy* which, escorted by the USCG *Ingham* (WPG–35), sailed for the Naval Gun Factory in Washington, D.C. The World War II soldier not chosen was then prepared for burial at sea while the *Canberra* moved eight miles offshore to meet the requirements for deep sea burial. As the body was committed to the sea, the bugler sounded taps and eight marines fired three volleys. The bugler then blew release and the *Canberra* turned back toward shore.

Plans for the Washington rites meanwhile had been completed, and between 12 and 23 May every ceremony, including one in full dress, and every administrative function had been rehearsed at least twice. Some phases, such as traffic and parking control, were rehearsed four times. For the lying in state ceremony at the Capitol, the U.S. Capitol Architect had provided the Lincoln catafalque and a second catafalque, identical in dimensions and drapings, that had been built at Fort Myer under supervision of the Military District of Washington. The two crypts at the Tomb of the Unknown Soldier also had been completed.

The *Blandy* arrived at the Naval Gun Factory at 1235 on 27 May. She was

TABLE 5—TROOP LIST, ARRIVAL CEREMONY AT THE NAVAL GUN FACTORY FOR THE UNKNOWN SOLDIERS OF WORLD WAR II AND THE KOREAN WAR

Duty	U.S. Army		U.S. Marine Corps		U.S. Navy		U.S. Air Force		U.S. Coast Guard		Total	
	Officers	Enlisted Men	Officers	Enlisted Men	Officers	Enlisted Men	Officers	Enlisted Men	Officers	Enlisted Men	Officers	Enlisted Men
Escort commander and staff	1										1	
Special honor guard	2		2		2		3		2		11	
Commander of troops and staff					1						1	
Honor cordon		20		20		20		20				80
National color detail		2		1		1		1		1		6
Clergy	2				1		1				4	
Body bearers		4		2		2		2		2		12
Band					1	56					1	56
Saluting battery					2	20					2	20
Security cordon					10	400					10	400
Floral detail	1	2									1	2
Communications					1	4					1	4
Total	6	28	2	23	18	503	4	23	2	3	32	580

moored stern in, starboard side to the south edge of Pier 1. A special gangplank was installed and other ceremonial fittings were erected. The caskets of the two unknown servicemen, accompanied by a guard of honor, then were brought from below to the fantail ceremonial area in preparation for the reception ceremony the next day.

On 28 May troops and officials began to take stations for the ceremony at 0840. (*Table 5*) Aboard ship sailors manned the rail while officers and petty officers formed ranks aft. On Pier 1 the commander of troops placed military participants at parade rest, and the U.S. Navy Band played hymns as attending dignitaries, led by the Secretaries of Defense and the Treasury, took their places. (*Diagram 17*) The colors arrived next and were presented to the honor cordon, the assembled dignitaries, and the unknown soldiers. At 0925, as the Navy Band concluded the hymns, the body bearers, divided into two groups, each led by two chaplains, boarded the ship to remove the caskets. All troops saluted when the bearers were in position. The Navy Band sounded four ruffles and flourishes, then played hymns as the caskets were borne from the *Blandy*; the World War II unknown soldier was taken ashore first. The caskets were carried to hearses at the end of the pier and placed inside simultaneously. Following another salute, participating dignitaries entered their automobiles and the procession started toward the Capitol. A 21-gun salute was fired by a Navy battery as the procession departed. (*Diagram 18*)

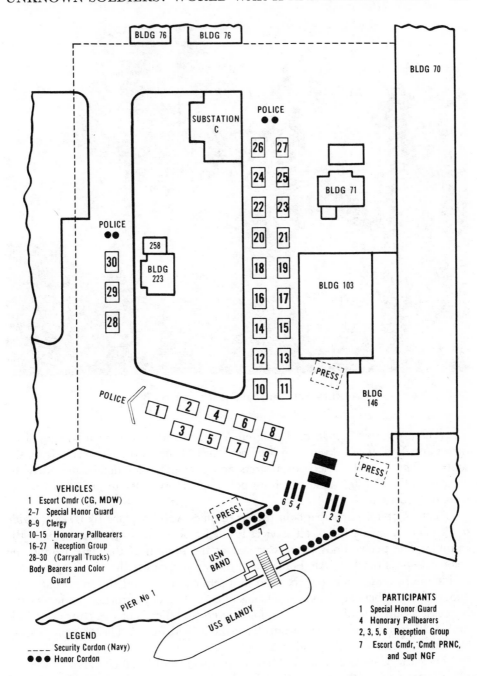

Diagram 17.   Reception formation at the Naval Gun Factory, Washington, D.C.

CASKETS ARE CARRIED FROM THE USS BLANDY

The procession moved up Dahlgren Avenue to M Street, then by way of M Street and New Jersey Avenue to the East Plaza of the Capitol, entering from the south. (*Diagram 19*) The body bearers and national color details preceded the cortege to the Capitol under separate police escort in order to arrive in time to meet the procession.

At the Capitol participants in the ceremonies were in place by 0945. (*Table 6*) A joint honor cordon of all services formed a corridor up the east steps to the rotunda. The twelve body bearers waited at the bottom of the steps behind the color details as the U.S. Air Force Band drew up opposite them. (*Diagram 20*) Inside the rotunda, standing six deep in a semicircle around the south end were about 150 members of Congress, officials of executive departments, justices of the Supreme Court, members of the diplomatic corps, officials of the District of Columbia, the press, and a large group from the armed forces. The two catafalques were in the center of the rotunda. (*Diagram 21*)

The cortege arrived at 0944. After the members had left their cars and were in place to proceed up the steps to the rotunda, the honor guard presented arms, and the Air Force Band sounded four ruffles and flourishes before beginning a hymn.

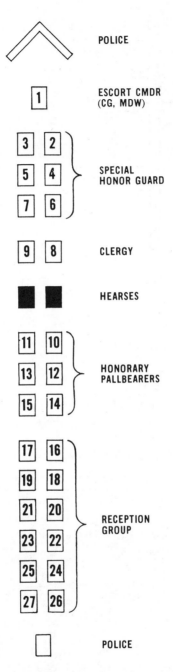

Diagram 18.   Order of march, Naval Gun Factory to the Capitol.

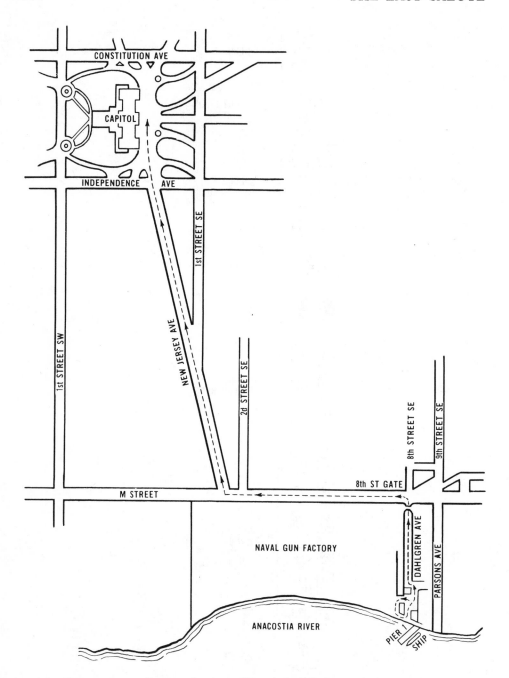

Diagram 19.   Route of march, Naval Gun Factory to the Capitol.

TABLE 6—TROOP LIST, ARRIVAL CEREMONY AT THE U.S. CAPITOL
FOR THE UNKNOWN SOLDIERS OF WORLD WAR II AND THE KOREAN WAR

Duty	U.S. Army		U.S. Marine Corps		U.S. Navy		U.S. Air Force		U.S. Coast Guard		Total	
	Officers	Enlisted Men	Officers	Enlisted Men	Officers	Enlisted Men	Officers	Enlisted Men	Officers	Enlisted Men	Officers	Enlisted Men
Escort commander and staff.....	1	....	....	....	....	....	....	....	....	....	1	....
Special honor guard.............	2	....	2	....	2	....	3	....	2	....	11	....
Commander of troops and staff...	1	....	....	....	....	....	....	....	....	....	1	....
Honor cordon....................	....	12	....	12	....	12	....	12	....	12	....	60
National color detail..............	....	2	....	1	....	1	....	1	....	1	....	6
Clergy.........................	2	....	....	....	1	....	1	....	....	....	4	....
Body bearers....................	....	4	....	2	....	2	....	2	....	2	....	12
Band...........................	....	....	....	....	....	....	1	56	....	....	1	56
Guard of honor.................	1	9	1	9	1	9	1	9	1	9	5	45
Floral detail....................	1	2	....	....	....	....	....	....	....	....	1	2
Communications.................	1	4	....	....	....	....	....	....	....	....	1	4
Information desk................	1	1	....	....	....	....	....	....	....	....	1	1
Total....................	10	34	3	24	4	24	6	80	3	24	26	186

As the hymn was played, the body bearers removed the caskets from the hearses and formed a column led by the clergy, with the unknown soldier of World War II to the front. (*Diagram 22*) The procession passed through the joint honor cordon at a slow cadence, and when it entered the rotunda divided to the right and left. The color details and body bearers made a semicircle to the rotunda's far side then turned back to the catafalques in the center of the hall. The clergy meanwhile took their positions at the foot of the biers. The caskets were then placed on the biers, the bearers were dismissed, and the first relief of the guard of honor was posted. (*Diagram 23*)

The honor guard comprised five reliefs and included troops from the Army, Navy, Marine Corps, Air Force, and Coast Guard. Each relief had four enlisted sentinels, a noncommissioned or petty officer, and a commissioned officer. (*Table 7*) A relief stood a one-hour tour, its members alternating between the positions of attention and parade rest. Off-duty reliefs were billeted in a room directly beneath the rotunda.

Vice President Richard M. Nixon, as president of the Senate, was escorted by an Army officer to a position directly in front of the caskets. An enlisted man acting as one of the wreath bearers met him and assisted him in placing a wreath at the head of the biers. After they had withdrawn, Speaker of the House Sam Rayburn and the dean of the diplomatic corps, Dr. Guillermo Sevilla-Sacasa of

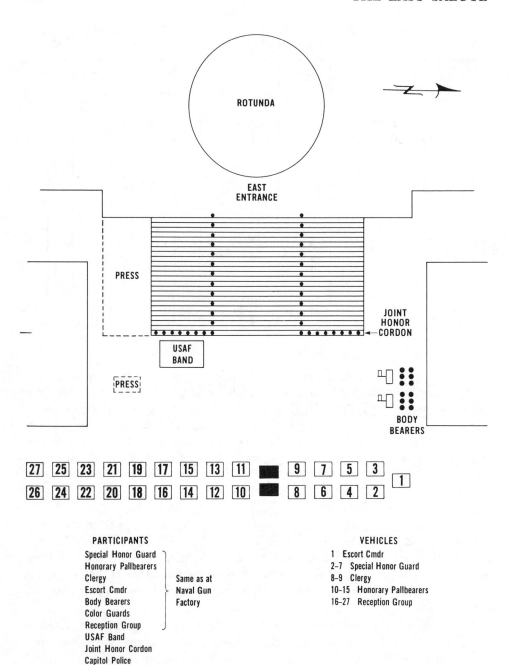

Diagram 20.   Arrival ceremony at the Capitol.

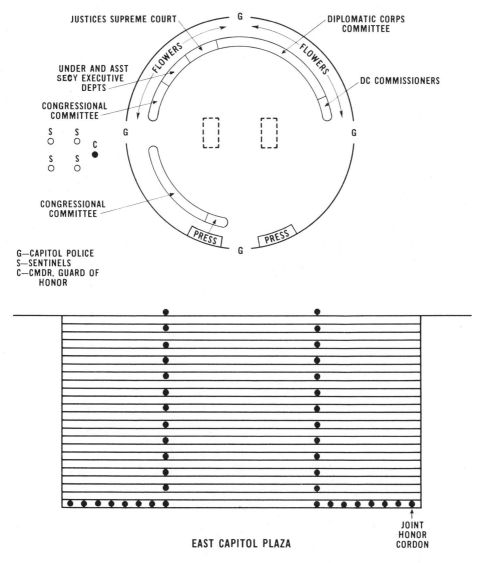

Diagram 21.   Positions for the ceremony in the rotunda.

Nicaragua, also placed wreaths. Shortly after the wreath-laying ceremony ended, the public was admitted to the rotunda.

The unknown dead lay in state from midmorning on 28 May to 1300 on 30 May. Tributes of flowers were accepted and arranged in the rotunda throughout this period. At 1200 on 29 May the caskets were switched so that the serviceman

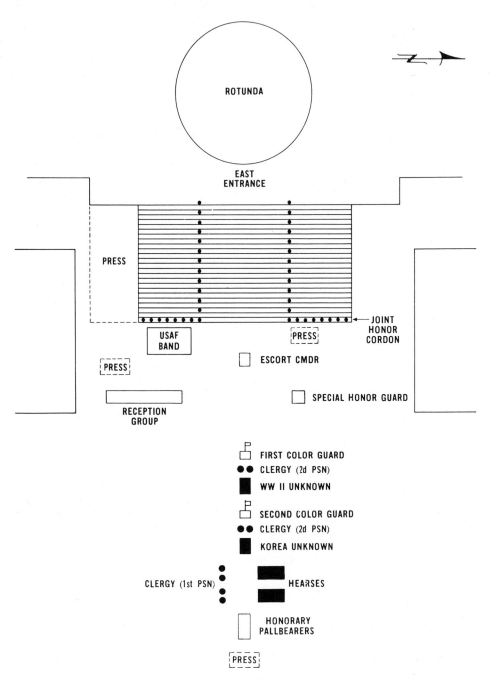

Diagram 22.   Formation of the procession in the rotunda.

CASKETS ARE CARRIED INTO THE CAPITOL

TABLE 7—TROOP LIST, LYING IN STATE PERIOD FOR THE UNKNOWN
SOLDIERS OF WORLD WAR II AND THE KOREAN WAR

Duty	U.S. Army		U.S. Marine Corps		U.S. Navy		U.S. Air Force		U.S. Coast Guard		Total	
	Officers	Enlisted Men	Officers	Enlisted Men	Officers	Enlisted Men	Officers	Enlisted Men	Officers	Enlisted Men	Officers	Enlisted Men
Commander of troops and staff...	1	....	....	....	....	....	....	....	....	....	1	....
Guard of honor...............	1	9	1	9	1	9	1	9	1	9	5	45
Floral detail..................	5	19	....	....	....	....	....	....	....	....	5	19
Information desk.............	3	7	1	1	1	1	1	1	1	1	7	11
Total.....................	10	35	2	10	2	10	2	10	2	10	18	75

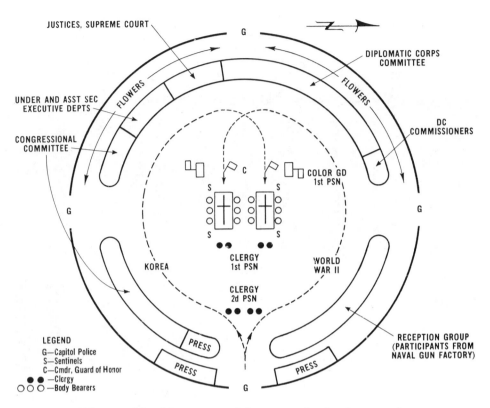

Diagram 23.   Movement of the procession in the rotunda.

of the Korean War rested on the Lincoln catafalque. At the same time, the catafalques were moved so that the World War II soldier kept the senior position on
the right. The public was admitted to the rotunda from 1000 until 1900 on 28
May and from 0800 on 29 May until 1200 on the 30th.

On 30 May in preparation for the procession, the caisson detail of the 3d Infantry left Fort Myer for the Capitol at 0730. At the same time, troops of the 3d
Infantry moved into Arlington National Cemetery to prepare for traffic and parking control. Some 250 officers and men were to occupy fifty-one posts to cope with
the 14,000 cars expected. The 400 officers and men of the regiment who were to
man rope and security cordons also arrived early. Part of them formed a cordon
around the Memorial Amphitheater to keep the ceremonial area clear and later to
direct movement from the amphitheater to the Tomb of the Unknown Soldier.
The rest manned a rope cordon along Roosevelt Drive, the route of the procession.
In all, troops manned about six miles of rope.

UNKNOWN SOLDIERS LIE IN STATE IN THE CAPITOL ROTUNDA

Twenty-four different kinds of parking stickers and seating tickets had been printed and distributed in order to allow guests to park and to be seated in the most expeditious manner. Since the cemetery lacked parking spaces for everyone, arrangements were made for shuttle buses to run between the Pentagon parking lots and the amphitheater. Of 3,000 seating tickets distributed, which approximated the capacity of the amphitheater, all went to members of Congress, the diplomatic corps, ranking military officials, press representatives, Medal of Honor holders, and veteran and patriotic groups. Both the Pentagon and the veteran's affairs adviser for the District of Columbia were besieged with requests for tickets from mothers or widows of men lost in the war—provisions had been made for mothers and widows during ceremonies for the Unknown Soldier of World War I —but all seats had been allocated.

Medical aid was available during all phases of the ceremonies. The Potomac River Naval Command provided medical facilities at the Naval Gun Factory. During the lying in state rites, the Congressional physician was available during his working hours, and at other times the Army provided medical care. For the ceremonies on 30 May, four aid stations were set up, each staffed by a medical officer, nurse, and attendant and each equipped with supplies and an ambulance. Anyone requiring hospitalization was to be evacuated to the George Washington University Hospital or to the U.S. Army Dispensary at Fort Myer. Medical attendants in sedans were to follow the procession to Arlington to pick up and treat anyone who became ill in the ranks of marchers. (As it turned out, some forty servicemen and women in the procession were overcome by the heat; others collapsed at the amphitheater, among them Supreme Court Justice Charles E. Whittaker.)

The General Services Administration had also provided five comfort stations in various buildings along the route of the procession, and the National Park Service had furnished two within buildings, three mobile stations along the route of march, and a station at the amphitheater.

Of the signal communications established, a radio net connected the Capitol and the amphitheater with net control at the Washington Monument grounds. Motor messengers were available at each radio station. Wire communications were established in four information booths at the cemetery and at the information desk in the rotunda of the Capitol.

Photographic coverage, both still and motion, was arranged. The Army covered all ceremonies except the arrival at the Naval Gun Factory, which was photographed by the Navy.

TABLE 8—TROOP LIST, DEPARTURE CEREMONY AT THE U.S. CAPITOL FOR THE UNKNOWN SOLDIERS OF WORLD WAR II AND THE KOREAN WAR

Duty	U.S. Army		U.S. Marine Corps		U.S. Navy		U.S. Air Force		U.S. Coast Guard		Total	
	Officers	Enlisted Men	Officers	Enlisted Men	Officers	Enlisted Men	Officers	Enlisted Men	Officers	Enlisted Men	Officers	Enlisted Men
Escort commander and staff	1	....	....	....	....	....	....	....	....	....	1	....
Special honor guard	2	....	2	....	2	....	3	....	2	....	11	....
Commander of troops and staff	1	....	....	....	....	....	....	....	....	....	1	....
Honor cordon	....	12	....	12	....	12	....	12	....	12	....	60
National color detail	....	2	....	1	....	1	....	1	....	1	....	6
Clergy	2	....	....	....	1	....	1	....	....	....	4	....
Body bearers	....	4	....	2	....	2	....	2	....	2	....	12
Caisson detail	....	8	....	....	....	....	....	....	....	....	....	8
Band	....	....	....	....	1	56	....	....	....	....	1	56
Saluting battery	2	20	....	....	....	....	....	....	....	....	2	20
Floral detail	3	33	....	....	....	....	....	....	....	....	3	33
Drivers	....	50	....	....	....	....	....	....	....	....	....	50
Information desk	1	1	....	....	....	....	....	....	....	....	1	1
Total	12	130	2	15	4	71	4	15	2	15	24	246

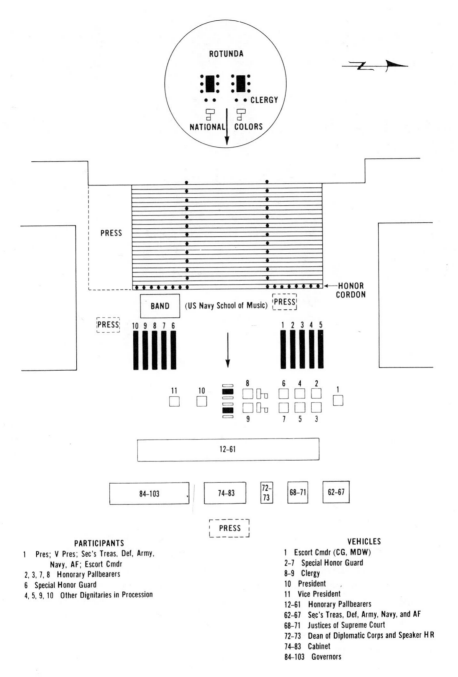

Diagram 24.   Formation of cortege at the Capitol.

CASKETS ARE PLACED ON CAISSONS

At midmorning on 30 May a saluting battery from Headquarters, Second U.S. Army, took station on the Washington Monument grounds where it was to fire a minute-gun salute during the procession and the ceremony at the cemetery. Escort units of the main procession began assembling along Delaware Avenue, N.E., just north of the Capitol, about noon; the groups that would move as part of the cortege from the Capitol were in place on the East Plaza by 1230. (*Diagram 24*) (*Table 8*)

At 1259 the U.S. Naval School of Music Band sounded attention. At 1300 the body bearers took up the caskets and, with those carrying the unknown soldier of World War II leading, moved out of the rotunda. At the same moment, the saluting battery on the Washington Monument grounds began firing minute guns. The firing continued until the close of ceremonies at the cemetery except for a pause during two minutes of silence observed at the amphitheater. The cease-fire signal for the minute guns was the firing of the first round of the final 21-gun salute at the cemetery.

As the procession moved out of the rotunda, each casket was preceded by a color guard and two clergymen. Maj. Gen. Patrick J. Ryan, the Army Chief of

TABLE 9—TROOP LIST, MAIN PROCESSION FOR THE UNKNOWN SOLDIERS OF WORLD WAR II AND THE KOREAN WAR

Duty	U.S. Army		U.S. Marine Corps		U.S. Navy		U.S. Air Force		U.S. Coast Guard		Total	
	Officers	Enlisted Men	Officers	Enlisted Men	Officers	Enlisted Men	Officers	Enlisted Men	Officers	Enlisted Men	Officers	Enlisted Men
Escort commander and staff	1										1	
Special honor guard	2		2		2		3		2		11	
Commander of troops and staff	2		1		1		1		1		6	
National color detail		2		1		1		1		1		6
Clergy	2				1		1				4	
Body bearers		4		2		2		2		2		12
Caisson detail		8										8
Band	1	99			1	99	1	99			3	297
Military escort												
Active	6	85	5	85	5	85	5	85	5	85	26	425
Cadet	4	85			4	85					8	170
Servicewomen	1	19	1	19	1	19	1	19			4	76
Army National Guard	6	85									6	85
Army Reserve	5	85									5	85
Marine Reserve			5	85							5	85
Navy Reserve					5	85					5	85
Air National Guard							5	85			5	85
Air Force Reserve							5	85			5	85
Coast Guard Reserve									5	85	5	85
Street cordon	13	490	12	490	13	490	13	490			51	1,960
Drivers		50									50	
Communications	1	6									1	6
Total	44	1,018	26	682	33	866	35	866	13	173	151	3,605

Chaplains, and Rear Adm. Edward B. Harp, the Navy Chief of Chaplains, walked ahead of the World War II unknown soldier and Maj. Gen. Charles I. Carpenter, the Air Force Chief of Chaplains, and Lt. Col. Philip Pincus, Air Force chaplain, ahead of the unknown soldier of the Korean War. The procession halted at the top of the steps while the U.S. Navy Band sounded four ruffles and flourishes and then began a hymn. During the hymn the procession descended the steps and the caskets were secured to the caissons.

Once the caskets were in place, the band stopped playing and the clergy entered automobiles in front of the caissons. The color details took post ten paces ahead of the clergy, while the body bearers stationed themselves three on each side of each caisson. The cortege then moved north from the plaza to join the escort of the procession on Constitution Avenue. (*Table 9*)

The full procession started toward the cemetery a few minutes after 1300 and moved via Constitution Avenue, 23d Street, Memorial Bridge, and Memorial Drive. Along the route was a joint honor cordon composed of Army, Navy, Marine, and Air Force troops. (*Diagrams 25 and 26*) When the procession arrived at the cemetery the caissons, which had been moving abreast, shifted into a column led by the caisson bearing the World War II Unknown Soldier. As the

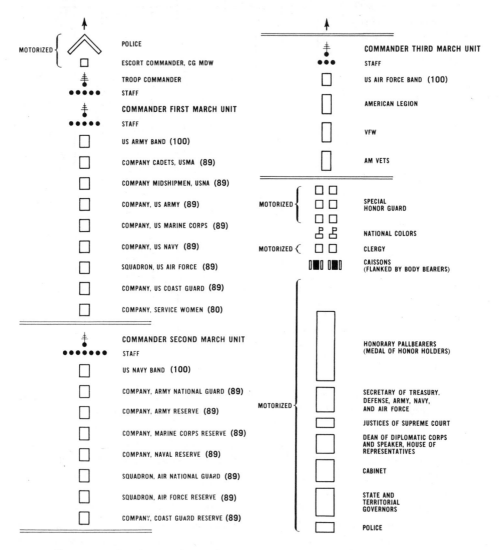

Diagram 25.   Order of march, procession from the Capitol to Arlington National Cemetery.

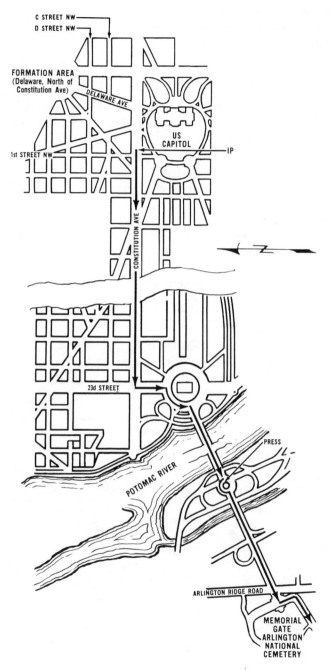

Diagram 26.   Route of march, Capitol to Arlington National Cemetery.

caissons entered the cemetery through Memorial Gate, twenty jet fighters and bombers passed overhead with one plane missing from each formation (a ceremonial feature used for the first time during the funeral for General Hoyt S. Vandenberg in 1954). The procession reached the west entrance of the Memorial Amphitheater at approximately 1440.

President Dwight D. Eisenhower and Vice President Nixon meanwhile had arrived from the White House but remained outside the amphitheater until dignitaries in the cortege had dismounted and taken seats. All others invited to attend the ceremony were already in their places. (*Diagram 27*) General Van Houten, commander of the Military District of Washington, escorted the Vice President to his seat, while Secretary of the Army Wilber M. Brucker escorted the President to his; both seats were in the apse. Members of the public were then allowed to fill any unoccupied spots.

After the audience was seated, the U.S. Army Band outside the amphitheater played four ruffles and flourishes, followed by a hymn. During the hymn the

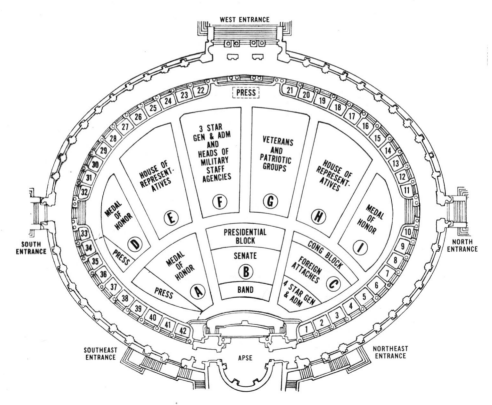

Diagram 27.   Memorial Amphitheater seating plan.

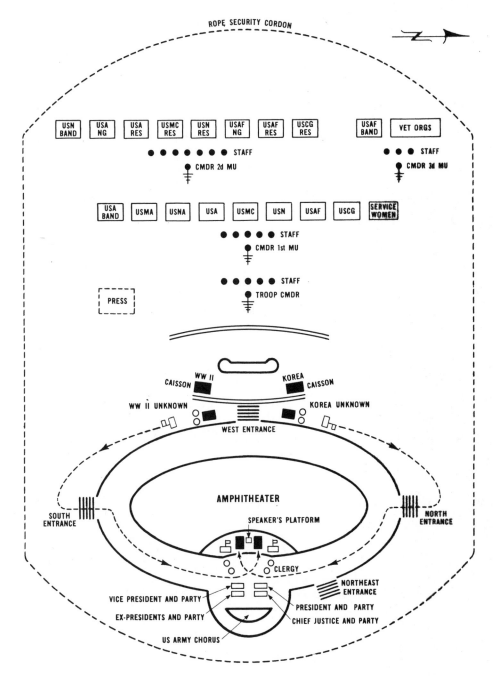

Diagram 28.   Arrival ceremony at Memorial Amphitheater.

bearers removed the caskets from the caissons and, led as before by clergy and colors, carried them inside. The Unknown Soldier of World War II was borne through the south entrance and the Korean War Unknown Soldier through the entrance on the north. Just inside the amphitheater, each casket was set on a movable bier and wheeled around the colonnade to the apse, where the World War II Unknown Soldier was placed in front of President Eisenhower and the Korean War Unknown Soldier in front of Vice President Nixon. While the caskets were being brought to the apse, the U.S. Marine Band, seated in the amphitheater, played religious music. After the caskets were situated, the Marine Band played the national anthem. (*Diagram 28*)

The Army Chief of Chaplains, General Ryan, then delivered the invocation. At its conclusion a bugler sounded attention three times and a two-minute period of silence followed. The Army Chorus and the audience sang "America," after which President Eisenhower arose and placed a Medal of Honor on each casket. The reading of scripture and singing to religious music followed. (*Table 10*) As the funeral service was brought to a close by the Marine Band's postlude, the Unknown Soldiers were taken to the amphitheater's Trophy Room. The Presidential party also withdrew to the Trophy Room, while the audience made its way to the plaza at the Tomb of the Unknown Soldier for the burial service.

TABLE 10—TROOP LIST, FUNERAL SERVICE FOR THE UNKNOWN SOLDIERS OF WORLD WAR II AND THE KOREAN WAR

Duty	U.S. Army		U.S. Marine Corps		U.S. Navy		U.S. Air Force		U.S. Coast Guard		Total	
	Officers	Enlisted Men	Officers	Enlisted Men	Officers	Enlisted Men	Officers	Enlisted Men	Officers	Enlisted Men	Officers	Enlisted Men
Escort commander and staff	1	....	....	....	....	....	....	....	....	....	1	....
Special honor guard	2	....	2	....	2	....	3	....	2	....	11	....
National color detail	....	2	....	1	....	1	....	1	....	1	....	6
Clergy	2	....	....	....	1	....	1	....	....	....	4	....
Body bearers	....	4	....	2	....	2	....	2	....	2	....	12
Band	....	....	1	56	....	....	....	....	....	....	1	56
Chorus	1	30	....	....	....	....	....	....	....	....	1	30
Site control	20	....	....	....	....	....	....	....	....	....	20	....
Security cordon	6	372	....	....	....	....	....	....	....	....	6	372
Ushers	4	45	3	44	2	42	2	42	2	15	13	188
Guides	21	....	....	....	....	....	....	....	....	....	21	....
Floral detail	3	33	....	....	....	....	....	....	....	....	3	33
Communications	1	4	....	....	....	....	....	....	....	....	1	4
Information desk	12	40	....	....	....	....	....	....	....	....	12	40
Total	73	530	6	103	5	45	6	45	4	18	94	741

PRESIDENT EISENHOWER PLACES MEDAL OF HONOR ON EACH CASKET

The Unknown Soldiers were taken from the Trophy Room, in a procession that included the Presidential party, to the head of the plaza steps. There the procession halted while the Army Band sounded four ruffles and flourishes. After this salute the procession descended the steps, and the body bearers placed the caskets over the crypts. (*Diagram 29*) They then took hold of the flags that had draped the caskets and held them taut above the caskets.

Three chaplains, General Ryan, a Catholic; Admiral Harp, a Protestant; and Colonel Pincus, a Jew, each conducted the burial service of his faith. The saluting battery of the 3d Infantry then fired twenty-one guns. At the first round, the minute-gun battery on the Washington Monument grounds ceased firing. After the gun salute, a squad of eight from the 3d Infantry fired the traditional three volleys and, immediately afterward, a 3d Infantry bugler sounded taps. The body bearers then folded the flags and presented them to the President and Vice President, who in turn gave them to cemetery officials for safekeeping. (*Table 11*)

The presentation of the flags completed the burial service. After the participants had left the plaza, the public, guided by members of the 3d Infantry, filed by the crypts. Later in the evening, about 2100, cemetery superintendent John C.

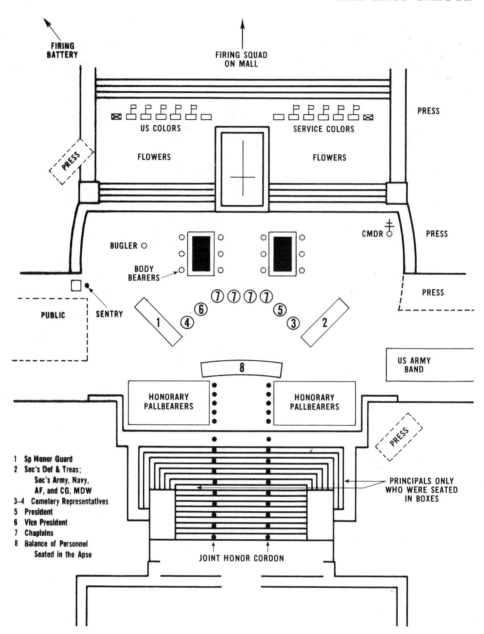

Diagram 29.   Formation for the burial service.

LAST RITES IN ARLINGTON NATIONAL CEMETERY

TABLE 11—TROOP LIST, BURIAL SERVICE FOR THE UNKNOWN
SOLDIERS OF WORLD WAR II AND THE KOREAN WAR

Duty	U.S. Army		U.S. Marine Corps		U.S. Navy		U.S. Air Force		U.S. Coast Guard		Total	
	Officers	Enlisted Men	Officers	Enlisted Men	Officers	Enlisted Men	Officers	Enlisted Men	Officers	Enlisted Men	Officers	Enlisted Men
Escort commander and staff	1	....									1	....
Special honor guard	2	....	2	....	2	....	3	....	2	....	11	....
Commander of troops and staff	1	....									1	....
Honor cordon	1	6	....	6	....	6	....	6	....	6	1	30
Color detail	....	3	....	3	....	3	....	3	....	2	....	14
Clergy	2	....			1	....	1				4	....
Body bearers	....	4	....	2	....	2		2	....	2	....	12
Band	1	56									1	56
Saluting battery	2	20									2	20
Firing party	....	8										8
Bugler	....	1										1
Security cordon	3	172									3	172
Floral detail	3	33									3	33
Total	15	303	2	11	3	11	4	11	2	10	26	346

Metzler and his assistant, F. A. Lockwood, lowered the caskets. The body bearers stood behind a guide chain and saluted as the caskets sank into their crypts. This was the last rite in the ceremonies that throughout the day had involved some 4,800 members of the armed forces.

The final act, not part of any planned ceremony, took place on 2 June 1958. On that date, each crypt was filled with a concrete slab and topped with white marble. The marble tops bore only dates: 1941–1945 for the Unknown American of World War II, 1950–1953 for the Unknown American of the Korean War. At the same time, the dates 1917–1918 were carved in the pavement in front of the tomb of the Unknown Soldier of World War I.

CHAPTER XV

Deputy Secretary of Defense Donald A. Quarles
Special Military Funeral
8-12 May 1959

Deputy Secretary of Defense Donald A. Quarles, at the age of sixty-four, died in his sleep at his home in Washington, D.C., 8 May 1959. An autopsy performed at Walter Reed General Hospital on 9 May revealed that Secretary Quarles had died of a heart attack. He was given a Special Military Funeral, the first such ceremony to be conducted under revised funeral policies and plans issued in September 1958. As provided for in the regulations, Headquarters, Military District of Washington, received the primary responsibility for funeral arrangements.

These arrangements, made with close attention to the wishes of the Quarles family, called for Secretary Quarles's body to lie in the Bethlehem Chapel of the Washington National Cathedral for twenty-four hours, beginning at noon on 11 May. The funeral service was to be held in the nave of the cathedral at 1400 on the 12th. By virtue of his service as an Army artillery officer in World War I, Mr. Quarles was to be buried in Arlington National Cemetery; the gravesite was in Section 2, about midway between Memorial Gate and the Memorial Amphitheater. Following the funeral ceremony, a hearse moving in a motor cortege was to carry the casket to the Memorial Gate of the cemetery. There, before a military escort standing in formation on the green, the casket was to be transferred to a caisson. The military escort was then to lead the cortege to the grave.

There were two departures from the 1958 regulations. The existing general plan called for the transfer of the casket from the hearse to the caisson at Constitution Avenue and 15th Street, N.W., in Washington and for the full procession to move to the burial site from that intersection. In this case, the transfer would take place at Memorial Gate and the full procession would march through the cemetery only. The general plan also called for an escort company from each of the armed services, but in the funeral of Mr. Quarles the military escort troop units consisted of one platoon each from the Army, Marine Corps, Navy, Air Force, and Coast Guard. These modifications (made without explanation in the Military District of Washington letter order for the funeral) emulated features of less elaborate "full honor" ceremonies employed by the Department of the Army under plans published in 1949 but now superseded.

Mr. Quarles's body was taken to the Bethlehem Chapel just before noon on

JOINT HONOR GUARD STANDS WATCH IN BETHLEHEM CHAPEL

11 May. Six body bearers (two Army, one Marine Corps, one Navy, one Air Force, and one Coast Guard), including the noncommissioned officer from the 3d Infantry who was in charge, handled the casket. The first relief of a joint guard of honor took post. The strength of the guard, forty-six, and its composition were precisely as prescribed in the 1958 plan. (*Table 12*)

TABLE 12—JOINT GUARD OF HONOR, LYING IN STATE CEREMONY FOR
DEPUTY SECRETARY OF DEFENSE DONALD A. QUARLES

Units	Commander of Troops	Commander of Guard	Noncom-missioned Officers	Enlisted Men
3d Infantry	1	1	5	4
Potomac River Naval Command	....	1	5	4
Headquarters Command, U.S. Air Force	....	1	5	4
Headquarters, U.S. Marine Corps	....	1	5	4
Headquarters, U.S. Coast Guard	....	1	2	2
Total	1	5	22	18

On 12 May, the body bearers and forty-seven commissioned officers (majors, lieutenant colonels, or men of equivalent grades) who were to serve as ushers and guides reported to the cathedral at 1230. The twenty officers appointed as guides for dignitaries attending the service were all Army officers while the ushers formed a joint service detail of nine Army, three Marine Corps, six Navy, six Air Force, and three Coast Guard officers. In charge of ushers and guides was an officer from the Military District of Washington. Another detail of one officer and six men from the 3d Infantry arrived somewhat later to be on hand to transfer floral pieces to Arlington National Cemetery after the funeral service.

The ushers and guides had been briefed the day before on the seating arrangements. About a fifth of the 2,800 seats in the cathedral were allotted to the general public, and a few were set aside for members of the press. The remainder were reserved for the Quarles family and personal friends, the official funeral party, and other individuals invited to attend the service. (*Diagram 30*)

Heading the official party attending the service was Vice President Richard M. Nixon; President Dwight D. Eisenhower had chosen to attend only the graveside rites. Twenty friends and associates of Mr. Quarles were asked to participate as honorary pallbearers:

Neil H. McElroy, Secretary of Defense
Wilber M. Brucker,
    Secretary of the Army
Thomas S. Gates, Jr.,
    Secretary of the Navy
James H. Douglas,
    Secretary of the Air Force
Robert B. Anderson,
    Secretary of the Treasury
Lewis L. Strauss, Secretary of Commerce
Charles E. Wilson,
    former Secretary of Defense
Dr. James R. Killian,
    Presidential Science Advisor

Reuben B. Robertson, former
    Deputy Secretary of Defense
William C. Foster, former Deputy
    Secretary of Defense
Allen W. Dulles, Director,
    Central Intelligence Agency
Robert Cutler
Maj. Gen. Robert W. Wilson (retired)
Malcolm J. Baber
Dr. W. R. Lovelace, Sr.
Admiral Arthur W. Radford
J. Wright Taussig
Floyd Coffin
Dr. Frank H. McCloskey
Maxwell M. Upson

Also present in the cathedral as a special honor guard were the Chairman of the Joint Chiefs of Staff and the military chief and his deputy or assistant of each of the uniformed services.

Shortly before 1400, the body bearers brought the casket from the Bethlehem Chapel to the nave where they placed it on a movable bier. The two Army bearers then moved the casket to a central position in the nave. The Reverend Donald W. Mayberry, rector of St. John's Episcopal Church in Washington, conducted the service, assisted by the Right Reverend Angus Dun, bishop of Washington,

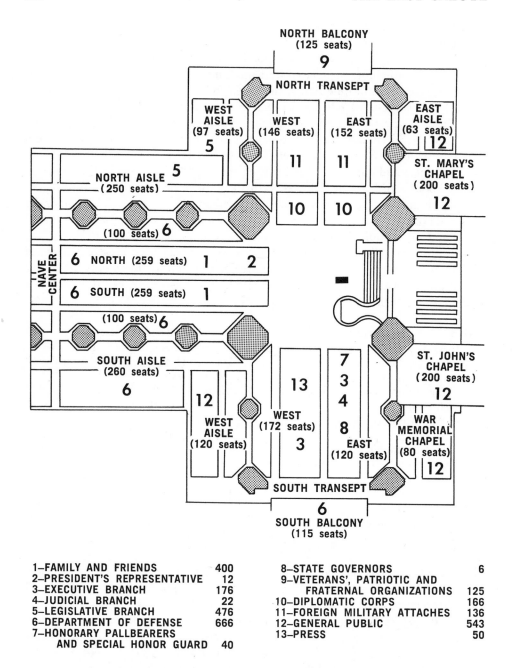

1—FAMILY AND FRIENDS	400	8—STATE GOVERNORS	6
2—PRESIDENT'S REPRESENTATIVE	12	9—VETERANS', PATRIOTIC AND	
3—EXECUTIVE BRANCH	176	FRATERNAL ORGANIZATIONS	125
4—JUDICIAL BRANCH	22	10—DIPLOMATIC CORPS	166
5—LEGISLATIVE BRANCH	476	11—FOREIGN MILITARY ATTACHES	136
6—DEPARTMENT OF DEFENSE	666	12—GENERAL PUBLIC	543
7—HONORARY PALLBEARERS		13—PRESS	50
AND SPECIAL HONOR GUARD	40		

Diagram 30.   Washington National Cathedral seating plan.

CAISSON AT MEMORIAL GATE, *above. Caisson moves through the cemetery, below.*

CASKET IS BORNE THROUGH CORDON OF HONORARY PALLBEARERS

the Very Reverend Francis B. Sayre, dean of the Washington National Cathedral, and Canon Luther D. Miller, former Army Chief of Chaplains.

After the cathedral service, the body bearers carried the casket to the hearse and the Quarles family and members of the official funeral party entered automobiles which were to take them to Arlington National Cemetery. The military escort had formed on line on the green before the Memorial Gate at 1430 to await the arrival of the cortege. A caisson stood on the street in front of the military escort.

When the cortege reached the gate, it halted for a brief ceremony during which the casket was transferred to the caisson. The commander of troops, who in this instance was the commanding officer of the 1st Battle Group, 3d Infantry, then led the way via Roosevelt Drive to the gravesite. Behind the commander of troops and his staff of five (one field grade officer or the equivalent from each of the uniformed services) marched the U.S. Air Force Band, which may have been chosen because Mr. Quarles once served as Secretary of the Air Force.

Behind the band was the column of Army, Marine Corps, Navy, Air Force, and Coast Guard platoons, each composed of a platoon leader, guide, and three squads of eight men each. Next came the joint color guard with the national colors and all of the service colors. The caisson itself, flanked by the body bearers, was followed by the personal flag, the honorary pallbearers, members of the Quarles family, and other mourners.

President Eisenhower arrived at the grave separately. Just as he took a seat behind the rows of chairs seating the Quarles family, two twelve-plane flights of jet fighters, one Air Force and one Navy, passed overhead. The flyover was planned and controlled by Headquarters Command, U.S. Air Force, a procedure prescribed whenever aircraft from more than one service rendered a salute from the air. The Navy flight was staged from the nearby Naval Air Station and the Air Force flight from Andrews Air Force Base. Each group, flying at an altitude of 1,500 feet, passed over the gravesite in a formation of four-ship diamonds in trail.

Dr. Mayberry and Canon Miller conducted the graveside service. At its close, the 3d Infantry battery fired a 19-gun salute. A 3d Infantry squad then fired the traditional three volleys and a bugler blew taps, concluding the military honors for Mr. Quarles.

CHAPTER XVI

Former Secretary of State
John Foster Dulles
Official Funeral
24-27 May 1959

After a long illness, former Secretary of State John Foster Dulles died at Walter Reed General Hospital just before 0800 on 24 May 1959. President Dwight D. Eisenhower received the word at his farm near Gettysburg, Pennsylvania. Returning to Washington, the President on the afternoon of the 24th directed that Mr. Dulles be given an Official Funeral with full military honors.

Before leaving Gettysburg, President Eisenhower ordered that the flags at the White House and all other government buildings in the United States, except the Capitol, and the flags at American embassies, legations, and consulates abroad be flown at half-staff until the burial service for Mr. Dulles had been held. Customarily the flag over the Capitol is lowered only at the death of a President, Vice President, or member of Congress. But at the prompting of Congressman William H. Ayres, Republican of Ohio, who was an ardent admirer of Mr. Dulles, the Congressional leadership—Vice President Richard M. Nixon, Senate Majority Leader Lyndon B. Johnson, and Speaker of the House Sam Rayburn—instructed the Capitol Architect, J. George Stewart, to fly the Capitol flag at half-staff for Mr. Dulles. Many foreign embassies including that of the Soviet Union voluntarily lowered their flags also.

The funeral for Mr. Dulles was the first one conducted after policies and general plans for the Official Funeral had been issued late in 1949 and published with revisions in 1958. (The funeral held for James V. Forrestal early in 1949 resembled the Official Funeral.) The ceremonies of the Official Funeral were only slightly less elaborate than those of the State Funeral; the main difference was that the Official Funeral did not include a period of lying in state in the rotunda of the Capitol.

Chief responsibility for arranging the funeral rested with the Department of State and Headquarters, Military District of Washington. As prescribed in the existing funeral policies, the Department of State was responsible for co-ordinating all funeral arrangements since it was the department of which Mr. Dulles had been a member. The Commanding General, Military District of Washington, as the representative of the Secretary of the Army, who in turn represented the Secretary of Defense, was in charge of arranging all armed forces participation in the ceremonies. President Eisenhower also instructed Brig. Gen. Andrew J. Goodpaster, White House Staff Secretary, to see that the wishes of Mrs. Dulles were followed implicitly.

According to the plans developed, Mr. Dulles's body was to lie at the Dulles residence in Washington from noon on 25 May until noon on the 26th, when it was to be moved to the Washington National Cathedral. There the body was to lie in the Bethlehem Chapel until noon on 27 May, and the funeral service was to be held in the nave of the cathedral at 1400 on the 27th. Mr. Dulles himself was a Presbyterian and had been an elder of the National Presbyterian Church in Washington. The cathedral, a Protestant Episcopal Church, was selected for the funeral service because of its large seating capacity of 2,800. The Reverend Roswell P. Barnes of New York, secretary of the World Council of Churches and long-time friend of Mr. Dulles, was to lead the clergymen officiating at the service. To assist him were the Reverend Paul A. Wolfe of the Brick Presbyterian Church, which was Mr. Dulles's church when he was in New York, and the Reverend Edward L. R. Elson of the National Presbyterian Church in Washington. Burial was to take place in Arlington National Cemetery, by virtue of Mr. Dulles's service as a commissioned officer on the War Trade Board during World War I. The gravesite, selected by Mrs. Dulles, was in Section 21, not far southwest of the Memorial Amphitheater.

Mr. Dulles's body was taken from Walter Reed General Hospital to the Dulles residence at noon on 25 May by morticians from Gawler's Funeral Home. At 1100 on the following day, the casket was moved by hearse to the Washington National Cathedral. Six military body bearers (two Army, one Marine Corps, one Navy, one Air Force, and one Coast Guard) handled the casket. In addition, the small motorized cortege moving to the cathedral included the mortician, the clergy, and members of the Dulles family. Mrs. Dulles herself remained at home.

The cortege halted on the drive at the south entrance to the cathedral. An honor cordon representing all services including the Coast Guard flanked the driveway curb and the walkway to the entrance. Inside this cordon was a second cordon of friends and associates of the former Secretary whom Mrs. Dulles had selected to act as honorary pallbearers:

Thomas E. Dewey	Edward H. Green
C. Douglas Dillon	Charles C. Glover
George M. Humphrey	Robert F. Hart, Jr.
Jean Monnet	C. D. Jackson
Herbert C. Hoover, Jr.	Joseph E. Johnson
John D. Rockefeller 3d	George Murnane
Admiral Arthur W. Radford	Herman Phleger
General Walter B. Smith	Dean Rusk

General C. Stanton Babcock   Eustace Seligman
Pemberton Berman   Henry P. Van Dusen
Arthur H. Dean   Morris Hadley
Harold Dodds

Near the double cordon stood a national color detail and the verger of the cathedral. Inside the Bethlehem Chapel waited some eighty members of the diplomatic
corps headed by Mr. Wiley Buchanan, the Chief of Protocol of the Department
of State. Also at hand was a joint honor guard, the first relief of which would take
post around the casket as soon as it was brought into the chapel.

When members of the cortege had left their automobiles, the body bearers removed the casket from the hearse and a small procession formed to escort the
body into the chapel, the national color detail leading the way. Dr. Barnes and
the cathedral verger preceded the casket and behind it came the honorary pallbearers and members of the Dulles family.

Moving through the honor cordon and a cathedral corridor, the body bearers
placed the casket on a velvet-covered bier in the center of the chapel. Floral tributes had been arranged earlier and a square of velvet rope surrounded the closed
casket. The first relief of the guard of honor took post inside the rope, one sentinel
at each corner of the bier, the officer in charge at the head of the casket. The
Dulles family, honorary pallbearers, and members of the diplomatic corps gathered outside the rope. In this setting, Dr. Barnes read from Psalms and offered a
prayer.

At the conclusion of this simple ceremony, about 1230, members of the public
were allowed to enter the chapel, which remained open through the night and
until 1100 on 27 May while thousands of people came to pay their respects.

On the 27th, in preparation for the funeral service at 1400, troops supplied by
the Military District of Washington reported at the cathedral at 1000 to complete
arrangements for controlling automobile traffic and parking. At noon twenty-
seven ushers and twenty guides arrived to prepare for handling the movement
and seating of persons attending the service. All were of the grades of major or
lieutenant colonel, or the equivalent. The ushers represented all the uniformed
services (nine Army, three Marine Corps, six Navy, six Air Force, and three
Coast Guard), while the guides were Army officers. In charge of both ushers and
guides was an officer from the Military District of Washington.

Troops to cordon off the ceremonial area around the entrance to the cathedral reported at 1230. An officer and six men of a floral detail also arrived to
handle the transfer of flowers within the cathedral and from the cathedral to
Arlington National Cemetery. About 1300 the body bearers, who again represented all the armed forces, arrived and Mr. Dulles's casket was borne from the
Bethlehem Chapel to the nave of the cathedral. At the same time the national
colors were posted in the main chapel and the guard of honor took post around the
casket.

Shortly afterward invited guests and the first members of the official funeral party, including members of the cabinet, justices of the Supreme Court, members of Congress, and state and territorial governors, arrived. About 1345 distinguished foreign dignitaries, the honorary pallbearers, and a special honor guard were ushered into the cathedral. Among the foreign dignitaries were Chancellor Konrad Adenauer and Mme. Chiang Kai-shek; the foreign ministers of Great Britain, France, West Germany, Turkey, Italy, the Netherlands, and the Soviet Union; and the Secretary General of the North Atlantic Treaty Organization, Paul-Henry Spaak. The special honor guard included the Chairman of the Joint Chiefs of Staff, the Army Chief of Staff and Vice Chief of Staff, the Chief of Naval Operations and the Vice Chief of Naval Operations, the Chief of Staff and Vice Chief of Staff of the Air Force, the Commandant and Assistant Commandant of the Marine Corps, and the Commandant and Assistant Commandant of the Coast Guard. Over the next fifteen minutes, Vice President Nixon and his party, President Eisenhower and his party, and Mrs. Dulles and her family were ushered to their seats. Upon the arrival of Mrs. Dulles, the guard of honor around the casket retired, and the funeral service was begun.

At the opening of the service a hymn, "O God, Our Help in Ages Past," was sung by a choir of thirty boys marching down the aisle from the north transept of the cathedral. Dr. Wolfe, Dr. Elson, and Dr. Barnes in turn offered prayers and read from the Old and New Testaments. As Mrs. Dulles had requested, no eulogies were delivered.

At the conclusion of the service, about 1430, the honorary pallbearers left the cathedral to form a cordon outside the entrance. When they were in position, the procession formed, the color detail leading. The clergy preceded the casket, which was followed by the personal flag bearer, the Dulles family, President Eisenhower and his party, Vice President Nixon and his party, the mortician, and the rest of the official funeral party. Members of the procession moved directly to vehicles for the journey to Arlington National Cemetery.

After the body bearers placed the casket in the hearse, they stood fast with the national color detail while the cortege formed and departed for the cemetery. The body bearers, the color detail, and the floral detail, escorted by police, then moved by a separate route to arrive at the cemetery ahead of the procession.

Except for the escort commander, Col. Milton S. Glatterer, the deputy commander of the Military District of Washington, the military escort did not participate in the move from the cathedral to the Memorial Gate of the cemetery. The following order of march was observed: police escort, escort commander, special honor guard, mortician, clergy, hearse, Dulles family, President Eisenhower, Vice President Nixon, honorary pallbearers, other dignitaries, police escort. The motorized cortege moved to Memorial Gate via Woodley Road, 34th Street, Massachusetts Avenue, Rock Creek Parkway, Memorial Bridge, and Memorial Drive. (*Diagram 31*) It took twenty-five minutes to reach the gate.

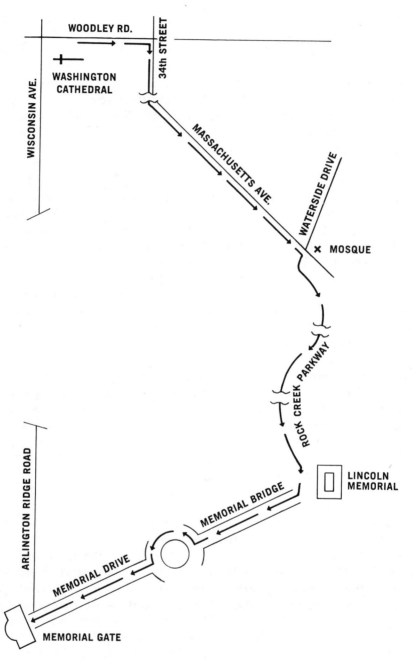

Diagram 31.   Route of march, Washington National Cathedral to
Arlington National Cemetery.

On the green at the gate, the military escort was on line facing the approaching cortege. The U.S. Army Band was at the right of the formation. To the left of the band, in order, stood a company-size contingent each from the Army, Marine Corps, Navy, Air Force, and Coast Guard. To the left of these troops was a composite company of servicewomen and, finally, a group composed of representatives of seven national veterans' organizations chartered by Congress. The caisson and body bearers were waiting in the street opposite the center of the escort formation for the casket transfer ceremony.

When the cortege reached the gate, guides directed each section to its proper position for the transfer ceremony. The special honor guard, leading the procession, formed three cars abreast on the left side of Memorial Drive. The car carrying the clergy joined this formation. The hearse was at first guided to a position on Schley Drive to the rear of the caisson. The cars bearing the Dulles family formed on the right side of the road, the one carrying Mrs. Dulles in front by itself, the others behind, three abreast. To the rear of the family cars were those of the Presidential and Vice Presidential parties, three abreast, and behind these, also three abreast, were the automobiles of the honorary pallbearers. The rest of the cortege was in column, two cars abreast, on the right side of Memorial Drive. (*Diagram 32*)

When all cars were in position, the hearse moved forward and halted at the left and a few feet ahead of the caisson. The body bearers and personal flag bearer then moved into position behind the hearse. The military escort presented arms and held the salute while the Army Band played ruffles and flourishes, a slow march, and then a hymn. As the hymn was begun, the body bearers removed the casket from the hearse and carried it to the caisson. The hearse left the area. After the casket was secured on the caisson, the band ceased playing and the military escort ordered arms, completing the transfer ceremony.

The procession then moved toward the gravesite, starting south on Roosevelt Drive. Behind the escort commander, the military units marched in column in the same order in which they had formed in line on the green at Memorial Gate. The cortege followed much the same arrangement as in the movement from the cathedral. The following order of march was observed: escort commander, U.S. Army Band, Army contingent (89), Marine Corps contingent (89), Navy contingent (89), Air Force contingent (89), Coast Guard contingent (89), servicewomen contingent (102), veterans' group, special honor guard, national colors, mortician, clergy, caisson, personal colors, Dulles family, President Eisenhower, Vice President Nixon, honorary pallbearers, other mourners. The procession reached the gravesite via Roosevelt, Wilson, Farragut, McPherson, and Lawton Drives. The cortege halted on Lawton Drive, which was just north of the gravesite. The military escort continued past the site, then turned back on Porter Drive to reach its assigned position just south of the grave. (*Diagram 33*) Upon reaching this

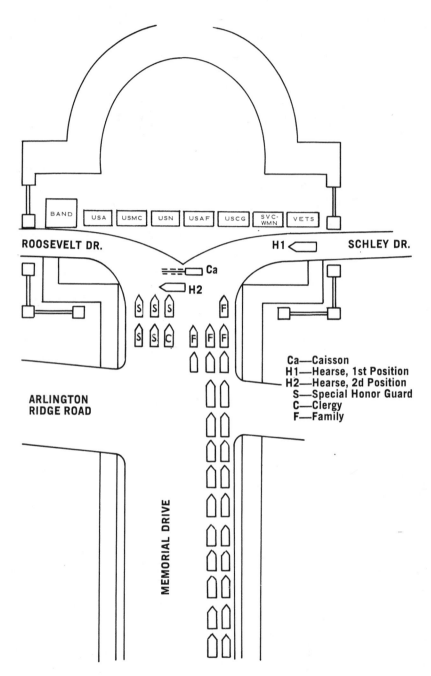

Diagram 32.   Formation for casket transfer ceremony (schematic).

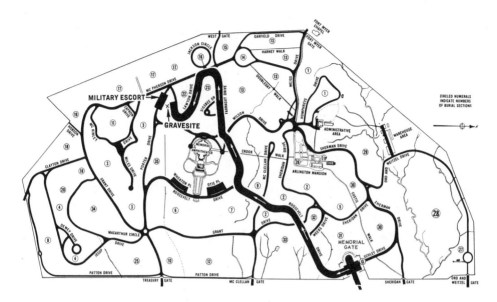

Diagram 33.   Route of march, Memorial Gate to gravesite.

position, the escort units halted facing the gravesite; the Army Band played a hymn while other members of the procession, on Lawton Drive, left their cars.

The grave chosen by Mrs. Dulles was on the brow of a shaded hill. On one side the floral detail had arranged over a hundred floral tributes. On the north side, a canopy had been erected to provide shelter from the sun for the Dulles family and the highest government officials; the temperature was·in the eighties. From the grave, a carpeted aisle reached to Lawton Drive, and the caisson had been halted beside it.

The honorary pallbearers, among the first to dismount, took position on either side of the aisle. At the same time, the special honor guard was guided to its graveside position. (*Diagram 34*) The remaining mourners stayed on the road-way after leaving their automobiles.

When the members of the Dulles family, last to dismount, were out of their cars, the military escort presented arms and held its salute throughout the procession to the grave. The band sounded ruffles and flourishes and played a march, then began a hymn. As the hymn was played the body bearers removed the casket from the caisson. Preceded by the national colors and the clergy, and followed by the personal flag; the casket was borne between the cordon of honorary pallbearers. When it had passed, the pallbearers fell in behind and moved to their graveside position. The body bearers placed the casket on the lowering device. At that

424-140 O - 72 - 11

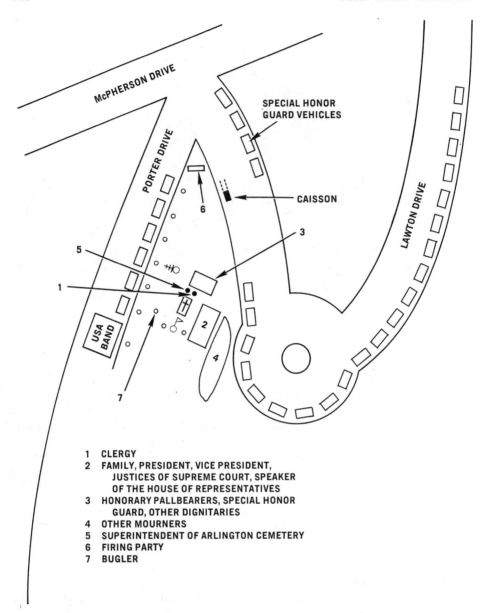

Diagram 34.   Formation at the graveside.

PROCESSION MOVES THROUGH THE CEMETERY, *above. Last rites at the graveside, below.*

time, the band stopped playing the hymn and the escort unit ordered arms. The body bearers then raised the flag that had draped the casket and held it over the casket throughout the graveside service.

Under the direction of the superintendent of Arlington National Cemetery, Mr. John C. Metzler, the Dulles family and the President and Vice President and their parties were escorted to seats under the canopy at the graveside. All other mourners then were guided to a position behind the seated group. When everyone had found his place, Dr. Elson read the Twenty-third Psalm. Dr. Barnes then continued the service. At its conclusion, the military escort presented arms while the battery of the 3d Infantry, from a distant position in the cemetery, fired a 19-gun salute. At the end of the cannon salute, a rifle squad from the 3d Infantry fired three volleys, and a bugler sounded taps. In the traditional manner the body bearers then folded the flag they had held over the casket and handed it to the cemetery superintendent. Mr. Metzler, in turn, gave it to a clergyman who presented it to Mrs. Dulles, thus concluding the funeral rites for former Secretary of State John Foster Dulles.

CHAPTER XVII

Former Chief of Naval Operations
Fleet Admiral William D. Leahy
Special Military Funeral
20-23 July 1959

Fleet Admiral William D. Leahy, former Chief of Naval Operations and personal Chief of Staff to Presidents Franklin D. Roosevelt and Harry S. Truman from 1942 to 1949, died at the U.S. Naval Hospital in Bethesda, Maryland, on 20 July 1959 at the age of eighty-four. He was given a Special Military Funeral on 23 July.

Under policies published the year before Admiral Leahy died, the service of which he was a member was responsible for co-ordinating arrangements for the Special Military Funeral. In this instance the responsibility rested with the Commandant of the Potomac River Naval Command, Rear Adm. Elonzo B. Grantham, Jr. Dignitaries asked to participate in or attend the ceremonies received invitations from the Secretary of the Navy; the Office of the Chief of Naval Personnel dispatched these invitations and recorded the responses.

The ceremonies planned by Admiral Grantham and his staff, with due regard for the wishes of Rear Adm. William H. Leahy, son of the fleet admiral, followed, with one exception, the general prescriptions for a Special Military Funeral. The body of Admiral Leahy was to lie in Bethlehem Chapel at the Washington National Cathedral from noon on 22 July until the same hour on the 23d; the funeral service was to be held in the nave of the cathedral at 1400 on 23 July; and burial was to take place in Arlington National Cemetery. The gravesite was in Section 2, about midway between Memorial Gate and the Memorial Amphitheater.

The exception to the prescribed ceremonies had to do with the formation of the main funeral procession, an exception for which there was precedent in the recent funeral for Deputy Secretary of Defense Donald A. Quarles. In the 1958 plan, the main procession for a funeral in which burial was to take place in Arlington National Cemetery was to form at Constitution Avenue and 15th Street, N.W., in Washington. The body was to be brought to this point by hearse from the place where the funeral service had been held, transferred to a caisson, and taken to Arlington National Cemetery in full procession. But in the ceremonies for

Admiral Leahy, as in the funeral for Secretary Quarles, a motorized cortege was to take the body of the admiral from the Washington National Cathedral to the Memorial Gate of the cemetery. The casket was to be transferred from hearse to caisson at that point in the presence of a military escort standing in formation on the lawn nearby. The full procession was then to enter the cemetery and proceed to the gravesite for the burial service.

On 22 July the body of Admiral Leahy was placed in Bethlehem Chapel of Washington National Cathedral. A Navy ceremonial guard from the U.S. Naval Air Station in Anacostia, D.C., formed the honor cordon and provided the personal flag bearer. The body bearers were a joint group of ten enlisted men, two each from the Military District of Washington, Headquarters Command of the Air Force at Bolling Air Force Base, Coast Guard headquarters in Washington, Marine Barracks in Washington, and the Naval Station. One of the two men from the Naval Station was the petty officer in charge of the group. Each of these agencies also provided one officer and nine men for the guard of honor to stand watch for the twenty-four hours that the body was to lie in Bethlehem Chapel.

Composing a special honor guard were General Lyman L. Lemnitzer, Army Chief of Staff; Admiral Arleigh A. Burke, Chief of Naval Operations; General Curtis E. LeMay, Air Force Vice Chief of Staff, who represented the Chief of Staff; General Thomas D. White; General Randolph M. Pate, Commandant of the Marine Corps; Rear Adm. James A. Hirshfield, Assistant Commandant of the Coast Guard; and General Nathan F. Twining, Chairman of the Joint Chiefs of Staff. Eleven friends of Admiral Leahy, one of whom was an academy classmate, served as honorary pallbearers. Officer escorts for the honorary pallbearers were furnished by the Naval Intelligence School at the U.S. Naval Air Station in Anacostia.

According to protocol, announcements of the funeral service for Admiral Leahy, which in effect were invitations to attend, were sent to all branches and principal agencies of the federal government and to the diplomatic corps. Invitations also were extended to all active and retired admirals of the Navy and Coast Guard, all active and retired generals of the Marine Corps, and all active generals of the Army and Air Force living in the Washington area. Among friends and associates of Admiral Leahy invited to attend, including those asked to serve as honorary pallbearers, those residing outside Washington received invitations by telegram. The honorary pallbearers were Fleet Admiral Chester W. Nimitz; Admiral Thomas C. Hart (retired); Admiral Charles P. Snyder (retired); Admiral Louis E. Denfeld (retired); Admiral Arthur W. Radford (retired); Admiral Jerauld Wright; Admiral Robert L. Dennison; Vice Adm. Edward L. Cochrane (retired); Rear Adm. Henry Williams (retired); Rear Adm. Joseph H. Wellings; and William D. Hassett.

Two Navy agencies located in the Washington area, the Navy Communication Station and the Naval Security Station, furnished officers and men to usher

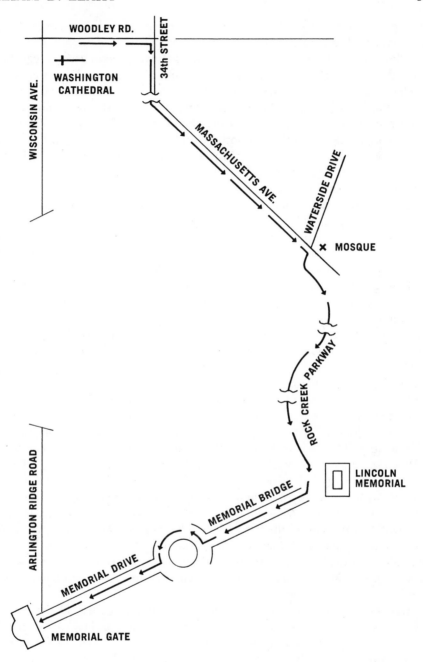

Diagram 35.   Route of march, Washington National Cathedral to Arlington National Cemetery.

guests to their seats for the funeral service. The service itself was conducted by a Navy chaplain, Capt. John B. Zimmerman.

Following the short service at 1400 on 23 July, a motorized cortege formed outside the cathedral to escort the body of Admiral Leahy to Arlington National Cemetery. As the body bearers carried the casket out of the cathedral and through the Navy honor cordon to the hearse, the U.S. Marine Band, in formation near the honor cordon, sounded ruffles and flourishes and played a hymn.

The cortege moved to the Memorial Gate of Arlington National Cemetery by way of Woodley Road, 34th Street, Massachusetts Avenue, Rock Creek Parkway, Memorial Bridge, and Memorial Drive. (*Diagram 35*) The military escort of some 550 officers and men, commanded by Admiral Grantham, stood on line on the green at the gate, facing the cortege as the motor column approached on Memorial Drive. In addition to the commander and a staff of four, one field grade officer or the equivalent from the Army, Marine Corps, Air Force, and Coast Guard, the escort consisted of the U.S. Navy Band and a company each from the Army (3d Infantry), Marine Corps (Marine Barracks), Navy (Navy Air Station), Air Force (Headquarters Command), and Coast Guard (Coast Guard headquarters). Each company had four officers and eighty-five men and was organized with a company commander, guidon bearer, and three platoons, each consisting of a platoon commander, right guide, and three nine-man squads. Also present at the gate were the national color detail of three men, an Army color bearer and one color guard each from the Marine Corps and Air Force, and a personal color bearer from the Navy.

On the street in front of the escort and facing south toward Roosevelt Drive in the cemetery were the caisson and caisson detail, furnished by the 3d Infantry, and the body bearers, who along with the color detail had come from the cathedral by a separate route in order to reach Memorial Gate ahead of the cortege.

When the motorcade reached the gate, the vehicles carrying the special honor guard and the clergy halted on the left side of the street. The others lined up on the right, with the family cars and those bearing the honorary pallbearers and dignitaries at the front. (*Diagram 36*) After the cortege was in place, the hearse was driven to a position at the left and slightly ahead of the caisson. As the Navy Band sounded ruffles and flourishes and played a hymn, the body bearers removed Admiral Leahy's casket from the hearse, which was then driven away, and placed it on the caisson. After this brief ceremony, the escort commander led the procession into the cemetery.

From a distant position in the cemetery, the saluting battery of the 3d Infantry fired a slow-paced 19-gun salute as the procession marched to the gravesite. The escort units moved via Roosevelt and Wilson Drives, then turned right and marched off the roadway across the grass to McClellan Drive. Moving on McClellan to a point almost due south of the gravesite, the escort units formed on line along the edge of the road facing north toward the grave. In front of them,

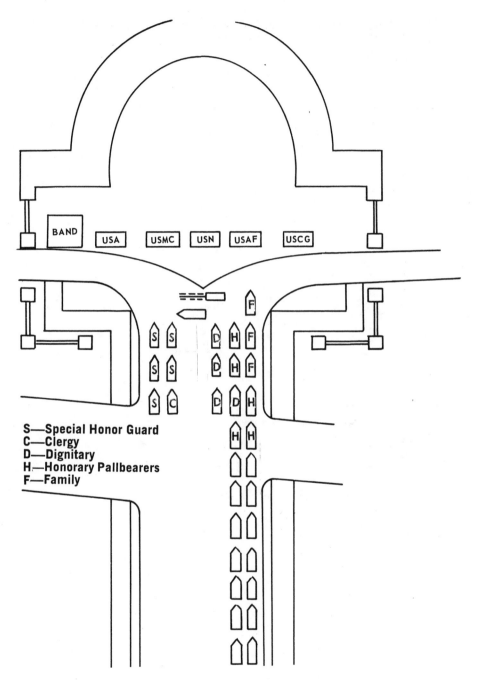

Diagram 36.   Formation at Memorial Gate.

on the grass between McClellan and Sheridan Drives, stood a squad ready to fire the traditional three volleys following the burial service. (*Diagram 37*)

The escort commander and the cortege continued on Wilson Drive, then turned right on Sheridan Drive, which passed immediately south of the gravesite. The clergy, caisson, and mourners halted on Sheridan, while the escort commander, special honor guard, and honorary pallbearers left their cars on a narrow unnamed roadway leading off Sheridan and passing north of the gravesite. (*Diagram 38*)

With the customary ceremony and honors, Admiral Leahy's casket was carried to the grave, where Chaplain Zimmerman read the burial service. A final cannon salute, the traditional three volleys, and the sounding of taps closed the final rites for the five-star admiral.

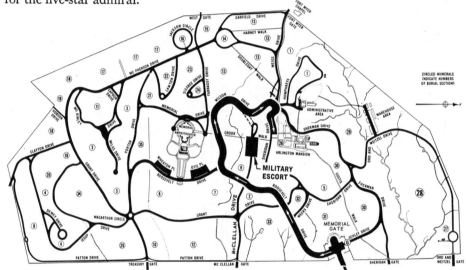

Diagram 37.   Route of march, Memorial Gate to gravesite.

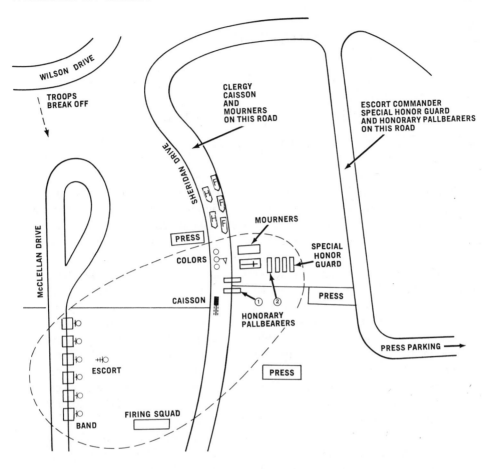

Diagram 38. Formation at the graveside.

CHAPTER XVIII

Fleet Admiral William F. Halsey, Jr.
Special Military Funeral
16-20 August 1959

On 16 August 1959, less than a month after the death of Fleet Admiral William D. Leahy, another five-star admiral, William F. Halsey, Jr., at the age of seventy-six died of a heart attack at Fishers Island, New York. For the second time within a month, the Potomac River Naval Command became responsible for arranging the ceremonies of a Special Military Funeral, which was held for Admiral Halsey on 20 August. The admiral's body was meanwhile taken from Fishers Island to the chapel of the Navy Receiving Station in Brooklyn.

According to plans, which incorporated the wishes of the Halsey family, the admiral's body was to be brought to Washington, D.C., for the funeral service and burial. The body was to lie in Bethlehem Chapel at the Washington National Cathedral from noon of 19 August until the same hour on the 20th. The funeral service was to be held in the nave of the cathedral at 1400 on 20 August, and burial was to follow in Arlington National Cemetery. The gravesite selected was in Section 2, near the grave of Admiral Leahy, and next to that of Admiral Halsey's father, who had been a Navy captain, and mother.

Announcements of the funeral service for Admiral Halsey, which served as invitations to attend, were issued by the Secretary of the Navy, but they were sent out and the responses were recorded by the Office of the Chief of Naval Personnel. Dignitaries and their wives who were invited to attend included the President, Vice President, members of the cabinet, justices of the Supreme Court, members of Congress, members of the diplomatic corps, officials of the Department of Defense, and representatives of patriotic organizations. Flag and general officers of all the uniformed services, active and retired, residing in the Washington area also were invited.

Among the friends and associates of Admiral Halsey who were asked to participate in the funeral and burial services as honorary pallbearers was Deputy Secretary of Defense Thomas S. Gates, Jr., who at one time had been Secretary of the Navy. Asked to serve as members of a special honor guard were General Nathan F. Twining, Chairman of the Joint Chiefs of Staff; General Lyman L. Lemnitzer, Chief of Staff of the Army; Admiral Arleigh A. Burke, Chief of Naval Operations; General Thomas D. White, Chief of Staff of the Air Force; General

Randolph M. Pate, Commandant of the Marine Corps; and Rear Adm. James A. Hirshfield, Commandant of the Coast Guard. Officer aides and escorts for the honorary pallbearers and members of the special honor guard were provided by the U.S. Naval Intelligence School at the U.S. Naval Air Station and the U.S. Naval Weapons Plant in Washington. Officers and enlisted men to usher guests to their seats for the funeral service were supplied by the Coast Guard headquarters, the Marine Barracks, the U.S. Naval Photographic Center, and the U.S. Naval Security Station, all in the Washington area.

On the morning of 19 August the admiral's body, accompanied by his son and daughter, was flown from Floyd Bennett Field, New York, to the U.S. Naval Air Station in Anacostia, D.C. Upon the arrival of the plane at 1100, the Ceremonial Guard from the Naval Air Station rendered military honors. After the ceremony the admiral's body was taken in a motor procession, led by Vice Adm. Ralph E. Wilson of the Navy who had been designated escort commander for all ceremonies, to the Washington National Cathedral.

Outside the cathedral a joint honor cordon of twenty men lined the entrance leading to Bethlehem Chapel. The cordon was made up of four men each from the Military District of Washington, the Headquarters Command of the Air Force at Bolling Air Force Base, the Coast Guard headquarters in Washington, the Marine Barracks in Washington, and the Naval Air Station. The body bearers and the joint guard of honor were from the same agencies. There were ten body bearers, with one of the two men from the Naval Air Station acting as petty officer in charge. The joint guard of honor, one officer and nine men from each agency, was to stand watch at the bier while the admiral's body lay in Bethlehem Chapel. Also standing outside the cathedral were the U.S. Navy Band; the national color deail, of which the military District of Washington had supplied the color bearer and the Air Force Headquarters Command and the Marine Barracks the two color guards; and a personal flag bearer from the Naval Air Station.

When the motorcade from the airfield arrived, the Navy Band sounded ruffles and flourishes and the honor cordon saluted as Admiral Wilson, followed by the national color detail, Navy Chaplain Capt. John D. Zimmerman, the body bearers with the casket, and the personal flag bearer entered the chapel. After the casket was placed on a bier in the chapel, the body bearers were dismissed and the first relief of the joint guard of honor took post. A constant vigil was maintained until 20 August.

Before 1400 on 20 August the joint guard of honor was dismissed and the body bearers moved Admiral Halsey's casket to the nave of the cathedral for the funeral service. Among the hundreds of guests who were arriving to attend the service was Fleet Admiral Chester W. Nimitz, the sole survivor of four fleet admirals appointed to five-star rank during World War II. Admiral Nimitz was the official representative of President Dwight D. Eisenhower. Last to enter the cathe-

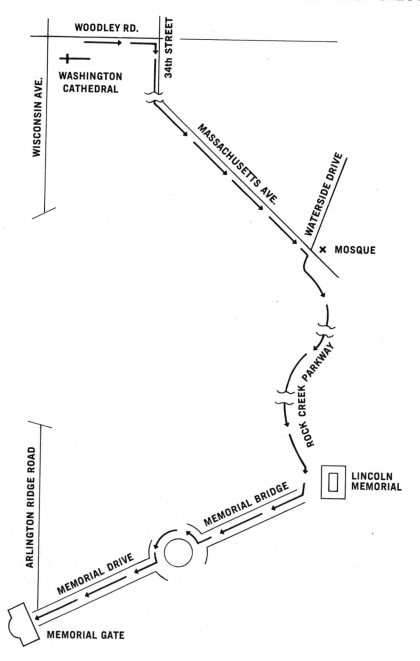

Diagram 39.   Route of march, Washington National Cathedral to
Arlington National Cemetery.

dral were Admiral Halsey's widow and his son and daughter. Chaplain Zimmerman then conducted the Protestant Episcopal funeral service.

Following the half-hour service, a procession formed to escort Admiral Halsey's body from the cathedral. As the bearers carried the casket out of the north door of the cathedral and through the joint honor cordon lining the steps, the Marine Band, posted across the driveway from the entrance, sounded ruffles and flourishes and began a hymn. While the hymn was played, the body bearers placed the casket in the hearse, which stood on the driveway. The Halsey family and others of the official funeral party then entered automobiles for the procession to Arlington National Cemetery.

As in Admiral Leahy's funeral, the motor cortege bearing Admiral Halsey's body to Arlington moved from the cathedral to the Memorial Gate of the cemetery via Woodley Road, 34th Street, Massachusetts Avenue, Rock Creek Parkway, Memorial Bridge, and Memorial Drive. (*Diagram 39*) On the lawn at Memorial Gate, facing the cortege as it approached on Memorial Drive, was the military escort, which would lead the procession from the gate to the gravesite. In addition to the escort commander and his staff of four, one field grade officer or the equivalent from the Army, Marine Corps, Air Force, and Coast Guard, the escort of some 550 officers and men consisted of the Navy Band and a company each from the Army (3d Infantry), Marine Corps (Marine Barracks), Navy (Naval Air Station), Air Force (Headquarters Command), and Coast Guard (Coast Guard headquarters). Each company had four officers and eighty-five men and was organized with a commander, a guidon bearer, and three platoons. Each platoon had a commander, a right guide, and three nine-man squads. Also at the gate were the national color detail and the personal flag bearer.

In preparation for the transfer of Admiral Halsey's casket at Memorial Gate, the caisson and caisson detail from the 3d Infantry were on the street in front of the military escort, facing south toward the cemetery's Roosevelt Drive. Also in position for the transfer ceremony were the body bearers, who along with the color detail had come from the cathedral by a separate route to reach Memorial Gate ahead of the cortege.

When the motorcade reached the gate, vehicles were halted at designated locations by site control personnel. Cars carrying the special honor guard and clergy were lined along the left side of Memorial Drive. The others took their places on the right, with the Halsey family cars and those bearing the honorary pallbearers and dignitaries at the front. (*Diagram 40*) After the cortege had halted, the hearse was driven to a position at the left and slightly ahead of the caisson. As the Navy Band sounded ruffles and flourishes and played a hymn, the body bearers removed Admiral Halsey's casket from the hearse, which was then driven away, and secured it on the caisson. After this brief ceremony, the escort commander, Admiral Wilson, led the procession into the cemetery.

The march to the gravesite in Section 2 took a somewhat circular route via

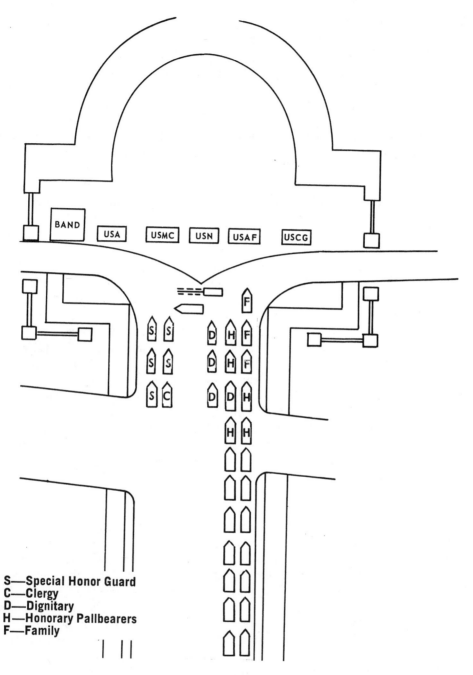

Diagram 40.   Formation at Memorial Gate.

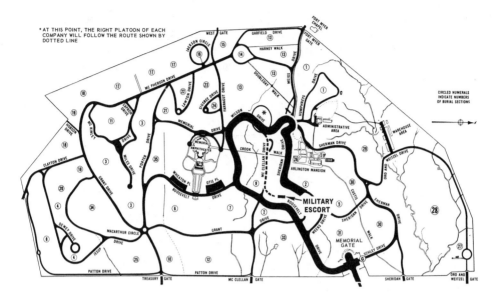

Diagram 41.   Route of march, Memorial Gate to gravesite.

Roosevelt, Wilson, and Sheridan Drives. (*Diagram 41*) As the military escort turned onto Wilson Drive and reached a point opposite the terminal circle of McClellan Drive, which lies east of and runs perpendicular to Wilson Drive, the band and right platoon of each escort company broke off from the procession, marched across the grass to McClellan Drive, then on it to a graveside position between Roosevelt and Sheridan Drives. To the right front of the escort's graveside position stood a firing squad from the Navy that had taken this position earlier to fire the traditional three volleys during the burial service. (*Diagram 42*)

The remaining escort troops, which were not scheduled to participate in the graveside rites, continued on Wilson Drive and out of the ceremonial area to dismissal points. The escort commander and the cortege turned right off Wilson Drive onto Sheridan Drive, which passed immediately south of the gravesite. The color detail, the clergy, the caisson, and the Halsey family and other mourners halted on Sheridan, while the escort commander, the special honor guard, and the honorary pallbearers stopped on a narrow unnamed roadway leading off Sheridan and passing north of the gravesite. During the movement of the procession from Memorial Gate to the gravesite, the 3d Infantry battery, from a distant position in the cemetery, fired a slow-paced 19-gun salute. The final round was fired as the cortege came to a halt at the gravesite.

Admiral Halsey's casket was borne to the grave through a cordon formed by the honorary pallbearers. After the Halsey family and other mourners had been conducted to the grave, Chaplain Zimmerman read the final service. At the close, the 3d Infantry battery delivered a second 19-gun salute, which was followed by three volleys from the firing squad. The sounding of taps by a Navy bugler closed the last rites for Admiral Halsey.

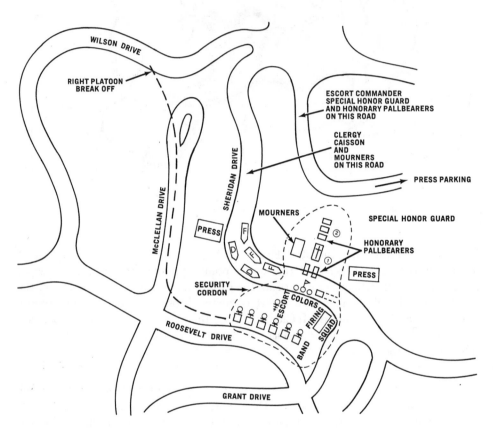

Diagram 42.   Formation at the graveside.

CHAPTER XIX

General of the Army George C. Marshall
Special Military Funeral
16-20 October 1959

General of the Army George C. Marshall died at Walter Reed General Hospital on 16 October 1959 at the age of seventy-eight. By virtue of his former positions as Chief of Staff of the Army and as Secretary of Defense, General Marshall was entitled to a Special Military Funeral and, as a former Secretary of State, he was entitled to the more elaborate honors of an Official Funeral. He received a Special Military Funeral, but in keeping with his known wishes and with what has been described as his "Spartan concept of propriety," the rites for General Marshall were among the simplest ever conducted for a man of his rank and prestige.

The Commanding General, Military District of Washington, Maj. Gen. Charles K. Gailey, was responsible for arranging the ceremonies. Through an officer of his staff appointed as aide to the next of kin, General Gailey worked closely with Katherine T. Brown Marshall, the general's widow, to see that all of her husband's and her own wishes were met.

According to the plan worked out, General Marshall's body was to lie in Bethlehem Chapel at the Washington National Cathedral for twenty-four hours, beginning at noon 19 October. On the 20th, the general's body was to be taken to the post chapel at Fort Myer, Virginia, for the funeral service, which would be attended by a limited number of invited guests. A private burial service in Arlington National Cemetery was to follow. The gravesite, in Section 7, a little to the east of the Memorial Amphitheater, had been selected by General Marshall some years earlier and already contained the grave of the general's first wife, Elizabeth Coles Marshall, and her mother.

On the day of the general's death, President Dwight D. Eisenhower issued a proclamation ordering the flag flown at half-staff on all public buildings except the Capitol, at all military posts and naval stations in the United States, and at American facilities abroad. The flag was to be so displayed until after the burial service.

On 17 October General Marshall's body was moved from Walter Reed General Hospital to the S. H. Hines Funeral Home, where it remained until 19 October. A half an hour before noon on the 19th, the commander of the Military District of Washington, General Gailey, accompanied by Armed Forces Police and

Metropolitan motorcycle police, arrived at the funeral home to escort the general's body to the Washington National Cathedral. The casket had already been placed in a hearse, and at 1145 General Gailey started the small motorized cortege toward the cathedral. Motorcycle police led the way, followed by Armed Forces Police, the escort commander, the hearse (accompanied by a mortician), and at the rear another Armed Forces Police car.

A few minutes before noon the military units taking part in the cathedral ceremonies were in position at the entrance to the Bethlehem Chapel. A joint honor cordon lined the walkway and entrance steps; a national color detail and personal flag bearer stood near the cordon; and the body bearers waited at the street end of the walkway. The body bearers included an enlisted man each from the Army, Marine Corps, Navy, Air Force, and Coast Guard and one cadet from Virginia

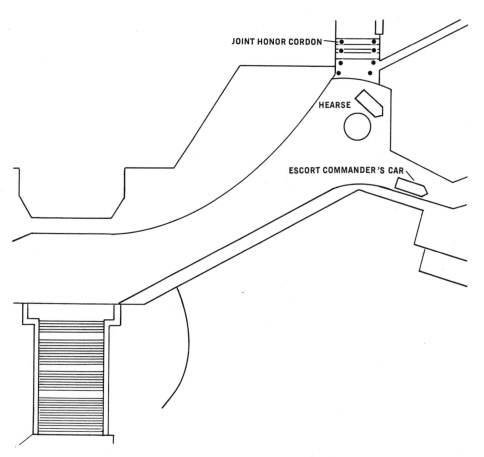

Diagram 43.   Arrival ceremony, Washington National Cathedral.

JOINT HONOR GUARD STANDS WATCH IN BETHLEHEM CHAPEL

Military Institute, General Marshall's alma mater. This same body bearer detail would participate in ceremonies at the cathedral and in the graveside service on 20 October. A second team of body bearers of the same composition would participate in the funeral service at Fort Myer. With the body bearers at the chapel walkway were two members of the clergy: Canon Luther D. Miller of the Washington National Cathedral, a long-time friend of General Marshall's and a former Army Chief of Chaplains, and the Reverend Franklin Moss, Jr., of General Marshall's home church, St. James Episcopal, in Leesburg, Virginia. Inside the cathedral, a joint guard of honor was ready to post its first relief around the casket after it was placed in the Bethlehem Chapel.

When the cortege arrived the hearse stopped in front of the chapel entrance. (*Diagram 43*) The body bearers and clergy then moved to the rear of the hearse, and the color teams took station nearby. The escort commander meanwhile took his place at the chapel entrance.

The honor cordon presented arms as the body bearers removed the casket from the hearse. Then, preceded by the escort commander, the clergy, and the national color detail, and followed by the personal flag bearer, General Marshall's

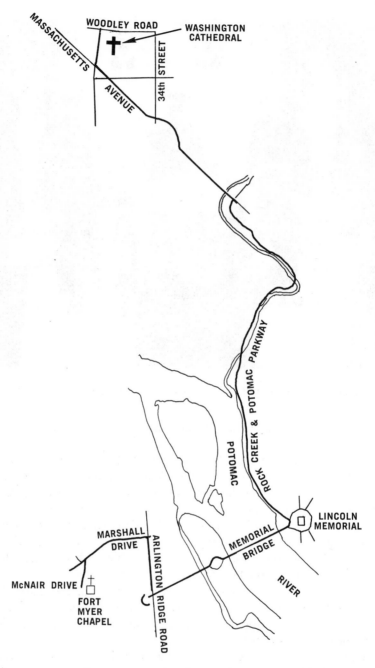

Diagram 44.   Route of march, Washington National Cathedral to
Fort Myer Chapel.

ARMED FORCES HONOR GUARD APPROACHES THE CHAPEL

casket was borne through the honor cordon into the chapel, where it was placed on a catafalque. The colors were posted without guards. The first relief of the guard of honor then entered the chapel, whereupon the guard commander dismissed the body bearers and posted his sentinels around the casket. General Marshall's body remained in the Bethlehem Chapel which the public was permitted to enter to pay respects until noon on 20 October.

At 1400 on the 20th, the general's body was taken from the cathedral for the movement to Fort Myer in a ceremony conducted by the same formation that had attended the arrival at the cathedral. Again the joint honor cordon formed along the steps and walkway outside the Bethlehem Chapel. The honor cordon saluted as Canon Miller and the Reverend Mr. Moss, followed by the national color detail, the body bearers with the casket, and the personal flag bearer, came out of the cathedral and moved to a hearse on the street. After the body bearers placed the casket in the hearse, General Gailey, the escort commander, and the clergy entered their vehicles (a mortician again was with the hearse), and the small cortege, accompanied by Metropolitan and Armed Forces Police, started for Fort Myer. (*Diagram 44*)

While the ceremony at the cathedral was in progress, some two hundred invited guests filed into the chapel at Fort Myer. Among them were President Eisenhower and former President Harry S. Truman, Secretary of State Christian A. Herter, former Secretary of State Dean G. Acheson, W. Averell Harriman, General of the Army Omar N. Bradley, General Alfred M. Gruenther, and General Matthew B. Ridgway. Members of the Marshall family entered after the President was seated; Mrs. Marshall, last to arrive, entered the chapel about 1425.

Outside the Fort Myer Chapel fourteen honorary pallbearers lined the entrance walkway: General Lyman L. Lemnitzer, Robert A. Lovett, General Wal-

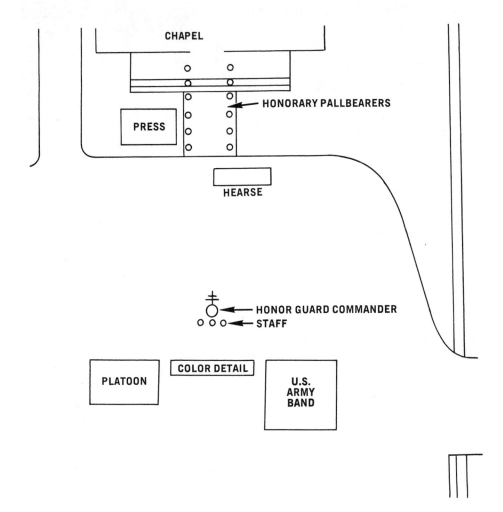

Diagram 45.   Formation at Fort Myer Chapel.

CASKET IS CARRIED INTO THE CHAPEL

ter Bedell Smith, Robert Woods Bliss, James Bruce, Admiral Harold R. Stark, General Charles D. Herron, Brig. Gen. Frank McCarthy, Col. Robert H. Fletcher, Col. William M. Spencer, Donald Cook, Lt. Col. Clarence J. George, M. Sgt. James W. Powder, and M. Sgt. William J. Heffner. In formation across the street from the entrance was an armed forces honor guard commanded by an Army captain with a staff of three: a lieutenant, junior grade, from the Navy, a lieutenant, junior grade, from the Coast Guard, and an Air Force lieutenant. The formation included the U.S. Army Band, an armed forces color detail, and an armed forces platoon of three squads. The color detail was made up of one color guard each from the Army and Marine Corps, two Army color bearers, one for the national colors and one for the Army colors, and one color bearer from each of the other services with the appropriate service colors. The armed forces platoon was commanded by a Marine Corps lieutenant. Each squad in the platoon had ten men, two each from the Army, Marine Corps, Navy, Coast Guard, and Air Force. One of the Army men in each squad was the leader. (*Diagram 45*)

The arriving motorcade halted on the street between the honor guard and Fort Myer Chapel, the hearse coming to a stop near the chapel entrance. After the clergy and body bearers had taken their positions at the rear of the hearse, the honor guard troops presented arms and the Army Band sounded ruffles and flourishes and played the "General's March." When the band began the hymn "Faith of Our Fathers," the body bearers removed the casket from the hearse. Canon Miller and the Reverend Mr. Moss then led the way through the cordon of honorary pallbearers to the chapel entrance. At the entrance the body bearers placed the casket on a movable bier, and from that point two of the bearers moved the casket, following the clergy, to a position at the front of the chapel. The honorary pallbearers then entered the chapel and took their seats.

Canon Miller conducted the funeral service from the Episcopal Order for the Burial of the Dead. There was no eulogy. At the conclusion of the twenty-minute service, the honorary pallbearers, led out of the chapel by General Bradley, reformed their cordon at the entrance. Two body bearers meanwhile had moved to the front of the chapel to handle the casket. The clergy then led the funeral party from the chapel. President Eisenhower left the chapel by a side entrance. When the clergy reached the front entrance, the honor guard troops, who had remained in formation across the way, presented arms; the band sounded honors, then began a hymn. During the hymn the body bearers lifted the casket from the movable bier and returned it to the hearse. The honorary pallbearers proceeded to their cars. The members of the Marshall family, who had remained at the chapel entrance while the casket was placed in the hearse, went to their cars, and the

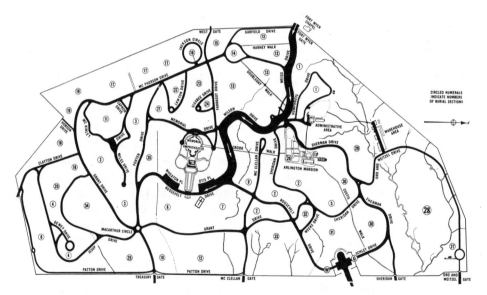

Diagram 46.   Route of march, Fort Myer Chapel to gravesite.

Casket Is Carried to the Grave, *above. Last rites at the graveside, below.*

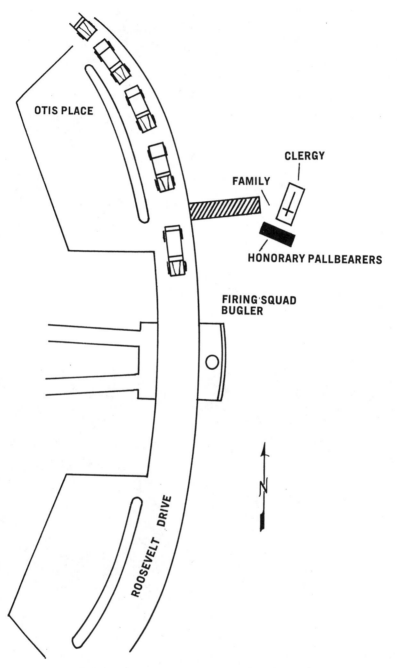

Diagram 47.   Formation at the graveside.

small cortege of eight vehicles formed and moved toward the gravesite. The other mourners then dispersed.

Since early afternoon, a security cordon of troops from the 3d Infantry had been on station around the gravesite. A principal duty of these troops was to keep members of the press and the public at least 150 feet away from the gravesite in order to ensure the privacy of the burial service. Also in position some time before the cortege left the chapel were the saluting battery of the 3d Infantry, a firing squad, a bugler, the national color detail, the personal flag bearer, and the body bearer team. The members of the body bearer team were those who earlier had participated in the ceremonies at the Washington National Cathedral. The body bearers who handled the casket at the Fort Myer Chapel did not accompany the cortege to the gravesite.

The small procession, in order of march, included Mr. John C. Metzler, superintendent of Arlington National Cemetery; General Gailey, escort commander; the honorary pallbearers; the clergy; the hearse (accompanied by a mortician); the Marshall family; and a second cemetery representative. To reach the gravesite, the motorcade moved via Meigs Drive, Wilson Drive, and Roosevelt Drive. (*Diagram 46*) It came to a halt so that the rear of the hearse was aligned with a mat that had been laid from Roosevelt Drive east to the grave.

The honorary pallbearers, first to leave their cars, formed a cordon along the mat. The members of the Marshall family got out next and stood while the clergy, body bearers, national color detail, and personal flag bearer took positions at the rear of the hearse. When all were in place, the body bearers removed the casket from the hearse. Then, in procession, the national color detail, mortician, clergy, body bearers with the casket, and personal flag bearer moved through the cordon of honorary pallbearers to the grave. As the casket passed by, the honorary pallbearers fell in behind and moved to their graveside position. The Marshall family was escorted to the graveside by the cemetery superintendent. (*Diagram 47*)

The clergy then conducted the burial service. At its conclusion, the battery fired a 19-gun salute, the firing squad discharged the traditional three volleys, and the bugler sounded taps. As the sound of the bugle died away, the body bearers folded the flag that had draped the casket, and one of them, the cadet from Virginia Military Institute, presented the flag to Mrs. Marshall, thus concluding the simple rites for General Marshall. Mrs. Marshall placed a small bouquet of flowers on her husband's casket and left the graveside.

CHAPTER XX

General Walter Bedell Smith
Special Full Honor Funeral
9-14 August 1961

On 9 August 1961 General Walter Bedell Smith suffered a heart attack at his home in Washington and died in the ambulance on the way to Walter Reed General Hospital. He was sixty-five years old and had retired. From the hospital his body was taken to Gawler's funeral establishment where it remained while funeral arrangements were completed.

By virtue of his rank, General Smith was entitled to a Special Full Honor Funeral, in which the Army was the sole military service to participate. But in deference to the wishes of Mary Cline Smith, the general's widow, a distinctly different ceremony was actually held.

Mrs. Smith made her wishes known on the morning of 10 August, when she conferred in the offices of Arlington National Cemetery with the officer appointed from Headquarters, Department of the Army, as the official aide to the next of kin, the ceremonies officer of the Military District of Washington, and the assistant superintendent of the cemetery. At that time she selected a gravesite for her husband in Section 7 of the cemetery, very near the grave of General of the Army George C. Marshall, and requested that his funeral be patterned after the simple joint service funeral given General Marshall in 1959.

In line with existing policy which states that the officer in charge of arranging a military funeral shall be from the same service as the deceased, the Commanding General, Military District of Washington, Maj. Gen. Paul A. Gavan, became responsible for planning the ceremonies for General Smith. An immediate requirement facing General Gavan, raised by Mrs. Smith's request that her husband's funeral be similar to General Marshall's, was to obtain Department of Defense clearance for joint service participation. This clearance was readily granted. General Gavan and his staff then made plans based largely on the records of General Marshall's funeral, but varying in several respects. The essential difference was that General Smith's body would not lie in the Washington National Cathedral as had the body of General Marshall.

General Smith's body was to remain at the funeral establishment until mid-morning on 14 August, when it was to be escorted to the chapel at Fort Myer, Virginia, for a requiem mass. Immediately following the chapel rites, a private

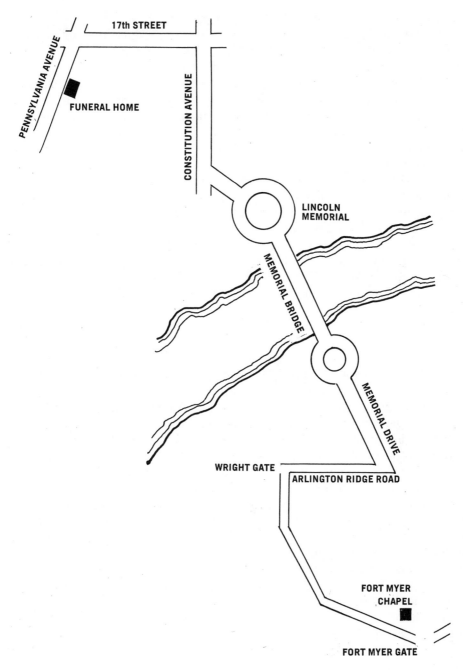

Diagram 48.   Route of march, funeral establishment to Fort Myer Chapel.

burial service was to be held at the Arlington gravesite.

At 1000 on 14 August a small escort arrived at the funeral establishment to take General Smith's body to the Fort Myer Chapel. The morticians had already placed the casket in the hearse, which one of them would accompany. The escort included Metropolitan motorcycle police, two cars of Armed Forces Police, and the escort commander, who in this instance was a field grade officer from the 3d Infantry. The motorcade left the funeral establishment at 1040, its departure timed so that it would reach the chapel a few minutes before 1100, the scheduled hour of the funeral service. (*Diagram 48*)

At Fort Myer most of the mourners were seated in the chapel before the arrival of the cortege. Among them were high military officials, members of Congress, and a number of foreign diplomats. President John F. Kennedy was represented by his Army, Navy, and Air Force aides. Outside the chapel fourteen honorary pallbearers formed a cordon at the entrance: Morehead Patterson, Carter L. Burgess, General of the Army Dwight D. Eisenhower, Louis Marx, David Marx, General George H. Decker, Robert A. Lovett, Samuel C. Waugh, A. F. Wechsler, Robert Murphy, John Snively, Marion Blazek, Paul Stone, and Allen W. Dulles. At 1055 the Smith family walked through the cordon and entered the chapel.

Waiting near the honorary pallbearers was Bishop William R. Arnold, Military Delegate to the Armed Forces of the United States from the Office of the Military Ordinariate of the Catholic Church. Bishop Arnold, who had been the Army Chief of Chaplains from 1937 to 1946, would conduct the mass. Nearby were the body bearers, a joint service group composed of two men from the Army and one man each from the Marine Corps, Navy, Air Force, and Coast Guard.

Across the street from and facing the chapel stood an armed forces honor guard, a joint service detail of seventy-six men which included an officer, a drum major, and thirty musicians from the U.S. Army Band, a color detail, and a platoon of troops. In command of the guard was an Army major with a staff of three, one officer each from the Navy, Air Force, and Coast Guard. The color detail was composed of one color guard each from the Army and Marine Corps, two Army color bearers for the national colors and Army colors, and one color bearer from each of the other services carrying appropriate service colors. The platoon of troops was commanded by a Marine Corps lieutenant and consisted of three ten-man squads, each of which included two men from the Army, Marine Corps, Navy, Air Force, and Coast Guard. One of the Army men in each squad was the leader, and one other Army man with the formation was the platoon guide. The honor guard elements were on line, the platoon in the center, the color detail at the left, and the band at the right. During the ceremonies for General Marshall the color detail was in the center and the platoon at the left. (*Diagram 49*)

The cortege came to a stop between the armed forces honor guard and the

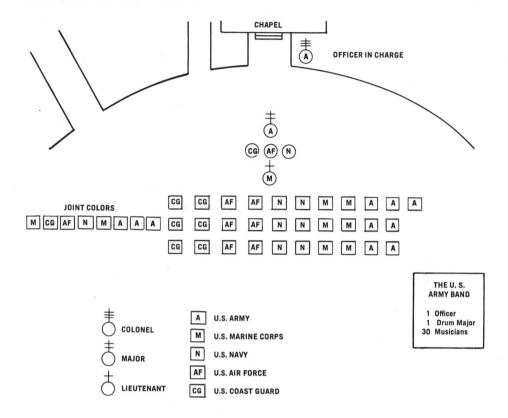

Diagram 49. Position of armed forces honor guard at Fort Myer Chapel.

chapel, the hearse at the chapel entrance. (*Diagram 50*) Bishop Arnold, the mortician, the body bearers, and Col. Richard M. Lee, the commanding officer of the 3d Infantry who was responsible for the ceremonies at the chapel site, then moved to the rear of the hearse. At Colonel Lee's signal the honor guard presented arms; the band sounded ruffles and flourishes, played the "General's March," and then began a hymn. While the hymn was played, the body bearers removed the casket from the hearse and, preceded by Bishop Arnold, carried it through the cordon of honorary pallbearers to the chapel entrance. There the casket was placed on a movable bier; with the bishop still leading, two of the bearers wheeled it to the front of the chapel. The honorary pallbearers followed the casket into the chapel and were taken to their seats.

Bishop Arnold then said the requiem mass. At its completion, the honorary pallbearers were first to be ushered from the chapel to allow them to re-form the cordon outside. Two body bearers moved to the front of the chapel to handle the

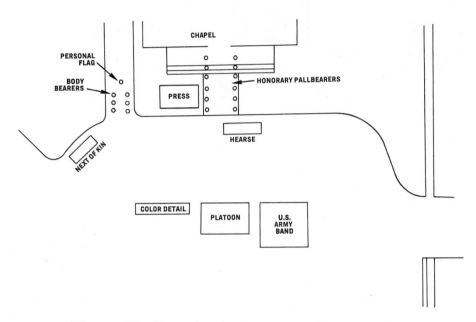

Diagram 50. Formation for ceremony at Fort Myer Chapel.

casket. Bishop Arnold then led the procession out of the chapel, the Smith family and other mourners following the casket.

The armed forces honor guard, which had remained in formation during the funeral service, presented arms when Bishop Arnold appeared at the chapel entrance, while the band sounded ruffles and flourishes and began a hymn. As the hymn was played, the casket was returned to the hearse. Those attending the private graveside rites then moved to their cars. Members of the Smith family, who had waited at the chapel entrance while the casket was carried to the hearse, were the last to enter their cars. The honor guard again presented arms as the cortege began to move through the gate into the cemetery. After the cortege had gone, the guard units, none of which were scheduled for further participation in ceremonies, were dismissed.

Since midmorning a detail of one officer and forty-four men from the 3d Infantry had been on station as a security cordon around the gravesite to ensure privacy for the burial service. Inside this ring of troops was another group of one officer and five men to control the press.

Also in position in the cemetery before the cortege reached the gravesite were a saluting battery, a firing squad, a bugler, a national color detail, and a personal

Diagram 51.   Route of march, Fort Myer Chapel to gravesite.

flag bearer, all from the 3d Infantry, and a second armed forces body bearer team
of the same composition as that which had served during the chapel rites.

Leading the cortege was the superintendent of Arlington National Cemetery,
Mr. John C. Metzler. Behind him came Colonel Lee, the honorary pallbearers,
Bishop Arnold, the hearse (accompanied by the mortician), and the Smith fam-
ily. To reach the gravesite the cortege moved via Meigs Drive, Wilson Drive, and
Roosevelt Drive. When it halted, the hearse was at the end of a mat that ran from
Roosevelt Drive to the grave. (*Diagram 51*)

The honorary pallbearers, who were the first to leave their cars, formed a
cordon along the mat. Bishop Arnold, the body bearers, the national color detail,
and the personal flag bearers took positions at the rear of the hearse. The body
bearers then removed General Smith's casket from the hearse, and the procession,
with the national color detail leading and the mortician, the bishop, the casket,
and the personal flag bearers following in that order, marched through the cordon
of pallbearers to the grave. The honorary pallbearers fell in behind and moved to
their graveside position. The Smith family was then escorted to the graveside by
Mr. Metzler. (*Diagram 52*)

Bishop Arnold conducted the burial service. After the benediction, the saluting battery fired seventeen guns, the firing squad discharged three volleys, and the
bugler sounded taps. As the last note faded, the body bearers performed the ritual
of folding the flag that had draped General Smith's casket. One of them handed

it to Mr. Metzler, who in turn passed it to Bishop Arnold. The bishop then presented it to Mrs. Smith. The rites for General Smith, as Mrs. Smith wished, had been conducted with the simplicity and dignity that had marked the ceremony tor General Marshall.

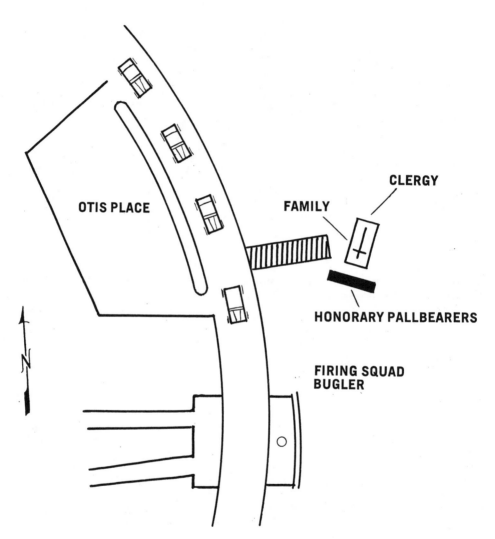

Diagram 52.   Formation at the graveside.

CHAPTER XXI

Senator Styles Bridges
Funeral Without Formal Classification
26-29 November 1961

Senator Styles Bridges, Republican from New Hampshire and former governor of the state, died in his sleep at his East Concord, New Hampshire, home on 26 November 1961 at the age of sixty-three. Although he had suffered a heart attack earlier in the fall, his death was unexpected.

Final tribute was paid Senator Bridges in a private service in East Concord on 28 November and in a public service held in the state capitol at Concord on the 29th. During the interval between the two services the senator's body lay in state in the rotunda of the capitol. In New Hampshire the public service was described as a State Funeral and was reported by newspapers to be the first conducted in the New Hampshire statehouse. The senator was buried in Pine Grove Cemetery in East Concord.

Military honors were accorded Senator Bridges at the wish of his widow. Mrs. Bridges made her request to the Sergeant at Arms of the United States Senate, Mr. Joseph C. Duke, who sent it through legislative liaison channels to Department of Defense officials.

The department arranged to send to New Hampshire two officers and nineteen enlisted men from the Washington area, most of them from ceremonial units and all of them experienced participants in military funerals. The group consisted of a commander, one other company officer, and thirteen enlisted men from the Honor Guard Company, 1st Battle Group, 3d Infantry, stationed at Fort Myer, Virginia; two enlisted men from the Ceremonial Guard, U.S. Naval Air Station in Washington; two enlisted men from the 1100th Security Squadron stationed at Bolling Air Force Base in the District of Columbia; and two enlisted men of the Ceremonial Guard Company from the Marine Barracks in Washington.

Of these troops, the six men furnished by the Marine Corps, Navy, and Air Force and two of the men supplied by the Army formed a joint service body bearer team, of which one of the Army men, a noncommissioned officer, was in charge. Four Army men were a part of the guard of honor that would watch over Senator Bridges' body while it lay in state; the company officer from the 3d Infantry, assisted by a noncommissioned officer, had charge of the guard. Of the remaining enlisted men from the 3d Infantry, four served as a national color detail

and two were alternates. The Ceremonial Officer of the Military District of
Washington and an officer from the Office of the Chief of Legislative Liaison,
Headquarters, Department of the Army, also went to Concord to help arrange
the military ceremonies. In addition to participating in the funeral ceremonies,
the experienced men from Washington organized and briefed six troop contingents from local installations which were also assigned by the Department of Defense to take part. Three of these installations furnished additional troops for the
guard of honor, which was to be a joint service group: the Portsmouth Naval
Base, Portsmouth, New Hampshire, one officer and six men; the Marine Barracks, Portsmouth, one officer and five men; and the Pease Air Force Base, New
Hampshire, one officer and four men.

The Combat Support Company, 1st Battle Group, 4th Infantry, stationed at
Fort Devens, Massachusetts, furnished a platoon to act as escort in the funeral
procession and during the graveside rites. Also sent from Fort Devens to serve
with the escort was the 18th U.S. Army Band. The New Hampshire Army National Guard, with headquarters in Concord, provided a firing squad of one officer
and eight enlisted men and a bugler for the graveside ceremony. (*Table 13*)

TABLE 13—TROOP LIST, CEREMONY FOR SENATOR STYLES BRIDGES

Duty	Officers	En-listed Men
Guard of honor		
3d Infantry (Virginia)	1	5
Portsmouth Naval Base (New Hampshire)	1	6
Marine Barracks (New Hampshire)	1	5
Pease Air Force Base (New Hampshire)	1	4
Ceremonial site control officer		
3d Infantry (Virginia)	1	....
Body bearers		
3d Infantry (Virginia)	....	2
U.S. Naval Station (Washington, D.C.)	....	2
Bolling Air Force Base (Washington, D.C.)	....	2
Marine Barracks (Washington, D.C.)	....	2
National color detail		
3d Infantry (Virginia)	....	4
Escort		
4th Infantry (Massachusetts)	2	30 (approx.)
18th Army Band (Massachusetts)	....	27
Firing squad		
Army National Guard (New Hampshire)	1	8
Bugler		
Army National Guard (New Hampshire)	....	1
Total	8	98

The private service for Senator Bridges took place on the morning of 28 November in the East Congregational Church in East Concord and was conducted by the Reverend Clifton G. Davis, pastor of the church. Six members of the senator's staff served as honorary pallbearers. Some hundred persons attended the half-hour service, among them Mayor Charles P. Johnson and Mrs. Johnson of Concord; New Hampshire Governor Wesley Powell; former Governor and Mrs. Robert O. Blood; and Vice President Lyndon B. Johnson. The Vice President came to the private service because previous commitments would prevent him from attending the public service on 29 November.

At the conclusion of the private service, the joint service body bearer team, the only military contingent at the ceremony, carried the casket to the hearse. The senator's family, the honorary pallbearers, other members of the funeral party, and the body bearers then entered automobiles for the journey to the capitol in Concord, where Senator Bridges' body would lie in state. The motorcade traveled via the Bridges Highway, which was named for the senator. Local police provided the only escort as far as the Bridge Street traffic circle in Concord. Assembled at that point were the 18th Army Band, the platoon of troops from the 4th Infantry, and the national color detail, which escorted the cortege the remaining distance to the capitol. This stage of the march was made at a slow cadence meted out by the band on muffled drums.

When the cortege arrived the escort units and mourners took their positions outside the statehouse. As the body bearers removed the casket from the hearse, the military escort presented arms. While the band played the hymn "Abide With Me," the senator's casket was carried in procession into the flower-banked rotunda, known as the Hall of Flags, and placed on a bier. The body bearers were then dismissed, and the first relief, one officer and four enlisted men, of the joint service guard of honor took post. In order to maintain a constant vigil at the bier, each relief of the guard of honor stood a thirty-minute watch. In the afternoon the Hall of Flags was opened to the public. From 1400 until 2200 on 28 November and from 0830 until 1100 on the 29th more than 4,000 persons passed by the bier.

No formal invitations to attend the public funeral were issued, but long before the service it was apparent to Maj. Gen. Francis B. McSwiney, the Adjutant General of the State of New Hampshire, who was in charge, that the representatives of the federal government, active and former officials of the New Hampshire government, local leaders, and other guests would constitute an audience far beyond the capacity of the Hall of Flags. He therefore arranged to have a public address system installed with speakers in Representatives Hall, the Senate Chamber, and other rooms near the Hall of Flags. He also had other speakers set up outside the capitol to allow the public to hear the services.

Since no formal invitations had been issued, there was no formal seating plan. The Hall of Flags itself was reserved for Senator Bridges' family, the representatives of the federal government, the highest state officials, and the members of the senator's staff. A nearby room was assigned to the senator's business associates and to official delegations of various political and patriotic organizations. Representatives Hall and the Senate Chamber were set aside for members and former members of the state legislature and their families.

Early on the morning of 29 November a large delegation from both houses of the United States Congress left Washington by plane for Concord to attend the public funeral. Transportation was provided by the Air Force, as arranged jointly by the staffs of the Sergeant at Arms of the Senate and the Department of the Air Force Legislative Liaison Office. Representatives of the Department of Defense, headed by Secretary of Defense Robert S. McNamara, also flew to Concord; among them were Secretary of the Navy John B. Connally, Jr., Secretary of the Air Force Eugene M. Zuckert, and Lt. Gen. Arthur G. Trudeau, acting for Secretary of the Army Elvis J. Stahr, Jr. Arriving in Concord on behalf of President Kennedy were the President's brother Edward and Lawrence O'Brien, White House assistant for legislative affairs.

The service began at noon, led by the Reverend Frederick W. Alden, minister of the New Hampshire Congregational Christian Conference. Eulogies were delivered by Governor Wesley Powell, U.S. Senate Minority Leader Everett M. Dirksen, and U.S. House Majority Leader John W. McCormack. Music was provided by an organist and the combined choirs of two local colleges. The Reverend Frederick Brown Harris, Chaplain of the U.S. Senate, pronounced the benediction.

Immediately following the hour-long service, Senator Bridges' body was taken from the capitol in procession, the joint service body bearer team again handling the casket and members of the senator's staff again acting as honorary pallbearers. After the casket was placed in the hearse, the Bridges family, the body bearers, and others in the funeral party entered automobiles and the cortege left for Pine Grove Cemetery in East Concord. The military escort had meanwhile taken its position at the gravesite to participate in the final rites. Some eighty-five automobiles made up the procession, which traveled over the Bridges Highway. From each overpass spanning the highway, people watched its passage. In East Concord the procession passed by Senator Bridges' residence.

Upon reaching the cemetery, the cortege moved to the family plot near the center of the cemetery, where Senator Bridges' previous wife had been buried in 1938. The grave was at the foot of a gentle rise of ground. On the rise, as viewed from the head of the grave, the Army National Guard firing squad stood in position at the left, the 18th Army Band in the center, and the 4th Infantry platoon at the right.

The military escort presented arms as the body bearers removed the casket from the hearse. The band then played "Abide With Me" as Senator Bridges' casket was borne in procession to the grave. After the Bridges family and other mourners had been guided to positions at the graveside, the Reverend Dr. Alden read a simple service. Standing with him as he conducted the rites were the Reverend Dr. Davis of the East Congregational Church and Chaplain Harris.

After the benediction, the firing squad delivered the traditional three volleys and the Army National Guard bugler sounded taps. As the band played "America the Beautiful," the body bearers folded the flag that had draped Senator Bridges' casket and handed it to the commanding officer of the Honor Guard Company of the 3d Infantry, Capt. Keith Bissell, Jr. Captain Bissell gave the flag to the Reverend Dr. Alden, who presented it to Mrs. Bridges, thus closing the final rites for the senator from New Hampshire.

CHAPTER XXII

Ambassador of Botswana, Zachariah K. Matthews
Ambassador of Spain, Mariano de Yturralde
Ambassador of Malagasy, Louis Rakotomalala
Ambassador of Poland, Edward Drozniak
Departure Ceremonies
1962-1968

When foreign dignitaries have died while in the United States, honors in keeping with their rank and national origin have been accorded them by the U.S. government. On most occasions these honors have taken the form of a departure ceremony when the body of the foreign official was returned to his homeland for burial.

Between 1962 and 1968 four foreign officials, each the ambassador of his country, died while stationed in the United States. Ambassador of Spain Mariano de Yturralde died in March 1962, Ambassador of Poland Edward Drozniak in November 1966, Ambassador of Botswana Zachariah K. Matthews in May 1968, and Ambassador of Malagasy Louis Rakotomalala in July 1968. All were in Washington at the time of their deaths, and all were returned to their countries by plane from Andrews Air Force Base.

The departure ceremony for the ambassador of Botswana on 14 May 1968 was arranged by Headquarters Command, U.S. Air Force, and carried out by Air Force troops. The troop formations included an honor cordon, a body bearer team, a national color detail, and the personal flag bearers. (*Table 14*) The body was escorted by Metropolitan and Armed Forces Police from Washington to Andrews Air Force Base. When the cortege arrived, the honor cordon, lining the way to the aircraft that would carry the ambassador's body to Botswana, presented arms as the body bearers removed the casket from the hearse. With the national color detail leading and the personal flag bearers at the rear, the ambassador's casket was carried through the honor cordon and put aboard the plane. This ceremony was the simplest of the four.

Responsibility for arranging and conducting the other three departure ceremonies was assigned by the Department of Defense to the Military District of Wash-

TABLE 14—TROOP LIST, DEPARTURE CEREMONY FOR AMBASSADOR OF
BOTSWANA ZACHARIAH K. MATTHEWS

Duty	U.S. Army		U.S. Marine Corps		U.S. Navy		U.S. Air Force		U.S. Coast Guard		Total	
	Offi-cers	En-listed Men	Offi-cers	En-listed Men	Offi-cers	En-listed Men	Offi-cers	En-listed Men	Offi-cers	En-listed Men	Offi-cers	En-listed Men
Honor cordon							1	18			1	18
Color detail								5				5
Body bearers								8				8
Personal flag bearer								3				3
Total							1	34			1	34

ington. The planning for all three was based on the portions of the current policy directives outlining departure honors in State, Official, and Special Military Funerals. The three ceremonies were not identical; variations occurred in the number of troops involved and in the composition and procedures of the ceremonies. But all of them resembled departure ceremonies for high-ranking U.S. civil and military officials, and each one was distinguished by recognition of the nationality of the ambassador being honored.

In the departure ceremony for Ambassador Mariano de Yturralde on 7 March 1962, a street cordon of 105 men lined both sides of the air base roadway leading to the ceremonial area at Andrews Field. Half an hour before the scheduled arrival of the ambassador's body from Washington, these troops were spaced at ten-step intervals facing the street. Within the ceremonial area, which was surrounded by a security cordon to keep it clear, an honor cordon of eighteen men lined the way from the point at which the hearse bearing the casket would stop to the aircraft itself. Also on hand were a band, a color detail of three men with the flag of Spain, and an eight-man body bearer team.

U.S. Park Police escorted the cortege that took the casket of Ambassador de Yturralde from Washington to the air base. Although members of the Military District of Washington staff had co-ordinated this movement with the police on 6 March, the police, for reasons not apparent, completed the move twenty minutes ahead of schedule. Air police at the gate, although they had been informed of the schedule of events, sustained the error in timing when they expedited rather than delayed the movement of the cortege from the base gate to the ceremonial site. Maj. Gen. Paul A. Gavan, commanding the Military District of Washington, fortunately had passed the cortege on his way to the air base. Realizing that it was ahead of schedule, he sped to the site of the ceremony to warn the troops. Thus the confusion that might have been caused by the early arrival of the cortege was averted. But as a result of the incident, Armed Forces Police were put in the police

HONOR CORDON FORMS FOR AMBASSADOR RAKOTOMALALA

escort in all subsequent ceremonies of this kind, and a communications vehicle was placed in the ceremonial area so that constant contact between the motorcade and the ceremonial troops could be maintained.

As the cortege moved toward the ceremonial site, the members of the street cordon presented arms individually without command as the lead vehicle of the police escort approached and ordered arms when the hearse had passed. In the ceremonial area, once the hearse had been parked in the proper position the site control officer directed the body bearers to move to the rear of the hearse. The honor cordon then presented arms and the band played the national anthem of Spain, the national anthem of the United States, and a hymn. As the hymn began, the body bearers took the casket from the hearse. With the color detail leading, the casket was carried through the honor cordon and taken aboard the aircraft. Once it was aboard, the band ceased playing and the honor cordon ordered arms, concluding the departure ceremony for Ambassador de Yturralde.

A ceremony quite similar to the one performed for the Ambassador of Spain was conducted at Andrews Field on 6 July 1968 when the body of Ambassador Louis Rakotomalala was returned to his African homeland, the Republic of Mala-

CASKET OF AMBASSADOR RAKOTOMALALA IS CARRIED TO AIRCRAFT

gasy. The main difference between the two ceremonies was in the troops participating. No street cordon was employed in the ceremony for the African official, but the honor cordon, a joint service group, was three times the size of the cordon for the Spanish ambassador. Further, the national colors of the United States and the Republic of Malagasy led the way as a joint service body bearer team took Ambassador Rakotomalala's casket through the honor cordon to the aircraft. Since the casket was unusually cumbersome, it was supported by a movable bier. (*Table 15*)

Of the four ceremonies, the most elaborate took place on 3 November 1966 at the departure of the body of Ambassador Edward Drozniak of Poland. The ceremony was unusual in that it took place at night.

Troops participating included the U.S. Army Band, a joint service honor cordon, a joint service body bearer team, a joint service color detail, and the 3d Infantry saluting battery, a total of four officers and 121 men. Supporting troops consisted of a security cordon, press cordon, parking detail, baggage detail, and Armed Forces Police in three radio vehicles. (*Table 16*) All troops were in their respective positions at 2125.

TABLE 15—TROOP LIST, DEPARTURE CEREMONY FOR AMBASSADOR OF
MALAGASY LOUIS RAKOTOMALALA

Duty	U.S. Army		U.S. Marine Corps		U.S. Navy		U.S. Air Force		U.S. Coast Guard		Total	
	Officers	Enlisted Men	Officers	Enlisted Men	Officers	Enlisted Men	Officers	Enlisted Men	Officers	Enlisted Men	Officers	Enlisted Men
Honor cordon	....	15	....	10	....	10	....	12	....	8	....	55
Color detail	....	4	....	2	....	....	....	....	....	....	....	6
Body bearers	....	2	....	2	....	2	....	1	....	1	....	8
Band	....	....	....	....	....	....	1	30	....	....	1	30
Total	....	21	....	14	....	12	1	43	....	9	1	99

TABLE 16—TROOP LIST, DEPARTURE CEREMONY FOR AMBASSADOR OF
POLAND EDWARD DROZNIAK

Duty	U.S. Army		U.S. Marine Corps		U.S. Navy		U.S. Air Force		U.S. Coast Guard		Total	
	Officers	Enlisted Men	Officers	Enlisted Men	Officers	Enlisted Men	Officers	Enlisted Men	Officers	Enlisted Men	Officers	Enlisted Men
Honor cordon	1	9	....	8	....	8	....	8	....	8	1	41
National color detail	....	1	....	1	....	1	....	....	....	....	....	3
Body bearers	1	2	....	2	....	2	....	1	....	1	1	8
Band	1	56	....	....	....	....	....	....	....	....	1	56
Saluting battery	1	13	....	....	....	....	....	....	....	....	1	13
Security cordon	....	....	....	....	....	....	1	27	....	....	1	27
Parking detail	....	5	....	....	....	....	....	....	....	....	....	5
Press cordon	....	5	....	....	....	....	....	....	....	....	....	5
Baggage detail	....	4	....	....	....	....	....	....	....	....	....	4
Total	4	95	....	11	....	11	1	36	....	9	5	162

The cortege of American and Polish officials accompanying the body of Ambassador Drozniak to Andrews Air Force Base left the Embassy of Poland at 2050. When the cortege drove into the ceremonial area at the airfield, the troops came to attention. A parking detail guided the cars to designated places on the airstrip, and the Polish and American dignitaries were then escorted from their cars to positions for the ceremony. The body bearers, meanwhile, had moved to the rear of the hearse.

The officer in charge of the honor cordon ordered the troops to present arms. At the same time, the Army Band sounded four ruffles and flourishes and played the national anthem of Poland and the national anthem of the United States. As

CASKET OF AMBASSADOR DROZNIAK IS CARRIED THROUGH HONOR CORDON, *above.*
Casket of Ambassador Drozniak is placed aboard aircraft, below.

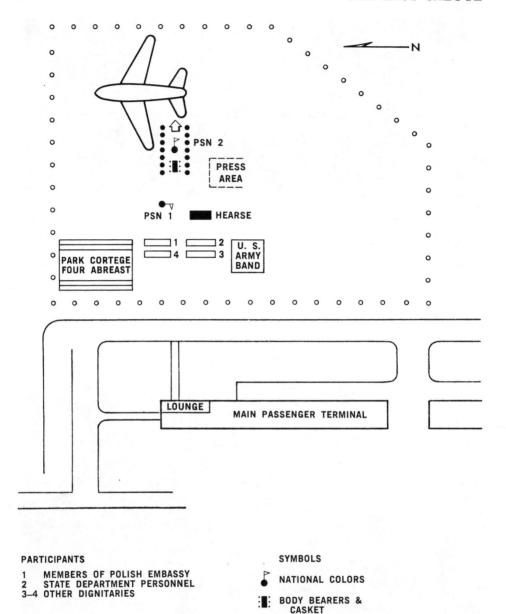

Diagram 53.   Departure ceremony, ambassador of Poland, Andrews Air
Force Base.

the band played, the battery fired nineteen guns, the salute for an ambassador. After the anthems, the band played Chopin's "Funeral March." As the march began, the body bearers removed the satin-draped casket from the hearse. Preceded by the national colors of Poland, the bearers then carried Ambassador Drozniak's casket through the honor cordon and placed it on the plane. (*Diagram 53*) After the casket was aboard the aircraft, the honor cordon presented arms and the color detail cased the Polish flag, thus concluding the departure ceremony.

CHAPTER XXIII

President John F. Kennedy
State Funeral
22-25 November 1963

About 1330 (eastern standard time) on 22 November 1963, President John F. Kennedy was shot by an assassin while riding in a motorcade through Dallas, Texas. The President was rushed to Parkland Memorial Hospital in Dallas for emergency treatment and at 1400 he was pronounced dead. An hour later President Kennedy's body was taken to the Dallas airport for transportation back to Washington aboard Air Force One, the Presidential plane. After a wait at the field while Lyndon B. Johnson was sworn in as President aboard Air Force One, the plane departed about 1540. There was no formal departure ceremony.

When the news of President Kennedy's death reached Washington, planning was begun immediately for a State Funeral. Frequently, officials entitled to State Funerals have been discreetly asked for their preferences in regard to the ceremonies and contingency plans have been framed accordingly, but no such information existed for President Kennedy. Responsibility for planning the funeral largely rested with Maj. Gen. Philip C. Wehle, commander of the Military District of Washington, who, under existing directives, was in charge of all State Funeral ceremonies held in Washington, D.C. General Wehle had as a basic guide the book of funeral plans and policies published in 1958, but there were to be numerous adjustments, some made with extremely brief notice, and most of them efforts to meet the wishes of the next of kin.

Upon receiving the first grim report from Dallas, Paul C. Miller, Chief of Ceremonies and Special Events for the Military District of Washington, notified the Office of the Military Aide to the President of the district's readiness to act. Shortly afterward, he was summoned to the White House office of Ralph A. Dungan, Special Assistant to the President. Already in the office when he arrived was R. Sargent Shriver, Director of the Peace Corps and brother-in-law of President Kennedy, who was there to represent the Kennedy family. These three men began at once the difficult task of arranging funeral ceremonies under the pressure of time and without direct contact with the immediate family.

By 1600 word reached Washington that Air Force One, bearing President Kennedy's body, was due at Andrews Air Force Base at 1800. From there, a helicopter furnished by the White House Executive Flight Detachment was to transport the body to the Naval Medical Center in Bethesda, Maryland, for autopsy. As plans stood at that moment, Gawler's morticians were then to take the body to their establishment for preparation. Afterward the President's body was to be escorted to the White House where it was to lie until 24 November. On the 24th the body was to be taken to the Capitol to lie in state in the rotunda. At this point neither the place of burial nor the exact wishes of the next of kin regarding the funeral service were known.

At Military District of Washington headquarters, General Wehle meanwhile had opened a funeral operations center, from which all funeral details, administrative as well as ceremonial, would be controlled. As the first order of business, members of the center staff flashed alerts to military and civil units and agencies which would be or were likely to be involved in the funeral. This task included communicating with Congressional officials whose permission and support were needed in order to use the rotunda of the Capitol for the lying in state ceremony.

Between 1600 and 1800, General Wehle organized a joint service ceremony for receiving President Kennedy's body at Andrews Air Force Base and made arrangements for its reception at the Naval Medical Center and at the White House. A Navy security guard was posted at the medical center, and a guard detail was set up to stay with the body until it was borne to the White House. An honor guard composed of members of all the armed services was to be stationed at the White House when the President's body arrived. In preparation for the ceremony at the White House, General Wehle requested that the replica of the Lincoln catafalque, used in 1958 during the ceremonies for the Unknown Soldiers of World War II and the Korean War, be brought from storage at Arlington National Cemetery and set up in the White House. At Andrews Base Air Force troops were posted as an honor cordon, and troops from all services were to act as body bearers. Finding that more men had reported than were needed, 1st Lt. Samuel R. Bird, a 3d Infantry officer in charge of all body bearers, formed two joint service body bearer teams and placed the remaining men with the honor cordon. General Wehle had also arranged to have military police from the Military District of Washington at the airfield. Although he had been informed that the President's body was to be taken to the medical center by helicopter, he asked that a Navy ambulance be provided at the field. (Jacqueline Kennedy, the President's widow, later decided to use the ambulance.)

Air Force One landed at Andrews Air Force Base at 1805. Dignitaries who waited at the field included the Secretary of Defense, Chairman of the Joint Chiefs of Staff, Chief Justice of the United States, some members of Congress, a number of diplomats, and Robert F. Kennedy, the Attorney General and brother of the slain President. As the plane came to a stop, a cargo lift carrying Lieutenant Bird and his first team of body bearers moved to the aircraft. After the hatch was opened, however, Brig. Gen. Godfrey T. McHugh, Air Force Aide to the President, who was on board, notified Lieutenant Bird that secret service men would carry the casket from the plane. The secret service men were obliged nevertheless to call on the trained body bearers for help in moving the casket from the lift to the ambulance.

The motorcade consisting of a police escort, General Wehle in his sedan, the ambulance, in which Mrs. Kennedy and Robert Kennedy rode, and three cars bearing members of the President's staff departed for the Naval Medical Center. General Wehle used the helicopter that was to have carried the President's body to send Lieutenant Bird and the second team of body bearers to the medical center so that they would be present when the ambulance arrived.

At the medical center there was some confusion when the President's body arrived by ambulance instead of by helicopter. As instructed, Navy troops had formed a cordon from the center's helipad to the rear (morgue) entrance to keep the way clear. But when the motorcade arrived it had no such protection and a crowd of spectators surged about it. With some difficulty, Lieutenant Bird and his body bearer team managed to reach the ambulance and carry the casket to the morgue. The team remained in the hallway as a guard.

After the autopsy the morticians from Gawler's, for reasons of security and speed, prepared the body at the center rather than at their own facility. At this time the body was transferred to a mahogany casket which the body bearer team draped with a flag supplied by the morticians. Mrs. Kennedy and the group that had accompanied her to the medical center then came from the hospital suite where they had waited, the casket was placed in the ambulance, and the motorcade, led by General Wehle, proceeded to the White House where the President's body would lie in the East Room.

The motorcade reached the White House at 0430 on 23 November, entering the grounds through one of the two gates on Pennsylvania Avenue. Posted at the gate to escort the ambulance to the North Portico was a detachment of twelve marines. A little more than an hour before, Mr. Shriver had asked for a small troop unit to act as escort and at 0330, a White House aide had telephoned the commanding officer of the Marine Barracks in Washington for twelve to twenty-four men in full-dress uniform. An Army bus supplied by the Military District of Washington with an Armed Forces Police escort went to the barracks and returned with twelve men of the Marine Drill Team in full dress in less than twenty minutes.

After the marines had escorted the ambulance to the North Portico entrance, the body bearer team, still led by Lieutenant Bird, carried the casket into the White House. Moving past a joint honor cordon lining the hallway, the body bearers took the casket to the East Room and placed it on the replica of the Lincoln catafalque. The first relief of an honor guard immediately took post at the four corners of the bier, facing outward. The honor guard included troops from the 3d Infantry and from the Army's Special Forces (Green Berets). The Special Forces troops had been brought hurriedly from Fort Bragg, North Carolina, at the request of Robert Kennedy, who was aware of his brother's particular interest in them.

Up to this point, as an inescapable result of the speed with which events had taken place and the state of shock that had overtaken a great number of the people involved, little of the existing general plan for a State Funeral had been followed. The ceremony at the White House, on the other hand, was nearly according to the plan. From the White House, invitations were sent by telegram and telephone to the official government family and the diplomatic corps to pay their respects following a private family mass in the East Room at 1030 on 23 November. From 1100 until 1900, the governmental and diplomatic officials presented themselves at the White House according to an established schedule:

1100–1400	Executive Branch Presidential Appointees White House Staff
1400–1430	Supreme Court
1430–1700	Senate House of Representatives State and Territorial Governors
1700–1900	Chiefs of Diplomatic Missions

Throughout the scheduled hours a joint service cordon positioned on North Portico Drive, at the North Portico entrance, and in the hallway guided visiting dignitaries to and through the East Room.

During the daylight hours of 23 November, gun salutes, one round each half hour, were fired at all U.S. Army installations equipped to do so, worldwide. These salutes had been ordered on the 22d by the Army Chief of Staff, who, at the same time, directed that the flags at all Army installations be flown at half-staff for thirty days.

By evening of 23 November, as direct liaison with Mrs. Kennedy and Robert Kennedy was established and their wishes were ascertained and incorporated into existing plans, arrangements for the remaining funeral ceremonies assumed definite shape. For the lying in state ceremony, the move from the White House to the Capitol was to begin at 1300 on 24 November. The route—from the North Portico entrance of the White House onto Pennsylvania Avenue, down 15th Street, again on Pennsylvania Avenue to Constitution Avenue, and then over Constitution Avenue to the Delaware Avenue entrance of the East Plaza—was to be lined by a joint service cordon. The President's body was to be borne to the Capitol on a horse-drawn caisson. The procession, as organized at that time, was to move in the following order: police (marching); commanding general, Military District of Washington; muffled drums (no other instruments); detail of Navy enlisted men as honorary pallbearers; special honor guard; national color detail; clergy; caisson, flanked by four members from each of the armed services; President's flag; body bearer detail; immediate family; President Johnson; other mourners; police (marching). Two features of the plan were distinct departures from the general concept of a State Funeral. One was the use of a caisson instead of a hearse at this point in the ceremonies; the other was the omission of a band in favor of muffled drums only. The ceremony at the Capitol itself, with one exception, was scheduled to follow the conventional plan. The exception was a series of eulogies to be delivered in the rotunda. Eulogies were by no means an innovation, but neither were they a customary part of the lying in state ceremony.

It was now firmly established that the funeral service would be held at St. Matthew's Cathedral in Washington and that burial would take place in Arlington National Cemetery. The composition and order of the main funeral procession had yet to be fully determined. In particular, provisions had to be made for the diplomatic corps and other representatives of foreign nations. But it was decided that in the move from the Capitol to St. Matthew's Cathedral the procession would halt at the White House. There, members of the Kennedy family were to leave the cars in which they had ridden from the Capitol and, joined by President Johnson and other dignitaries, were to proceed on foot to the cathedral.

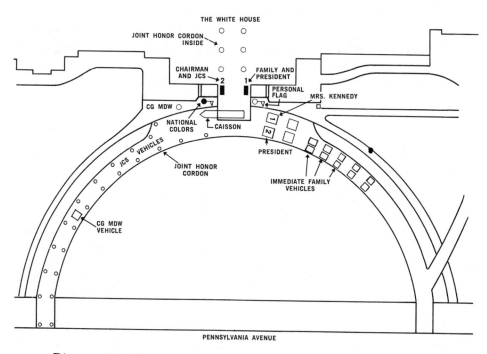

Diagram 54. Formation for departure from the White House.

On 22 November, in anticipation of a decision that President Kennedy would be buried in Arlington National Cemetery, John C. Metzler, the cemetery superintendent, selected three possible gravesites. One was at Dewey Circle in the southeastern corner of the cemetery; the second was near the grave of John Foster Dulles, southwest of the Memorial Amphitheater; and the third was on the slope east of the Custis-Lee Mansion. About noon on 23 November, Robert Kennedy and other members of the family, accompanied by Secretary of Defense Robert S. McNamara, toured these sites with Mr. Metzler. They made no decision but appeared to favor the site near the mansion. At midafternoon the same day, the group returned with Mrs. Kennedy and at this time the mansion site was chosen. Over the next two days the work of surveying, marking, and otherwise preparing the gravesite continued almost to the hour of the burial service.

In preparation for the procession from the White House to the Capitol on 24 November, the joint service honor cordon lined both sides of the route of march by 1230. The Army, Marine Corps, Navy, and Air Force each furnished 240 officers and men for the cordon. The men were spaced twenty-five feet apart and faced toward the street.

The procession formed on the North Portico Drive, which also was lined by an honor cordon. (*Diagram 54*) About 1300, the body bearers carried President Kennedy's casket from the East Room, passed through an honor cordon posted in the hallway and on the portico itself, and placed the casket on the caisson. No music was played during the departure ceremony, nor would there be any during the march—only the beat of the muffled drums.

Metropolitan Police on foot headed the procession, followed by General Wehle and a joint service drum detail with four snare drummers from each service, one bass drummer each from the Army and Marine Corps, and a drum major and leader from the Army. After the drummers came a Navy escort company of four officers, three petty officers, and eighty-six enlisted men. Next came a special honor guard composed of the Joint Chiefs of Staff and led by General Maxwell D. Taylor. The White House military aides, Maj. Gen. Chester V. Clifton of the Army, Capt. Tazewell Shepard of the Navy, and Brig. Gen. Godfrey T. McHugh of the Air Force, followed them. Behind these officers was the national color detail, two men from the Army and one each from the Marine Corps, Navy, Air Force, and Coast Guard. Three members of the clergy were next in the procession: the Very Reverend Francis B. Sayre, Jr., dean of Washington National Cathedral; the Right Reverend John S. Spencer of Sacred Heart Shrine; and the Very Reverend K. V. Kazanjian, rector of St. Mary's Armenian Apostolic Church. After the clergy came the caisson, drawn by matched grays. Twenty servicemen flanked the caisson, ten on a side. Each group of ten included two men from each of the services, these ordered front to rear according to the seniority of the service: Army, Marine Corps, Navy, Air Force, and Coast Guard. Behind the caisson President Kennedy's personal flag was carried by Seaman E. Nemuth of the Navy, who was

PROCESSION MOVES ALONG PENNSYLVANIA AVENUE TO THE CAPITOL

followed by the body bearer team under Lieutenant Bird and Pfc. Arthur A. Carlson of the 3d Infantry, leading the caparisoned horse, Black Jack.

A column of ten automobiles followed: The first carried Mrs. Kennedy, her two children, John and Caroline, Robert F. Kennedy, and President and Mrs. Johnson; the second, two of President Kennedy's sisters and their husbands; the third, the widow's stepfather and mother, Mr. and Mrs. Hugh D. Auchincloss, and others of the Auchincloss family; the fourth, Mrs. Robert F. Kennedy, several of her children, and Sargent Shriver. (Mrs. Shriver, another of President Kennedy's sisters, Rose Kennedy, the President's mother, and Edward M. Kennedy, the President's younger brother, were en route from Hyannisport, Massachusetts, at this time.) In the remaining automobiles were a number of employees of the Kennedy family and of the White House, and security officials.

At the press corps' own request, a large delegation of the press followed the cars in the procession on foot. Bringing up the rear was another detail of Metropolitan Police on foot. During the march, many in the large crowd of spectators evidently interpreted the presence of the press corps group as an invitation for the public to join the procession. At first police and troops blocked off the marching spectators, but as the procession drew nearer the Capitol they allowed the people to fall in behind the police.

In preparation for the ceremony at the Capitol, government and diplomatic corps officials meanwhile had been ushered to designated positions in the rotunda. Outside, an honor cordon of seventy Army, Marine Corps, Navy, Air Force, and Coast Guard members lined the east steps. Thirty of President Kennedy's aides and advisers stood aligned at the top of the steps. On the plaza, the U.S. Air Force Band formed at the south side of the steps.

The procession from the White House arrived at the Capitol about 1350 where part of it halted at the east steps. The drummers, the Navy escort company, and the joint group of twenty servicemen that had flanked the caisson continued marching and left the ceremonial area. After those who had ridden in automobiles had dismounted, the chauffeurs drove the cars to a holding area on the south side of the plaza. The members of the procession meanwhile were guided to positions for the procession into the rotunda. (*Diagram 55*)

After the participants were in place, and on signal from the site control officer, the joint honor cordon presented arms. The Air Force Band then sounded four ruffles and flourishes and played "Hail to the Chief." Ordinarily this music is played at 120 beats to the minute; but at Mrs. Kennedy's request, it was played dirge adagio, or at 86 beats to the minute. The band then began the Navy hymn "Eternal Father, Strong to Save." The saluting battery from the 3d Infantry had been posted near the Senate garage at Louisiana Avenue and D Street. At the first note of the Navy hymn, the battery began a 21-gun salute, spacing the rounds five seconds apart. At the same time, the body bearers removed the casket from the caisson.

The escort commander, General Wehle, led the way up the steps. Behind him came the special honor guard, the national color detail, the clergy, the casket, the personal flag, and the Kennedy family and other mourners. After the procession entered the rotunda, the band ceased playing the hymn and the honor cordon ordered arms.

Upon entering the rotunda, the special honor guard turned left and stopped at a position near the east entrance. The national color detail, the clergy, the body bearers and casket, and the personal flag bearer turned right, moved in a semicircle, then turned back toward the east entrance to reach the Lincoln catafalque in the center of the hall. The family party also turned right after entering and stopped at a position near the east entrance. (*Diagram 56*)

After placing the casket on the catafalque, the body bearers stood fast while the colors were posted. (Because the base for the President's flag was inadequate, the flag bearer had to hold the flag in place throughout the ceremony.) The commander and first relief of the guard of honor came in next through the west entrance; the commander immediately dismissed the body bearers and posted his first

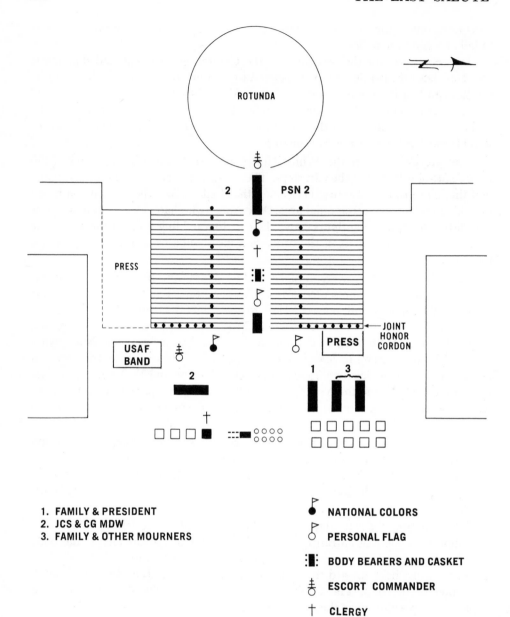

Diagram 55.   Positions for arrival ceremony at the Capitol.

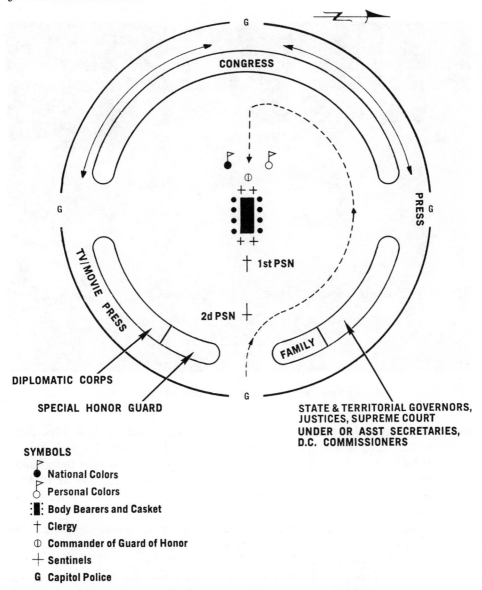

Diagram 56.   Positions for ceremony in the rotunda.

relief at the bier. The full guard was a joint group of five officers and thirty-two men representing all five uniformed services.

Following the posting of the guard, Senate Majority Leader Mike Mansfield, Chief Justice Earl Warren, and Speaker of the House John W. McCormack, in

BODY OF THE PRESIDENT LIES IN STATE IN THE CAPITOL

that order, delivered short eulogies. When the speakers had finished, Mrs. Kennedy went forward, knelt briefly at the bier, and left the rotunda with Robert Kennedy by the east entrance. The other mourners then left and after the rotunda was clear it was opened to the public. People began filing by the bier at 1400; a great number were still waiting to enter when the rotunda was closed to the public at 0930 on 25 November.

After the ceremony at the Capitol, final plans for the remaining ceremonies were completed during meetings held at the White House, Arlington National Cemetery, and Headquarters, Military District of Washington. The composition and movement of the main funeral procession were two of the first matters settled. In the process several changes were made to a preliminary organization of the military escort as a result of requests by the President's widow. Whereas the preliminary plan called for the Army Band to lead the first march unit of the escort, Mrs. Kennedy asked that the Marine Band be used. The Army Band subsequently was scheduled to participate in the arrival ceremony at St. Matthew's Cathedral. Mrs. Kennedy also wanted a company of marines that had been earmarked to move in the first march unit to be relocated at the rear of the escort, hence close to the

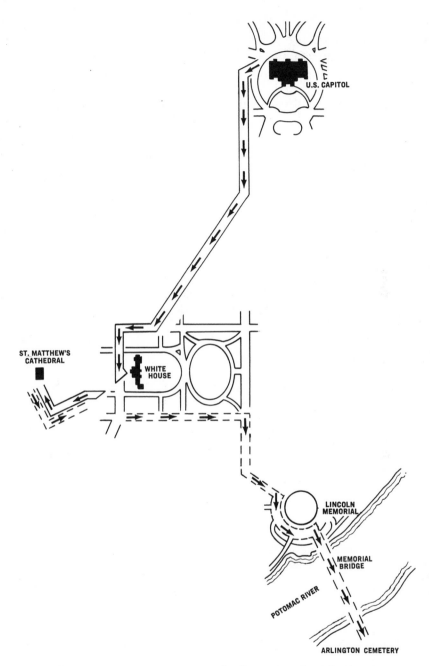

Diagram 57. Route of march, Capitol to St. Matthew's
Cathedral; Cathedral to Arlington National Cemetery.

caisson, and requested that a platoon of Army Special Forces troops be added to the procession and positioned just ahead of the Marine company.

The route of the funeral procession from the Capitol to St. Matthew's Cathedral lay over Constitution Avenue, Pennsylvania Avenue, 15th Street, and again over Pennsylvania Avenue to the White House, then over 17th Street, Connecticut Avenue, and Rhode Island Avenue to the cathedral. (*Diagram 57*) The composi-

TABLE 17—ORDER OF MARCH, PROCESSION FROM THE U.S. CAPITOL
TO THE WHITE HOUSE, CEREMONY FOR PRESIDENT JOHN F. KENNEDY

Police escort
Escort commander
Commander of troops
First march unit
  U.S. Marine Band (91)
  Company, cadets, U.S. Military Academy (89)
  Company, midshipmen, U.S. Naval Academy (89)
  Company, cadets, U.S. Air Force Academy (89)
  Company, cadets, U.S. Coast Guard Academy (89)
  Company, U.S. Army (89)
  Company, U.S. Navy (89)
  Squadron, U.S. Air Force (89)
  Company, U.S. Coast Guard (89)
  Company, servicewomen, composite (82)
Second march unit
  U.S. Navy Band (91)
  Company, Army National Guard (89)
  Company, Army Reserve (89)
  Company, Marine Corps Reserve (89)
  Company, Navy Reserve (89)
  Squadron, Air National Guard (89)
  Squadron, Air Force Reserve (89)
  Company, Coast Guard Reserve (89)
Third march unit
  U.S. Air Force Band (91)
  Representatives, 22 national veterans' organizations
  Platoon, Special Forces, U.S. Army (38)
  Company, U.S. Marine Corps (89)
Cortege
  Special honor guard
  National color detail
  Clergy
  Caisson and body bearers
  Personal flag bearers
  Caparisoned horse
  Kennedy family
Police escort

---

tion and order of the procession was now set for the move from the Capitol as far as the White House. (*Table 17*)

The special honor guard, the clergy, and the Kennedy family were to ride in automobiles as far as the White House, then, except for the President's two children who would remain in an automobile, were to continue to the cathedral on foot. Other persons scheduled to join the cortege at the White House also were to proceed on foot. These included President and Mrs. Johnson, cabinet members and military service secretaries, members of Congress, justices of the Supreme Court, members of the White House staff, personal friends, members of the diplomatic corps, and a large assemblage of foreign dignitaries.

The Department of State, which was responsible for arranging the presence of representatives of foreign governments, at first had decided not to invite foreign dignitaries to attend or participate in the ceremonies. The department reasoned that since there was very little time to send out invitations before the funeral, some invitations might reach their destinations late and cause deep embarrassment. The department maintained this position until the morning of 23 November. By then, however, certain foreign dignitaries had announced their intention of attending the ceremonies as private persons, among them President Eamon de Valera of Ireland, Chancellor Ludwig Erhard of West Germany, and Prime Minister Sir Alec Douglas-Home of England. Around midday on the 23d, after word was received that General Charles de Gaulle, President of France, and King Baudouin I of Belgium planned to attend, the Department of State hastily cabled formal invitations. A flood of acceptances followed. In all, ninety-two representatives of foreign governments accepted, including eight heads of state and ten prime ministers.

After the final plans were drafted on 24 November, only one more change was made in the composition of the procession to St. Matthew's Cathedral: a small contingent of bagpipers, the Black Watch of the Royal Highland Regiment, was to join the procession at the White House. This unprecedented participation of a foreign unit in the funeral for a President of the United States was the result of another of Mrs. Kennedy's requests. The pipers were to fall in behind the Marine company at the rear of the military escort. The procession would be further lengthened when the persons assembled at the White House joined the march. The full cortege would then observe the following order of march from the White House to St. Matthew's Cathedral:

Special honor guard	Kennedy children (in limousine)
National color detail	Foreign delegations
Clergy	Supreme Court justices
Caisson	Cabinet members
Personal flag bearer	Members of the Congress
Caparisoned horse	Presidential assistants
Kennedy family	Personal friends
President and Mrs. Johnson	White House staff

The organization of the procession would undergo other changes for the movement from St. Matthew's Cathedral to Arlington National Cemetery. The Black Watch pipers were to leave the military escort at the cathedral, as were the representatives of veterans' organizations moving with the escort's third march unit. Originally, these representatives were scheduled to attend the funeral service, but a lack of sufficient seating space in the cathedral forced a cancellation of this plan. As an alternative, they were allotted space at the graveside rites, and transportation was provided them from the cathedral to the cemetery. A motorcade of 107 vehicles also was organized for the movement of the cortege to the cemetery. To join the cortege at the cathedral were former Presidents Truman and Eisenhower and state and territorial governors, all of whom were invited to attend the funeral service. (*Diagram 58*)

Beyond plans for the composition and movement of the funeral procession on 24 November, other arrangements were made to carry out further wishes of Mrs. Kennedy: the U.S. Naval Academy Choir was scheduled to perform two selections at the White House during the time the funeral procession was halted there while en route from the Capitol to the cathedral; the 3d Infantry's Colonial Fife and Drum Corps, which Mrs. Kennedy wanted somewhere along the procession's route of march to the cemetery, was assigned a position on the green at the Memorial Gate entrance to the cemetery, although it was not scheduled to play.

In a wide departure from customary graveside procedure in which a band, standing fast in formation, plays an appropriate hymn as the casket is carried from the caisson to the grave, Mrs. Kennedy preferred that the Air Force Bagpipe Band march past the gravesite playing "Mist Covered Mountain" while the movement of the casket was taking place. The Air Force group was so scheduled, and a route permitting the group to perform as requested was marked out at the gravesite.

Out of awareness of President Kennedy's admiration of a silent drill he had seen performed by Irish Guards (military cadets) while visiting Ireland, Mrs. Kennedy also asked that this group perform the same drill during the graveside rites. Accordingly, after arranging to have the Irish Guards present, it was scheduled that they would perform their drill at the foot of the grave and then join the military escort at its more distant graveside position.

Of two further requests made by Mrs. Kennedy, both of which concerned the graveside ceremony, one was that the only flowers at the grave itself be a basket of blossoms taken from the White House garden. All other floral pieces were to be banked on the hillside above the grave and were to be arranged by the White House gardener.

The last request was difficult to meet. About 1500 on 24 November, the superintendent of Arlington National Cemetery, John Metzler, received word from the White House through the Military District of Washington funeral operations center that Mrs. Kennedy wished to have constructed at the gravesite an "eternal flame" which she would light during the burial service. Mr. Metzler turned to the

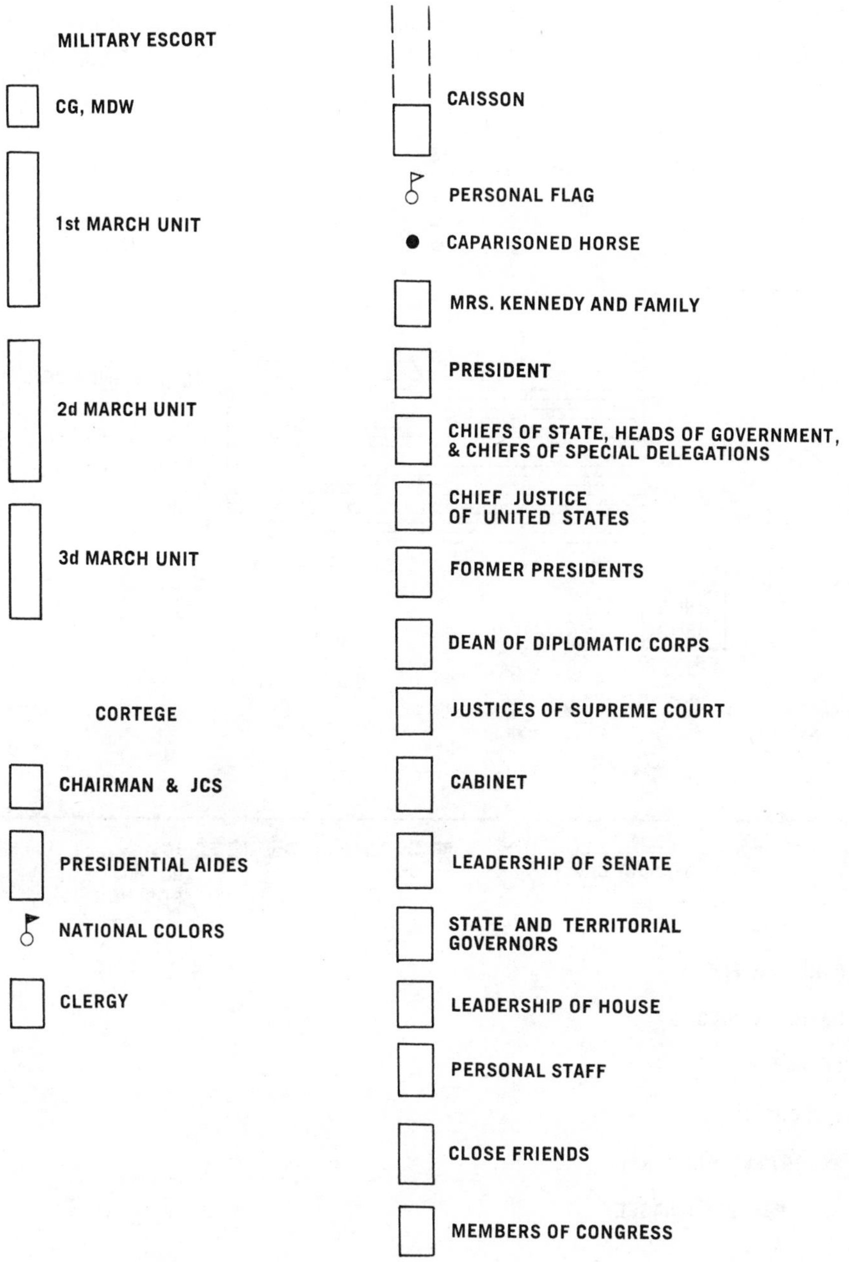

MILITARY ESCORT

CG, MDW

1st MARCH UNIT

2d MARCH UNIT

3d MARCH UNIT

CORTEGE

CHAIRMAN & JCS

PRESIDENTIAL AIDES

NATIONAL COLORS

CLERGY

CAISSON

PERSONAL FLAG

CAPARISONED HORSE

MRS. KENNEDY AND FAMILY

PRESIDENT

CHIEFS OF STATE, HEADS OF GOVERNMENT, & CHIEFS OF SPECIAL DELEGATIONS

CHIEF JUSTICE OF UNITED STATES

FORMER PRESIDENTS

DEAN OF DIPLOMATIC CORPS

JUSTICES OF SUPREME COURT

CABINET

LEADERSHIP OF SENATE

STATE AND TERRITORIAL GOVERNORS

LEADERSHIP OF HOUSE

PERSONAL STAFF

CLOSE FRIENDS

MEMBERS OF CONGRESS

Diagram 58.   Main funeral procession, St. Matthew's
Cathedral to Arlington National Cemetery.

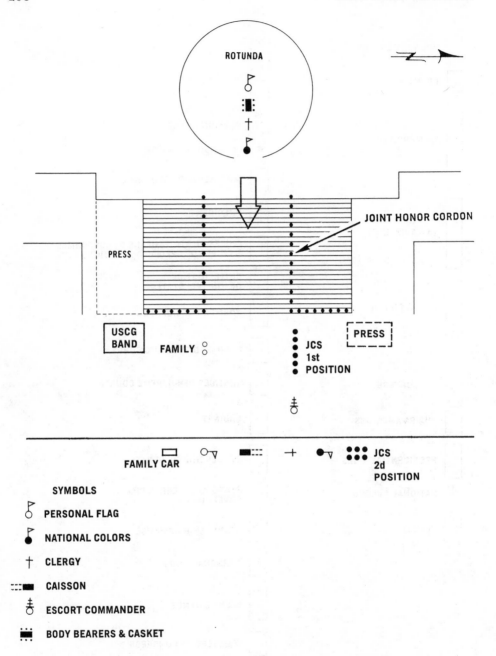

ROTUNDA

JOINT HONOR CORDON

PRESS

USCG
BAND   FAMILY

JCS
1st
POSITION

PRESS

FAMILY CAR

JCS
2d
POSITION

SYMBOLS

PERSONAL FLAG

NATIONAL COLORS

✝ CLERGY

CAISSON

ESCORT COMMANDER

BODY BEARERS & CASKET

Diagram 59.   Departure ceremony at the Capitol.

post engineer at Fort Myer, Lt. Col. Bernard G. Carrol, for help. Using commercial components Colonel Carrol, assisted by several other engineers and specialists, constructed and installed the mechanism by midnight. From wire, they made a frame shaped like half a ball, three feet in diameter at the base and eighteen inches high, which was later covered with evergreen boughs. This frame supported a Hawaiian torch. Over three hundred feet of copper tubing ran from the torch to a tank of propane gas. (Later a permanent gas line was installed.)

On the evening of 24 November, General Wehle's headquarters published and distributed the final plans for the remaining ceremonies. General Wehle then instructed representatives of all government agencies and the commanders of all military units scheduled to participate. The meeting lasted until 0200 on 25 November.

Ceremonies were to begin at the Capitol at 1030 on the 25th. Before that hour, 1,200 troops cordoned the route of the funeral procession from the Capitol to the cathedral. The Army, Marine Corps, Navy, and Air Force each supplied three hundred men for the street cordon and provided an additional forty-four men each to cordon the longer route from the cathedral to the cemetery. The plan called for the necessary repositioning and adding of troops to be accomplished while the funeral service was in progress.

At the Capitol, a joint honor cordon lined the east steps for the ceremony of carrying President Kennedy's body from the rotunda. Inside the rotunda waited the clergy, body bearers, and color bearers. On the plaza, the caisson was in a central position at the foot of the steps. To the immediate south was the U.S. Coast Guard Band. To the north were the special honor guard (the Joint Chiefs of Staff and the military aides to the President) and the escort commander, General Wehle. The escort units were along Constitution Avenue, from 3d Street eastward, aligned for the procession.

Mrs. Kennedy and other members of the Kennedy family in five cars arrived at the Capitol from the White House at 1038. Mrs. Kennedy, accompanied by her husband's two brothers, Robert and Edward, entered the rotunda for a final visit, then returned to the plaza and joined other family members near the band.

Inside the rotunda the guard of honor was dismissed after the Kennedy visit. The body bearers secured the casket and, preceded by the national color detail and the clergy and followed by the personal flag bearer, carried it from the hall. (*Diagram 59*) The formation halted at the top of the east steps. The honor cordon presented arms while the band sounded ruffles and flourishes, played "Hail to the Chief," and then began the hymn "O God of Loveliness." On the hymn's first note, the procession moved down the steps to the caisson. After the body bearers secured the casket on the caisson the band stopped playing and those who were to move with the procession went to their assigned positions for the march. The body bearers did not join the cortege but were sent by bus to the cathedral to be on hand when the procession arrived.

When the funeral procession reached the White House, all escort units save the company of marines at the very rear moved past it, turned right off Pennsylvania Avenue onto 17th Street, and halted after the last unit had made the turn. In accord with another of Mrs. Kennedy's wishes the left platoon of the Marine company, as it reached the White House, turned in the northeast gate and led the cortege onto North Portico Drive. As the cortege moved around the drive, the U.S. Naval Academy Choir on the White House lawn sang "Londonderry Air" and "Eternal Father, Strong to Save." The remainder of the Marine company meanwhile continued on Pennsylvania Avenue, then halted at the northwest gate just in front of its left platoon now halted on the drive. At this point the Black Watch pipers, who had waited near the northwest gate, took position immediately behind the Marine platoon. (*Diagram 60*)

The halt at the White House lasted only a few minutes. The members of the Kennedy family left the vehicles that had brought them from the Capitol and took their places behind the caisson, the Presidential flag, and the caparisoned horse. President and Mrs. Johnson took positions behind the Kennedy family, but ahead of a limousine bearing Caroline and John Kennedy; the other dignitaries who had assembled at the White House fell in behind in the scheduled order. The Black Watch pipers played "The Brown Haired Maiden" as the cortege then moved to rejoin the procession. When it reached the military escort on 17th Street, the full procession resumed the march to the cathedral.

The escort units turned off Connecticut Avenue onto Rhode Island Avenue to

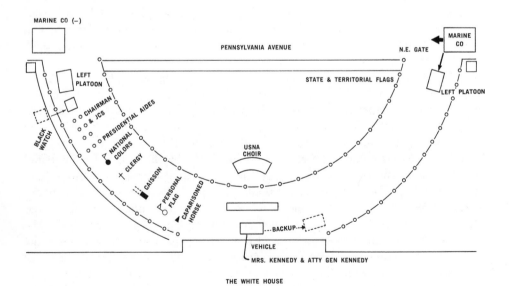

Diagram 60.   Halt at the White House.

reach St. Matthew's, marched past the cathedral, made three left turns to circle the irregular block, and halted on Connecticut Avenue facing south. The Black Watch group and the representatives of veterans' organizations then left the formation, the latter proceeding to Arlington National Cemetery to attend the graveside rites. The remainder of the escort stood fast, awaiting the conclusion of the funeral service.

As the cortege reached the cathedral, the caisson was stopped at the entrance. A joint honor cordon of one officer and twenty-five men lined the steps, and the U.S. Army Band was in formation at the base and to the right side of the steps. After the caisson came to a stop, Mrs. Kennedy, without pause, led the marchers through the honor cordon into the cathedral. Other family members, family friends, and invited dignitaries, none of whom had marched in the procession, already were seated. Among them were Mrs. Rose Kennedy, the state and territorial governors, and former Presidents Truman and Eisenhower.

After the President's widow and the other mourners had been seated, and after the special honor guard had formed at the base of the cathedral steps opposite the Army Band, the body bearers moved to a position behind the caisson. The cordon troops then presented arms and the band played ruffles and flourishes, "Hail to the Chief," and the hymn "Prayer for the Dead." On the hymn's first note, the body bearers took the casket from the caisson. General Wehle then led the way up the cathedral steps, followed by the national color detail, clergy, casket, personal flag, and special honor guard. (*Diagram 61*)

When the body bearers had carried the casket part of the way up the steps Cardinal Richard J. Cushing, who would celebrate the pontifical requiem mass for President Kennedy, appeared before them to bless the casket, a normal part of the mass. The body bearers were obliged to halt in an awkward position on the steps, with the weight of the casket distributed unevenly, and were able to maintain their position only with difficulty. After the blessing, the procession continued into the cathedral where the casket was placed on a movable bier and wheeled to the front of the room. Cardinal Cushing then conducted the requiem mass.

At the end of the service, the body bearers moved the casket up the center aisle of the cathedral to join the national color detail at the main door. The joint honor cordon on the steps outside presented arms, and the Army Band played ruffles and flourishes, "Hail to the Chief," and the hymn "Holy God, We Praise Thy Name." As the hymn was begun, the body bearers carried the casket through the joint honor cordon and placed it on the caisson. The family and others observed this ceremony from the cathedral entrance. Once the casket was on the caisson the honor cordon ordered arms and the family and guests were escorted to their cars for the procession to Arlington National Cemetery.

The departure from the cathedral was somewhat confused. Because of the mistaken, if well intended, intervention of a Presidential aide, few of the cars were in the proper order; and because the cathedral stood within a limited street network,

Caisson Arrives at St. Matthew's Cathedral, *above. Procession enters the cathedral, below.*

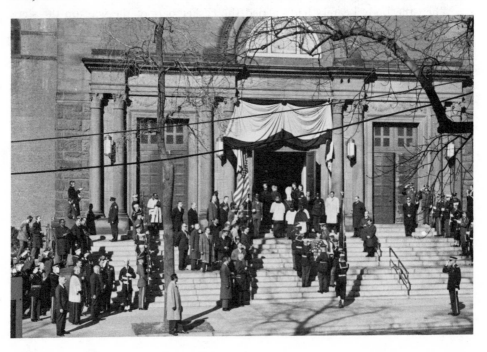

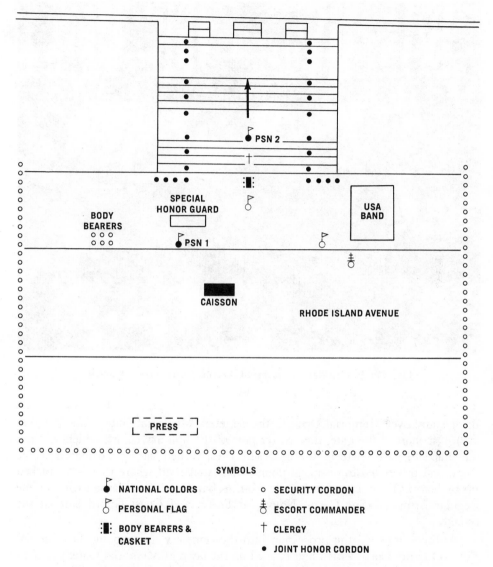

Diagram 61.   Arrival ceremony at St. Matthew's Cathedral.

there was little that could be done to correct the situation without undue delay. Thus, with many of the cars still out of prescribed order, the cortege proceeded by way of Connecticut Avenue, 17th Street, Constitution Avenue, and Henry Bacon Drive, then counterclockwise around the Lincoln Memorial, across Memorial

CASKET IS CARRIED FROM THE CATHEDRAL TO THE CAISSON

Bridge, and over Memorial Drive to the cemetery Memorial Gate. (*See Diagram 57.*) Just short of the gate, the greater part of the military escort, which was not scheduled to participate in the graveside rites, turned left on Arlington Ridge Road and proceeded to dismissal points along that road where they were picked up by buses. Of the escort units, the Marine Band and one platoon each of the Regular Army, Marine Corps, Navy, Air Force, and Coast Guard entered the cemetery.

As these units led the procession into the cemetery, moving by the Colonial Fife and Drum Corps which had formed on the lawn at Memorial Gate, the cemetery superintendent met the column and guided it to the gravesite. The procession moved via Schley, Sherman, and Sheridan Drives. The route was roped off and cordoned by troops from the 3d Infantry, who presented arms in ripples as the procession passed. Upon reaching the gravesite, the Marine Band and five platoons of escort troops immediately moved to their graveside positions. Already in position was a group of Army Special Forces troops lining both sides of a cocomat that ran from Sheridan Drive to the grave, and at the foot of the grave stood the

IRISH GUARDS STAND FAST AT GRAVESITE AS MILITARY ESCORT APPROACHES

thirty members of the Irish Guard. Also in place to perform, as Mrs. Kennedy had requested, was the Air Force Bagpipe Band. In addition, an Army bugler, a 3d Infantry firing party, and the 3d Infantry saluting battery were in their positions, ready to participate in the final rites. (*Diagram 62*)

The caisson was halted at the cocomat runner. The automobiles bearing the Kennedy family, President Johnson and his party, and the foreign dignitaries parked farther to the rear along Sheridan Drive. The foreign officials dismounted and moved to the graveside. Under the guidance of Superintendent Metzler, the Kennedy family and President Johnson and his party remained for the time being in their automobiles in order that their arrival at the grave would coincide with a flyover by Air Force and Navy jet fighters and by the Presidential plane, Air Force One. After about four minutes, the cemetery superintendent assisted the members of the Kennedy family from their cars and signaled secret service men to help President Johnson and his party.

The Marine Band opened the graveside rites with ruffles and flourishes and played the national anthem. When the anthem ended, the Air Force pipers began

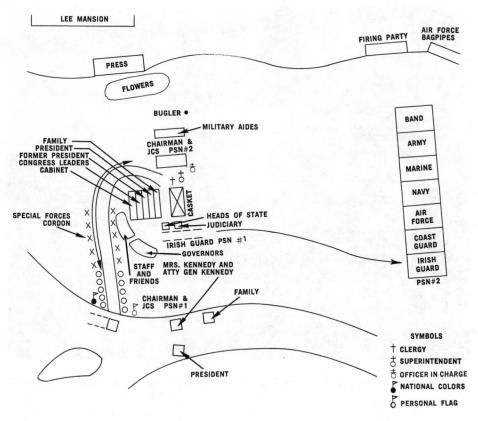

Diagram 62.   Formation at the graveside.

a slow march past the gravesite as they played "Mist Covered Mountain." At the same time the body bearers removed the casket from the caisson. With General Wehle leading, the national color detail, clergy, casket, personal flag, and special honor guard following, the procession moved through the cordon of Army Special Forces troops to the grave. The cemetery superintendent followed, escorting the Kennedy family.

When they reached the grave, the body bearers backed the casket onto the placer, since the hurriedly constructed torch at the head of the grave prevented use of the conventional method. At this moment, while the superintendent was showing members of the family to their graveside positions, the flyover took place. Fifty fighter aircraft, thirty Air Force F–105's and twenty Navy F–4B's, passed overhead in three V formations, one plane missing from the last V in tribute to the fallen leader. Following the fighters came Air Force One, piloted by Col. James B.

CASKET IS CARRIED TO THE GRAVE, *above. Body bearers emplace the casket at the grave, below.*

MEMBERS OF KENNEDY FAMILY ARRIVE AT THE GRAVESIDE, *above. Troops salute at the graveside as firing party delivers three volleys, below.*

Swindal. After the tribute from the air the Irish Guards executed their silent drill; at its conclusion they left the graveside and stood with the escort units.

Cardinal Cushing then conducted the service. When he had finished, the escort troops saluted while the 3d Infantry battery fired twenty-one guns. Cardinal Cushing pronounced the benediction. The troops again saluted while the 3d Infantry firing party delivered three volleys. The bugler sounded taps.

The U.S. Marine Band began to play the hymn "Eternal Father, Strong to Save," and at the same time the body bearers folded the flag and handed it to Mr. Metzler. Then, as the hymn was concluded, Cardinal Cushing stepped forward and blessed the eternal flame. Mr. Metzler presented the folded flag to Mrs. Kennedy. Maj. Stanley P. Converse, executive officer of the 1st Battalion, 3d Infantry, then lighted a taper and handed it to Mrs. Kennedy, who lighted the torch that would become the eternal flame, thus ending the ceremonies for her husband. Army Special Forces troops, although they were not scheduled to do so, posted themselves at the four corners of the grave.

CHAPTER XXIV

General of the Army Douglas MacArthur
State Funeral
5-11 April 1964

General of the Army Douglas MacArthur died on 5 April 1964 in Walter Reed General Hospital at the age of eighty-four. Earlier President Kennedy had authorized a State Funeral, and President Johnson confirmed the directive when he ordered that General MacArthur be buried "with all the honor a grateful nation can bestow on a departed hero."

Plans for the funeral, which had been made some time before in consultation with the general himself, specified that the ceremonies should occupy seven days instead of the four days prescribed in the plan of 1958 for a State Funeral. In accordance with the wishes of the general he was to be buried in Norfolk, Virginia, rather than in Arlington National Cemetery and his body was to lie in the 7th Regiment Armory in New York City and in the MacArthur Memorial in Norfolk as well as in the Capitol in Washington.

Maj. Gen. Philip C. Wehle, commander of the Military District of Washington, was responsible for arranging and conducting ceremonies taking place in Washington and for co-ordinating all funeral ceremonies. From his resources in the Washington area he was to provide whatever assistance and support were necessary in New York City and Norfolk. The Commanding General, First U.S. Army, Lt. Gen. Garrison H. Davidson, was in charge of ceremonies in New York City, and the Commanding General, U.S. Continental Army Command, General Hugh P. Harris, had charge of ceremonies in Norfolk. In each command area, a center was established from which funeral operations, administrative and ceremonial, were controlled.

When he was notified of General MacArthur's death, General Wehle, in accordance with plans, went to Walter Reed General Hospital, accompanied by John C. Metzler, superintendent of Arlington National Cemetery, who provided a casket, a flag, and a hearse. With him also were the body bearers—one officer, one noncommissioned officer, and three enlisted men from the 3d Infantry—and Armed Forces Police in two escort vehicles. Shortly after General Wehle reached the hospital, the Army officer assigned as military aide to the next of kin, Col. Neil Robinson, arrived to accompany the cortege to New York City.

The cortege left Washington about 1730 on 5 April. An Armed Forces Police sedan led the way, followed by a limousine carrying General Wehle and Mr. Metz-ler; the hearse; a limousine and two sedans with members of the family, the per-sonal staff, and Colonel Robinson; a station wagon bearing the casket detail; and an Armed Forces Police sedan bringing up the rear. For use in case of mechanical difficulty with the hearse, a second hearse trailed the cortege by twenty minutes.

In each state local police escorted the cortege as it passed through. During a scheduled halt on the New Jersey Turnpike, Mrs. MacArthur was upset by the sight of the hearse being refueled before a crowd of curious onlookers; otherwise, the trip was made without mishap. Reaching New York City about 2330, the cor-tege separated, the hearse and escort proceeding to the Universal Funeral Parlor and the family cars directly to the MacArthur apartment in the Waldorf Towers. General Davidson, the First Army commander, was present at the funeral estab-lishment to meet the hearse and to relieve General Wehle as escort commander.

At 1700, before the cortege left Washington, the Military District of Washing-ton had dispatched a joint service guard of honor, made up of four officers and thirteen enlisted men, and a joint service casket detail to New York from Andrews Air Force Base. These troops arrived at the Universal Funeral Parlor at 2100. The 3d Infantry sent a caisson detail and a caparisoned horse and a handler from Fort Myer, Virginia, at 2230; they reached New York at 0530 on 6 April. All were to participate in the ceremonies, those in the guard of honor joining other members of the guard furnished by First Army.

General MacArthur's body was prepared for burial at the funeral establish-ment under the direction of Capt. G. R. Rubin, the First Army mortuary officer. The general was dressed in a tropical worsted uniform adorned only with the U.S. and grade insignia. The casket was draped with a flag and, with the top cover open, was placed in the main chapel of the funeral establishment at 0500 on 6 April. The guard of honor posted a relief at the bier at 0800 and maintained a vigil until 0200 on the 7th. The public was not admitted to the chapel.

At 0900 on the 6th, Maj. Gen. Courtney Whitney, long-time aide and close friend of General MacArthur's, viewed the body and made the decision to leave the casket open during subsequent periods of lying in state. Later in the morning General Whitney conferred in his office with Colonel Robinson and Brig. Gen. Howard McCrum Snyder, Jr., the Chief of Staff, First Army. General Snyder ex-plained the details of events to take place on 7 April and together the three officers decided that the family group—the immediate family, close friends, and aides—would number twenty-six during the ceremonies in New York.

The guard of honor meanwhile was having difficulty. By 1230 on 6 April the sixteen officers and 126 enlisted men, including a seventeen-man detail furnished by the Military District of Washington, had arrived in New York and had been billeted at the 7th Regiment Armory on Park Avenue. First the billeting arrange-ment proved inadequate for the number of men. Second, and of more conse-quence, the food, handled by a caterer, was unsanitary. After fifteen of the guard

PRIVATE MEMORIAL SERVICE IN 7TH REGIMENT ARMORY

detail became ill with food poisoning and required medical treatment, a change was made to obtain food service from a First Army mess.

At 0400 on 7 April General MacArthur's body was moved to the 7th Regiment Armory, where it was to lie in the Clark Room throughout the day. A relief of the guard of honor was posted immediately after the casket was placed on the bier. Later in the morning at 0915, Mrs. MacArthur and the family group arrived at the armory for a private interfaith memorial service. Waiting to greet the widow in the family room adjoining the Clark Room, and then to attend the memorial service, were several dignitaries, including New York Governor Nelson A. Rockefeller, New York City Mayor Robert F. Wagner, and former New York Governor Thomas E. Dewey, and a group of diplomats.

A ten-minute memorial service was conducted by clergymen of three faiths: Cardinal Francis Spellman; the Right Reverend H. W. B. Donegan, Episcopal bishop of New York City; the Reverend T. J. Finlay, pastor of St. Bartholomew's Episcopal Church, of which MacArthur was a member; and Rabbi Max Schenk, president of the New York Board of Rabbis. After the service Colonel Robinson, the military aide to the next of kin, escorted the group back to the family room, where Mrs. MacArthur received the condolences of those who had attended. No other ceremonies were held on 7 April. At approximately 1000 the armory was opened to the public and remained open until 2315. Some 35,000 people passed by the bier.

Early on 8 April, a rainy day, troops assembled by the First Army began to form three security cordons: one at the armory, another at Pennsylvania Station, and a third at the station's loading platform. The troops for the cordons came from all five uniformed services: 6 officers and 300 enlisted men from the Army; 3 officers and 150 enlisted men from the Marine Corps; 1 officer and 50 enlisted men from the Navy; 2 officers and 75 enlisted men from the Air Force; and 1 officer and 25 enlisted men from the Coast Guard. In addition, the Corps of Cadets from the U.S. Military Academy, less one battalion, formed in a line of battalions on Seventh Avenue opposite and facing Pennsylvania Station.

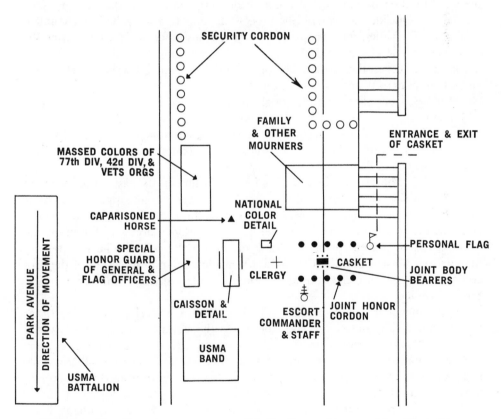

Diagram 63.   Departure ceremony, 7th Regiment Armory, New York City.

424-140 O - 72 - 16

Troops that would march in the procession assembled at the armory about 0715. The military escort troops included the escort commander, General Davidson, and his staff, the troop commander and his staff, the U.S. Military Academy Band, and a battalion of West Point cadets. To march with the cortege were a special honor guard of general and flag officers from all five services; a national color detail and joint body bearer team provided by the Military District of Washington; and a caisson, a caisson detail, and a caparisoned horse with an attendant from the 3d Infantry. Cadet Captain H. P. Kindleberger of the U.S. Military Academy was the personal flag bearer. Also in the cortege were the massed colors of veterans' organizations, of the 42d Infantry (Rainbow) Division of the New York Army National Guard, and of the 77th Infantry Division of the Army Reserve.

At 0745 members of the family group began to assemble in the family room of the armory. Fifteen minutes later, when they had taken their positions outside, General MacArthur's casket was borne from the armory in procession, the casket preceded by the national color detail and the clergy and followed by the personal flag bearer. Outside the armory, the procession came to a halt, the band sounded ruffles and flourishes, and troop units presented arms. (*Diagram 63*) After the band played one chorus of "The Corps," a West Point song, the body bearers placed the casket on the caisson. The procession then formed for the march of two and a half miles to Pennsylvania Station.

Mounted city police led and brought up the rear of the procession. (*Diagram 64*) The rain fell harder as the column left the armory at Park Avenue and 66th Street, followed Park Avenue to 57th Street, turned west across Fifth Avenue, and then went south on Broadway. After crossing Times Square, it moved along Seventh Avenue to Pennsylvania Station.

The U.S. Military Academy cadets forming a line on the east side of Seventh Avenue opposite the station stood at attention as the procession approached. After the police and military escort passed in front of the cadet formation, the police continued to march until they were out of the ceremonial area and the marching cadet battalion moved to the far flank of the cadets in line. The escort commander and his staff and the U.S. Military Academy Band turned out of the procession as they reached the railroad station and took positions at the station's 31st Street entrance.

When they had moved past the cadet battalions, the special honor guard, national color detail, and clergy also stopped at the station entrance. The caisson and body bearers, personal flag bearer, horse and attendant, and massed colors formation halted at the near flank of the cadet line and remained there while members of the family group descended from their cars in front of the station and took positions at the entrance (*Diagram 65*)

After all participants were in their places, the U.S. Military Academy Band sounded ruffles and flourishes and played the "General's March." When the

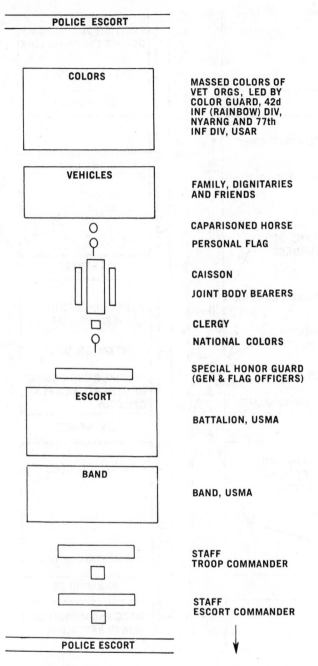

POLICE ESCORT

COLORS — MASSED COLORS OF VET ORGS, LED BY COLOR GUARD, 42d INF (RAINBOW) DIV, NYARNG AND 77th INF DIV, USAR

VEHICLES — FAMILY, DIGNITARIES AND FRIENDS

CAPARISONED HORSE

PERSONAL FLAG

CAISSON

JOINT BODY BEARERS

CLERGY

NATIONAL COLORS

SPECIAL HONOR GUARD (GEN & FLAG OFFICERS)

ESCORT — BATTALION, USMA

BAND — BAND, USMA

STAFF
TROOP COMMANDER

STAFF
ESCORT COMMANDER

POLICE ESCORT

Diagram 64. Order of march of funeral procession, New York City.

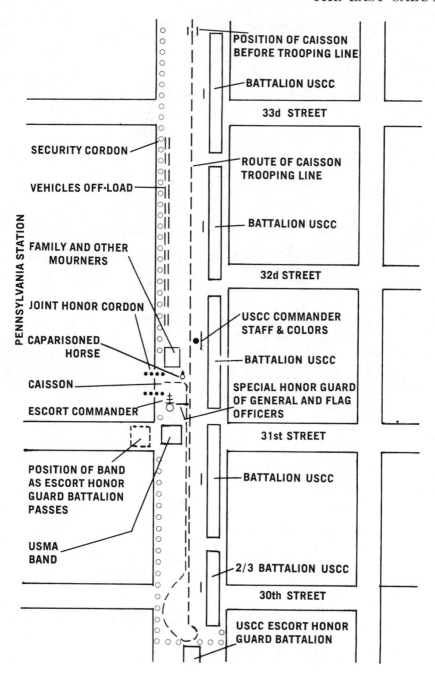

Diagram 65.   Formation at Pennsylvania Station, New York City.

CASKET IS CARRIED THROUGH HONOR CORDON AT PENNSYLVANIA STATION

band began a hymn, the caisson and body bearers, personal flag bearer, and caparisoned horse with its attendant trooped the line of cadets, moving to the far flank of the formation and returning to the 31st Street entrance of the station. The body bearers then transferred General MacArthur's casket to a hearse at the entrance. The family group entered the station and walked through the concourse to the funeral train, which was below street level. The hearse, accompanied by the escort commander, special honor guard, body bearers, and personal flag bearer, moved via the 31st Street taxi ramp to an elevator that lowered the casket to the loading platform below. The body bearers then placed the casket in the funeral car, where they were joined by the personal flag bearer. The family group entered the car ahead. (*Diagram 66*) Scores of floral tributes were placed in the funeral car, whose side doors were left open so that the flag-draped casket could be seen from outside. The train left New York for Washington at 0935.

Most of the troops who had participated in the ceremonies then returned to their home stations. The members of the guard of honor furnished by the Military District of Washington, however, left at 1030 on 8 April for Norfolk, Virginia, where they would participate in further ceremonies beginning on the 9th. At 1130

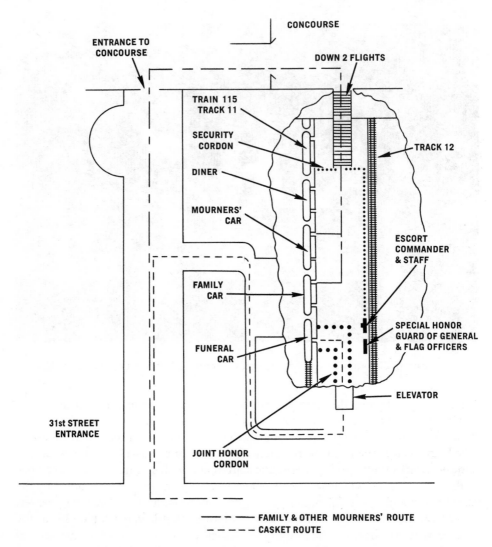

Diagram 66. Approach to funeral train, Pennsylvania Station,
New York City.

the caisson detail and the caparisoned horse with an attendant also left for Norfolk.

The funeral train slowed down at several points where crowds had gathered
and made a few stops. On these occasions, Mrs. MacArthur came to the door to
acknowledge the tribute paid the general. During the stop at Trenton, New Jer-

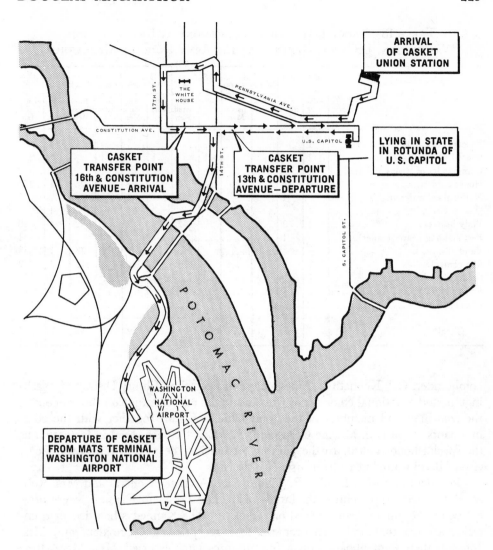

Diagram 67.   Route of march and ceremonial sites, Washington, D.C.

sey, the governor came aboard to greet Mrs. MacArthur. It was 1320 when the train reached Washington and entered Union Station on Track 17. (*Diagram 67*)

Ceremonial troops arranged for by the Military District of Washington were on hand at Union Station. A joint service honor cordon lined the platform and station concourse; on the platform at Track 17 were General Wehle, the escort

TABLE 18—TROOP LIST, ARRIVAL CEREMONY AT UNION STATION, WASHINGTON, D.C., FOR GENERAL OF THE ARMY DOUGLAS MACARTHUR

Duty	U.S. Army		U.S. Marine Corps		U.S. Navy		U.S. Air Force		U.S. Coast Guard		Total	
	Officers	Enlisted Men	Officers	Enlisted Men	Officers	Enlisted Men	Officers	Enlisted Men	Officers	Enlisted Men	Officers	Enlisted Men
Escort commander and staff	1										1	
Special honor guard	2		1		1		1		1		6	
Commander of troops and staff	1										1	
Honor cordon	1	26		26		26		26		26	1	130
National color detail		1				1		1				3
Clergy	1										1	
Body bearers	1	2		2		2		2		2	1	10
Personal flag bearer (cadet)		1										1
Band									1	33	1	33
Site control	3	2									3	2
Security cordon	1	11									1	11
Press cordon	1	13									1	13
Baggage detail		12										12
Total	12	68	1	28	1	29	1	29	2	61	17	215

commander, Col. Kenneth L. Ames, chaplain from the Military District of Washington, and a national color detail. Just inside the east entrance on the concourse, the chairman and members of the Joint Chiefs of Staff together with the commandants of the U.S. Marine Corps and U.S. Coast Guard stood in formation as the special honor guard. In the parking lot outside the east entrance, the Coast Guard Band waited near the hearse. (*Table 18*)

President and Mrs. Lyndon B. Johnson and Attorney General and Mrs. Robert F. Kennedy, representing the family of the late President Kennedy, were present when the funeral train arrived on Track 17. The Kennedys boarded first, entering a diner that had been prepared as a reception car. President and Mrs. Johnson then went aboard and a few minutes later escorted Mrs. MacArthur from the train. With the rest of the family group following, they led the way through the honor cordon, which stood at attention, to the concourse just inside the east entrance.

The body bearers meanwhile removed General MacArthur's casket from the funeral car and placed it on a movable bier. After the family was in position, the casket, preceded by General Wehle, the national color detail, and the chaplain and followed by the personal flag bearer, was taken through the concourse as far as the east entrance. As the procession moved, the members of the honor cordon presented arms in ripples.

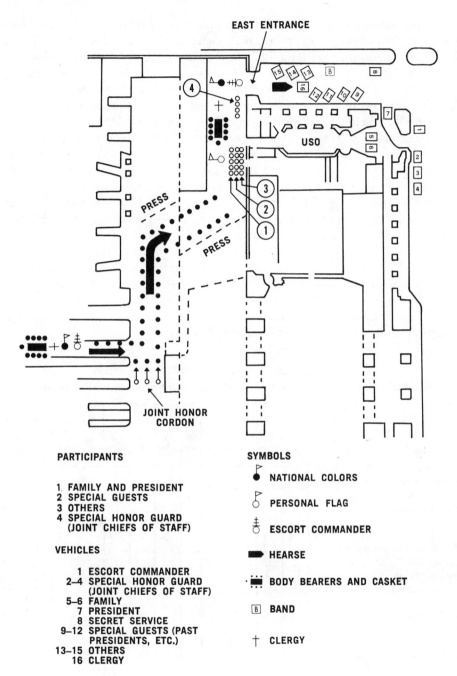

Diagram 68.   Arrival ceremony, Union Station, Washington, D.C.

When the procession came to a stop at the east entrance, the Coast Guard Band played ruffles and flourishes, the "General's March," and "Lead Kindly Light." As the hymn began, the body bearers lifted the casket from the bier and the procession made its way to the hearse. After the casket had been placed in the hearse, the band ceased playing and the honor cordon came to order arms. The family and others then entered automobiles and joined the procession that would circle the White House and come to an end at the Capitol. (*Diagram 68*)

The cortege left Union Station shortly after 1400, led by local police, who were followed by the escort commander, the special honor guard in three vehicles, the clergy, and the hearse. Behind the hearse were two cars bearing the family, two cars carrying the President and his party, seven cars with other mourners, and police bringing up the rear. The cortege moved down Delaware Avenue, turned right onto Constitution Avenue, and followed Constitution onto Pennsylvania Avenue. After circling the White House via Pennsylvania Avenue, 14th Street, and New York Avenue, it turned left at 17th Street and left again onto Constitution Avenue, proceeding east to the intersection of Constitution and 16th Street where the general's casket was to be transferred to a caisson. (*See Diagram 67.*) While military escort units waited ahead on Constitution Avenue to lead the procession the remaining distance to the Capitol, cars containing dignitaries stood ready to join the cortege between 17th and 18th Streets.

TABLE 19—TROOP LIST, CASKET TRANSFER CEREMONY, WASHINGTON, D.C., FOR GENERAL OF THE ARMY DOUGLAS MACARTHUR

Duty	U.S. Army		U.S. Marine Corps		U.S. Navy		U.S. Air Force		U.S. Coast Guard		Total	
	Offi-cers	En-listed Men	Offi-cers	En-listed Men	Offi-cers	En-listed Men	Offi-cers	En-listed Men	Offi-cers	En-listed Men	Offi-cers	En-listed Men
Escort commander and staff	1	....	....	....	....	....	....	....	....	....	1	....
Special honor guard	2	....	1	....	1	....	1	....	1	....	6	....
National color detail	....	1	....	1	....	1	....	....	....	....	....	3
Clergy	1	....	....	....	....	....	....	....	....	....	1	....
Body bearers	1	2	....	2	....	2	....	2	....	2	1	10
Personal flag bearer (cadet)	....	1	....	....	....	....	....	....	....	....	....	1
Caisson detail	....	5	....	....	....	....	....	....	....	....	....	5
Site control	2	6	....	....	....	....	....	....	....	....	2	6
Security cordon	5	285	....	....	....	....	....	....	....	....	5	285
Guides	....	2	....	2	....	2	....	2	....	....	....	8
Traffic guides	....	1	....	1	....	1	....	1	....	....	....	4
Parking detail	....	2	....	2	....	2	....	2	....	....	....	8
Communications	....	5	....	....	....	....	....	....	....	....	....	5
Information desk	....	1	....	....	....	....	....	....	....	....	....	1
Total	12	311	1	8	1	8	1	7	1	2	16	336

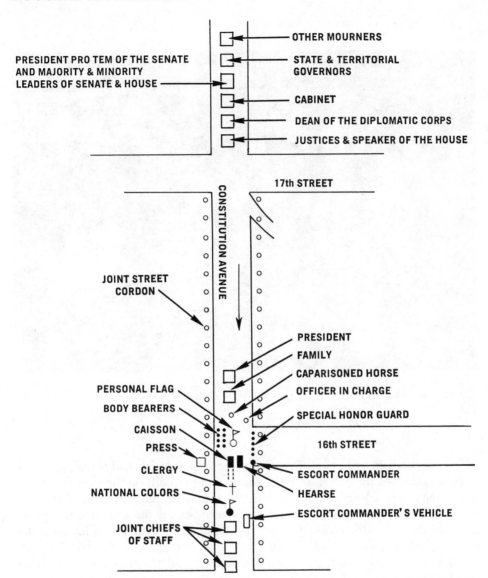

Diagram 69. Formation for the casket transfer ceremony, Washington, D.C.

When the cortege reached 16th Street the hearse halted to the left of and parallel to the caisson, which stood in the middle of the intersection of Constitution Avenue and 16th Street. The escort commander, special honor guard, and clergy left their vehicles and took their positions for the transfer ceremony. All others in the cortege remained in their cars. (*Diagram 69*) At a signal from the site control

CASKET IS TRANSFERRED TO CAISSON ON CONSTITUTION AVENUE, *Washington, D.C.*

officer, the body bearers (a different team from that which had served at Union Station) removed the casket from the hearse and placed it on the caisson; as they did so the troops saluted. Chaplain Ames then took his place in front of the caisson, which he would precede on foot, and members of the special honor guard returned to their automobiles. The escort commander was driven in his car to the head of the full procession. (*Table 19*)

Behind a police escort, the escort commander and the commander of troops and his joint service staff of five led the military escort troops, which were organized into three march units. The commander of the first unit was an Army field grade officer with a joint service staff of five; his troops included the Army Band, one officer and eighty-two enlisted men; a company, four officers and eighty-five enlisted men, from each of the four service academies; a company, four officers and eighty-five enlisted men, each from the active Army, Marine Corps, Navy, Air Force, and Coast Guard; and a composite company of servicewomen, five officers and seventy-seven enlisted women.

The second march unit was led by an Army National Guard field grade officer and a staff composed of a field grade officer each from the Army Reserve, Marine Corps Reserve, Navy Reserve, Air National Guard, and Coast Guard Reserve. In this unit were the Marine Band, one officer and eighty-two enlisted men, and a company, four officers and eighty-five enlisted men, each from the Army National Guard, Army Reserve, Marine Corps Reserve, Navy Reserve, Air National Guard, Air Force Reserve, and Coast Guard Reserve. The third march unit was composed of the Air Force Band, one officer and eighty-two enlisted men, and the commanders, or their representatives, of twenty-seven veterans' organizations. Six of the delegates acted as the march unit commander and staff. Although it was not the usual procedure, the special honor guard also marched to the Capitol as part of the third unit.

With the addition of dignitaries who joined at the transfer point, the cortege now included the national color detail, clergy, caisson, personal flag bearer, caparisoned horse, MacArthur family group, President and his party, Speaker of the House of Representatives, justices of the Supreme Court, dean of the diplomatic corps, cabinet officials, president pro tempore of the Senate with the Senate and House majority and minority leaders, state and territorial governors, and other mourners. A police escort brought up the rear of the procession. (*Diagram 70*).

From the casket transfer point to the East Plaza of the Capitol a joint service street cordon lined both sides of Constitution Avenue. (*Table 20*) As the procession moved, the members of the street cordon presented arms individually when the national color detail approached and ordered arms after the President had passed.

Just before they reached the Capitol most of the escort units, including the delegations from veterans' organizations, turned left on Louisiana Avenue and proceeded to dismissal points. Only the Army Band and the right flank platoon of each company of the Army, Marine Corps, Navy, Air Force, and Coast Guard of the first march unit moved into formation on the East Plaza.

The escort commander, special honor guard, national color detail, clergy, caisson, personal flag bearer, caparisoned horse and his handler, family group, and President Johnson and his party turned out of the line of march as they reached the Capitol driveway entrance opposite New Jersey Avenue. This group waited on the driveway until the escort units reached positions on the plaza and other dignitaries in the cortege got out of their cars at the east steps of the Capitol and entered the rotunda. General Wehle then led those waiting on the drive to their ceremonial positions on the plaza. (*Diagram 71*)

Besides the troops arriving with the procession, those participating in the ceremony included a joint service honor cordon, which lined the east steps, and the 3d Infantry saluting battery, in position on the grounds near Louisiana Avenue and D Street. Inside the Capitol waited a joint service guard of honor, which would

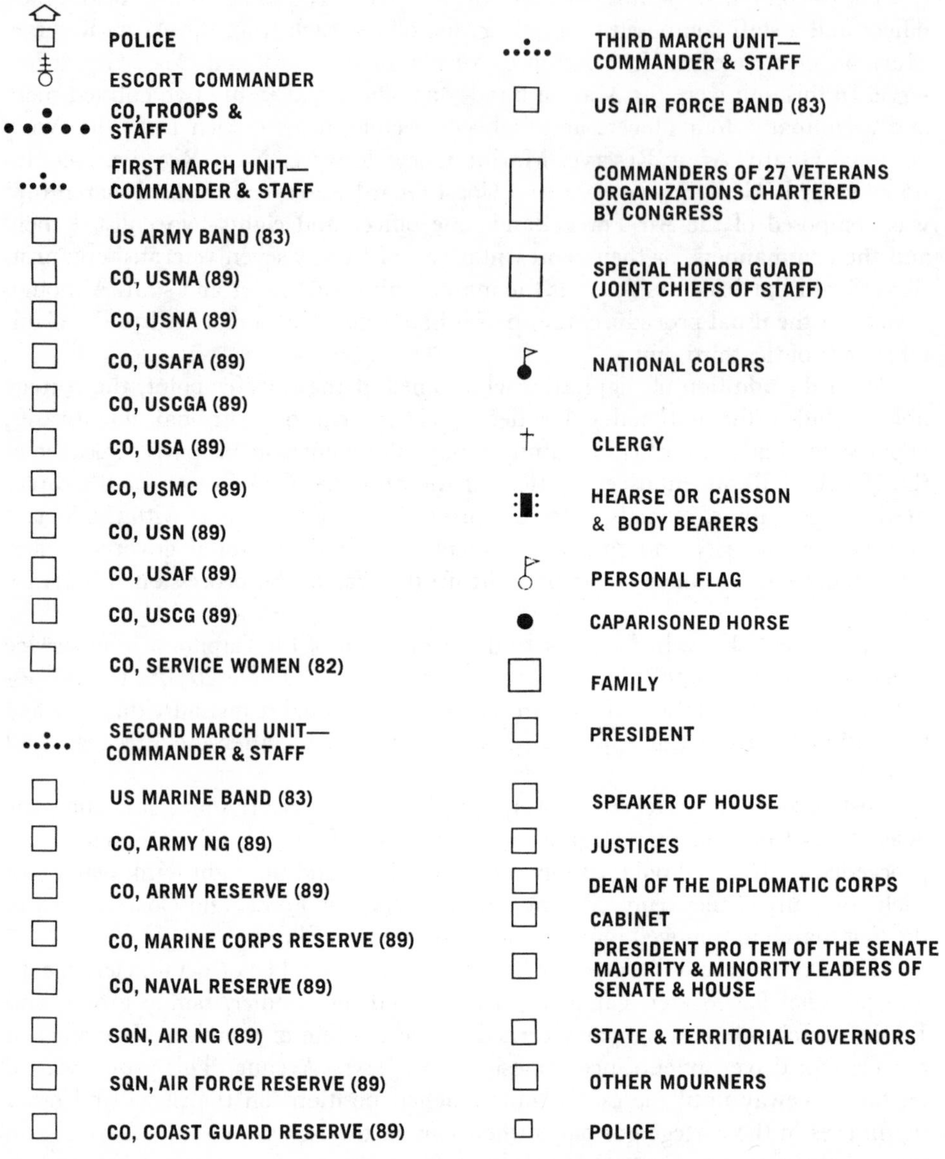

POLICE	
ESCORT COMMANDER	
CO, TROOPS & STAFF	
FIRST MARCH UNIT— COMMANDER & STAFF	
US ARMY BAND (83)	
CO, USMA (89)	
CO, USNA (89)	
CO, USAFA (89)	
CO, USCGA (89)	
CO, USA (89)	
CO, USMC (89)	
CO, USN (89)	
CO, USAF (89)	
CO, USCG (89)	
CO, SERVICE WOMEN (82)	
SECOND MARCH UNIT— COMMANDER & STAFF	
US MARINE BAND (83)	
CO, ARMY NG (89)	
CO, ARMY RESERVE (89)	
CO, MARINE CORPS RESERVE (89)	
CO, NAVAL RESERVE (89)	
SQN, AIR NG (89)	
SQN, AIR FORCE RESERVE (89)	
CO, COAST GUARD RESERVE (89)	

THIRD MARCH UNIT— COMMANDER & STAFF	
US AIR FORCE BAND (83)	
COMMANDERS OF 27 VETERANS ORGANIZATIONS CHARTERED BY CONGRESS	
SPECIAL HONOR GUARD (JOINT CHIEFS OF STAFF)	
NATIONAL COLORS	
CLERGY	
HEARSE OR CAISSON & BODY BEARERS	
PERSONAL FLAG	
CAPARISONED HORSE	
FAMILY	
PRESIDENT	
SPEAKER OF HOUSE	
JUSTICES	
DEAN OF THE DIPLOMATIC CORPS	
CABINET	
PRESIDENT PRO TEM OF THE SENATE MAJORITY & MINORITY LEADERS OF SENATE & HOUSE	
STATE & TERRITORIAL GOVERNORS	
OTHER MOURNERS	
POLICE	

Diagram 70.   Order of march, full procession, Washington, D.C.

TABLE 20—TROOP LIST, MAIN PROCESSION IN WASHINGTON, D.C., FOR GENERAL OF THE ARMY DOUGLAS MACARTHUR

Duty	U.S. Army		U.S. Marine Corps		U.S. Navy		U.S. Air Force		U.S. Coast Guard		Total	
	Officers	Enlisted Men	Officers	Enlisted Men	Officers	Enlisted Men	Officers	Enlisted Men	Officers	Enlisted Men	Officers	Enlisted Men
Escort commander and staff	1										1	
Special honor guard	2		1		1		1		1		6	
Commander of troops and staff	2		1		1		1		1		6	
National color detail		1		1		1						3
Clergy	1										1	
Body bearers		2		2		2		2		2		10
Personal flag bearer (cadet)		1										1
Caisson detail		5										5
Band	1	82	1	82			1	82			3	246
Military escort												
Active	6	85	5	85	5	85	5	85	5	85	26	425
Cadet	4	85			4	85	4	85	4	85	16	340
Servicewomen	2	20	1	19	1	19	1	19			5	77
National Guard	5	85					4	85			9	170
Reserve	5	85	5	85	5	85	5	85	5	85	25	425
Street cordon			3	217	3	217	3	217			9	651
Site control	5	6		5		5	1	5			6	21
Total	34	457	17	496	20	499	26	665	16	257	113	2,374

maintain a vigil at the bier during the lying in state period. (*Table 21*)

When all participants were in position, the troop formations presented arms, the Army Band played ruffles and flourishes and the "General's March," and the battery fired a 19-gun salute. At the last round of the salute the band began the hymn "God of Our Fathers," and the body bearers took the casket from the caisson. General Wehle then led the way up the steps into the rotunda, followed by the special honor guard, national color detail, clergy, body bearers with the casket, personal flag bearer, MacArthur family, and President Johnson and his party.

When the procession entered the rotunda the national color detail, clergy, body bearers with the casket, and personal flag bearer turned right and, making a semicircle, proceeded to the center of the rotunda. The others moved to positions along the outer edge of the circular room. After the body bearers placed the casket on the Lincoln catafalque they remained at their stations while the colors were posted and the color bearers dismissed. The first relief of the guard of honor then came into the rotunda through the west entrance and took post at the bier; the body bearers left by the east entrance. (*Diagram 72*)

CAISSON BEARING THE CASKET ARRIVES AT THE CAPITOL, *above. Body of the general lies in state in the rotunda, below.*

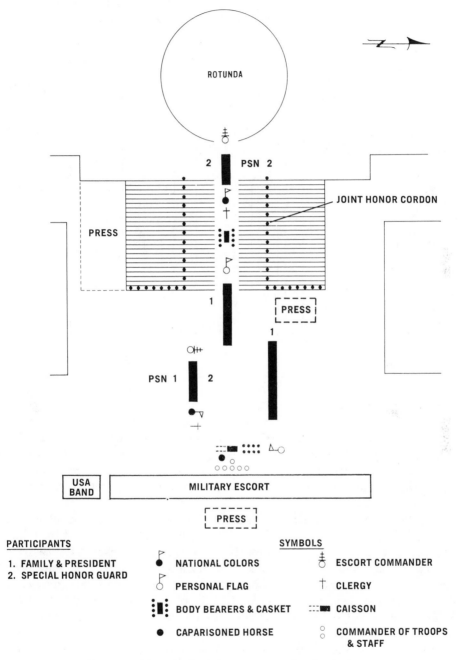

ROTUNDA

2   PSN 2

PRESS

JOINT HONOR CORDON

1

PRESS

1

PSN 1   2

USA
BAND   MILITARY ESCORT

PRESS

PARTICIPANTS   SYMBOLS

1. FAMILY & PRESIDENT   ⚑ NATIONAL COLORS   ESCORT COMMANDER
2. SPECIAL HONOR GUARD
                            ⚑ PERSONAL FLAG   † CLERGY

                            BODY BEARERS & CASKET   CAISSON

                            ● CAPARISONED HORSE   COMMANDER OF TROOPS
                                                        & STAFF

Diagram 71.   Arrival ceremony at the Capitol.

TABLE 21—TROOP LIST, ARRIVAL CEREMONY AT THE U.S. CAPITOL
FOR GENERAL OF THE ARMY DOUGLAS MACARTHUR

Duty	U.S. Army		U.S. Marine Corps		U.S. Navy		U.S. Air Force		U.S. Coast Guard		Total	
	Officers	Enlisted Men	Officers	Enlisted Men	Officers	Enlisted Men	Officers	Enlisted Men	Officers	Enlisted Men	Officers	Enlisted Men
Escort commander and staff	1	....	....	....	....	....	....	....	....	....	1	....
Special honor guard	2	....	1	....	1	....	1	....	1	....	6	....
Commander of troops and staff	2	....	1	....	1	....	1	....	1	....	6	....
Honor cordon	1	14	....	14	....	14	....	14	....	14	1	70
National color detail	....	1	....	1	....	1						3
Clergy	1	....		..	....	....					1	....
Body bearers	....	2	....	2	....	2	....	2	....	2	....	10
Personal flag bearer (cadet)	....	1										1
Band	1	82	....	....	....	....	....	....	....	....	1	82
Military escort, active	1	28	1	28	1	28	1	28	1	28	5	140
Guard of honor	3	13	1	11	1	11	1	11	1	11	7	57
Saluting battery	2	65	....	....	....	....	....	....	....	....	2	65
Site control	4	11	....	....	....	....	....	....	....	....	4	11
Security cordon	1	21	....	21	....	21	....	21	....	....	1	84
Ushers	....	8									....	8
Floral detail	3	9									3	9
Traffic guides	....	12									....	12
Parking detail	....	5									....	5
Information desk	....	5									....	5
Total	22	277	4	77	4	77	4	76	4	55	38	562

House Chaplain Bernard Braskamp and Senate Chaplain Frederick B. Harris delivered eulogies. President Johnson then stepped forward and placed a wreath at the base of the catafalque. Chaplain Ames pronounced the benediction, after which the rotunda was cleared and the MacArthur family retired to a private room in the Capitol.

Captain Rubin, the First Army mortuary officer, who was responsible for the care of the general's body until 9 April, when he would be relieved by John C. Metzler, superintendent of Arlington National Cemetery, opened the casket, redraped the flag, and completed other preparations for the lying in state period. Returning to the rotunda, the family expressed satisfaction with the arrangements that had been made and then left. At 1645 the rotunda was opened to the public. When it was closed at 1230 on the 9th, an estimated 150,000 people had filed by the bier.

On 9 April at 1300, a departure ceremony was held at the Capitol and General MacArthur's body was escorted to Washington National Airport, where he

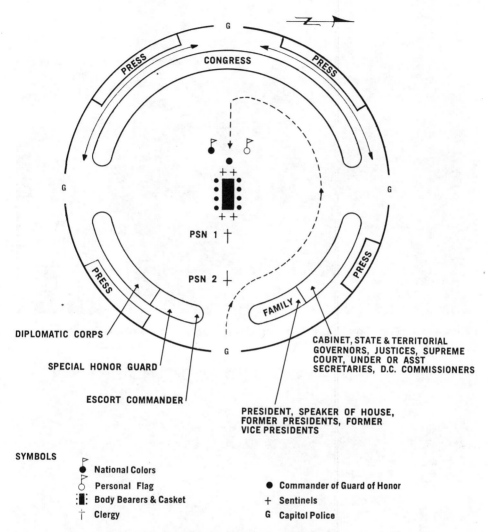

Diagram 72.   Arrival ceremony in the rotunda.

was again honored. Before the ceremony at the Capitol began the escort commander, General Wehle, the special honor guard (the chairman and members of the Joint Chiefs of Staff including the commandants of the Marine Corps and Coast Guard), the Coast Guard Band, and a joint service honor cordon took their positions on the East Plaza and steps. The caisson, caparisoned horse and his handler, and automobiles for those accompanying the cortege were also aligned on

Procession Halts on East Capitol Steps, *above. Full procession turns onto Constitution Avenue, below.*

the plaza. Inside the Capitol waited the body bearers, national color detail, personal flag bearer, and Colonel Ames, the chaplain from the Military District of Washington. (*Table 22*)

At 1245 members of the MacArthur family arrived at the Capitol and went into the rotunda to say a prayer. They then took their places on the plaza. At 1300, after the guard of honor was dismissed from the vigil at the bier, the body bearers took up the casket and carried it in procession, led by the national color detail and clergy and followed by the personal flag bearer. The procession left the rotunda through the east door; when the national color detail appeared at the top of the steps, the honor cordon presented arms. The procession halted when the body bearers reached the top landing and the band sounded ruffles and flourishes. As it began to play "Abide With Me," the procession moved on to the caisson. After the casket was placed on the caisson, the band ceased playing, the troops ordered arms, and the members of the cortege went to their automobiles. (*Diagram 73*)

The full procession was to form on Constitution Avenue between Delaware and New Jersey Avenues where the cortege, proceeding from the East Plaza, was to join the military escort units—the commander of troops and his staff, the Army Band, and a company of four officers and eighty-five men each from the active Army, Marine Corps, Navy, Air Force, and Coast Guard. A joint service cordon

TABLE 22—TROOP LIST, DEPARTURE CEREMONY AT THE U.S. CAPITOL
FOR GENERAL OF THE ARMY DOUGLAS MACARTHUR

Duty	U.S. Army		U.S. Marine Corps		U.S. Navy		U.S. Air Force		U.S. Coast Guard		Total	
	Officers	Enlisted Men	Officers	Enlisted Men	Officers	Enlisted Men	Officers	Enlisted Men	Officers	Enlisted Men	Officers	Enlisted Men
Escort commander and staff	1	....	....	....	....	....	....	....	....	....	1	....
Special honor guard	2	....	1	....	1	....	1	....	1	....	6	....
Honor cordon	1	14	....	14	....	14	....	14	....	14	1	70
National color detail	....	1	....	1	....	1	....	....	....	....	....	3
Clergy	1	....	....	....	....	....	....	....	....	....	1	....
Body bearers	1	2	....	2	....	2	....	2	....	2	1	10
Personal flag bearer (cadet)	....	1	....	....	....	....	....	....	....	....	....	1
Band	....	....	....	....	....	....	....	....	1	55	1	55
Site control	4	11	....	....	....	....	....	....	....	....	4	11
Security cordon	1	21	....	21	....	21	....	21	....	....	1	84
Traffic guides	....	12	....	....	....	....	....	....	....	....	....	12
Parking detail	....	5	....	....	....	....	....	....	....	....	....	5
Information desk	....	5	....	....	....	....	....	....	....	....	....	5
Total	11	72	1	38	1	38	1	37	2	71	16	256

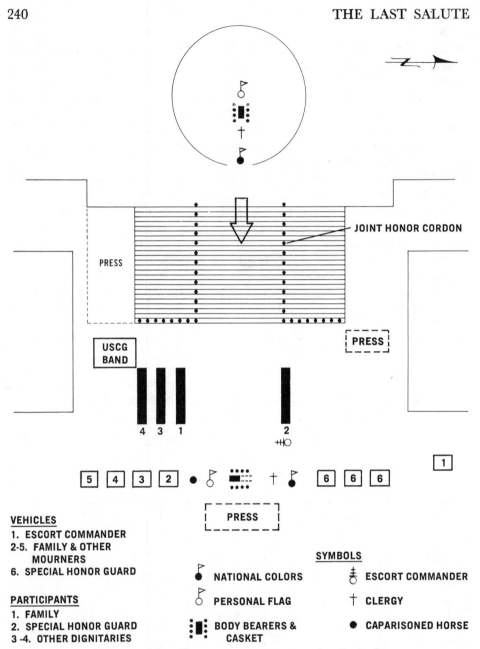

VEHICLES
1. ESCORT COMMANDER
2-5. FAMILY & OTHER
     MOURNERS
6. SPECIAL HONOR GUARD

PARTICIPANTS
1. FAMILY
2. SPECIAL HONOR GUARD
3-4. OTHER DIGNITARIES

SYMBOLS

⚑ NATIONAL COLORS   ⚐ ESCORT COMMANDER
⚐ PERSONAL FLAG   † CLERGY
▪▪▪ BODY BEARERS &   ● CAPARISONED HORSE
    CASKET

Diagram 73.   Departure ceremony at the Capitol.

lined Constitution Avenue from New Jersey Avenue to 14th Street, the end of the
route of the full procession. (*Table 23*) The procession was to observe the follow-

ing order of march: police; escort commander; commander of troops and his staff; U.S. Army Band; Army, Marine Corps, Navy, Air Force, and Coast Guard units; special honor guard; national colors; clergy; caisson; personal flag; caparisoned horse with attendant; family and other mourners; and police.

When the cortege from the Capitol reached the military units the full procession marched on Constitution Avenue, members of the street cordon presenting arms individually as the national color detail approached and ordering arms as the personal flag bearer passed. Fifty Air Force planes flew over the column in salute as the procession neared the site of the casket transfer.

Upon reaching 14th Street the cortege halted so that the caisson was approximately in the middle of the two blocks of Constitution Avenue between 12th and 14th Streets. The hearse, which had been parked on a nearby driveway, was then driven onto the avenue and stopped at the left of and parallel to the caisson. The escort troops of the cortege did not pause at 14th Street but marched directly to dismissal points. Members of the special honor guard meanwhile left their cars and took their positions near the escort commander for the transfer ceremony. The MacArthur family and other mourners remained in their cars. (*Diagram 74*)

While the troops stood at salute, the body bearers transferred the casket from the caisson to the hearse. The caisson was then driven off the avenue onto a

TABLE 23—TROOP LIST, PROCESSION FROM THE U.S. CAPITOL
FOR GENERAL OF THE ARMY DOUGLAS MACARTHUR

Duty	U.S. Army		U.S. Marine Corps		U.S. Navy		U.S. Air Force		U.S. Coast Guard		Total	
	Officers	Enlisted Men	Officers	Enlisted Men	Officers	Enlisted Men	Officers	Enlisted Men	Officers	Enlisted Men	Officers	Enlisted Men
Escort commander and staff.....	1	.....	.....	.....	.....	.....	.....	.....	.....	.....	1	.....
Special honor guard............	2	.....	1	.....	1	.....	1	.....	1	.....	6	.....
Commander of troops and staff...	2	.....	1	.....	1	.....	1	.....	1	.....	6	.....
National color detail............	.....	1	.....	1	.....	1	.....	.....	.....	.....	.....	3
Clergy........................	1	.....	.....	.....	.....	.....	.....	.....	.....	.....	1	.....
Body bearers..................	1	2	.....	2	.....	2	.....	2	.....	2	1	10
Personal flag bearer (cadet)......	.....	1	.....	.....	.....	.....	.....	.....	.....	.....	.....	1
Caisson detail.................	.....	5	.....	.....	.....	.....	.....	.....	.....	.....	.....	5
Band.........................	1	82	.....	.....	.....	.....	.....	.....	.....	.....	1	82
Military escort, active..........	4	85	4	85	4	85	4	85	4	85	20	425
Street cordon.................	.....	.....	2	163	2	163	2	163	.....	.....	6	489
Site control..................	5	6	.....	5	.....	5	1	5	.....	.....	6	21
Security cordon...............	2	204	.....	.....	.....	.....	.....	.....	.....	.....	2	204
Guides.......................	.....	2	.....	2	.....	2	.....	2	.....	.....	.....	8
Total..................	19	388	8	258	8	258	9	257	6	87	50	1,284

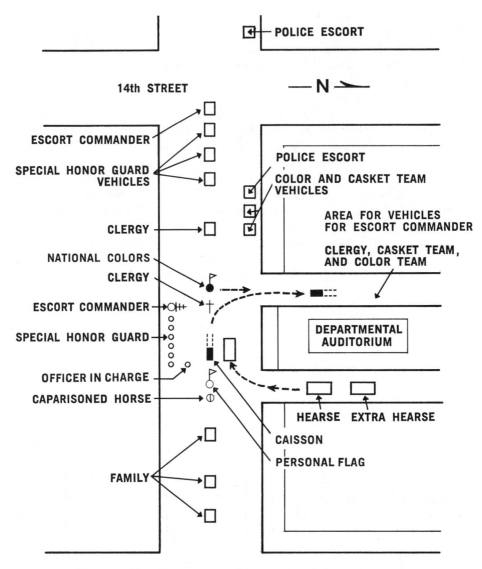

Diagram 74.   Ceremony at the transfer of the casket to the
hearse, Washington, D.C.

nearby roadway. The body bearers, national color detail, and personal flag bearer
boarded two buses and proceeded separately under police escort to Washington
National Airport in order to be in position for the departure ceremony before the
cortege arrived. The escort commander, clergy, and special honor guard entered

automobiles and General Wehle moved to the head of the cortege, which resumed the journey to the airfield. (*For route see Diagram 67.*)

As the cortege moved over the access road to the Military Air Transport Service Terminal, members of the joint service cordon which lined the road presented arms individually when the hearse approached and ordered arms when it had passed. When the hearse reached the first man of the cordon, the 3d Infantry battery on the airfield began a 19-gun salute. (*Table 24*) The last round was fired as the hearse stopped in the ceremonial area opposite a waiting C–130 plane. (*Diagram 75*) At the same time, President Johnson arrived from the White House by helicopter to participate in the ceremony. All other vehicles meanwhile were parked on the ramp behind the ceremonial area, and the occupants went directly to their assigned positions. A joint service honor cordon stretched from the hearse to the aircraft and the U.S. Air Force Band stood nearby. Just outside the ceremonial area was a second plane that was to take the family and others to Norfolk, Virginia.

After everyone was in position, all troops presented arms, and the Air Force Band played ruffles and flourishes, the "General's March," and "Faith Of Our Fathers." When the hymn began, the body bearers removed the casket from the

TABLE 24—TROOP LIST, DEPARTURE CEREMONY AT WASHINGTON NATIONAL AIRPORT FOR GENERAL OF THE ARMY DOUGLAS MACARTHUR

Duty	U.S. Army		U.S. Marine Corps		U.S. Navy		U.S. Air Force		U.S. Coast Guard		Total	
	Officers	Enlisted Men	Officers	Enlisted Men	Officers	Enlisted Men	Officers	Enlisted Men	Officers	Enlisted Men	Officers	Enlisted Men
Escort commander and staff	1										1	
Special honor guard	2		1		1		1		1		6	
Honor cordon	1	9		8		8		8		8	1	41
National color detail		1				1		1				3
Body bearers	1	2		2		2		2		2	1	10
Personal flag bearer (cadet)		1										1
Band							1	54			1	54
Street cordon		24		24		24		24		24		120
Saluting battery	1	14									1	14
Site control	3										3	
Security cordon	1	78									1	78
Floral detail	1	15									1	15
Traffic guides		4										4
Parking detail		6										6
Press cordon	1	10									1	10
Baggage detail		10										10
Total	12	174	1	34	1	35	2	89	1	34	17	366

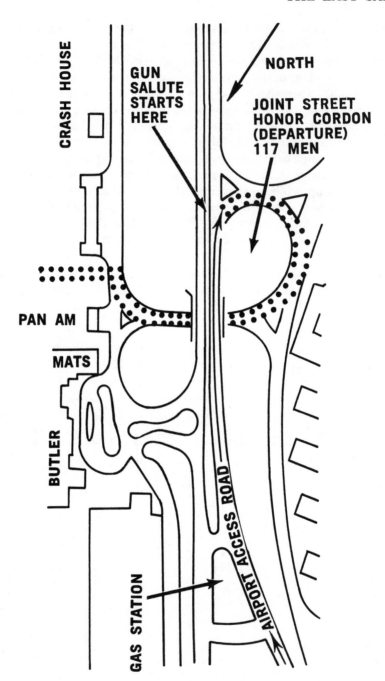

Diagram 75.   Street cordon, Washington National Airport.

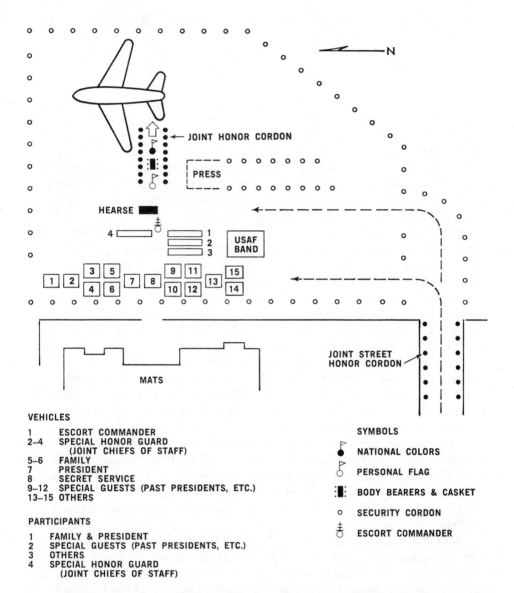

VEHICLES

1	ESCORT COMMANDER
2–4	SPECIAL HONOR GUARD (JOINT CHIEFS OF STAFF)
5–6	FAMILY
7	PRESIDENT
8	SECRET SERVICE
9–12	SPECIAL GUESTS (PAST PRESIDENTS, ETC.)
13–15	OTHERS

SYMBOLS

PARTICIPANTS

1	FAMILY & PRESIDENT
2	SPECIAL GUESTS (PAST PRESIDENTS, ETC.)
3	OTHERS
4	SPECIAL HONOR GUARD (JOINT CHIEFS OF STAFF)

Diagram 76. Departure ceremony, Washington National Airport.

hearse. In procession, with the national color detail leading, the casket and the personal flag bearer following, General MacArthur's body was borne through the honor cordon and placed in the C–130. (*Diagram 76*) General Whitney followed the personal flag bearer into the aircraft. After he was aboard the band stopped playing and the troops ordered arms and marched away. The C–130 meanwhile was towed away from the ceremonial area as the second plane was pulled into its place to take aboard the family and other passengers. President Johnson escorted Mrs. MacArthur and her son to the plane; the rest of the group then boarded, and both planes left for Norfolk about 1430.

Events scheduled for 9 April in Norfolk were to begin with the arrival ceremony at the Norfolk Naval Air Station. A motorized cortege escorting the hearse was then to proceed via Granby Street and Monticello Avenue to 21st Street, in the heart of the city, where General MacArthur's casket was to be transferred to a caisson. A military escort assembled at the transfer site was to lead the procession to the MacArthur Memorial near the intersection of City Hall Avenue and Bank Street. In the final ceremony of the day, the casket was to be placed in the rotunda of the memorial, where it would remain until 11 April. (*Diagram 77*)

The two aircraft from Washington reached Norfolk about 1530 on the 9th. The troops participating in the arrival ceremony, who had taken positions at the Naval Air Station a half-hour earlier, were the escort commander, Maj. Gen. Hugh M. Exton of the Continental Army Command staff; a special honor guard of two general or flag officers from each of the five uniformed services; a joint service honor cordon, one officer and fifteen enlisted men, flanking the route from the aircraft to the hearse; a 56-piece Navy band provided by the Atlantic Fleet; and an Army saluting battery of one officer and nine enlisted men. Five clergymen were present: the Reverend Walton W. Davis, rector of St. Paul's Episcopal Church; the Right Reverend George P. Gunn, bishop of Southern Virginia; the Right Reverend David S. Rose, bishop coadjutor of Southern Virginia; the Right Reverend William A. Brown (retired), bishop of Southern Virginia; and Col. William J. Reiss, chaplain from the Continental Army Command.

. Upon landing, the aircraft carrying the family taxied to the ceremonial area, stopping in line with the honor cordon. Escort officers met the passengers as they descended and guided them to positions for the ceremony. The plane then moved away as the C–130 bearing General MacArthur's body, General Whitney, the body bearers, the national color detail, and the personal flag bearer taxied into position.

After the rear loading ramp of the C–130 had been lowered, the national color detail, followed by the body bearers with the casket, marched part of the way down the ramp and halted. The ceremonial troops presented arms, the band played ruffles and flourishes and the "General's March," and the battery fired a 19-gun salute. As the last round was fired, the band began the hymn "God of Our Fathers." In procession, the national color detail and clergymen leading, the casket and the personal flag bearer following, General MacArthur's casket was carried through the honor cordon and placed in the hearse. (*Diagram 78*) The ceremony concluded, escort officers guided the family group and special honor guard to waiting cars, and the cortege formed for the journey to the casket trans-

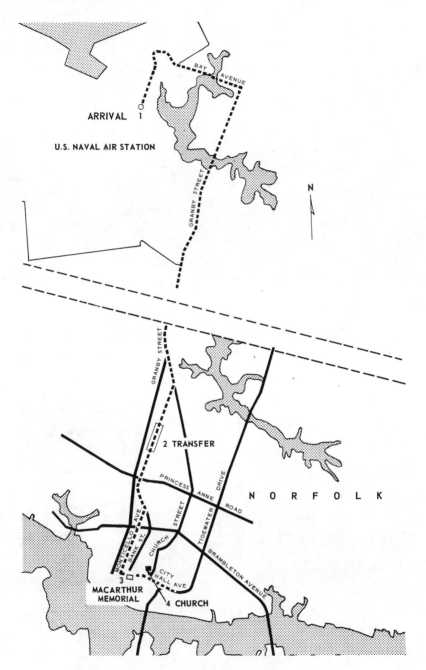

Diagram 77. Ceremonial sites, Norfolk, Virginia.

Casket Is Carried From Plane at Naval Air Station, Norfolk, Virginia, *above.*
Cortege leaves the Naval Air Station, below.

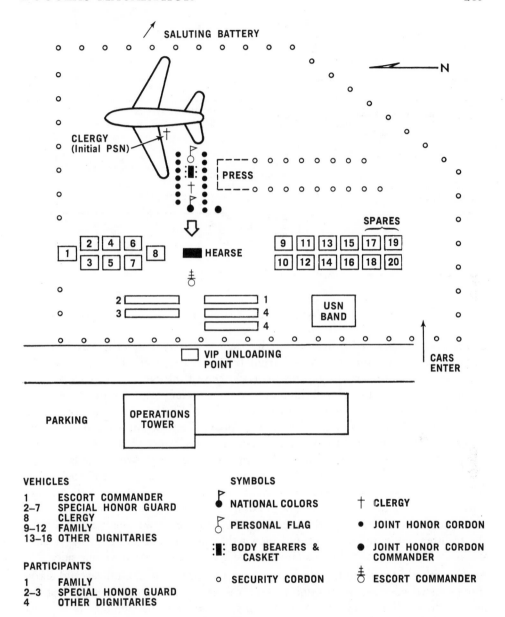

SALUTING BATTERY

N

CLERGY
(Initial PSN)

PRESS

SPARES

2 4 6
1   8
3 5 7

9 11 13 15 17 19
10 12 14 16 18 20

HEARSE

2
3

1
4
4

USN
BAND

VIP UNLOADING
POINT

CARS
ENTER

PARKING

OPERATIONS
TOWER

VEHICLES

1 ESCORT COMMANDER
2–7 SPECIAL HONOR GUARD
8 CLERGY
9–12 FAMILY
13–16 OTHER DIGNITARIES

PARTICIPANTS

1 FAMILY
2–3 SPECIAL HONOR GUARD
4 OTHER DIGNITARIES

SYMBOLS

NATIONAL COLORS

PERSONAL FLAG

BODY BEARERS &
CASKET

○ SECURITY CORDON

† CLERGY

● JOINT HONOR CORDON

● JOINT HONOR CORDON
COMMANDER

ESCORT COMMANDER

Diagram 78.   Arrival ceremony, Norfolk Naval Air Station.

fer site. The body bearers and color bearers meanwhile entered other vehicles and
left the field immediately in order to reach the transfer site ahead of the cortege.
The military escort troops waited in column on Monticello Avenue below 21st

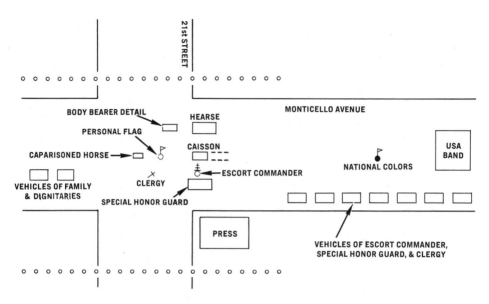

Diagram 79.   Casket transfer ceremony, Norfolk.

Street in the prescribed order of march: the escort commander's staff; a drum corps of twenty drummers selected from bands in the Second Army area; the Army commander of troops and his joint service staff of five; a company of eighty-nine cadets from the U.S. Military Academy; a company of four officers and eighty-five enlisted men each from the Army (Fort Eustis), Marine Corps (Atlantic Fleet), Navy (Atlantic Fleet), Air Force (Tactical Air Command), and Coast Guard (Atlantic Fleet); and a special Army band of seventy musicians selected from the Continental Army Command and Second Army Bands.

Behind the military escort at 21st Street and in the center of Monticello Avenue stood the caisson, and to its rear were the caparisoned horse and its handler sent down by the Military District of Washington. When the body and color bearers from the airfield reached the site, the national color detail took its position for the transfer ceremony ahead of and facing the caisson. The personal flag bearer stationed himself behind the caisson while the body bearers waited to one side.

On either side of the transfer site, a security cordon of one officer and sixty-three enlisted men was in position to keep the ceremonial area clear. At first the men in the cordon stood on the curb facing the street in the manner of a street honor cordon. With their backs to the spectators and lacking restraining ropes, the troops were having trouble keeping the public out of the ceremonial area. Before the cortege arrived, however, the site control officer rearranged the cordon, placing the troops in the street just off the curb and having them face the spectators.

PROCESSION MOVES THROUGH NORFOLK TO MACARTHUR MEMORIAL

As the cortege halted at the transfer site, the commander of troops called the escort troops to attention. The escort commander, special honor guard, and clergy left their cars and took their places for the ceremony; members of the family remained in their cars. The hearse meantime had been driven to a position left of and parallel to the caisson. (*Diagram 79*) At a signal from the site control officer, the body bearers went to the hearse where they secured the casket and placed it on the caisson. General Exton then walked to the head of the military escort to lead the procession. At the same time, the members of the special honor guard took their positions ahead of the national color detail, which turned about in preparation for the march. Those of the clergy who were to go on foot took their places behind the colors and in front of the caisson while the others re-entered their cars. General Exton, at a signal from the site control officer, led the procession forward. The column moved along Monticello Avenue as far as City Hall Avenue, turned left, and proceeded to the MacArthur Memorial. (*See Diagram 77.*)

Upon reaching the memorial, General Exton and his staff and the special honor guard moved to the west entrance; the drum corps and the escort troops

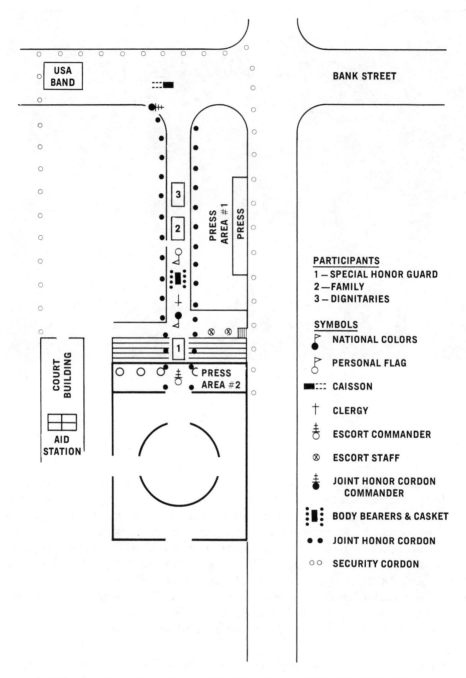

Diagram 80.   Arrival ceremony, MacArthur Memorial, Norfolk.

continued along City Hall Avenue to dismissal points. The band and the cortege turned right onto Bank Street and halted, the caisson drawn up at the end of a long walkway which led from Bank Street to the west entrance of the memorial. The walkway was lined on both sides by a joint service honor cordon consisting of one Army officer and eight enlisted men from each of the five uniformed services.

Escort officers helped the family and other mourners from their cars and guided them to their appointed positions for the ceremony. The honor cordon then presented arms and the band played ruffles and flourishes, the "General's March," and "Abide with Me." As the hymn began, the body bearers removed the casket from the caisson and in procession it was carried into the memorial. (*Diagram 80*)

The memorial building itself had once been the Norfolk courthouse, begun in 1847 and completed in 1850. The consulting architect was Thomas V. Walter of Philadelphia, designer of the dome and the House and Senate wings of the Capitol in Washington. In 1960 the mayor of Norfolk proposed remodeling the courthouse, using funds raised by public contribution, as a memorial to General MacArthur and as a repository for his papers, decorations, and mementos. General MacArthur accepted. Although he had no other ties with the state, his mother was a Virginian, born in Norfolk. Restored and remodeled, the building contains nine museum galleries whose contents reflect the general's fifty years of military service. At the heart of the memorial is a rotunda, and in its center a circular sunken crypt holding two marble sarcophagi, one for General MacArthur, the other for his wife.

As the cortege entered the rotunda, the body bearers placed the casket on a catafalque erected over the crypt. When the other members of the procession were in position around the catafalque, the first relief of an honor guard, furnished by the Military District of Washington, took post at the bier and the body bearers were dismissed. (*Diagram 81*) The mayor of Norfolk, in behalf of the people of the city, laid a wreath at the bier. Everyone then left the rotunda except the family, the clergy, and the mortician, who departed after the family approved the arrangements in the rotunda.

The memorial was open to the public from 1800 on 9 April until 0700 on the 11th. During that time, about 62,000 people filed through the rotunda to pay their respects, entering by the west door and leaving by the south door.

On the morning of 11 April, troops that were to participate in the ceremonies were in their positions by 0915. General Exton and the special honor guard stationed themselves just outside the west entrance of the memorial while the body bearers, national color detail, personal flag bearer, and clergy assembled in the rotunda. Lining the walkway to the caisson on Bank Street was a joint service honor cordon of one officer and forty-two enlisted men. The composite Army band was in formation on City Hall Avenue just below the Bank Street intersection. On the grounds north of the band stood the Army saluting battery which would not par-

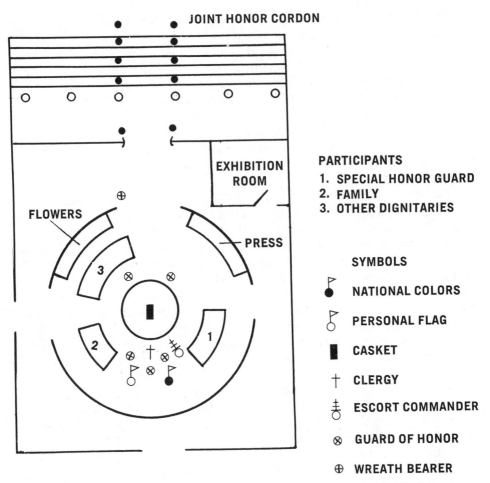

Diagram 81.   Formation, rotunda of MacArthur Memorial, Norfolk.

ticipate until the procession returned to the memorial after the service at St. Paul's Episcopal Church. Lining both sides of City Hall Avenue from the Mac-Arthur Memorial to the church were eighty troops—twenty each from the Army, Marine Corps, Navy, and Air Force—bearing the flags of the United Nations, all states and territories except the District of Columbia, and the twenty-eight military commands in which the general had served. (*Diagram 82*)

The MacArthur family and other mourners arrived in the rotunda of the memorial at 0920; ten minutes later the ceremony began. General Exton and the special honor guard moved onto the walkway outside the west entrance. The national color detail then led the way out of the rotunda, followed by the clergy, the

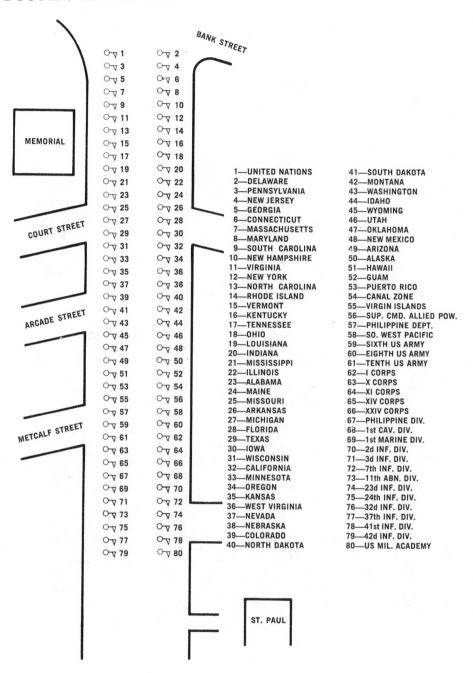

Diagram 82. Flag cordon, Norfolk.

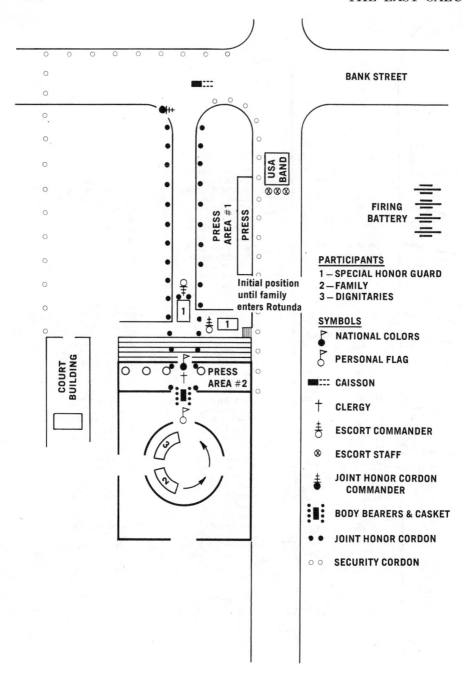

Diagram 83.   Departure ceremony, MacArthur Memorial, Norfolk.

body bearers with the casket, the personal flag bearer, the family, and other mourners. When the national color detail reached the west entrance it halted; the honor cordon presented arms and the band played ruffles and flourishes and the "General's March." As the band began the hymn "God of Our Fathers," the procession moved down the walkway to Bank Street where the body bearers secured the casket to the caisson. (*Diagram 83*) Other members took their places and the march to the church began.

As the procession passed through the cordon of flags, the flag bearers, facing each other across the street, dipped their flags in pairs as the national color detail approached and held the salute until the personal flag bearer had passed. When the head of the cortege reached the south gate of the churchyard on City Hall Avenue, General Exton turned in while his staff and the band continued to the intersection of the avenue with St. Paul Boulevard, where they turned and halted. (*Diagram 84*) The special honor guard followed General Exton through the church gate and half the distance from the gate to the church, where they placed themselves along the edge of the walk, five on each side. The national color detail and the clergy also entered and halted just inside the gate. The caisson and personal flag bearer meanwhile had stopped on the avenue opposite the gate.

When the family and other mourners reached the gate, they were escorted down the walkway and into the church where some 400 invited guests were already seated. These included officials of the federal, state, and local governments, members of the diplomatic corps, foreign dignitaries, and a large number of military men from all of the armed forces. Attorney General and Mrs. Robert F. Kennedy attended as the representatives of President Johnson.

After the family had been ushered into the church the band, at a signal from the site control officer, played ruffles and flourishes and the "General's March." At the first note, the escort commander, special honor guard, body bearers, and color bearers presented arms; they held the salute until the march was over. When the band began "Rock of Ages," the body bearers lifted the casket from the caisson. Led by General Exton, the procession of special honor guard, national color detail, clergy, body bearers with the casket, and personal flag bearer entered the church. Just inside the door the body bearers placed the casket on a movable bier. Preceded by the Reverend Walton W. Davis, rector of St. Paul's, two of the bearers wheeled the casket to the front of the church, then retired. The colors were posted in the church foyer.

The Reverend Mr. Davis, assisted by the Right Reverend George P. Gunn, bishop of Southern Virginia, conducted a brief religious service. At the conclusion two body bearers went forward to the casket. The clergymen leading, the family group following, the casket was wheeled to the church entrance. General Exton, the special honor guard, and the national color detail meanwhile left the church and took their places on the sidewalk for the departure ceremony.

When all the body bearers had taken their positions around the casket at the

CAISSON HALTS OUTSIDE ST. PAUL'S EPISCOPAL CHURCH, NORFOLK, *above. Casket is moved to front of St. Paul's Episcopal Church, below.*

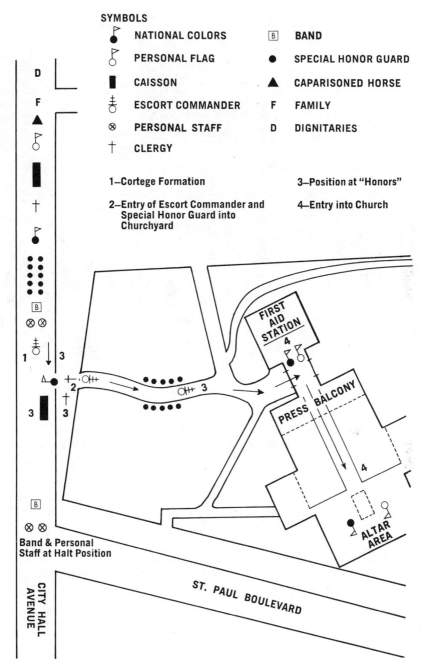

Diagram 84.   Arrival at St. Paul's Episcopal Church, Norfolk.

TROOPS FORM OUTSIDE MACARTHUR MEMORIAL FOR LAST RITES

church entrance, the band again sounded ruffles and flourishes and played the "General's March." As it began the hymn "Lead Kindly Light," General Exton led the procession from the church. Behind the general came the national color detail, clergy, body bearers with the casket, personal flag bearer, family, and other mourners. At City Hall Avenue the casket was secured to the caisson, which had been turned around during the funeral service for the return trip to the Mac-Arthur Memorial. In the same order as before the procession marched along City Hall Avenue.

The members of the flag cordon again dipped their flags in salute. At the MacArthur Memorial, the participants took the same positions they had occupied during the arrival ceremony on 9 April. An Army firing squad had been added to the troop formations and stood on the memorial grounds near the west entrance. Following the same procedure as on the 9th, General MacArthur's body was then taken in procession to the rotunda. (*Diagram 85*)

Bishop Gunn conducted a brief service in the rotunda. At its conclusion the honor cordon outside the memorial presented arms, the battery on the grounds north of City Hall Avenue began a 19-gun salute, and the members of the flag

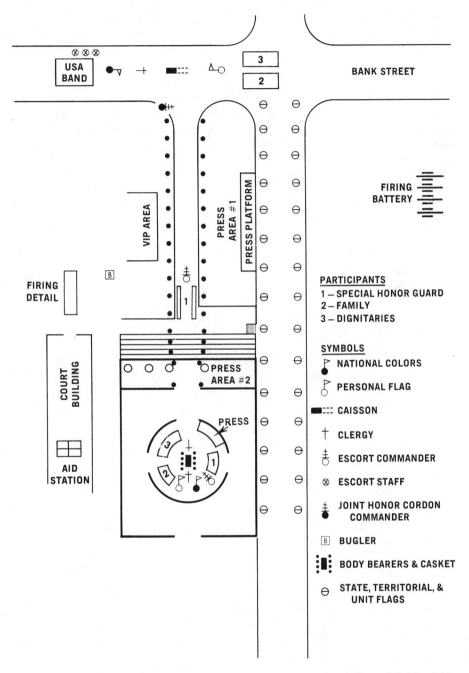

Diagram 85.   Arrival and burial ceremonies, MacArthur Memorial, Norfolk.

cordon along the avenue dipped their colors. When the last round of the gun salute had been fired, Bishop Gunn pronounced the benediction. The traditional three volleys were then discharged by the firing party and the bugler from the band sounded taps. The body bearers folded the flag that had draped the casket and handed it to General Exton who presented it to Mrs. MacArthur.

After the ceremony, about noon, the MacArthur family group was flown back to New York City. The period of national mourning for General MacArthur ended at sunset on 11 April when a battery at Fort Monroe, across Hampton Roads from Norfolk, fired a final 19-gun salute.

CHAPTER XXV

Former President Herbert C. Hoover
State Funeral
20-25 October 1964

At the age of ninety Herbert Clark Hoover, the thirty-first President of the United States, died in his suite at the Waldorf Astoria Hotel in New York City shortly before noon on 20 October 1964. The former President would be accorded a State Funeral with full military honors.

At the time of Mr. Hoover's death contingency funeral plans following policies established in 1958 and incorporating the wishes of the Hoover family already had been prepared. According to the scheduled sequence of events, Mr. Hoover's body was to be moved under escort on 21 October from the funeral home to St. Bartholomew's Episcopal Church in New York City, where it was to remain until the funeral service took place in the late afternoon of the 22d. On the 23d the body of the former President was to be escorted from the church to Pennsylvania Station for movement by special train to Washington, D.C. Upon arrival in Washington, the casket was to be taken in procession to the Capitol, and there the former President was to lie in state in the rotunda until the morning of 25 October. At that time the body was to be escorted to Washington National Airport and then flown to Cedar Rapids, Iowa. From there a motor procession would escort the body to West Branch, Iowa, Mr. Hoover's home town, where burial would take place on the grounds of the Herbert Hoover Library during the afternoon of the 25th.

Responsibility for arranging and conducting the ceremonies rested with the major Army commands in which the three ceremonial sites were located. The Commanding General, First U.S. Army, Lt. Gen. Robert W. Porter, Jr., was responsible for the ceremonies in New York City; Maj. Gen. Philip C. Wehle, commanding the Military District of Washington, had charge of ceremonies in Washington; and responsibility for the ceremonies in Iowa fell to Lt. Gen. Charles G. Dodge, the Commanding General, Fifth U.S. Army. General Wehle had the added responsibility of co-ordinating all the ceremonies.

According to plan, trained ceremonial troops from the Washington area were sent to New York City to assist the First Army commander as body bearers, color guards, and part of the guard of honor. Other troops for the guard of honor, which totaled seventy men, were provided by First Army. The Washington contingent was a joint service group of two officers and eleven enlisted men from the Army; one officer and ten enlisted men each from the Marine Corps, Navy, and Air Force; and one officer and eight enlisted men from the Coast Guard. These troops left Andrews Air Force Base at 1400 and arrived at St. Bartholomew's Church at 1630 on 20 October. Along with the First Army guard of honor troops, they were billeted in the Community House, adjacent to the church; their meals were provided by the First Army Senior Noncommissioned Officer and Specialist Mess at Governors Island.

Under police escort Mr. Hoover's body was taken from the hotel suite to the Presbyterian Memorial Hospital for an autopsy supervised by the First Army mortuary officer. At 1635 on the 20th the mortuary officer and a police escort took the body to the Universal Funeral Chapel; at 2145 it was placed in the main chapel of the funeral home, and a relief of the guard of honor was posted. The casket was left open. A few minutes later Herbert C. Hoover, Jr., arrived; after his visit the casket was sealed and would not be opened again.

At 0300 on 21 October, the casket, accompanied by the First Army mortuary officer and police, was moved by hearse from the chapel to St. Bartholomew's Church. The body bearer team, which was waiting at the church entrance, carried it into the chancel and placed it on the replica of the Lincoln catafalque that had been sent from Washington. A relief of the guard of honor took post immediately. Later in the morning, at 0900, the church was opened to the public and remained open until 1530. On 22 October the church again was open to the public from 0900 until 1500 and from 1700 until 2100. It was closed for two hours during the afternoon for the funeral service. Some 22,000 people paid their respects.

In executing the plans for the funeral service at St. Bartholomew's on 22 October, a possible seating problem arose. Before Mr. Hoover's death a list of persons who would be invited to attend the various funeral ceremonies had been prepared in the office of the Secretary of the General Staff, First Army. Copies with later changes made by the Hoover family had been sent to the family and to agencies involved in the funeral arrangements. Some 1,400 invitations were issued: 1,000 by the Hoover family, 300 by the Department of State to diplomatic personnel, and 100 by the White House for the Presidential representative and his group. Since the invitations had not required an answer, there was no way of estimating the number that would attend, and the church held 1,100. As it turned out, only 15 of the 300 diplomatic personnel actually appeared at the church, and only 583 of the invitations issued by the Hoover family were used. As a result, the church was scarcely two-thirds full during the service.

On 21 October when President Johnson announced that he would attend the service at St. Bartholomew's elaborate security preparations suddenly became necessary. These preparations involved the secret service, Armed Forces Police, and New York City Police Department and necessitated closing the church at

1500 on 22 October while the building was thoroughly inspected before the funeral service.

President Johnson and his party arrived at the church about 1620. Other distinguished guests attending included Hubert H. Humphrey, Barry M. Goldwater, William E. Miller, Thomas E. Dewey, Richard M. Nixon, John B. Connally, and Robert F. Kennedy. In the family group were Mr. Hoover's two sons, their wives, and the former President's six grandchildren. The Reverend Terence J. Finlay, rector of St. Bartholomew's and personal friend and neighbor of the Hoover family, conducted a brief funeral service; at its conclusion, the church was reopened to the public.

On 23 October, in preparation for the motorcade to Pennsylvania Station, troops began to assemble outside St. Bartholomew's at 0730. They included a joint service honor cordon, which would line the church steps, a company of cadets from the U.S. Military Academy, and the U.S. Military Academy Band. (*Table 25*)

Members of the Hoover family and their friends arrived at the church between 0815 and 0845. The body bearer team from the Military District of Washington, preceded by the national color detail and the clergy and followed by the President's flag bearer, then brought the casket out of the church. At the top of the steps leading from the church to Park Avenue, the body bearers halted while the band sounded ruffles and flourishes and played "Hail to the Chief." When the band began the hymn "Lord, Thou Hast Been Our Dwelling Place," the body bearers carried the casket down the steps through the honor cordon and placed it in a hearse.

The family and friends entered automobiles, as did the escort commander, Maj. Gen. John F. R. Seitz, Acting Commander, First Army, his staff, the clergy, the national color detail, the personal flag bearer, and the body bearers. The motorcade of eighteen limousines and hearse then left for Pennsylvania Station.

At the station, the body bearers removed the casket from the hearse and carried it to an elevator to be lowered to the track platform. The escort commander and his staff, the clergy, the national color detail, and the personal flag bearer also reached the track by elevator but the family group used a different route. On the platform, a joint service honor cordon lined the way from the elevator to the funeral car in the special train. After the family group and the escort commander and staff took positions near the funeral car, the body bearers, preceded by the national color detail and clergy, and followed by the personal flag bearer, took the casket through the honor cordon and placed it aboard the funeral car. The car was then sealed. The family group of about 150 people boarded the train, which departed for Washington at 0935.

The train was scheduled to reach Washington at 1335. A half hour ahead of the arrival time, troops organized by the Military District of Washington to participate in the arrival ceremony took position at Union Station. (*Table 26*) From

TABLE 25—TROOP LIST, CEREMONY IN NEW YORK CITY FOR FORMER
PRESIDENT HERBERT C. HOOVER

Troops
U.S. Army.. 270
U.S. Military Academy.. 200
U.S. Marine Corps... 100
U.S. Navy.. 25
U.S. Air Force.. 50
U.S. Coast Guard... 25

Total.. 670

Units

U.S. Army
    Headquarters and Headquarters Company, First U.S. Army, Governors Island, New York
    Headquarters and Headquarters Company, Fort Jay, New York
    Company E, 1st Battalion, 3d Infantry, Fort Myer, Virginia
    Headquarters, Fort Dix, New Jersey
    Corps of Cadets, U.S. Military Academy
    U.S. Military Academy Band

U.S. Marine Corps
    Headquarters, Marine Barracks, Washington, D.C.
    Headquarters, 1st Marine Corps Detachment, Garden City, New York
    1st Marine Reserve and Recruiting District, New York

U.S. Navy
    U.S. Naval Station, Washington, D.C.
    U.S. Navy Recruiting Station, Brooklyn, New York
    3d Naval District, New York, New York

U.S. Air Force
    Headquarters, McGuire Air Force Base
    1100th Air Police Squadron, Washington, D.C.

U.S. Coast Guard
    Headquarters, U.S. Coast Guard, Washington, D.C.
    3d Coast Guard District, New York, New York

Track 17, on which the immediate family and funeral cars would enter the station, a joint service honor cordon lined the platform and station concourse to and through the east entrance. Waiting on the platform along Track 17 were General Wehle, who was the escort commander, the clergy, national color detail, personal flag bearer, and a joint service body bearer team. In formation outside the station entrance were the special honor guard, composed of the chairman and members of the Joint Chiefs of Staff; the U.S. Coast Guard Band; the caisson and caisson detachment from the 3d Infantry; and a 3d Infantry soldier with a caparisoned

TABLE 26—TROOP LIST, ARRIVAL CEREMONY AT UNION STATION, WASHINGTON, D.C., FOR FORMER PRESIDENT HERBERT C. HOOVER

Duty	U.S. Army		U.S. Marine Corps		U.S. Navy		U.S. Air Force		U.S. Coast Guard		Total	
	Officers	Enlisted Men	Officers	Enlisted Men	Officers	Enlisted Men	Officers	Enlisted Men	Officers	Enlisted Men	Officers	Enlisted Men
Escort commander and staff	1										1	
Special honor guard	2		1		1		1		1		6	
Honor cordon	1	26		26		26		26		26	1	130
National color detail		1		1		1						3
Clergy	1										1	
Body bearers	1	2		2		2		2		2	1	10
Personal flag bearer								1				1
Caisson detail		4										4
Band									1	46	1	46
Site control	3	2									3	2
Security cordon	1	16									1	16
Press cordon	1	13									1	13
Baggage detail		12										12
Total	11	76	1	29	1	29	1	29	2	74	16	237

horse. Other troops, all from the 3d Infantry, included a security cordon and a group to control members of the press.

Two elements of the military escort for the procession from Union Station to the Capitol also were at the station in position to lead the way. These were the commander of troops, Col. Joseph Conmy, Jr., commanding officer of the 3d Infantry, and his joint service staff of five and the U.S. Army Band. The troop units themselves had begun to assemble at noon on the three blocks of Delaware Avenue between the station and the East Plaza of the Capitol, the route to be taken by the procession. Since the distance was short, the troop units were to remain stationary instead of marching in the procession. (*Table 27*)

The escort troops, organized as two march units, were on line along the east side of the avenue, facing the center of the street. At the north end of the line, adjacent to the Union Station Plaza, were the first march unit commander (Army) and a joint service staff of five. In order, to the south, were a company from each of the service academies; a company each from the Army, Marine Corps, Navy, Air Force, and Coast Guard; and a composite company of servicewomen. Next, to the south, were the second march unit commander (Army National Guard) and a staff of five representing the reserve components of all five uniformed services. Below them was a company each from the Army National Guard, Army Reserve, Marine Corps Reserve, Navy Reserve, Air National

TABLE 27—TROOP LIST, MAIN PROCESSION IN WASHINGTON, D.C., FOR FORMER PRESIDENT HERBERT C. HOOVER

Duty	U.S. Army		U.S. Marine Corps		U.S. Navy		U.S. Air Force		U.S. Coast Guard		Total	
	Officers	Enlisted Men	Officers	Enlisted Men	Officers	Enlisted Men	Officers	Enlisted Men	Officers	Enlisted Men	Officers	Enlisted Men
Escort commander and staff	1										1	
Special honor guard	2		1		1		1		1		6	
Commander of troops and staff	2		1		1		1		1		6	
National color detail		1		1		1						3
Clergy	1										1	
Body bearers	1	2		2		2		2		2	1	10
Personal flag bearer								1				1
Caisson detail		4										4
Band	1	55									1	55
Military escort												
Active	7	77	6	77	6	77	6	77	6	77	31	385
Cadet	5	77			5	77	5	77	5	77	20	308
Servicewomen	2	20	1	19	1	19	1	19			5	77
National Guard	6	77					6	77			12	154
Reserve	6	77	6	77	6	77	5	77	6	77	29	385
Saluting battery	1	14									1	14
Site control	6	6		5		5	1	5			7	21
Security cordon	2	79	2	79	2	79	2	79			8	316
Guides		2		2		2		2				8
Communications		5										5
Information desk		1										1
Total	43	497	17	262	22	339	28	416	19	233	129	1,747

Guard, Air Force Reserve, and Coast Guard Reserve. Completing the line at the southern end were representatives of eight veterans' organizations. (*Diagram 86*) On either side of Delaware Avenue was a cordon of security troops to keep the route clear. To the west of the avenue, the 3d Infantry battery was in position at Louisiana Avenue and D Street where it was to fire a 21-gun salute as the procession moved to the Capitol.

The funeral train reached Union Station at 1325, ten minutes ahead of schedule, but the timing of the ceremonies was not affected. President and Mrs. Johnson were on the platform to greet the Hoover family when the funeral cars were brought in on Track 17. The group moved through the honor cordon to positions outside the east entrance. The body bearer team meanwhile removed the casket from the train and placed it on a church truck. In procession, the escort commander leading, followed by the national color detail, the clergy, the body bearers with the casket, and the personal flag bearer, Mr. Hoover's body was taken be-

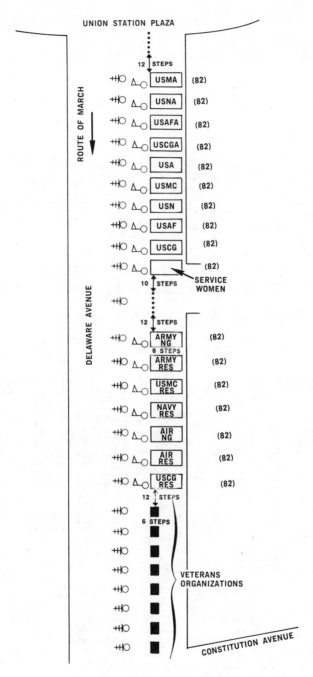

Diagram 86.   Military escort formation.

tween the ranks of the honor cordon to the area outside the east entrance. The members of the honor cordon presented arms in ripples as the national color detail approached and ordered arms when the personal flag bearer had passed. Outside, the procession moved to positions near the Hoover family and waited. (*Diagram 87*)

As the procession halted, the honor cordon presented arms. The Coast Guard

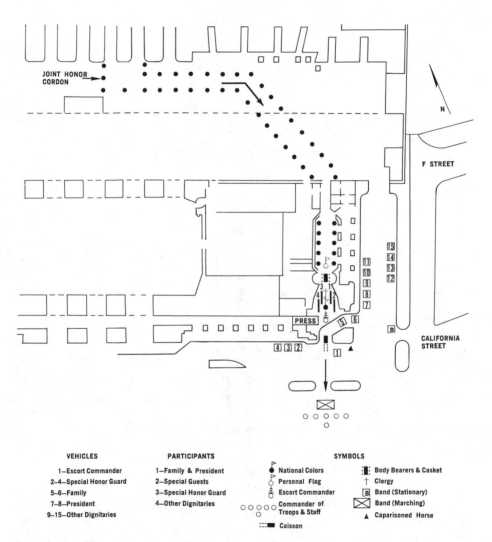

VEHICLES	PARTICIPANTS	SYMBOLS	
1—Escort Commander	1—Family & President	● National Colors	▮ Body Bearers & Casket
2-4—Special Honor Guard	2—Special Guests	○ Personal Flag	† Clergy
5-6—Family	3—Special Honor Guard	⚲ Escort Commander	B Band (Stationary)
7-8—President	4—Other Dignitaries	○○○○○ Commander of	⊠ Band (Marching)
9-15—Other Dignitaries		Troops & Staff	▲ Caparisoned Horse
		▪ Caisson	

Diagram 87.   Arrival ceremony, Union Station, Washington, D.C.

PROCESSION LEAVES UNION STATION

Band then sounded ruffles and flourishes and played "Hail to the Chief" and the hymn "The Light of God is Falling." On the first note of the hymn, the national color detail moved to a position in front of the caisson, and the body bearers, accompanied by the personal flag bearer, transferred the casket from the church truck to the caisson. When the casket was on the caisson, the band stopped playing, the honor cordon ordered arms, and the procession formed for the move to the Capitol.

General Wehle, as escort commander, led the procession, followed by the commander of troops with his staff, the Army Band, the special honor guard in three limousines, and the national color detail, clergy, and caisson. Following the caisson were the personal flag bearer, the groom with the caparisoned horse, the Hoover family in two limousines, President Johnson with a secret service escort, former Vice President Nixon, and five cars of other dignitaries. Former Presidents Truman and Eisenhower had planned to participate in the ceremonies, but illness prevented their attendance. (*Diagram 88*)

As the column moved south on Delaware Avenue across the front of the escort units, each escort company presented arms when the national color detail was

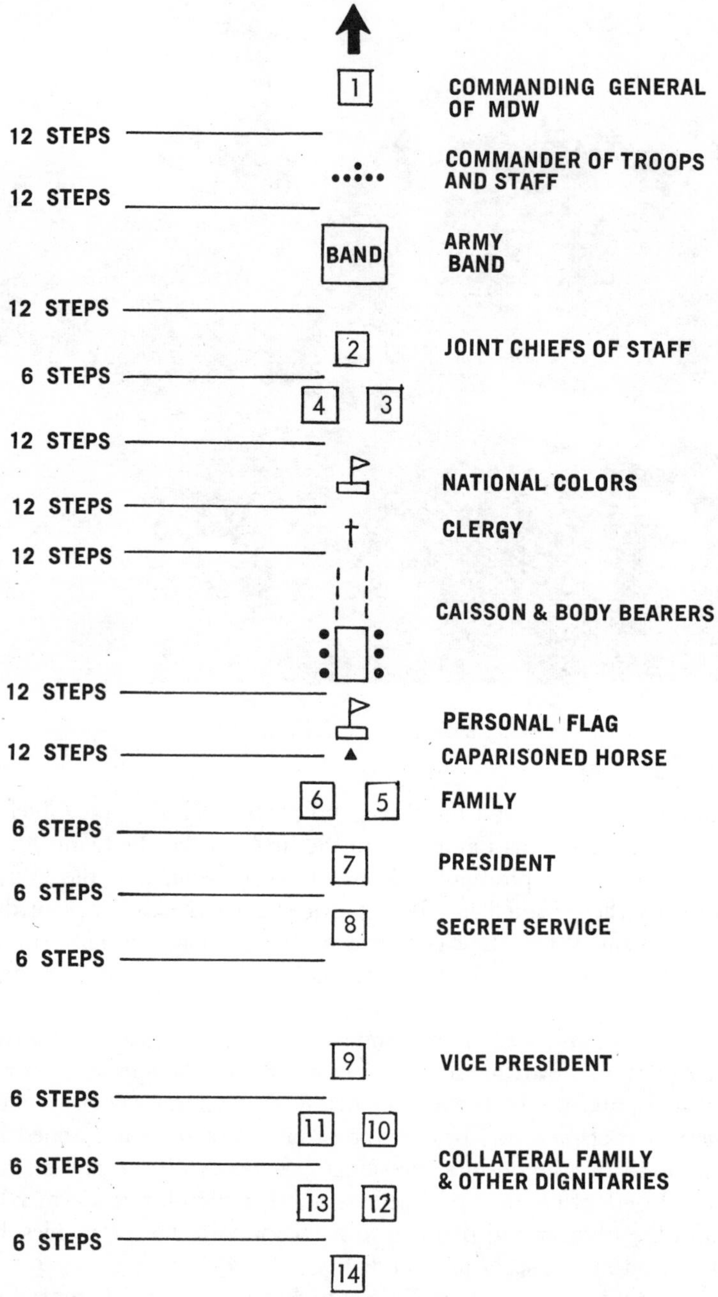

	COMMANDING GENERAL OF MDW
12 STEPS	COMMANDER OF TROOPS AND STAFF
12 STEPS	
	ARMY BAND
12 STEPS	
2	JOINT CHIEFS OF STAFF
6 STEPS	
4 3	
12 STEPS	
	NATIONAL COLORS
12 STEPS	
†	CLERGY
12 STEPS	
	CAISSON & BODY BEARERS
12 STEPS	
	PERSONAL FLAG
12 STEPS	CAPARISONED HORSE
6 5	FAMILY
6 STEPS	
7	PRESIDENT
6 STEPS	
8	SECRET SERVICE
6 STEPS	
9	VICE PRESIDENT
6 STEPS	
11 10	
6 STEPS	COLLATERAL FAMILY & OTHER DIGNITARIES
13 12	
6 STEPS	
14	

Diagram 88. Order of march, Union Station to the Capitol.

PROCESSION MOVES ALONG DELAWARE AVENUE

twelve steps to the company's right flank and ordered arms when the rear of the caisson passed the company's left flank. As the lead horse pulling the caisson entered Delaware Avenue from the Union Station Plaza, the 3d Infantry battery fired the first round of the 21-gun salute. The rounds were spaced so that the last was fired when the caisson was about to cross Constitution Avenue and enter the East Plaza of the Capitol. As the caisson crossed the avenue, forty-eight Air Force jet fighter planes in clusters of three passed overhead. When the cortege entered the East Plaza, the commander of troops, Colonel Conmy, and his staff and the Army Band continued to march until they were out of the ceremonial area. The remainder of the cortege halted in front of the Senate wing steps, which would be used in taking the former President's casket into the Capitol. The main stairway leading directly to the rotunda could not be used because inaugural platforms were under construction there.

Military formations not with the cortege but scheduled to participate in the ceremony at the Capitol had taken position at 1400. (*Table 28*) A joint service honor cordon lined the Senate wing steps, and the U.S. Marine Band was in for-

CAISSON ARRIVES AT EAST PLAZA

mation on the plaza just to the left of the steps. Inside the Capitol a joint service guard of honor was ready to post its first relief as soon as the casket was placed on the Lincoln catafalque, which had been set up in the center of the rotunda. Already in the rotunda were committees representing the various departments and agencies of the federal government, and representatives of the diplomatic corps.

By 1430 the Hoover family and others who had accompanied the procession from Union Station were in their respective positions at the foot of the Senate wing steps. (*Diagram 89*) At the signal of the site control officer, the officer in charge of the honor cordon ordered his troops to present arms. The Marine Band then sounded ruffles and flourishes, played "Hail to the Chief," and began "America the Beautiful." At the first note, the body bearers removed the casket from the caisson. The escort commander, General Wehle, led the special honor guard up the Senate wing steps to start the procession into the Capitol. Joining the column in order were the national color detail, the clergy, the body bearers with the casket, the personal flag bearer, the Hoover family, and other mourners. When the procession had entered the Capitol, the band ceased playing and the honor cordon ordered arms.

TABLE 28—TROOP LIST, ARRIVAL CEREMONY AT THE U.S. CAPITOL
AND LYING IN STATE PERIOD FOR FORMER PRESIDENT
HERBERT C. HOOVER

Duty	U.S. Army		U.S. Marine Corps		U.S. Navy		U.S. Air Force		U.S. Coast Guard		Total	
	Officers	Enlisted Men	Officers	Enlisted Men	Officers	Enlisted Men	Officers	Enlisted Men	Officers	Enlisted Men	Officers	Enlisted Men
Escort commander and staff.....	1	....	....	....	....	....	....	....	....	....	1	....
Special honor guard.............	2	....	1	....	1	....	1	....	1	....	6	....
Honor cordon..................	1	13	....	13	....	13	....	13	....	13	1	65
National color detail............	....	1	....	1	....	1	....	....	....	....	....	3
Clergy........................	1	....	....	....	....	....	....	....	....	....	1	....
Body bearers..................	1	2	....	2	....	2	....	2	....	2	1	10
Personal flag bearer............	....	....	....	....	....	....	....	....	....	1	....	1
Band.........................	....	....	1	91	....	....	....	....	....	....	1	91
Guard of honor................	3	13	1	11	1	11	1	11	1	11	7	57
Wreath bearer.................	....	1	....	....	....	....	....	....	....	....	....	1
Site control...................	4	11	....	....	....	....	....	....	....	....	4	11
Security cordon................	1	22	....	....	....	....	....	....	....	....	1	22
Ushers........................	....	8	....	....	....	....	....	....	....	....	....	8
Guides........................	....	8	....	....	....	....	....	....	....	....	....	8
Floral detail..................	1	15	....	....	....	....	....	....	....	....	1	15
Traffic guides.................	....	12	....	....	....	....	....	....	....	....	....	12
Medical support...............	....	1	....	....	....	....	....	....	....	....	....	1
Total..................	15	107	3	118	2	27	2	27	2	26	24	305

Inside the Senate wing entrance, the body bearers placed the casket on a church truck. The procession then continued through the east hallway to the east entrance foyer to the rotunda. There the body bearers lifted the casket from the church truck and the procession entered. Inside the rotunda the Hoover family and other mourners were guided to positions while the national color detail, clergy, and personal flag bearer accompanied the casket as the body bearers carried it in a semicircular route to the center of the rotunda and placed it on the Lincoln catafalque. The Reverend Frederick Brown Harris, chaplain of the Senate, took a position near the foot of the bier; the national colors and personal flag were posted, the first relief of the guard of honor took position at the bier, and the body bearers were dismissed. (*Diagram 90*)

Chaplain Harris delivered a short eulogy, after which President Johnson placed a wreath at the base of the bier. Chaplain (Lt. Col.) Kenneth L. Ames of the Military District of Washington pronounced the benediction, concluding the brief rotunda ceremony a few minutes after 1500. While the rotunda cleared, the Hoover family inspected the arrangements for the lying in state period. After the

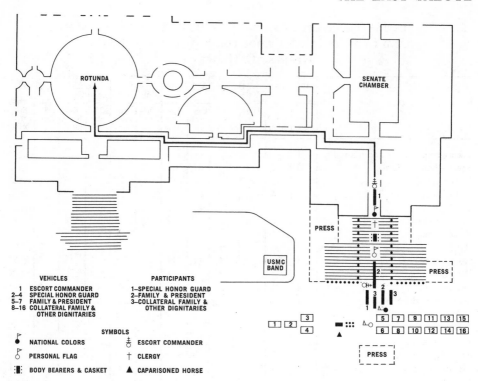

VEHICLES

1   ESCORT COMMANDER
2–4   SPECIAL HONOR GUARD
5–7   FAMILY & PRESIDENT
8–16 COLLATERAL FAMILY &
         OTHER DIGNITARIES

PARTICIPANTS

1–SPECIAL HONOR GUARD
2–FAMILY & PRESIDENT
3–COLLATERAL FAMILY &
   OTHER DIGNITARIES

SYMBOLS

NATIONAL COLORS   ESCORT COMMANDER

PERSONAL FLAG   CLERGY

BODY BEARERS & CASKET   CAPARISONED HORSE

Diagram 89.   Arrival ceremony at the Capitol.

departure of the family, the rotunda was opened to the public from 1530 until 2100.

On 24 October the rotunda again was opened to the public between the hours of 0900 and 2100. Over the two days approximately 30,000 people filed past the bier. Throughout the lying in state period the joint service guard of honor maintained a constant vigil, changing reliefs each thirty minutes.

On 25 October the last ceremonies in Washington for former President Hoover were scheduled to begin at 0930. At that time the casket was to be carried from the rotunda of the Capitol and taken in a motorized procession to Washington National Airport, where a departure ceremony would be conducted as the casket was put aboard an Air Force C–130 transport for the flight to Cedar Rapids, Iowa.

Participating troops at both the Capitol and the airport were in position by 0900. Those at the Capitol included the escort commander, General Wehle, and a special honor guard, this time composed of two general or flag officers from each of the uniformed services. A joint service honor cordon again lined the Senate

CASKET IS CARRIED THROUGH JOINT HONOR CORDON

wing steps. The U.S. Navy Band was in formation on the plaza to the left of the steps. Waiting inside the Capitol were the body bearers, national color detail, personal flag bearer, and Chaplain Ames. A hearse and other vehicles for the motorcade also were in place on the plaza, and the entire ceremonial area outside the Capitol was cordoned off by troops to keep it clear. (*Table 29*)

The Hoover family group and other dignitaries began to arrive at the Capitol at 0915. President Johnson, who was unable to attend the ceremony, designated as his representatives Secretary of State Dean Rusk and Under Secretary of Commerce Clarence D. Martin. By 0930 all of these participants had been guided to positions at the base of the Senate wing steps. (*Diagram 91*)

At that hour, the guard of honor at the bier in the rotunda was dismissed, and the body bearers secured the casket and placed it on a church truck. Then the procession, with the national color detail and clergy preceding the casket and the personal flag bearer following it, left by the east door of the rotunda and moved down the east hallway to the Senate wing entrance.

As the national color detail appeared in the doorway, the honor cordon pre-

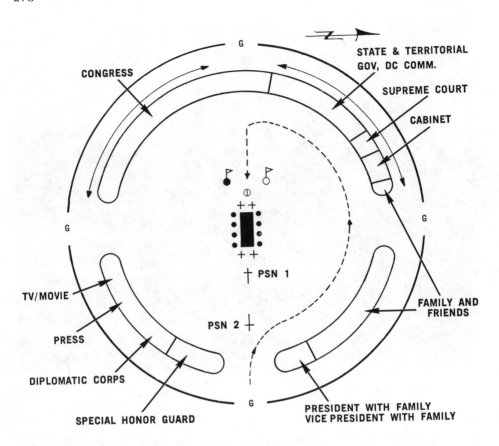

CONGRESS

STATE & TERRITORIAL
GOV, DC COMM.

SUPREME COURT

CABINET

PSN 1

TV/MOVIE

FAMILY AND
FRIENDS

PRESS

PSN 2

DIPLOMATIC CORPS

SPECIAL HONOR GUARD

PRESIDENT WITH FAMILY
VICE PRESIDENT WITH FAMILY

SYMBOLS
National Colors
Personal Flag
Body Bearers & Casket
† Clergy
① Commander of Guard of Honor
+ Sentinels
G Capitol Police

Diagram 90. Formation in the rotunda.

PRESIDENT JOHNSON PLACES A WREATH DURING CEREMONY IN THE ROTUNDA

TABLE 29—TROOP LIST, DEPARTURE CEREMONY AT THE U.S. CAPITOL
for FORMER PRESIDENT HERBERT C. HOOVER

Duty	U.S. Army		U.S. Marine Corps		U.S. Navy		U.S. Air Force		U.S. Coast Guard		Total	
	Officers	Enlisted Men	Officers	Enlisted Men	Officers	Enlisted Men	Officers	Enlisted Men	Officers	Enlisted Men	Officers	Enlisted Men
Escort commander and staff	1	....	....	....	....	....	....	....	....	....	1	....
Special honor guard	2	....	2	....	2	....	2	....	2	....	10	....
Honor cordon	1	13	....	13	....	13	....	13	....	13	1	65
National color detail	....	1	....	1	....	1	....	....	....	....	....	3
Clergy	1	....	....	....	....	....	....	....	....	....	1	....
Body bearers	....	2	....	2	....	2	....	2	....	2	....	10
Personal flag bearer	....	....	....	....	....	....	....	1	....	....	....	1
Band	....	....	....	....	1	91	....	....	....	....	1	91
Security cordon	....	16	....	16	....	16	1	16	....	16	1	80
Floral detail	1	15	....	....	....	....	....	....	....	....	1	15
Total	6	47	2	32	3	123	3	32	2	31	16	265

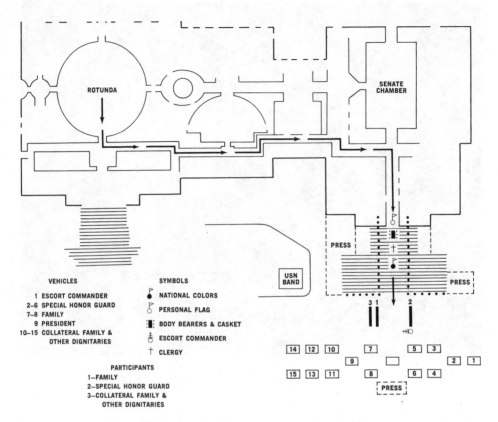

VEHICLES

1 ESCORT COMMANDER
2–6 SPECIAL HONOR GUARD
7–8 FAMILY
9 PRESIDENT
10–15 COLLATERAL FAMILY &
      OTHER DIGNITARIES

SYMBOLS

NATIONAL COLORS
PERSONAL FLAG
BODY BEARERS & CASKET
ESCORT COMMANDER
CLERGY

PARTICIPANTS

1–FAMILY
2–SPECIAL HONOR GUARD
3–COLLATERAL FAMILY &
  OTHER DIGNITARIES

Diagram 91.   Departure ceremony at the Capitol.

sented arms. After the body bearers had taken the casket to the top of the steps, they halted while the Navy Band sounded honors. When the band started the hymn "Abide With Me," the body bearers lifted the casket from the church truck and the procession continued down the steps through the honor cordon to the hearse. After the casket had been placed in the hearse, the music ceased, the honor cordon ordered arms, and the Hoover family and others scheduled to accompany the cortege to the airport entered their automobiles.

General Wehle occupied the lead vehicle of the motorcade. In the cars behind him were the special honor guard followed by the hearse, then cars carrying the Hoover family, President Johnson's representatives, and other dignitaries. The motorcade reached the Military Air Transport Service Terminal at Washington National Airport at 0955. (*Diagram 92*)

A street cordon lined the access road to the terminal, and at the airport a security cordon ringed the ceremonial area to keep it clear. (*Diagram 93*) Inside

CASKET IS CARRIED FROM THE CAPITOL

this area the U.S. Air Force Band was in formation and a joint service honor cordon lined the way from the point at which the hearse would stop to the aircraft itself. In a position near the ceremonial area was the 3d Infantry saluting battery. (*Table 30*)

As the motorcade traveled the access road to the terminal, the members of the street cordon presented arms individually when the hearse was twelve paces away and ordered arms when it had passed. The 3d Infantry battery fired the first round of a 21-gun salute as the hearse began its passage through the street cordon; the remaining rounds were spaced so that the last was fired as the hearse stopped in the ceremonial area.

After the hearse stopped, the body bearers, who, along with the national color detail and personal flag bearer, had traveled from the Capitol to the airfield separately to arrive ahead of the cortege, took position at the rear of the hearse. The other vehicles in the cortege were driven to a parking area on a ramp to the rear of the ceremonial area. The passengers then dismounted and were guided to positions for the departure ceremony.

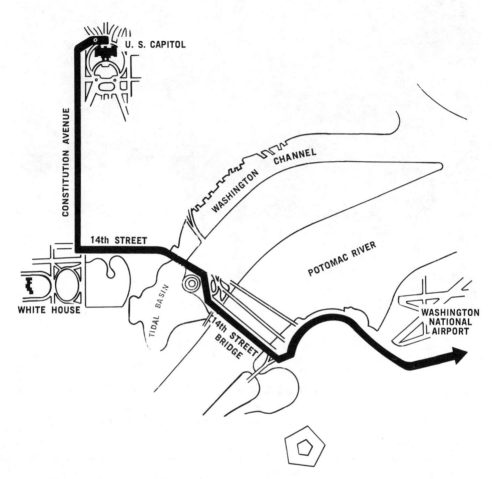

Diagram 92. Route of march, Capitol to Washington National Airport.

When all participants were in position, the honor cordon presented arms and the band sounded honors. As the band began the hymn "Now the Day is Over," the body bearers removed the casket from the hearse and in procession, the national color detail leading, the casket and the personal flag bearer following, the casket was carried through the honor cordon and aboard the plane. (*Diagram 94*) The music stopped and the troops ordered arms. The ceremonial troops, except the body bearers, national color detail, and personal flag bearer, then marched away from the cordoned area.

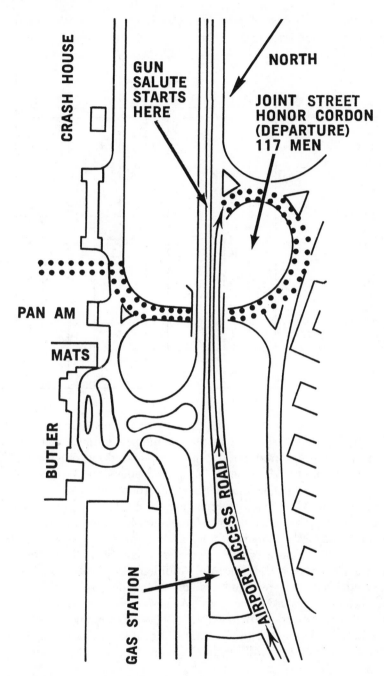

Diagram 93. Street cordon, Washington National Airport.

TABLE 30—TROOP LIST, DEPARTURE CEREMONY AT THE WASHINGTON NATIONAL AIRPORT FOR FORMER PRESIDENT HERBERT C. HOOVER

Duty	U.S. Army		U.S. Marine Corps		U.S. Navy		U.S. Air Force		U.S. Coast Guard		Total	
	Officers	Enlisted Men	Officers	Enlisted Men	Officers	Enlisted Men	Officers	Enlisted Men	Officers	Enlisted Men	Officers	Enlisted Men
Escort commander and staff	1	....	....	....	....	....	....	....	....	....	1	....
Special honor guard	2	....	2	....	2	....	2	....	2	....	10	....
Honor cordon	1	9	....	8	....	8	....	8	....	8	1	41
National color detail	....	1	....	....	....	1	....	1	....	....	....	3
Clergy	1	....	....	....	....	....	....	....	....	....	1	....
Body bearers	1	2	....	2	....	2	....	2	....	2	1	10
Personal flag bearer	....	....	....	....	....	....	....	1	....	....	....	1
Band	....	....	....	....	....	....	1	91	....	....	1	91
Street cordon	....	24	....	24	....	24	....	24	....	24	....	120
Saluting battery	1	14	....	....	....	....	....	....	....	....	1	14
Site control	3	....	....	....	....	....	....	....	....	....	3	....
Security cordon	1	78	....	....	....	....	....	....	....	....	1	78
Floral detail	1	15	....	....	....	....	....	....	....	....	1	15
Traffic guides	....	4	....	....	....	....	....	....	....	....	....	4
Parking detail	....	6	....	....	....	....	....	....	....	....	....	6
Press cordon	1	10	....	....	....	....	....	....	....	....	1	10
Baggage detail	....	10	....	....	....	....	....	....	....	....	....	10
Total	13	173	2	34	2	35	3	127	2	34	22	403

The body bearers, color detail, and flag bearer all boarded the plane bearing the casket; they would participate in the ceremonies in Iowa. After they were aboard, the plane was towed out of the area, and three other aircraft were brought in to take aboard the Hoover family and others, in all sixty-four people, making the flight to Iowa. The four planes were airborne by 1030.

Lt. Gen. Charles G. Dodge, commanding the Fifth U.S. Army, directed the ceremonies in Iowa. To carry out his responsibility, he established the Fifth Army Detachment at the Cedar Rapids Municipal Airport, staffing it with officers and men from Army headquarters in Chicago and placing it under his deputy commander, Brig. Gen. Joseph E. Bastion, Jr. Additional officers for such functions as liaison and information were made available from the XIV U.S. Army Corps, which had headquarters in Minneapolis, Minnesota. Besides these staff members, the Fifth U.S. Army Band participated in the Iowa ceremonies. All other troops involved were provided by the Iowa Army National Guard, as arranged through Maj. Gen. Junior Franklin Miller, the Adjutant General of the state of Iowa. (Table 31)

For the arrival ceremony at the Cedar Rapids airport, a security cordon of

CASKET ARRIVES AT WASHINGTON NATIONAL AIRPORT, *above. Casket is carried to the plane, below.*

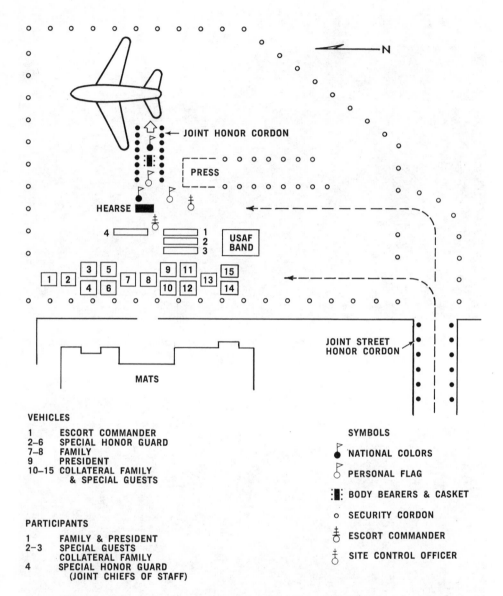

Diagram 94.   Departure ceremony, Washington National Airport.

Army National Guard troops sealed off the area. These troops along with the 34th U.S. Army Band and General Dodge, the escort commander, were in position at the airfield by 1300. Contrary to custom, no honor cordon was organized for the arrival ceremony.

The four aircraft from Washington landed at Cedar Rapids shortly before 1400. The plane bearing Mr. Hoover's body, the body bearers, the national color detail, the personal flag bearer, and floral tributes that had been on display during the ceremonies in Washington was guided to the proper position in the ceremonial area, while the three aircraft carrying the family group and other mourners were parked near the terminal building outside the area.

While the site control officer went aboard the plane to brief the body bearers and color bearers, General Dodge and other escort officers guided the family and friends to positions for the ceremony. As the body bearers appeared at the door of the plane with the casket, the band sounded ruffles and flourishes and played "Hail to the Chief." When the hymn "Fight the Good Fight" was begun, the body bearers carried the casket from the plane. The procession formed, with the national color detail leading off and followed by Dr. D. Elton Trueblood, professor of philosophy at Earlham College in Richmond, Indiana, and a friend of the Hoover family, the casket, and the personal flag bearer. (*Diagram 95*)

TABLE 31—TROOP LIST, IOWA, CEREMONY FOR
FORMER PRESIDENT HERBERT C. HOOVER

Troops	Officers	Enlisted Men	Total
Active Army	58	45	103
National Guard	61	694	755
Total	119	739	858

Units

Active Army
  Headquarters, Fifth U.S. Army
  Headquarters, XIV U.S. Army Corps
  Fifth U.S. Army Band

Iowa Army National Guard
  Headquarters and Headquarters Battery, 1st Howitzer Battalion, 185th Artillery
  Battery A, 1st Howitzer Battalion, 185th Artillery
  Battery B, 1st Howitzer Battalion, 185th Artillery
  Battery C, 1st Howitzer Battalion, 185th Artillery
  Service Battery, 1st Howitzer Battalion, 185th Artillery
  Company B, 234th Signal Battalion
  Headquarters and Headquarters Company, 224th Engineer Battalion
  Company A, 1st Battalion, 113th Armor
  Headquarters and Headquarters Detachment, 109th Medical Battalion
  209th Medical Company
  34th Army Band

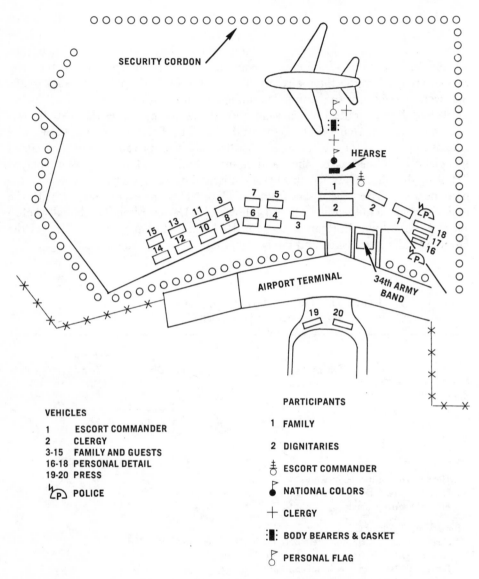

Diagram 95. Arrival ceremony, Municipal Airport, Cedar Rapids, Iowa.

When the procession reached the hearse and the casket was placed inside, the body bearers and color bearers immediately moved to vehicles reserved for them at the edge of the ceremonial area. At the same time, floral vans furnished without charge by local funeral directors were driven to the plane and loaded with the flowers brought from Washington. Police then escorted these vehicles to West Branch so that they would reach the gravesite ahead of the cortege.

Meanwhile General Dodge and escort officers ushered the family and other mourners to their vehicles for the motorcade to West Branch. The procession left the airfield about 1415, General Dodge leading, followed by the clergy, the hearse, and the family and other mourners in thirteen limousines also provided by local funeral directors. Moving over State Route 84, U.S. 218, and Interstate 80, the motorcade reached the gravesite a few minutes after 1500. (*Diagram 96*)

On the grounds of the Herbert Hoover Library some 75,000 people had assembled for the service. A security cordon of National Guard troops surrounded the gravesite and a small group of Guardsmen controlled the movement of members of the press. The Fifth U.S. Army Band stood in formation at the grave, and shortly before 1500 the body bearers and color bearers, arriving from Cedar Rapids, joined the band. All were in position for the ceremony when the procession entered the library grounds. (*Diagram 97*)

The cortege halted on the circular driveway at the library, with the hearse

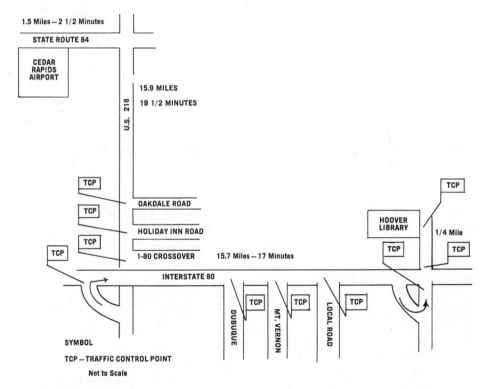

Diagram 96.   Route of march, Cedar Rapids to West Branch, Iowa.

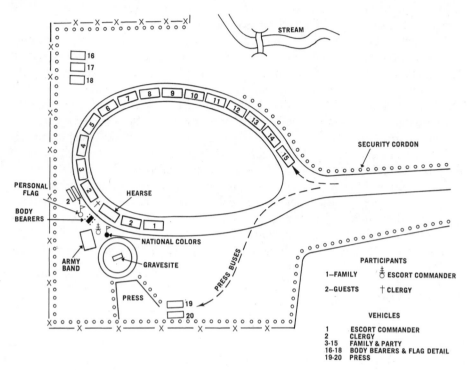

Diagram 97.   Arrival of cortege at the Hoover Library.

standing at the pathway to the grave. General Dodge and his assistants escorted the Hoover family and other mourners from their automobiles to the hearse. When they were in place, the band sounded honors, then played "The Battle Hymn of the Republic." As the hymn began, the body bearers took the casket from the hearse. The procession then moved to the grave, with General Dodge leading, and the national color detail, clergy, body bearers with the casket, personal flag bearer, the Hoover family, and other mourners following. Escort officers guided the family group and other mourners to their positions at the graveside. (*Diagram 98*)

Dr. Trueblood opened the service by asking for a period of meditation and then offered a prayer. He next delivered a short eulogy at the end of which he pronounced the benediction. General Dodge laid a Presidential wreath at the head of the grave, and a bugler from the Fifth Army Band sounded taps. A 21-gun salute had been scheduled but was canceled at the request of the Hoover family. When the bugler finished, the body bearers folded the flag that had draped the casket and presented it to General Dodge, who in turn handed it to

CASKET IS CARRIED TO THE GRAVE ON GROUNDS OF HERBERT HOOVER LIBRARY, *above. Dr. Trueblood conducts the burial service, below.*

Herbert Hoover, Jr., concluding the final rites for former President Hoover. At 1535 the family members and other mourners went to the cars that would take them to the Cedar Rapids airport from which they would leave for their homes.

After the library grounds were clear a security guard was posted at the grave, which would not be sealed until the late Mrs. Hoover, who had been buried in California, could be reburied beside her husband. (This was accomplished on 31 October.) When the guard had taken post, the public was permitted to file past the grave. At sunset on 25 October, a winding line of people still was moving slowly past the final resting place of the nation's thirty-first President.

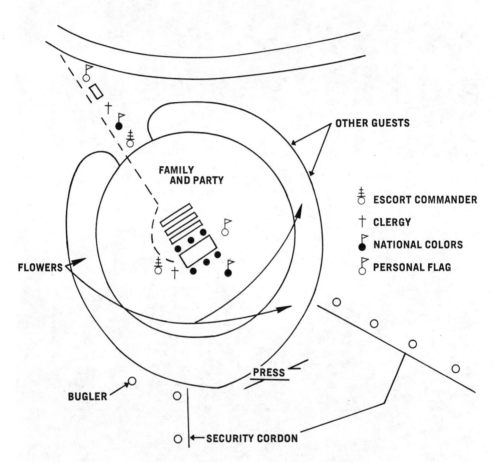

Diagram 98. Formation at the graveside.

CHAPTER XXVI

U.S. Representative to the United Nations
Adlai E. Stevenson
Official Funeral
14-19 July 1965

On 14 July 1965, Adlai E. Stevenson, U.S. Representative to the United Nations, died suddenly of a heart attack in London. Mr. Stevenson's body was taken to the U.S. Embassy where it lay, watched over by an American soldier, an American sailor, and two British soldiers from the King's Regiment, until the Stevenson family arrived from the United States. The embassy was not open to the public during this period.

Word of Mr. Stevenson's death was passed immediately from the embassy in London to the Department of State in Washington, and from the department to the White House and the Military District of Washington. Officials of the State Department at once communicated with the Stevenson family in Illinois, proposing that Mr. Stevenson be given an Official Funeral. The family accepted.

President Lyndon B. Johnson ordered the flags on all public buildings in the United States and on all U.S. ships at sea to be flown at half-staff until after the funeral services. He then appointed Vice President Hubert H. Humphrey, Secretary of Labor W. Willard Wirtz, Senator Eugene McCarthy of Minnesota, Under Secretary of State George W. Ball, and Mayor Richard J. Daley of Chicago to make up an official party which would accompany the Stevenson family to London and escort Mr. Stevenson's body to the United States. Mr. Stevenson's three sons and their wives meanwhile were flown from Illinois to Andrews Air Force Base, Maryland. The family and the official party then left for London aboard the Presidential plane, Air Force One, at 2300 on 14 July.

On the 15th, after the Stevenson family and the official party had arrived at the embassy in London, Prime Minister Harold Wilson and other British dignitaries called to pay their respects. Her Majesty, Queen Elizabeth II, sent a private message of condolence to the family, and later had her personal representative, Lord Nugent, attend to their needs at the airfield during preparations for the return flight. A Royal Air Force color squadron stood on the field as an honor guard while Mr. Stevenson's casket was taken aboard Air Force One. The departure of the plane was timed so that it would arrive at Andrews Air Force Base during the late afternoon of the 15th.

Plans for the funeral ceremonies were completed on 14 and 15 July by the Department of State, where Mr. Stevenson had been an official. Members of the department's Office of Protocol had talked to Mr. Stevenson's sons directly and by telephone as they traveled to Washington and went on to London, and from these consultations a schedule of ceremonies was drawn up. Mr. Stevenson's body was to rest in the Washington National Cathedral in Washington, D.C., until midmorning on 16 July, and a funeral service was to be conducted in the nave of the cathedral at 1100. Immediately after the service, the body was to be flown to Springfield, Illinois, where it would lie in state in the rotunda of the capitol until the morning of 18 July. A motor procession was then to escort the body to Bloomington, Illinois, the Stevenson family home, where a funeral service was to be held on 19 July. Burial was to take place in Evergreen Memorial Cemetery. Those responsible for making arrangements, besides the Department of State, included the Commanding General, Military District of Washington (for military ceremonies in Washington, D.C.), the governor of Illinois (for events in his state), and the Commanding General, Fifth U.S. Army, with headquarters in Chicago (for military ceremonies in Springfield and Bloomington).

TABLE 32—TROOP LIST, ARRIVAL CEREMONY AT ANDREWS AIR FORCE BASE FOR U.S. REPRESENTATIVE TO THE UNITED NATIONS ADLAI E. STEVENSON

Duty	U.S. Army		U.S. Marine Corps		U.S. Navy		U.S. Air Force		U.S. Coast Guard		Total	
	Officers	Enlisted Men	Officers	Enlisted Men	Officers	Enlisted Men	Officers	Enlisted Men	Officers	Enlisted Men	Officers	Enlisted Men
Escort commander and staff	1	....	....	....	....	....	....	....	....	....	1	....
Special honor guard	2	....	2	....	2	....	2	....	2	....	10	....
Honor cordon	1	9	....	8	....	8	....	8	....	8	1	41
National color detail	....	1	....	1	....	1	....	....	....	....	....	3
Clergy	1	....	....	....	....	....	....	....	....	....	1	....
Body bearers	1	2	....	2	....	2	....	2	....	2	1	10
Band	....	....	....	....	....	....	1	46	....	....	1	46
Street cordon	1	31	....	31	....	31	....	31	....	31	1	155
Site control	....	....	....	....	....	....	1	....	....	....	1	....
Security cordon	1	81	....	....	....	....	....	....	....	....	1	81
Floral detail	1	4	....	....	....	....	....	....	....	....	1	4
Parking detail	1	6	....	....	....	....	....	....	....	....	1	6
Press cordon	....	9	....	....	....	....	....	....	....	....	....	9
Baggage detail	1	10	....	....	....	....	....	....	....	....	1	10
Total	11	153	2	42	2	42	4	87	2	41	21	365

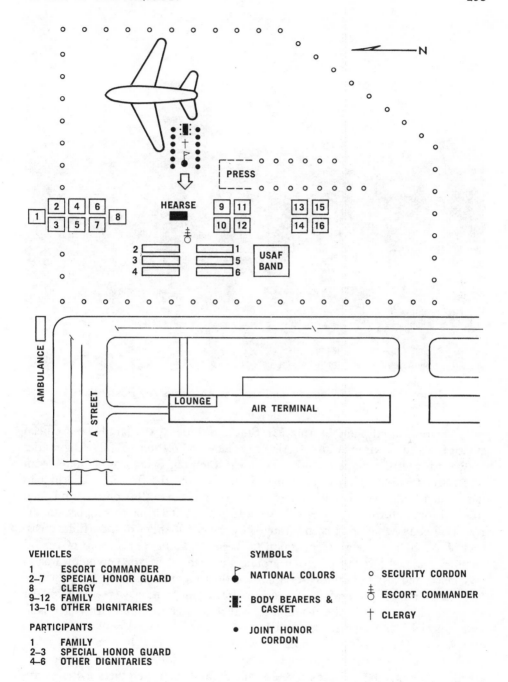

Diagram 99.   Arrival ceremony, Andrews Air Force Base.

VEHICLES

1   ESCORT COMMANDER
2–7   SPECIAL HONOR GUARD
8   CLERGY
9–12 FAMILY
13–16 OTHER DIGNITARIES

PARTICIPANTS

1   FAMILY
2–3   SPECIAL HONOR GUARD
4–6   OTHER DIGNITARIES

SYMBOLS

NATIONAL COLORS

BODY BEARERS &
CASKET

JOINT HONOR
CORDON

○ SECURITY CORDON

ESCORT COMMANDER

† CLERGY

BODY ARRIVES IN PRESIDENTIAL PLANE AT ANDREWS AIR FORCE BASE

The Presidential plane bearing Mr. Stevenson's body, the family, and official escorts touched down at Andrews Air Force Base at 1740 on 15 July. Dignitaries present to meet the plane included President Johnson, Secretary of State Dean Rusk, Secretary of the Treasury Henry H. Fowler, and the British ambassador to the United States, Sir Patrick Dean. Also on hand were 386 officers and men from all the uniformed services who were to participate in or to support the arrival ceremony, which had been arranged by the commander of the Military District of Washington, Maj. Gen. Philip C. Wehle. (*Table 32*) Troops of the 3d Infantry manned a security cordon around the area where the ceremony was to take place, and a joint honor cordon flanked the route by which the casket was to be carried from the aircraft to a hearse. Already in position were the U.S. Air Force Band, a national color detail, a joint body bearer team, an Army chaplain, and a special honor guard composed of two officers of general or flag rank from each service. General Wehle served as escort commander. (*Diagram 99*)

As the plane's passengers disembarked, President Johnson moved forward to greet first the members of the Stevenson family and then the others. After everyone had been guided to positions facing the aircraft, the body bearer team removed the casket from the plane. Preceded by the clergy, the body bearers carried the casket a few steps toward the hearse. At this point they halted while the joint honor cordon presented arms, and the U.S. Air Force Band sounded ruffles and flourishes and played part of the march "Stars and Stripes Forever." As the band began "America the Beautiful," the body bearers resumed their march; passing through the joint honor cordon, they placed the casket in the hearse. The band then ceased playing, the honor cordon ordered arms, and the participants went to their automobiles for the journey to Washington National Cathedral.

The band, color team, body bearers, honor cordon, and security cordon did not accompany the cortege to the cathedral; duplicate details had been stationed at the entrance of Bethlehem Chapel. (*Table 33*) The joint honor cordon of twelve men lined the steps at the chapel; the U.S. Marine Band was on the lawn nearby; the national color detail and the joint body bearer team stood close to the point where the hearse would stop; and the security cordon of troops from the 3d Infantry enclosed the whole ceremonial area. (*Diagram 100*)

The cortege from Andrews Air Force Base reached the cathedral at 1840. After members of the Stevenson family and the official party had taken their positions at the chapel entrance, the body bearer team moved to the rear of the hearse. The Marine Band played ruffles and flourishes followed by "Stars and Stripes Forever." As it began the hymn "Abide With Me," the body bearers lifted

TABLE 33—TROOP LIST, ARRIVAL CEREMONY AT WASHINGTON NATIONAL CATHEDRAL FOR U.S. REPRESENTATIVE TO THE UNITED NATIONS ADLAI E. STEVENSON

Duty	U.S. Army		U.S. Marine Corps		U.S. Navy		U.S. Air Force		U.S. Coast Guard		Total	
	Officers	Enlisted Men	Officers	Enlisted Men	Officers	Enlisted Men	Officers	Enlisted Men	Officers	Enlisted Men	Officers	Enlisted Men
Escort commander and staff	1	....	....	....	....	....	....	....	....	....	1	....
Special honor guard	2	....	2	....	2	....	2	....	2	....	10	....
Commander of troops and staff	1	....	....	....	....	....	....	....	....	....	1	....
Honor cordon	1	3	....	2	....	2	....	2	....	2	1	11
National color detail	....	1	....	1	....	1	....	....	....	....	....	3
Clergy	1	....	....	....	....	....	....	....	....	....	1	....
Body bearers	1	2	....	2	....	2	....	2	....	2	1	10
Band	....	....	1	50	....	....	....	....	....	....	1	50
Guard of honor	2	10	1	10	1	10	1	10	1	10	6	50
Site control	1	....	....	....	....	....	....	....	....	....	1	....
Security cordon	2	39	....	....	....	....	....	....	....	....	2	39
Floral detail	1	4	....	....	....	....	....	....	....	....	1	4
Total	13	59	4	65	3	15	3	14	3	14	26	167

the casket from the hearse. In procession the escort commander, special honor guard, national color detail, clergy, casket, Stevenson family, and other mourners passed through the honor cordon and entered the cathedral.

Inside the Bethlehem Chapel, the casket was placed on a movable bier in the center of the room. After the Stevenson family and the official party had entered the chapel, the clergy conducted a brief service. At its conclusion, the body bear-

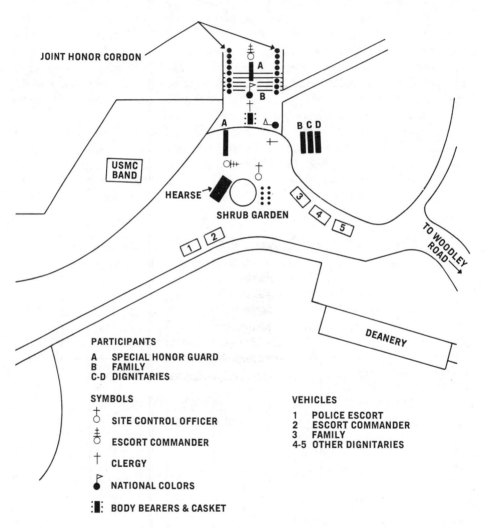

Diagram 100.   Formation for the reception ceremony, Bethlehem
Chapel, Washington National Cathedral.

CASKET IS TAKEN FROM HEARSE AT WASHINGTON NATIONAL CATHEDRAL, *above.*
Procession enters the cathedral, below.

JOINT HONOR GUARD STANDS WATCH IN BETHLEHEM CHAPEL

TABLE 34—TROOP LIST, FUNERAL SERVICE AND DEPARTURE CEREMONY AT WASHINGTON NATIONAL CATHEDRAL FOR U.S. REPRESENTATIVE TO THE UNITED NATIONS ADLAI E. STEVENSON

Duty	U.S. Army		U.S. Marine Corps		U.S. Navy		U.S. Air Force		U.S. Coast Guard		Total	
	Officers	Enlisted Men	Officers	Enlisted Men	Officers	Enlisted Men	Officers	Enlisted Men	Officers	Enlisted Men	Officers	Enlisted Men
Escort commander and staff.....	1	....	....	....	....	....	....	....	....	....	1	....
Special honor guard.............	2	....	1	....	1	....	1	....	1	....	6	....
Honor cordon..................	1	5	....	4	....	4	....	4	....	4	1	21
National color detail............	....	1	....	1	....	1	....	....	....	....	....	3
Clergy........................	1	....	....	....	....	....	....	....	....	....	1	....
Body bearers..................	1	2	....	2	....	2	....	2	....	2	1	10
Band.........................	....	....	1	50	....	....	....	....	....	....	1	50
Site control...................	4	....	....	....	....	....	....	....	....	....	4	....
Security cordon................	2	39	....	....	....	....	....	....	....	....	2	39
Ushers........................	6	50	5	50	5	50	5	50	5	50	26	250
Total..................	18	97	7	107	6	57	6	56	6	56	43	373

ers were dismissed, and the first relief of a joint guard of honor took post. The chapel was opened to the public at 1900 and remained so until 1000 on 16 July. At 1000 the joint guard of honor was dismissed. Two Army body bearers then wheeled Mr. Stevenson's casket from the chapel to the cathedral nave and remained standing at either end of the bier until the beginning of the funeral service, scheduled for 1100.

As the guests arrived, an usher detail of over 200 officers and men representing all of the uniformed services seated them according to a predetermined plan. (*Table 34*) Hundreds of persons attended including President and Mrs. Johnson, Vice President and Mrs. Humphrey, members of the cabinet, justices of the Supreme Court, members of Congress, diplomats and foreign dignitaries, and the Joint Chiefs of Staff. Shortly before 1100 the members of the Stevenson family entered the cathedral and were ushered to their seats.

The Reverend Richard Paul Grabel, pastor of the First Presbyterian Church in Springfield, Illinois, and a personal friend of Mr. Stevenson's, conducted the funeral service from the Book of Common Worship of the United Presbyterian Church. Another of Mr. Stevenson's close friends and associates, Judge Carl McGowan of the U.S. Court of Appeals for the District of Columbia, delivered a eulogy.

When the service ended, at 1145, General Wehle, the escort commander, left the cathedral and joined the national color detail at the north transept exit for the departure ceremony. A joint honor cordon had already lined the route from the cathedral to the street, where the hearse and other automobiles of the cortege waited to take Mr. Stevenson's body to Andrews Air Force Base for the flight to Springfield, Illinois. Across the street, directly opposite the northern exit of the cathedral, the Marine Band was in formation. (*Diagram 101*)

After General Wehle had left the cathedral, two Army body bearers wheeled Mr. Stevenson's casket to the north exit. There the full joint body bearer team took the casket from the movable bier and prepared to carry it to the hearse. In the meantime ushers directed the departure of the audience in such a way that the procession could form in proper order and that those who were to ride in the cortege could reach their automobiles quickly.

The joint honor cordon came to attention as the procession moved to the exit with the national color detail leading, followed by the clergy, the casket, the Stevenson family, President Johnson and his party, a special honor guard composed of general and flag officers (two from the Army and one each from the Marine Corps, Navy, Air Force, and Coast Guard), foreign dignitaries, and others in the official party. When the body bearers had brought the casket through the archway, they came to a halt. The Marine Band then played ruffles and flourishes and "Stars and Stripes Forever." As the hymn "Faith of Our Fathers" was begun, the procession again moved forward; the body bearers took the casket to the hearse and placed it inside; other members of the procession stopped at the

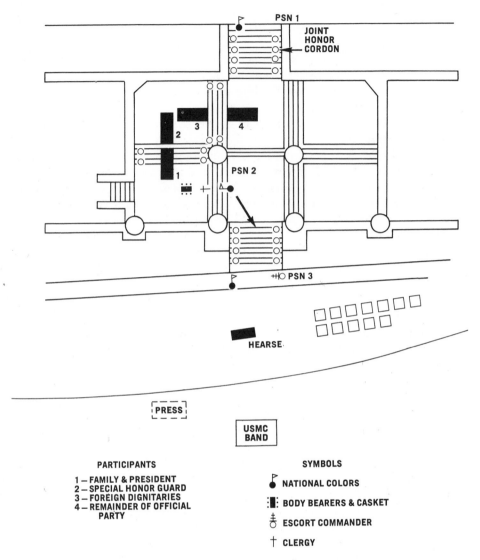

Diagram 101. Departure ceremony, Washington National Cathedral.

bottom of the cathedral steps. The honor cordon then ordered arms, and members of the cortege went to their cars. Shortly before noon, the cortege left for Andrews Air Force Base. A police escort led the way followed by the escort commander, the special honor guard, the hearse, the Stevenson family, President Johnson and his party, foreign dignitaries, Vice President Humphrey and his guests, and other officials, in that order.

CASKET IS CARRIED FROM THE CATHEDRAL

At Andrews Air Force Base a contingent of troops, distinct from that which had been used at the cathedral, was in position for the departure ceremony. A joint honor street cordon of more than 150 men lined both sides of the road to the terminal. Within the ceremonial area, which was enclosed by a security cordon of one officer and eighty-one men from the 3d Infantry, a joint honor cordon of one officer and forty-one men flanked the route that would be followed when the casket was taken from the hearse to the Presidential aircraft, Air Force One. The Air Force Band, a national color detail, and a joint body bearer team were also on hand. (*Table 35*)

The cortege reached the air base at 1240. Each member of the street cordon saluted as the hearse approached him and ordered arms as the last car of the cortege passed. Upon their arrival at the ceremonial area, the Stevenson family and the official party were escorted to their positions in the formation. At the same time the body bearer team moved to the rear of the hearse, which had stopped on line with the honor cordon and the aircraft. (*Diagram 102*)

The Air Force Band sounded ruffles and flourishes, then played "Stars and

TABLE 35—TROOP LIST, DEPARTURE CEREMONY AT ANDREWS AIR FORCE BASE FOR U.S. REPRESENTATIVE TO THE UNITED NATIONS ADLAI E. STEVENSON

Duty	U.S. Army		U.S. Marine Corps		U.S. Navy		U.S. Air Force		U.S. Coast Guard		Total	
	Offi-cers	En-listed Men	Offi-cers	En-listed Men	Offi-cers	En-listed Men	Offi-cers	En-listed Men	Offi-cers	En-listed Men	Offi-cers	En-listed Men
Escort commander and staff	1										1	
Special honor guard	2		1		1		1		1		6	
Honor cordon	1	9		8		8		8		8	1	41
National color detail		1		1		1						3
Body bearers	1	2		2		2		2		2	1	10
Band							1	50			1	50
Street cordon	1	31		31		31		31		31	1	155
Site control							1				1	
Security cordon	1	81									1	81
Floral detail	1	4									1	4
Press cordon		9										9
Baggage detail	1	10									1	10
Total	9	147	1	42	1	42	3	91	1	41	15	363

Stripes Forever." When the band began the hymn "God of Our Fathers," the body bearers removed the casket from the hearse and, preceded by the national color detail and the clergy, carried it through the honor cordon to the plane. After the casket was taken into the aircraft, the band stopped playing. The Stevenson family and some of the official party then boarded Air Force One, which took off for Capitol Airport in Springfield, Illinois, a few minutes after 1300.

The ceremonies in Illinois, as planned under the supervision of Governor Otto Kerner and the Commanding General, Headquarters, Fifth U.S. Army, Lt. Gen. Charles G. Dodge, would mark the arrival of Mr. Stevenson's body at the Springfield airport; the reception of the body at the state capitol; the period of lying in state, including a prayer service in the rotunda of the capitol on 18 July; the removal of the body from the capitol and movement to Bloomington on the 18th; and the funeral and burial services in Bloomington on 19 July. A control headquarters was established in the office of Maj. Gen. Leo M. Boyle, the Adjutant General of Illinois. There, with the assistance of the Senior Advisor and two other members of the Fifth U.S. Army Advisory Group, Army National Guard, Illinois, detailed plans were developed for joint service participation in the ceremonies, involving Army and Air Force National Guard units and Navy and Coast Guard Reserve units (the Marine Corps was not represented). One active Army unit, the 399th U.S. Army Band of Fort Leonard Wood, Missouri, was also included.

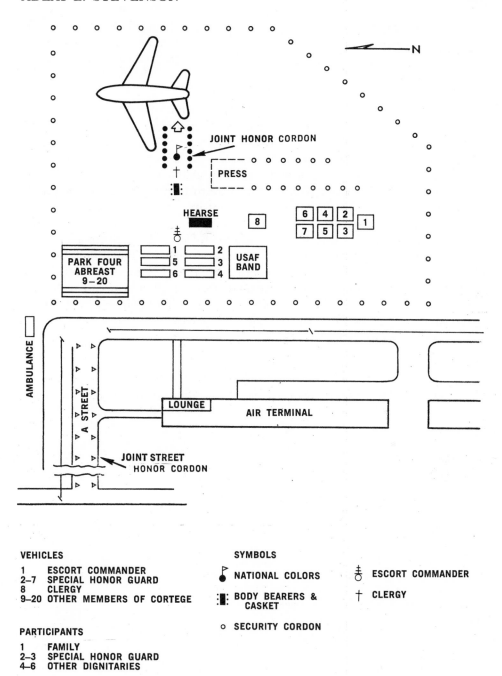

N

JOINT HONOR CORDON

PRESS

HEARSE

PARK FOUR ABREAST 9–20

USAF BAND

AMBULANCE

A STREET

LOUNGE   AIR TERMINAL

JOINT STREET HONOR CORDON

VEHICLES

1 ESCORT COMMANDER
2–7 SPECIAL HONOR GUARD
8 CLERGY
9–20 OTHER MEMBERS OF CORTEGE

PARTICIPANTS

1 FAMILY
2–3 SPECIAL HONOR GUARD
4–6 OTHER DIGNITARIES

SYMBOLS

● NATIONAL COLORS
▮ BODY BEARERS & CASKET
○ SECURITY CORDON

⚥ ESCORT COMMANDER
† CLERGY

Diagram 102.   Departure ceremony, Andrews Air Force Base.

At the time of Mr. Stevenson's death, the major unit scheduled to participate, the 33d Infantry Division of the Illinois Army National Guard, was engaged in its annual field training at Camp McCoy, Wisconsin; rapid preparations had to be made, therefore, to move the participating elements of the division to Springfield. (*Table 36*)

Air Force One landed at Springfield Capitol Airport at 1405 (central standard time) on 16 July. As the wheels of the Presidential plane touched ground, the salute detail from the 33d Infantry Division, using two 105-mm. howitzers, began a 19-gun salute. Firing the rounds at twelve-second intervals, the detail completed the salute during the plane's roll and taxi time of four minutes. As soon as the ramp was in place, Governor Kerner went forward to greet the Stevenson family and other members of the group as they disembarked. The body bearers meanwhile boarded the plane from the opposite side and brought the casket to the plane entrance. The 399th Army Band played ruffles and flourishes and "Stars and Stripes Forever." As the band started the hymn "These Things Shall Be," the body bearers carried Mr. Stevenson's casket from the plane and through the honor cordon formed by the Air National Guard troops to a hearse. The cortege of eighteen cars then formed and, escorted by Illinois State Police, set out for the state capitol. The route followed took the cortege past Abraham Lincoln's tomb in the Oak Ridge Cemetery of Springfield.

TABLE 36—TROOP LIST, ILLINOIS, CEREMONY FOR U.S. REPRESENTATIVE
TO THE UNITED NATIONS ADLAI E. STEVENSON

Participating units
  33d Infantry Division, Illinois Army National Guard
    Salute detail (3 officers, 12 enlisted men)
    Body bearers (1 officer, 8 enlisted men)
    Guard of honor (2 officers, 35 enlisted men)
  399th Army Band (1 chief warrant officer, 32 enlisted men)
  183d Tactical Fighter Group, Illinois Air National Guard
    Honor cordon and guard of honor (2 officers, 50 enlisted men)
  U.S. Naval Reserve Training Center, Springfield, Illinois
    Guard of honor (7 enlisted men)
  U.S. Coast Guard Reserve Training Center, Peoria, Illinois
    Guard of honor (1 officer, 3 enlisted men)
Supporting units
  Headquarters and Headquarters Detachment, Illinois Army National Guard (administrative and
    logistical support of all participating units)
  33d Infantry Division, Illinois Army National Guard (motor transportation)
  U.S. Army Reserve Training Center, Springfield, Illinois (motor transportation)
  126th Air Refueling Wing, Illinois Air National Guard (air transportation)

DEPARTURE CEREMONY AT ANDREWS AIR FORCE BASE

When the procession reached the state capitol, the body bearers carried Adlai Stevenson's casket into the rotunda and placed it on the same walnut table that had once held the casket of Abraham Lincoln nearly a century before. The body bearers were then dismissed and four men, the first relief of the joint guard of honor, took post inside the rope cordon that surrounded the bier, stationing themselves at the corners of the casket, facing outward. All round surveillance was maintained constantly by the guard, each relief standing a twenty-minute watch. At 1700 on the 16th the public was admitted to the rotunda, which remained open until midmorning on the 18th. During that time some 75,000 persons passed by the bier.

Shortly before 1000 on 18 July, a prayer service was conducted in the rotunda by the Reverend Corneal A. Davis, who was also a representative to the state legislature from Chicago. Only the immediate family, a few close friends, and state officials, including Governor Kerner, were present. As soon as the service ended, the guard of honor was dismissed, and the body bearers carried the casket to the hearse, which was drawn up just outside the entrance to the capitol. The Stevenson family, a few friends, and the body bearers then entered automobiles, and the cortege left for Bloomington, some sixty miles away. When it arrived at the Unitarian Church in Bloomington, the body bearers carried the casket into the Jesse Fell Assembly Room, where it would remain until the funeral service was held in the sanctuary at 1100 on 19 July.

Originally, the family had planned a private funeral service; however, on the evening of 17 July it was announced from the White House that President and Mrs. Johnson, Vice President and Mrs. Humphrey, and Chief Justice and Mrs. Warren would attend. This announcement prompted changes. Dignitaries of both the national and state governments were invited; six press representatives were permitted to attend; and the Stevenson family agreed to allow one television crew to make a tape of the service (without the use of artificial lighting) which could be made available to the three national networks. Invited dignitaries included Justice and Mrs. Arthur J. Goldberg; Governor and Mrs. Kerner; Illinois Senator and Mrs. Paul H. Douglas; Secretary of Labor W. Willard Wirtz; R. Sargent Shriver, head of the Peace Corps and the Office of Economic Opportunity; Governor and Mrs. Edmund G. Brown of California; Governor and Mrs. Karl F. Rolvaag of Minnesota; Newton N. Minow, former chairman of the Federal Communications Commission, and Mrs. Minow; J. Edward Day, former Postmaster General, and Mrs. Day; William McCormick Blair, Ambassador to the Philippines and a former law partner of Mr. Stevenson's, and Mrs. Blair; Judge Carl McGowan and Mrs. McGowan; and Illinois Representative Sydney Yates and Mrs. Yates.

The Reverend Robert Reed, pastor of the Unitarian Church, officiated at the service on 19 July. He was assisted by the Reverend Martin D. Hardin, an associate minister of the Presbyterian Church of Buffalo, New York, and a cousin of Mr. Stevenson's, and by Dr. Dana McLean Greeley, president of the Unitarian Universalist Association. Twenty-one members of the Children's Choir of the First Unitarian Church of Chicago sang hymns.

Immediately following the service, those who had attended took their places in the cortege for the three-mile journey to Evergreen Memorial Cemetery where Mr. Stevenson would be buried in the family plot. The body bearers from the 33d Infantry Division brought the casket to the hearse, then joined the cortege to the cemetery where they would handle the casket during the graveside ceremony.

Reverend Robert Reed also conducted the burial service. After the last prayer, the body bearers folded the flag that had draped the casket. The officer in charge then presented it to Mrs. Ernest Ives, the sister of Mr. Stevenson, who in turn gave it to one of his sons, thus concluding the final rites for the American delegate to the United Nations, who had been governor of his state and twice a candidate for the Presidency of the United States.

CHAPTER XXVII

Secretary of the Navy-Designate John T. McNaughton, Sarah McNaughton, and Theodore McNaughton Special Military Funeral 19-25 July 1967

Near noon on 19 July 1967, a Piedmont Airlines Boeing 727 and a private plane that was off its course collided and exploded over the Blue Ridge foothills in western North Carolina near Hendersonville, not far from the city of Asheville where the Piedmont plane had taken off only minutes before. All persons aboard both planes were killed. Among the passengers on the airliner were Secretary of the Navy-designate John T. McNaughton, his wife, Sarah, and the younger of his two sons, Theodore.

Mr. McNaughton was to have taken office as Secretary of the Navy on 1 August. At the time of his death he was Assistant Secretary of Defense for International Security Affairs, a post he had held since 1964. As Department of Defense officials considered formal funeral honors for Mr. McNaughton, a question arose as to his exact official status at the time of his death. As Assistant Secretary of Defense, he was entitled, under existing policies, to an Armed Forces Full Honor Funeral. As Secretary of the Navy, he was entitled to the more elaborate ceremonies of a Special Military Funeral. The decision, based on the fact that the Senate had confirmed his appointment as Secretary of the Navy, was that Mr. McNaughton was entitled to the greater honor of a Special Military Funeral.

Secretary and Mrs. McNaughton were survived by their eighteen-year-old son, Alexander, their parents, and the Secretary's two brothers and his sister. In consultations between Department of Defense officials and the next of kin, it was tentatively decided that a funeral service for Secretary McNaughton, his wife, and his son would be held in Pekin, Illinois, where the Secretary's parents resided, and that burial would take place in Arlington National Cemetery. Mr. McNaughton was eligible for burial in a national cemetery by virtue of World War II service as a commissioned officer in the Navy. Mrs. McNaughton also had served during World War II as an ensign in the WAVES. The final decision, however, was that a funeral service for the three members of the McNaughton family would be held in Washington, D.C., at the Washington National Cathedral on 25 July, with burial in Arlington Cemetery.

The commandant of the Naval District Washington, Rear Adm. Elliott Loughlin, would automatically have become responsible for completing funeral arrangements, in accordance with the current policy that the responsibility fell to the service with which the deceased had been associated. But at the specific request of the Naval District, the Commanding General, Military District of Washington, Maj. Gen. Curtis J. Herrick, accepted the responsibility for arranging and co-ordinating the ceremonies.

According to the plan, a Navy transport plane was to bring the bodies of Secretary and Mrs. McNaughton and their son from North Carolina to Andrews Air Force Base on 24 July. From there, the bodies were to be taken to Gawler's funeral establishment in Washington, D.C. A joint service arrival ceremony, based on the current prescriptions for a Special Military Funeral published in 1965, was to be conducted at the airfield. But since the arrival and transfer of the bodies to the funeral home were considered primarily administrative moves, some of the usual procedures of an arrival ceremony, including the presence of a band, special honor guard, and honorary pallbearers, were to be eliminated.

The site control officer at the field was to be from the 3d Infantry. One officer and thirty-eight enlisted men of the Navy were to form a security cordon surrounding the ceremonial area, and the Navy was also to furnish three body bearer teams of six men each (plus two supernumeraries) and the petty officer in charge. A joint honor cordon, which would line the route from the parked aircraft to the three hearses from Gawler's, was to be commanded by a Navy officer and to include eight men each from the Army, Marine Corps, Navy, Air Force, and Coast Guard. An Army color bearer and a guard each from the Marine Corps and the Air Force would make up the national color detail; the personal flag bearer would be a Navy man.

The plane bearing the bodies of Secretary McNaughton and his wife and son landed at Andrews field a few minutes after 1400 on 24 July. When the lift truck was brought up to lower the caskets from the plane, it was discovered that the platform would hold only two of the three caskets. The body bearer teams were consequently under considerable strain, being obliged to hold the first two caskets while the third was removed from the plane separately. The caskets were then carried in procession through the joint honor cordon to the hearses and taken to Gawler's funeral establishment, where they remained until the funeral service at the Washington National Cathedral on 25 July.

The service was held at 1300. During the morning of 25 July, troops that were to support or participate in the ceremony reported to the site control officer, who was from the 3d Infantry, at the cathedral. After briefing and rehearsal, all troops were in position by 1230. A security cordon of one officer, one noncommissioned officer, and thirty-five enlisted men from the 3d Infantry took post around the north transept entrance of the cathedral to keep the ceremonial area clear. A parking and traffic control detail of five officers, eleven noncommissioned officers,

CASKETS ARE PLACED IN HEARSES AT ANDREWS AIR FORCE BASE

and thirty-three enlisted men, also from the 3d Infantry, was on station, with a member of the cathedral police and two members of the Metropolitan Police assisting. A smaller detail of one officer, one noncommissioned officer, and five enlisted men from the 3d Infantry was on hand to control the movement of members of the press. One of the earliest to arrive at the cathedral was a detail of six men furnished by the Navy to handle all floral pieces.

An Army officer was in charge of a joint service detail of seventy-five officers and men (one officer, two noncommissioned officers, and twelve men from each service), who were to escort those attending the cathedral service to their seats. Escort officers also were present to assist and guide the honorary pallbearers during the ceremonies.

Persons invited to attend the service began to take their places in the cathedral about half an hour before the scheduled time. Members of the McNaughton family arrived at 1250, the honorary pallbearers, Vice President Hubert H. Humphrey and his party, and President Lyndon B. Johnson and his party in the next ten minutes. The arrival of the family and dignitaries, all at the north transept entrance and all at approximately the same time, caused some confusion, but with

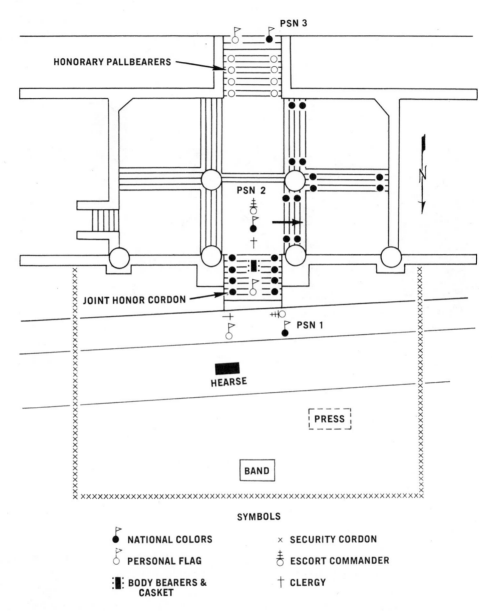

HONORARY PALLBEARERS

PSN 3

PSN 2

JOINT HONOR CORDON

PSN 1

HEARSE

PRESS

BAND

SYMBOLS

● NATIONAL COLORS   × SECURITY CORDON

○ PERSONAL FLAG   ♯○ ESCORT COMMANDER

▮ BODY BEARERS &   † CLERGY
  CASKET

Diagram 103.   Standard formation, arrival ceremony, Washington, D.C.

CASKETS ARE TAKEN INTO WASHINGTON NATIONAL CATHEDRAL

the help of the site control officer, who performed as an usher himself, all were seated without undue delay.

The arrival ceremony was based on procedures in the 1965 policy book, although no escort commander participated. (*Diagram 103*) The honorary pallbearers, among whom was Secretary of Defense Robert S. McNamara, formed a cordon on the steps of the north transept entrance to the cathedral. A joint honor cordon of troops lined the remaining steps to the street. At the foot of the steps stood the clergy, national color detail, and personal flag bearer, and across the street, opposite the cathedral entrance, the U.S. Marine Band was in formation. Nearby were three joint service body bearer teams.

Ten minutes before the scheduled beginning of the service, hearses bearing the bodies of the three members of the McNaughton family, accompanied only by a police escort, arrived at the cathedral and halted in column along the side of the driveway leading to the north transept entrance. At the scheduled hour, they were driven to the north transept entrance and parked abreast. The U.S. Marine Band sounded ruffles and flourishes, and as it began to play a hymn the three body bearer teams removed the three caskets from the hearses simultaneously. They

FUNERAL SERVICE IN THE CATHEDRAL

were then borne in procession through the honor cordon into the cathedral, the national color detail leading, the clergy, the caskets of Secretary McNaughton, Mrs. McNaughton, and Theodore McNaughton and the personal flag bearer following. Inside the cathedral entrance the caskets, those of the Secretary and Mrs. McNaughton draped with flags, that of their son undraped, were placed on movable biers and taken forward for the service.

Mr. Adam Yarmolinsky, who had been a deputy to Mr. McNaughton during his tenure as Assistant Secretary of Defense, opened the funeral service by delivering a eulogy. Religious services were then conducted by Canon William G. Workman of the Washington National Cathedral, Dr. Joseph A. Mason of the Grace Methodist Church (the McNaughton family church) in Pekin, Illinois, and the Right Reverend Paul Moore, Jr., suffragan bishop of Washington. Two hymns were sung during the service, one of them the Navy hymn, "Eternal Father, Strong to Save." These were led by the U.S. Navy Band Sea Chanters. The service ended about 1345. The caskets were then taken from the cathedral in procession, and the motor cortege, without military escort, departed for Arlington National Cemetery. The departure ceremony followed established procedure, but

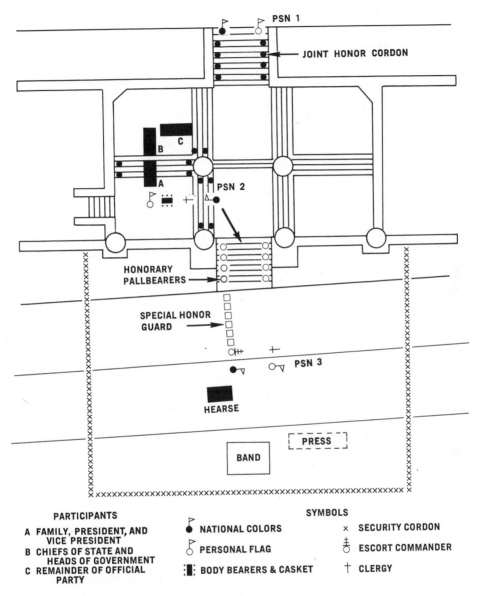

Diagram 104.   Standard formation, departure ceremony,
Washington National Cathedral.

without the participation of an escort commander or special honor guard. (*Diagram 104*)

According to plan, the cortege was to proceed to Memorial Gate of the cemetery. There, before a military escort drawn up on the green, the casket of Secretary McNaughton was to be transferred from the hearse to a caisson. After the transfer ceremony, the military escort was to lead the cortege into the cemetery to the gravesite in Section 5, northeast of the Custis-Lee Mansion.

In preparation for the casket transfer at the cemetery gate, all troops who were to participate in or support the ceremony were in position by 1330. The military escort included a Navy officer as commander, with a joint service staff of four, and five companies of troops, one each from the Army, Marine Corps, Navy, Air Force, and Coast Guard. Each escort company had a commander, two other officers, and sixty-three enlisted men. The escort also included the U.S. Navy Band. The entire formation was on line on the lawn at the gate, facing Memorial Drive over which the cortege would approach.

In front of and facing the escort, the caisson and caisson detail from the 3d Infantry were in the center of Memorial Drive. To the left front of the caisson a handler stood with a caparisoned horse that was to march in the cortege through the cemetery to the gravesite. To the right of the caisson stood a joint national color detail and a Navy enlisted man with the personal flag of Secretary McNaughton. Along the edge of Memorial Drive to the rear of the color bearers waited three body bearer teams, all from the Navy. (*Diagram 105*)

On the lawn across the street from the body bearer teams, an area cordoned by four enlisted men from the 3d Infantry had been reserved for members of the press. Other supporting troops included a 3d Infantry parking detail of one officer and four noncommissioned officers. These men were to guide the vehicles of the cortege to their positions for the casket transfer ceremony. Finally, one noncommissioned officer and twenty men from the 3d Infantry were posted as a security cordon to keep the ceremonial area clear.

Near 1430, as the cortege approached Memorial Gate, the cars were halted in a double column a short distance below the ceremonial area. Those carrying the clergy and honorary pallbearers were then signaled forward and were brought to a stop just after they turned north off Memorial Drive onto Schley Drive. The clergy and honorary pallbearers then dismounted and were guided to their positions for the transfer ceremony.

The three hearses and the cars carrying the family were next signaled forward. The hearse bearing the casket of Secretary McNaughton was halted to the right and even with the caisson; the other two hearses drew up abreast immediately behind the caisson. Immediately behind them the cars of the family were arranged in a single column. The family remained in the cars while the casket transfer ceremony took place. (*Diagram 106*)

After the hearses and family vehicles had been brought forward, the three

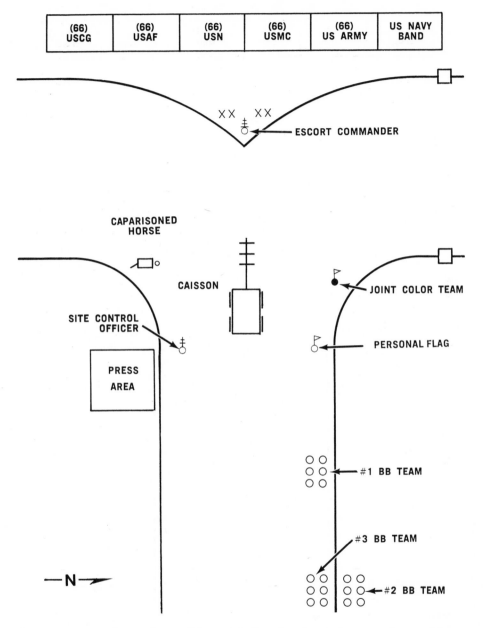

(66) USCG	(66) USAF	(66) USN	(66) USMC	(66) US ARMY	US NAVY BAND

ESCORT COMMANDER

CAPARISONED
HORSE

CAISSON

JOINT COLOR TEAM

SITE CONTROL
OFFICER

PERSONAL FLAG

PRESS
AREA

#1 BB TEAM

#3 BB TEAM

—N→

#2 BB TEAM

Diagram 105.   Formation at Memorial Gate for the casket transfer ceremony.

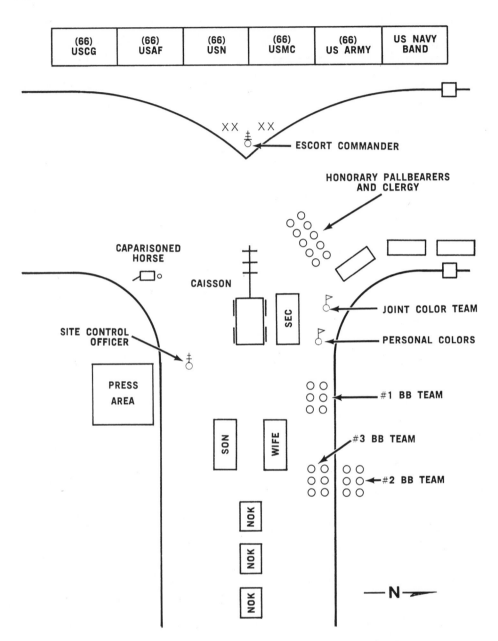

Diagram 106.   Casket transfer ceremony, arrival of cortege.

MILITARY ESCORT RENDERS HONORS *as casket of John McNaughton is transferred to caisson at Memorial Gate, above. Military escort marches through cemetery, below.*

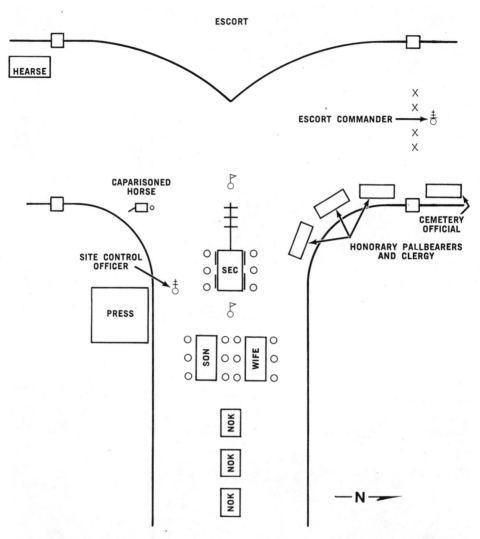

Diagram 107.   Formation at Memorial Gate after the casket transfer ceremony.

body bearer teams took position. One team moved to the rear of the hearse bearing the casket of Secretary McNaughton. Those assigned to carry the other two caskets took a position flanking the hearse, three men on either side. The U.S. Navy Band sounded ruffles and flourishes and the escort troop units presented arms. The band then played a hymn.

While the hymn was played, the body bearers transferred Secretary McNaughton's casket from the hearse to the caisson. After the hearse was driven away from the ceremonial area, the body bearers took positions flanking the caisson, three men on each side. The escort units then ordered arms, the clergy and honorary pallbearers returned to their cars on Schley Drive, and the escort commander and his staff moved off the green to a position on Schley Drive to lead the procession into the cemetery. Mr. John C. Metzler, cemetery superintendent, meanwhile had arrived to guide the procession to the gravesite. (*Diagram 107*)

Since the gravesite in Section 5 was very near the grave of President John F. Kennedy, troops from the 3d Infantry formed a cordon between the two sites to separate persons attending the McNaughton rites from those visiting the Kennedy grave. Additional troops from the 3d Infantry, who brought the number assigned to security duty to one officer and fifty-four men, cordoned a larger perimeter around the McNaughton gravesite to keep the ceremonial area clear. The 3d Infantry also supplied one officer and nineteen men to control traffic along the route of the procession to the gravesite.

As the procession marched via Schley, Sherman, and Sheridan Drives, the 3d Infantry battery, from its distant position in the cemetery, fired a 17-gun salute, spacing the rounds so that the last was fired close to the time that the procession reached the gravesite. (*Diagram 108*) When they were near the gravesite, the Navy Band and one platoon of each of the escort companies broke off from the formation and moved to their assigned positions at the graveside. The remainder

Diagram 108.   Route of march, Memorial Gate to gravesite.

NAVY BODY BEARERS CARRY CASKET OF
JOHN MCNAUGHTON TO GRAVE

of the escort units, not scheduled to participate in the graveside ceremony, continued to march, moving out of the ceremonial area to dismissal points.

When the cortege reached the gravesite, the caisson and two hearses were halted near a coco-mat runner leading to the graves. The national color team moved to a position between the caisson and the gravesite and the honorary pallbearers, after they had left their cars, were escorted forward to form a cordon along the cocomat runner. The remainder of the funeral party assembled behind the caisson and the two hearses.

At signals from the cemetery superintendent and the site control officer, the escort units at the grave presented arms and the Navy Band sounded ruffles and

flourishes. The band then began a hymn and the body bearers removed the caskets from the caisson and the hearses. The three caskets were taken in procession through the cordon of honorary pallbearers to the graves. As the procession passed, the honorary pallbearers fell in behind and were guided to their graveside position by the site control officer. The cemetery superintendent and his assistants then led the next of kin and other members of the funeral party to their positions. (*Diagram 109*)

At the conclusion of the graveside service, the battery delivered a second 17-gun salute, firing the rounds at five-second intervals. After the last round was fired the benediction was pronounced. A firing squad then delivered three volleys and a Navy bugler sounded taps, thus concluding the final rites for John T. McNaughton, who would have been the fifty-ninth Secretary of the Navy, and for his wife and son.

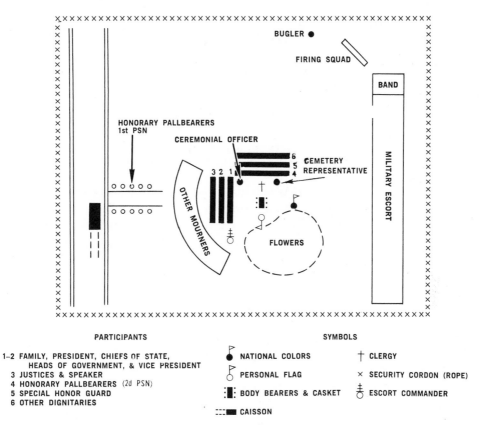

PARTICIPANTS

1–2 FAMILY, PRESIDENT, CHIEFS OF STATE,
    HEADS OF GOVERNMENT, & VICE PRESIDENT
3 JUSTICES & SPEAKER
4 HONORARY PALLBEARERS (2d PSN)
5 SPECIAL HONOR GUARD
6 OTHER DIGNITARIES

SYMBOLS

NATIONAL COLORS   † CLERGY
PERSONAL FLAG   × SECURITY CORDON (ROPE)
BODY BEARERS & CASKET   ESCORT COMMANDER
CAISSON

Diagram 109.   Formation at the graveside (schematic).

CHAPTER XXVIII

Senator Robert F. Kennedy
Funeral Without Formal Classification
5-8 June 1968

During the first minutes of Wednesday, 5 June 1968, Senator Robert F. Kennedy, while campaigning for nomination as candidate for the Democratic party in the coming Presidential election, was shot and critically wounded by an assassin in the Ambassador Hotel in Los Angeles, California. Senator Kennedy was rushed to Good Samaritan Hospital in Los Angeles, but intensive efforts failed to save his life. He died at 0144 (Pacific daylight time) on 6 June.

As it became less and less likely that the medical efforts to save Senator Kennedy would succeed, his brother, Edward, a brother-in-law, Stephen Smith, and a close friend, John Seigenthaler, outlined a funeral and burial plan. The plan called for a requiem mass at St. Patrick's Cathedral in New York City, the movement of the senator's body to Washington, D.C., by train, and burial in Arlington National Cemetery, all to take place on Saturday, 8 June. Ethel Kennedy, the widow, approved this outline shortly after her husband's death. The family then completed plans to take Senator Kennedy's body to New York City.

Upon receiving the news of Senator Kennedy's death, President Lyndon B. Johnson in Washington directed that all flags on federal buildings, installations, and naval vessels in the United States and abroad be flown at half-staff until after the senator's burial and proclaimed Sunday, 9 June, a day of national mourning. After learning later that burial would take place on 8 June, he extended the period in which flags were to be at half-staff to include the day of mourning.

When the President was informed of the general plan for the funeral ceremony for Senator Kennedy, he ordered an Air Force 707 jet transport sent to Los Angeles to carry the body, members of the Kennedy family, and close friends to New York City. The transport reached the Los Angeles terminal in time for an early afternoon return flight on 6 June. With the body and more than seventy people aboard, the plane touched down at La Guardia Airport at 2057 (eastern daylight time).

During the afternoon of the 6th, Secretary of Defense Clark M. Clifford formally directed that military support be furnished Senator Kennedy's family in connection with the funeral and designated the Department of the Army as the agency primarily responsible. Within the Office of the Secretary of Defense, the official in charge was Alfred B. Fitt, Assistant Secretary of Defense for Manpower and Reserve Affairs. Under Secretary of State Nicholas deB. Katzenbach was to work with Mr. Fitt and together they would co-ordinate funeral arrangements and provide liaison between the Kennedy family and authorities in Washington. The work of making ceremonial arrangements fell to the Military District of Washington.

Early on 6 June, in anticipation of the task eventually assigned to the Army, Maj. Gen. Charles S. O'Malley, Jr., commanding the Military District of Washington, opened a funeral operations center at his headquarters and established liaisons with other agencies that were likely to be called upon to participate in the funeral arrangements. As had been the case in 1963 when President John F. Kennedy was assassinated, no contingency funeral plans for Senator Kennedy existed, and again planning would have to be completed within a short time and started with little direct contact with the next of kin.

During the morning of the 6th, before the wishes of the next of kin were known, the Chief of Staff and other officials briefed Secretary of the Army Stanley R. Resor on the funeral arrangements. At the same time, the extent of military participation and the question of whether the senator's body should lie in state in the rotunda of the Capitol were discussed. Subsequently, Barrett E. Prettyman, Jr., a Washington attorney and close friend of the Kennedy family, delivered to Washington officials a message from Mrs. Kennedy: she wished a minimum of military participation in the ceremonies and did not favor a lying in state ceremony at the Capitol. Mr. Prettyman, along with Herbert Schmertz of Senator Kennedy's Washington office represented the Kennedy family during the planning of the Washington ceremonies and would handle the details of the arrival of Senator Kennedy's body in Washington and the movement to Arlington National Cemetery. Military officials would be in charge of only those ceremonies taking place inside the cemetery.

At a time when the exact military support that the Kennedy family would require in either New York City or Washington was still unknown, Paul C. Miller of the Military District of Washington, Maj. Robert C. Bacon of the Office of the Army Chief of Staff, John C. Metzler, the superintendent of Arlington National Cemetery, Mr. Fitt from the Office of the Secretary of Defense, and Robert E. Jordan III, Special Assistant to the Secretary of the Army for Civil Functions, met at Arlington National Cemetery. They considered four possible gravesites for Senator Kennedy, all of them in the vicinity of President Kennedy's grave, and took pictures which could be useful to the widow or her representative in making a final choice.

The group next met in Mr. Metzler's cemetery office to discuss possible ceremonies in Washington for Senator Kennedy, in particular, ceremonies at the cemetery. During the discussion, Mr. Metzler mentioned that a precedent existed for holding no ceremonies in Arlington National Cemetery beyond 1500 on Saturdays and asked by what means this precedent could be broken. Mr. Jordan replied that the large audience anticipated for the graveside rites was sufficient justification for holding the ceremony after the traditional closing hour. He also pointed out that holding the ceremony late Saturday would prevent rescheduling other funerals for the following week.

Since Senator Kennedy had served as a seaman in the Navy, Mr. Miller recommended Navy Special Full Honor ceremonies, which included use of Navy body bearers, a Navy firing squad, and a Navy bugler. The decision could not be made, however, until the wishes of the next of kin were known. Lt. Col. Hugh G. Robinson, an Army officer, had been sent on the plane to Los Angeles by the President to act as military aide to the family, and it was hoped that he would soon provide the needed information.

Mr. Fitt himself was scheduled to fly to New York City later in the afternoon of the 6th and would be at La Guardia Airport to meet the plane bringing the body of Senator Kennedy and the Kennedy family from Los Angeles. He had wanted to take with him the full plans for ceremonies in Washington, but, as Mr. Miller explained, plans could not be completed until the wishes of the next of kin were known. As an alternative, Mr. Miller proposed that Lt. Col. Robert H. Clark, from the Ceremonies and Special Events Office of the Military District of Washington, should accompany Mr. Fitt to New York to advise him and the Kennedy family during any discussion of the Washington ceremonies. Further, Mr. Miller promised to arrange for military participation in the ceremonies in New York if the Kennedy family wished. As it turned out, the only family request was made by Senator Edward M. Kennedy, who asked for four members of the Army Special Forces (Green Berets) to serve with an otherwise civilian guard of honor at the bier while the body lay in St. Patrick's Cathedral. On 7 June four Special Forces sergeants arrived in New York from Fort Bragg, North Carolina, to complete the guard of honor.

Mr. Fitt, accompanied by Mr. Katzenbach of the Department of State and Colonel Clark, left Andrews Air Force Base for New York City at 1730 on the 6th. Landing at Kennedy Airport, Mr. Fitt and Colonel Clark remained there to meet the plane bearing former Secretary of Defense Robert S. McNamara, now president of the World Bank, and his wife, who were coming from Europe to attend the Kennedy rites. Mr. Katzenbach meanwhile went into the city to Kennedy Campaign Headquarters at 200 Park Avenue, where a meeting with members of the Kennedy family would be held later.

Mr. and Mrs. McNamara arrived at 2000 and went with Mr. Fitt and Colonel Clark to La Guardia field. Also there to meet the Air Force plane bearing Senator Kennedy's body were New York Governor Nelson A. Rockefeller, New York Senator Jacob K. Javits, Mayor of New York City John V. Lindsay, and U.S. Representative to the United Nations Arthur Goldberg. About a thousand persons watched the proceedings from behind a fence some 200 feet away.

When the plane arrived, the Kennedy family stood close by as the casket, handled by persons who had accompanied the body from Los Angeles, was taken off the plane. There was a pause while Archbishop Terrence J. Cooke of New York delivered a prayer. The casket was then placed in the hearse, the family, friends, and dignitaries entered automobiles, and the cortege proceeded to St. Patrick's Cathedral. When it arrived about 2145, Archbishop Cooke offered another prayer as the casket was carried up the steps. Afterward Senator Kennedy's body was taken inside and the archbishop conducted a short service. Most of the people who had been in attendance then left the cathedral, but some took post at Senator Kennedy's bier as a guard of honor.

After the cathedral ceremony, Edward Kennedy, Stephen Smith, Mr. Fitt, Mr. Katzenbach, and Colonel Clark conferred at Kennedy Campaign Headquarters on the ceremonies to be held in Washington, especially on the extent of military participation. The family representatives presented their plans to take Senator Kennedy's body in a motorcade from Union Station to Arlington National Cemetery. En route the procession was to pause at the Department of Justice building on Constitution Avenue in recognition of Senator Kennedy's position as Attorney General during his brother's tenure as President; a second pause was to be made at the Lincoln Memorial, where a choir was to sing. The family representatives asked that a military band, joint service honor cordon, and Navy body bearer team meet the funeral train at Union Station, but they wanted no military escort or other troops in the procession to Arlington National Cemetery. Nor did they wish military participation or support at the cemetery beyond that required for traffic control. They also announced that they were making arrangements to have the Harvard University Band participate in the graveside rites. During the meeting there was some discussion of the selection of the gravesite but no final decision was made.

Mr. Fitt, Mr. Katzenbach, and Colonel Clark returned to Washington after this meeting. Before leaving New York, Mr. Fitt instructed Colonel Clark to take the precaution of having a Navy body bearer team stand by in Arlington National Cemetery at the time of the burial rites. Arriving at Andrews Air Force Base at 0330 on 7 June, the three men had all the necessary information for detailed planning of the funeral except the choice of the cemetery plot.

Mrs. Kennedy selected a gravesite late on 7 June. During the day Mr. McNamara had flown to Washington, inspected the four recommended sites, and returned to New York City to present his findings to the widow. Mrs. Kennedy then chose the site, which, when viewed from President Kennedy's grave, was just to the left. (*Diagram 110*) Her choice was communicated to Washington officials at 2200 on the 7th.

During several meetings held on the 7th meanwhile, the Washington planners completed the work of setting the sequence and composition of the ceremonies in Washington and of designating the military units that would participate. The fu-

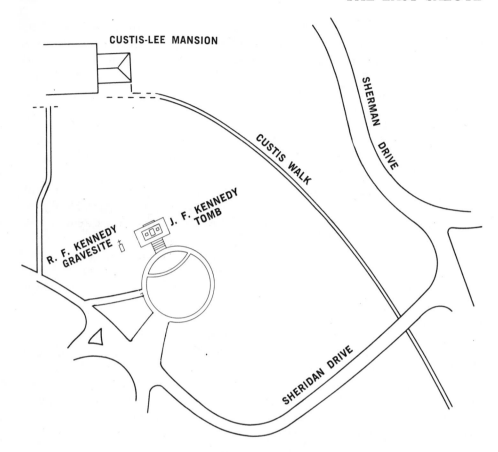

Diagram 110.   Location of the gravesite.

neral train from New York was scheduled to reach Union Station in Washington about 1620 on 8 June. One section of cars bearing dignitaries, family friends, members of the Kennedy staff, and members of the press was to arrive first on Track 16; the second section, the funeral car and cars bearing the Kennedy family and close friends, was to arrive next on Track 17. A Navy body bearer team of eight, supervised by a petty officer, from the Ceremonial Guard, Naval District Washington, was to wait on the platform. The casket was to be removed through a window of the funeral car by persons inside the car; the Navy body bearers were to receive it, carry it halfway through a joint service honor cordon, then halt to wait for all passengers to leave the train.

The honor cordon of 211 officers and men was to be provided in almost equal contingents by the 3d Infantry, Fort Myer, Virginia; the Ceremonial and Guard

Company, Marine Barracks, Washington; the Ceremonial Guard, Naval District Washington; the Air Force Honor Guard, Bolling Air Force Base, Washington; and the Coast Guard Ceremonial Honor Guard from Washington Radio Station, Alexandria, Virginia. An officer from the 3d Infantry would command the cordon troops.

When all passengers had left the train and after the family group had reached a position near the hearse, the body bearers were to carry the casket to the hearse while the U.S. Navy Band, standing near the hearse, was to play the Navy hymn "Eternal Father, Strong to Save." After Senator Kennedy's casket had been placed in the hearse, the body bearer team was to step aside as the family and others in the funeral party entered automobiles for the motorcade to Arlington National Cemetery. Including site control officials and supporting troops, all from the 3d Infantry, the officers and men performing duty during the arrival ceremony at Union Station would total 299. (*Table 37*)

In deference to the wishes of the Kennedy family, no military units would move with the procession to the cemetery. During the march ten musicians from the U.S. Marine Band were to accompany two local choirs that the Kennedy family had arranged to have sing together at the Lincoln Memorial when the motorcade paused there.

On the other hand, a large number of troops would assist civil police units in securing the route of march as far as the cemetery gate. District of Columbia civil authorities had requested 1,390 members of the District of Columbia National Guard, 1,284 from the Army, and 106 from the Air Force, who were to assemble for training early on 8 June at the District of Columbia Armory and at Camp Sims, the guard training camp in Southeast Washington. (*Table 38*) In addition, the Military District of Washington was to furnish 300 members of the active

TABLE 37—TROOP LIST, ARRIVAL CEREMONY AT UNION STATION, WASHINGTON, D.C., FOR SENATOR ROBERT F. KENNEDY

Duty	U.S. Army		U.S. Marine Corps		U.S. Navy		U.S. Air Force		U.S. Coast Guard		Total	
	Officers	Enlisted Men	Officers	Enlisted Men	Officers	Enlisted Men	Officers	Enlisted Men	Officers	Enlisted Men	Officers	Enlisted Men
Honor cordon	1	50	.....	42	....	42	.....	42	....	34	1	210
Body bearers	.....	.....	.....	.....	....	9	.....	.....	....	.....	.....	9
Band	.....	.....	.....	.....	1	48	.....	.....	....	.....	1	48
Site control	2	1	.....	.....	....	.....	.....	.....	....	.....	2	1
Press cordon	....	11	.....	.....	....	.....	.....	.....	....	.....	.....	11
Medical support	1	7	.....	.....	....	.....	.....	.....	....	.....	1	7
Door openers	1	7	.....	.....	....	.....	.....	.....	....	.....	1	7
Total	5	76	.....	42	1	99	.....	42	....	34	6	293

TABLE 38—SUPPORTING NATIONAL GUARD UNITS, WASHINGTON, D.C.,
CEREMONY FOR SENATOR ROBERT F. KENNEDY

District of Columbia Army National Guard

Headquarters and Headquarters Detachment, District of Columbia Army National Guard
Headquarters and Headquarters Detachment, 260th Military Police Group
Headquarters and Headquarters Detachment, 163d Military Police Battalion
Company A, 163d Military Police Battalion
Company B, 163d Military Police Battalion
Company C, 163d Military Police Battalion
Company D, 163d Military Police Battalion
Headquarters and Headquarters Detachment, 171st Military Police Battalion
Company A, 171st Military Police Battalion
Company B, 171st Military Police Battalion
Company C, 171st Military Police Battalion
104th Light Maintenance Company
115th Evacuation Hospital
140th Engineer Detachment
257th Army Band

District of Columbia Air National Guard

231st Mobile Communications Squadron
231st Flight Facilities Flight

armed forces to participate in safeguarding the route. These Regulars, most of the
National Guard troops, 900 Metropolitan Police, and Washington's entire Park
Police force were to cordon the full route from Union Station to Memorial Gate
of the cemetery. Part of the National Guard contingent was to constitute a reserve
force available in the event of civil disturbances.

Some 350 officers and men of the 3d Infantry were to support the ceremonies
at Arlington National Cemetery; most of them—three companies—were to form
a security cordon surrounding a large area centered on the gravesite. (*Diagram
111*) The others were assigned to traffic control or were to assist members of the
funeral party. Two platoons of the 3d Infantry were to stand by at Fort Myer in
case of civil disturbance. Also, as Mr. Fitt had directed, eight Navy body bearers
were to be on hand near the gravesite, prepared to carry the casket from the
hearse to the grave if their help was requested. Finally, in a precautionary move
that proved unnecessary, the Military District of Washington on 8 June alerted
the U.S. Army Band to be prepared to play at the graveside if the Harvard University Band was unable to be present.

Besides the troops, an important feature of military support arranged for the
ceremonies in Washington was motor transportation. Under the supervision of the
Military District of Washington, forty-six passenger cars, twenty-five buses, five

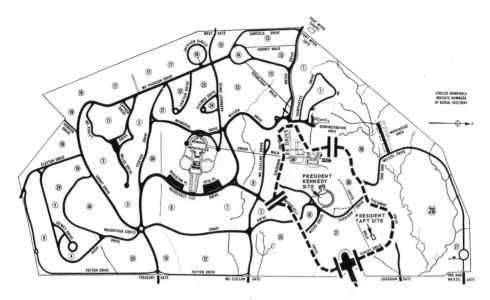

Diagram 111.   Cordon at the gravesite, Arlington National Cemetery.

station wagons, two trucks, and an ambulance were reserved for the ceremonies. These included limousines, sedans, and 45-passenger buses for transporting the Kennedy family and others in the funeral party to and from Arlington National Cemetery, buses of varying capacity for carrying members of the press to and from the ceremonial sites, and vehicles to meet the transportation needs of various officials and dignitaries. The motor pools at Fort Myer, Fort McNair, and the Army Service Center for the Armed Forces supplied most of the vehicles, and drivers were provided from the same sources. Some commercial buses were chartered. Eventually, five civilian and eighty military drivers were employed; twenty-eight additional military drivers were held in readiness but were not used.

Preparations were made to set up audio systems at the Lincoln Memorial to carry the choir music and at Arlington National Cemetery for the graveside service. Six Army photographers were assigned to cover the ceremonies, two each to be posted at Union Station, the entrance to the cemetery, and the gravesite. Army engineers were to erect press stands and to install electric circuits at Union Station and Arlington Cemetery. In addition, arrangements were made with the telephone company to put in lines at the ceremonial sites.

The method by which the motorcade from Union Station to the cemetery was to be televised received special attention. Network representatives would have preferred to broadcast the event as they would have an inaugural parade, that is, to employ mobile units on the streets, one at the head of the cortege and others "wrapped around" it. But military officials restricted coverage to cameras in fixed locations or carried along the sidewalks, a restriction that also had been applied to televising President Kennedy's funeral procession.

In New York City, where Senator Kennedy's body lay in St. Patrick's Cathedral, long lines of people passed by the bier until 0500 on 8 June, when the cathedral was closed to the public in preparation for the pontifical requiem mass. Invitations to the mass had been extended by the Kennedy family and its representatives to more than 2,000 persons, including President and Mrs. Johnson, Vice President and Mrs. Hubert H. Humphrey, government and military officials, professional people, and friends. Of those attending the mass, some 700 were invited to travel in the funeral train to Washington and to be present at the graveside rites. President and Mrs. Johnson and Vice President and Mrs. Humphrey, who

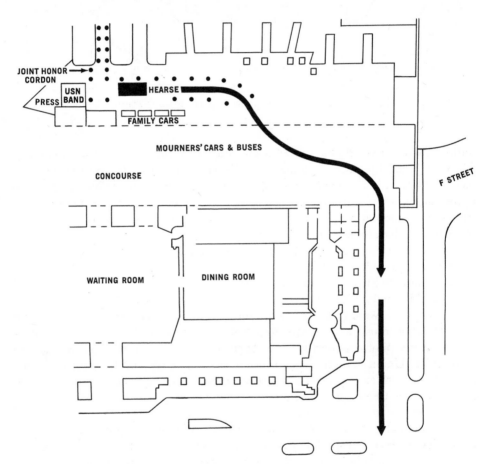

Diagram 112.   Arrival ceremony, Union Station.

were to return to Washington by air, would meet the funeral train at Union Station and accompany the cortege to the gravesite.

The mass began at 0955 on 8 June. Archbishop Cooke, the celebrant, was assisted by four other priests. Reflecting recent liturgical changes in the Roman Catholic Church, the clergymen wore purple instead of the traditional black vestments and Archbishop Cooke said the mass in English. When the mass ended, about 1035, Senator Kennedy's casket was carried out of the cathedral by thirteen bearers, among them a son of the senator and the senator's brother, Edward. A cortege of seventy-five cars made the fifteen-minute trip to Pennsylvania Station, the widow and the senator's brother riding in the hearse. At the station, after the casket was placed in the funeral car, the family, friends, associates, dignitaries, and newsmen, numbering about 1,000, boarded the 21-car train. The train was scheduled to leave at 1230 and to arrive in Washington at 1620. But because crowds of people lined the railroad right of way to pay their respects, the train started late and traveled at a slower pace than was expected. Its posted time of arrival in Washington became later and later.

In Washington the troops who were to participate in the arrival ceremony at Union Station were in place by 1600. By that hour it was clear that the funeral train would be late, and at 1645 General O'Malley, the commander of the Military District of Washington, arranged to have the troops at the station fed.

As the waiting time lengthened, making it obvious that the Washington ceremonies would take place after dark, the Kennedy family made a final request. From the funeral train, which was equipped with radiotelephones, Mr. Katzenbach called Mr. Fitt in his Washington office at 1900 to submit the family's request for 200 torches to be used at the gravesite. Since torches were not available, 200 candles were obtained from Fort Myer and 1,500 from St. Matthew's Cathedral; these were delivered to the cemetery about 2000. Army technicians also installed a bank of floodlights to illuminate the gravesite.

After a delay of almost five hours, the funeral train reached Washington at 2109. Within twenty minutes the train was brought into Union Station in two sections, the one with the funeral car and the cars carrying the Kennedy family, aides, and close friends on Track 17. The Navy body bearers waited nearby on the platform, which was covered by a red carpet extending to the station concourse where the honor cordon, the U.S. Navy Band, and the hearse were in position. President and Mrs. Johnson and Vice President and Mrs. Humphrey, who had arrived at the station by limousine a few minutes earlier, reached the ceremonial area about 2130. (*Diagram 112*)

At Track 17 the family, aides, and close friends left the train first. Then thirteen bearers, twelve of Senator Kennedy's friends and his son Robert, brought the casket off the train and carried it toward the concourse. For some reason the Navy body bearers were not used.

The Navy Band played the Navy hymn "Eternal Father, Strong to Save" as

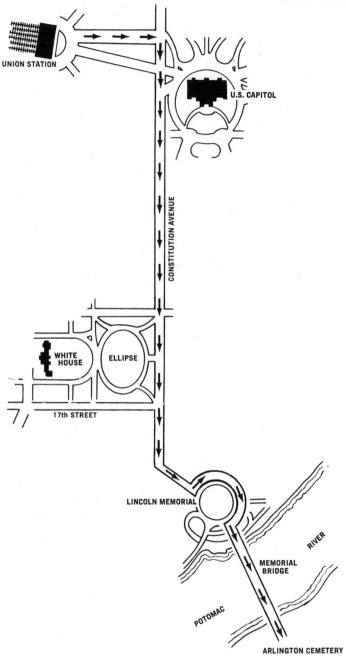

Diagram 113.   Route of march, Union Station to
Arlington National Cemetery.

the casket was borne through the honor cordon and placed in the hearse. Afterward, President Johnson, Vice President Humphrey, and other dignitaries spoke briefly with the widow and other members of the family. Mrs. Kennedy, her eldest son, Joseph, and the senator's brother, Edward, then got into the hearse; the others entered automobiles for the procession to Arlington National Cemetery.

The route to the cemetery was heavily lined with police and troops. Some police had taken position on the roofs of buildings verging on the road of march. The procession moved on 1st Street, N.E., then right on Constitution Avenue to the Department of Justice building, where it paused briefly. It then continued on Constitution Avenue, turned left on Henry Bacon Drive to reach the Lincoln Memorial, and moved clockwise around the memorial to the steps, where it came to a second halt. During a pause of four minutes, the choir on the steps of the Lincoln Memorial, backed by the brass section of the U.S. Marine Band, sang

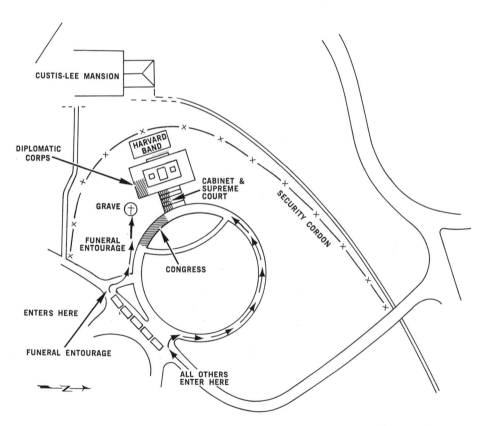

Diagram 114.   Movement of cortege, Memorial Gate to the gravesite.

"The Battle Hymn of the Republic." Several thousand people had assembled on the grounds around the memorial. Among them were some of the residents of Resurrection City, the symbolic shanty town that had been erected on the nearby mall under the sponsorship of the Southern Christian Leadership Conference as part of the organization's civil rights program. The procession then continued around the memorial, crossed Memorial Bridge, and entered Arlington National Cemetery. Mr. Metzler, the cemetery superintendent, met the motorcade at Memorial Gate to guide it to the gravesite. (*Diagram 113*)

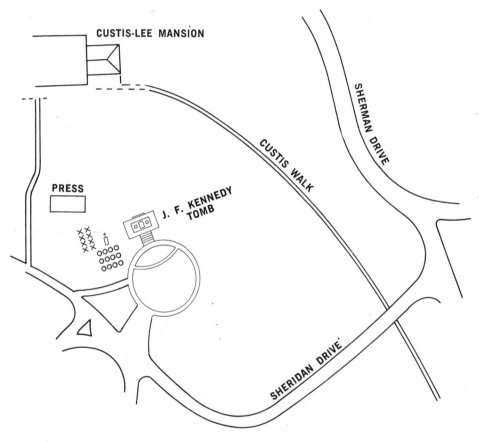

SYMBOLS

† CLERGY

× FAMILY

○ FRIENDS

Diagram 115.   Formation at the graveside.

The cortege moved through the cemetery via Schley, Sherman, and Sheridan Drives. Mr. Metzler, with assistance from the 3d Infantry traffic control detail, guided the cars to positions on Sheridan Drive adjacent to the grave of President Kennedy. He stopped the hearse and cars bearing the family, aides, and close friends beside the walkway nearest the gravesite chosen for Senator Kennedy. Other cars in the cortege were halted farther to the rear; their passengers were to reach the gravesite by way of the circular walk in front of President Kennedy's grave. Earlier, persons not in the cortege but attending the burial service had arrived in cars and buses and had been guided to graveside positions. (*Diagram 114*)

The family, aides, and close friends left their cars and moved to positions behind the hearse. After all were assembled there, the friends and son of Senator Kennedy who had been acting as body bearers removed the casket from the hearse. Guided by Mr. Metzler and preceded by the clergy, they bore the casket to the gravesite, the family and other mourners following.

When those accompanying the casket had reached their graveside positions, Archbishop Cooke of New York and Cardinal Patrick O'Boyle of Washington, read the brief burial service. (*Diagram 115*) At the close the body bearers, assisted by astronaut Col. John H. Glenn, folded the flag that had draped the casket. Colonel Glenn presented the flag to Senator Kennedy's eldest son, Joseph, who handed it to his mother. To conclude the graveside rites, the Harvard University Band played "America the Beautiful" while the Kennedy family and other mourners, carrying lighted candles, went up to the casket to pay their last respects.

The funeral for Senator Robert Kennedy conformed to no prescribed rules; except for the arrival ceremony at Union Station, it followed none of the precedents for an Official Funeral. It was rather a ceremony that reflected the effort of the nation to pay respect to Senator Kennedy in accordance with the wishes of his family.

CHAPTER XXIX

Former President Dwight D. Eisenhower
State Funeral
28 March-2 April 1969

At 1225 on 28 March 1969, after a long battle against a heart ailment, Dwight David Eisenhower, General of the Army and thirty-fourth President of the United States, died at the age of seventy-eight in Walter Reed Army Medical Center, Washington, D.C. President Richard M. Nixon immediately ordered flags at American installations everywhere to be flown at half-mast for the following thirty days. He designated Monday, 31 March, a day of national mourning for General Eisenhower.

Plans for honoring the former President with a State Funeral had been prepared in 1966; later modified somewhat, they incorporated the wishes of the general and his immediate family. The plans called for ceremonies in Washington and in Abilene, Kansas, the general's home town. In Washington the general's body was to lie in the Washington National Cathedral, then be taken in a full funeral procession to the U.S. Capitol to lie in state in the rotunda. After a funeral service in the Washington National Cathedral, the body was to be taken by train to Abilene, where a second funeral service was to be held on the steps of the Dwight D. Eisenhower Library. General Eisenhower was to be buried in a crypt in the Place of Meditation, a small chapel on the library grounds.

Responsibility for conducting ceremonies in Washington and for co-ordinating all funeral arrangements rested with the commanding general of the Military District of Washington, Maj. Gen. Charles S. O'Malley, Jr. In Abilene the commanding general of the Fifth U.S. Army, in whose territorial jurisdiction Abilene lay, had responsibility.

At 1700 on 28 March General O'Malley and Armed Forces Police escorted General Eisenhower's body from the hospital to Gawler's funeral establishment. A joint service body bearer detail handled the casket, and there was no ceremony. The body of the former President was placed in the Jefferson Room, on the basement level of the funeral home. Army guards took station at each of the three entrances to the room, and a joint honor guard kept vigil at the casket until late morning of 29 March.

On the 29th, General Eisenhower's casket was taken from the funeral establishment to the Washington National Cathedral. Mortuary attendants brought

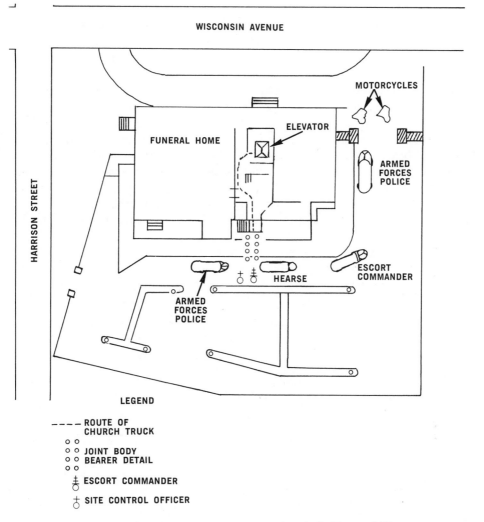

WISCONSIN AVENUE

MOTORCYCLES

ELEVATOR

FUNERAL HOME

ARMED
FORCES
POLICE

HARRISON STREET

ESCORT
COMMANDER

HEARSE

ARMED
FORCES
POLICE

LEGEND

- - - - ROUTE OF
CHURCH TRUCK

○ ○
○ ○ JOINT BODY
○ ○ BEARER DETAIL
○ ○

ESCORT COMMANDER

SITE CONTROL OFFICER

Diagram 116.   Departure formation, Gawler's Funeral Home.

the casket to the rear entrance of the establishment at 1045 and a joint body bearer team carried it to a hearse with no ceremony except the salutes of the site control officer, Capt. Jeffrey L. Dalia of the 3d Infantry, and General O'Malley, the escort commander. A small cortege formed for the short drive to the cathedral. Two members of the Metropolitan Police on motorcycles led the way, followed by a sedan carrying Armed Forces Police, another bearing General

O'Malley, the hearse, and at the rear a car carrying more Armed Forces Police. (*Diagram 116*)

The cortege was scheduled to reach the entrance of Bethlehem Chapel of the cathedral at 1100. In preparation for the arrival ceremony, participating troops took their positions at 1030. (*Table 39*) Inside the cathedral, a relief of the joint honor guard, one officer and six enlisted men, waited to stand watch at the bier. Outside, the U.S. Marine Band, fifty-four musicians and their leader, formed on the lawn near the Bethlehem Chapel entrance. A joint honor cordon, one officer and eleven enlisted men, lined both sides of the walkway and steps to the entrance, while along the walk at the curb were the national color detail, the personal flag bearer, and the chaplain of the Military District of Washington, Col. Wayne E. Soliday. In the driveway, just off the curb, ten general and flag officers of the five uniformed services stood as special honor guard. Beside a shrub garden in the center of the driveway, near the point at which the hearse bearing General Eisenhower's casket would stop, waited a joint body bearer team and the site control officer.

The ceremonial area was secured by a cordon of Army troops; other troops were on duty to handle traffic and parking. An Army detail of one officer and four enlisted men was also present to handle floral offerings. (The Eisenhower

TABLE 39—TROOP LIST, ARRIVAL CEREMONY AT BETHLEHEM CHAPEL, WASHINGTON NATIONAL CATHEDRAL, FOR FORMER PRESIDENT DWIGHT D. EISENHOWER

Duty	U.S. Army		U.S. Marine Corps		U.S. Navy		U.S. Air Force		U.S. Coast Guard		Total	
	Officers	Enlisted Men	Officers	Enlisted Men	Officers	Enlisted Men	Officers	Enlisted Men	Officers	Enlisted Men	Officers	Enlisted Men
Escort commander and staff	1										1	
Special honor guard	2		2		2		2		2		10	
Honor cordon	1	3		2		2		2		2	1	11
National color detail		1		1		1						3
Clergy	1										1	
Body bearers	1	2		2		2		1		1	1	8
Personal flag bearer		1										1
Band			1	54							1	54
Guard of honor	2	11	1	11	1	11	1	11	1	11	6	55
Site control	2	3									2	3
Security cordon	2	39									2	39
Floral detail	1	4									1	4
Traffic guides	1	12									1	12
Parking detail		6										6
Total	14	82	4	70	3	16	3	14	3	14	27	196

HEARSE ARRIVES AT WASHINGTON NATIONAL CATHEDRAL

family asked that instead of flowers, contributions be made to charities; nevertheless, floral tributes arrived in abundance.)

A few minutes before 1100, dignitaries invited by the Eisenhower family to serve as honorary pallbearers arrived and took position at the chapel entrance. Among them were General of the Army Omar N. Bradley; Generals J. Lawton Collins, Lauris Norstad, Wade H. Haislip, and Alfred M. Gruenther; Admiral Arthur W. Radford; the former President's brothers, Milton and Edgar Eisenhower; Col. G. Gordon Moore (Mrs. Eisenhower's brother-in-law); and M. Sgt. John Moaney, long-time aide to General Eisenhower. The Eisenhower family and other dignitaries reached the cathedral at the same time and were guided to positions for the arrival ceremony.

The cortege arrived at the chapel entrance shortly after 1100. As soon as the escort commander, General O'Malley, had left his car and taken a position near the entrance, the site control officer, Capt. Patrick D. Mulroy of the 3d Infantry, gave the signal for the ceremony to begin. (*Diagram 117*) The body bearers took their places at the rear of the hearse and the honor cordon presented arms. The

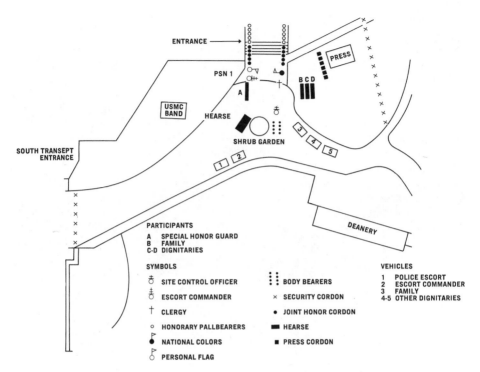

Diagram 117.   Arrival ceremony, Bethlehem Chapel,
Washington National Cathedral.

U.S. Marine Band sounded ruffles and flourishes and played "Hail to the Chief"
then began the hymn, "God of Our Fathers." The body bearers removed the
casket from the hearse and as the hymn was played the procession moved into the
cathedral. General O'Malley led. He was followed by the special honor guard, the
national color detail, the clergy, the body bearers with the casket (which was
placed on a movable bier just inside the cathedral), the personal flag bearer, the
honorary pallbearers, the Eisenhower family, and officials.

As the last of the procession entered the cathedral, the Marine Band stopped
playing and the honor cordon ordered arms. Inside, the national color detail and
personal flag bearer left the procession when it reached the doorway of Bethlehem
Chapel. (A national flag and a personal flag had already been posted in the
chapel.) The rest entered the chapel and took positions around the casket, which
the body bearers had placed on a catafalque. The first relief of the honor guard,
one officer and four enlisted men, was posted and the body bearers were dismissed. The Very Reverend Francis B. Sayre, Jr., dean of the Washington Na-

tional Cathedral, then conducted a brief prayer service, after which the family and other mourners left the chapel.

When the chapel had been cleared, it was opened to the public and remained open during the night and through the day of 30 March until shortly before 1500. Despite unseasonably cold weather, people waited in long lines outside the cathedral for the opportunity to pass through the chapel and pay their respects.

Plans for 30 March called for a ceremony of departure at the cathedral in mid-afternoon. General Eisenhower's casket was then to be taken in a motor cortege to Constitution Avenue at 16th Street, N.W., and transferred from the hearse to a caisson. The military escort, assembled nearby, was to lead the full procession to the Capitol. After an arrival ceremony, the general's body was to lie in state in the rotunda, which was to be open to the public until 1330 on 31 March.

The departure ceremony at the cathedral began at 1500 on the 30th; the participating troops had taken their positions half an hour earlier. (*Table 40*) Outside the Bethlehem Chapel entrance were the escort commander; the special honor guard made up of the chairman and members of the Joint Chiefs of Staff and the commandant of the Coast Guard; the U.S. Coast Guard Band, consisting of one officer and forty-five musicians; and a joint honor cordon, one officer and eleven enlisted men, that lined the steps and walkway. Inside, the national color detail, the personal flag bearer, the chaplain, and a joint body bearer team waited

TABLE 40—TROOP LIST, DEPARTURE CEREMONY FROM BETHLEHEM CHAPEL, WASHINGTON NATIONAL CATHEDRAL, FOR FORMER PRESIDENT DWIGHT D. EISENHOWER

Duty	U.S. Army		U.S. Marine Corps		U.S. Navy		U.S. Air Force		U.S. Coast Guard		Total	
	Officers	Enlisted Men	Officers	Enlisted Men	Officers	Enlisted Men	Officers	Enlisted Men	Officers	Enlisted Men	Officers	Enlisted Men
Escort commander and staff	1										1	
Special honor guard	2		1		1		1		1		6	
Honor cordon	1	3		2		2		2		2	1	11
National color detail		1		1		1						3
Clergy	1										1	
Body bearers	1	2		2		2		1		1	1	8
Personal flag bearer		1										1
Band									1	45	1	45
Site control	2	3									2	3
Security cordon	2	39									2	39
Floral detail	1	4									1	4
Traffic guides	2	14									2	14
Parking detail	1	14									1	14
Total	14	81	1	5	1	5	1	3	2	48	19	142

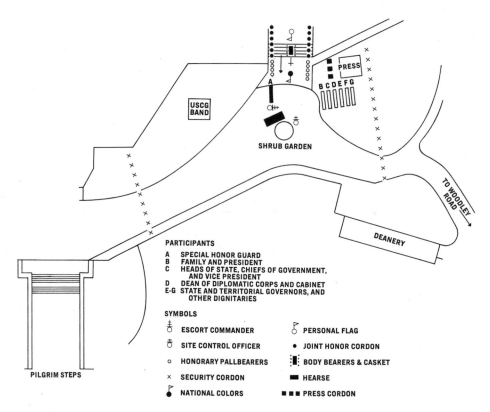

Diagram 118. Departure ceremony, Washington National Cathedral.

to form a procession that would accompany General Eisenhower's casket out of the cathedral.

Participating in the departure ceremony were President and Mrs. Nixon and their daughter Tricia, Vice President Spiro T. Agnew, chiefs of state and heads of government from foreign nations, cabinet members, justices of the Supreme Court, the dean of the diplomatic corps, state and territorial governors, and the honorary pallbearers. The last of these and members of the Eisenhower family took their positions outside the cathedral a few minutes before the ceremony began. (*Diagram 118*)

In the Bethlehem Chapel the joint guard of honor was dismissed and the body bearers posted themselves at the casket. At 1500 the procession began to move toward the cathedral entrance, led by the national color detail, which was followed by the clergy, the body bearers with the casket, and the personal flag bearer.

The body bearers halted at the door; the honor cordon presented arms and the Coast Guard Band sounded ruffles and flourishes and played "Hail to the Chief." As the band began "Onward Christian Soldiers" the procession resumed its march to the hearse. When the casket had been placed in the hearse the band ceased playing and the honor cordon ordered arms, concluding the ceremony. The Eisenhower family and others who were to travel in the funeral cortege returned to their cars.

The cortege proceeded north on Wisconsin Avenue, east on Woodley Road, south on 34th Street, southeast over Massachusetts Avenue, then along Rock Creek Parkway. Turning off the parkway onto Virginia Avenue, it continued to Constitution Avenue and on Constitution to its intersection with 16th Street. Traveling at twenty miles an hour, it reached the site of the casket transfer ceremony in about twenty minutes.

Long before the cortege began its journey from the cathedral, troops scheduled to participate in the main funeral procession had assembled along Constitution Avenue. Ten minutes before the arrival of the cortege, the caisson was driven to its ceremonial position on the right side of Constitution Avenue at its intersection with 16th Street. In column behind the caisson stood a new joint body bearer

TABLE 41—TROOP LIST, MAIN PROCESSION FOR FORMER PRESIDENT DWIGHT D. EISENHOWER

Duty	U.S. Army		U.S. Marine Corps		U.S. Navy		U.S. Air Force		U.S. Coast Guard		Total	
	Officers	Enlisted Men	Officers	Enlisted Men	Officers	Enlisted Men	Officers	Enlisted Men	Officers	Enlisted Men	Officers	Enlisted Men
Escort commander and staff	3	.....	.....	.....	.....	.....	.....	.....	.....	.....	3	.....
Special honor guard	2	.....	1	.....	1	.....	1	.....	1	.....	6	.....
Commander of troops and staff	2	.....	1	.....	1	.....	1	.....	1	.....	6	.....
National color detail	.....	1	.....	1	.....	1	.....	.....	.....	.....	.....	3
Clergy	1	.....	.....	.....	.....	.....	.....	.....	.....	.....	1	.....
Body bearers	1	2	.....	2	.....	2	.....	1	.....	1	1	8
Personal flag bearer	.....	1	.....	.....	.....	.....	.....	.....	.....	.....	.....	1
Caisson detail	.....	5	.....	.....	.....	.....	.....	.....	.....	.....	.....	5
Band	1	91	.....	.....	1	91	1	91	.....	.....	3	273
Military escort												
Active	6	85	5	85	5	85	5	85	5	85	26	425
Cadet	4	85	.....	.....	4	85	4	85	4	85	16	340
Servicewomen	2	19	1	19	1	19	1	19	.....	.....	5	76
National Guard	5	85	.....	.....	.....	.....	4	85	.....	.....	9	170
Reserve	5	85	5	85	5	85	5	85	5	85	25	425
Street cordon	4	160	4	160	4	160	4	160	.....	.....	16	640
Site control	2	.....	.....	.....	.....	.....	2	.....	.....	.....	4	.....
Traffic guides	1	28	.....	.....	.....	.....	.....	.....	.....	.....	1	28
Total	39	647	17	352	22	528	28	611	16	256	122	2,394

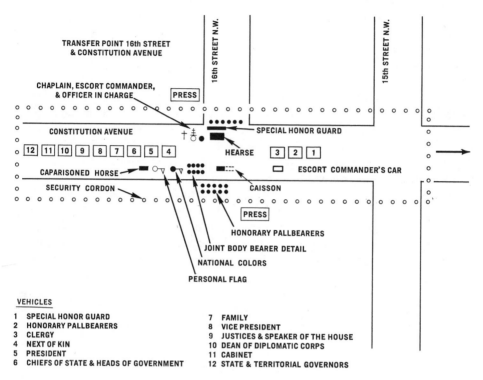

TRANSFER POINT 16th STREET
& CONSTITUTION AVENUE

CHAPLAIN, ESCORT COMMANDER,
& OFFICER IN CHARGE
PRESS

CONSTITUTION AVENUE   SPECIAL HONOR GUARD

12 11 10 9 8 7 6 5 4   HEARSE   3 2 1

CAPARISONED HORSE   ESCORT COMMANDER'S CAR

SECURITY CORDON

CAISSON

PRESS

HONORARY PALLBEARERS

JOINT BODY BEARER DETAIL

NATIONAL COLORS

PERSONAL FLAG

16th STREET N.W.

15th STREET N.W.

VEHICLES

1	SPECIAL HONOR GUARD	7	FAMILY
2	HONORARY PALLBEARERS	8	VICE PRESIDENT
3	CLERGY	9	JUSTICES & SPEAKER OF THE HOUSE
4	NEXT OF KIN	10	DEAN OF DIPLOMATIC CORPS
5	PRESIDENT	11	CABINET
6	CHIEFS OF STATE & HEADS OF GOVERNMENT	12	STATE & TERRITORIAL GOVERNORS

Diagram 119.   Formation for the casket transfer ceremony.

team, national color detail, and personal flag bearer, and a groom with a caparisoned horse. In order to keep the ceremonial area clear, a security cordon of
Army troops lined both sides of Constitution Avenue, stretching a block in both
directions from 16th Street.

On Constitution Avenue from 15th Street to 12th Street, the military escort
units were in formation for the main funeral procession. There were three bands
and seventeen companies, precisely the number specified in the current directive
governing the conduct of a State Funeral. The U.S. Army Band, the U.S. Navy
Band, and the U.S. Air Force Band each had a leader, a drum major, and ninety
musicians. Of the companies, there was one each from the four military academies; one each from the active Army, Marine Corps, Navy, Air Force, and Coast
Guard; one was a composite company of servicewomen; and seven represented all
the reserve components of the five uniformed services. Each unit numbered four
officers and eighty-five enlisted men, except the company of servicewomen which
comprised five officers and seventy-six enlisted members. Also preparing to march

with the military escort were the national commanders, or their representatives, of eight veterans' organizations.

A joint honor cordon of troops from the Army, Marine Corps, Navy, and Air Force lined both sides of Constitution Avenue from 15th Street eastward to Delaware Avenue opposite the Capitol, which was the complete route of the main funeral procession. Each of these four services furnished for the cordon four officers and 160 men. From west to east, the services occupied equal segments of the route in the reverse order of their seniority, that is, the Air Force, Navy, Marine Corps, and Army. (*Table 41*)

As the cortege reached the casket transfer site, the leading cars carrying the escort commander, special honor guard, honorary pallbearers, and clergy came to a standstill on Constitution Avenue just east of 16th Street. The hearse, immediately behind, stopped parallel to and on the left of the caisson. The rest of the cortege formed a column behind the hearse. (*Diagram 119*)

The escort commander, special honor guard, honorary pallbearers, and clergy left their cars and took their places around the hearse and caisson. The remaining members of the cortege stayed in their automobiles. When the participants were in position, the site control officer, Capt. John R. Thomas of the 3d Infantry, gave the order to present arms. As all other military participants saluted, the joint body bearer team marched to the rear of the hearse, removed the casket, and carried it to the caisson. No music was played during the transfer. When the casket was secured to the caisson and the body bearers had taken their marching positions behind it, the site control officer gave the command to order arms. Those who had taken part in the ceremony then returned to their automobiles. The national color detail, at the same time, moved in front of the clergy, and the personal flag bearer and the groom with the caparisoned horse took positions behind the caisson. As General O'Malley, the escort commander, walked to the head of the military escort, the troops came to attention and those bearing weapons shouldered arms. The main funeral procession then moved off toward the Capitol in normal cadence which was meted on the muffled drums of the three bands. (*Diagram 120*)

The street cordon saluted in ripples as the procession went by, each man presenting arms when the national colors were twelve steps from his position and ordering arms after the car bearing Vice President Agnew passed. When the caisson reached the midpoint of the journey, twenty-one Air Force F–4 Phantom jets flew over the procession in several wedge formations, with one plane missing from each formation to symbolize the loss of a leader.

On reaching the Delaware Avenue intersection, designated elements of the military escort turned onto the East Plaza where they would participate in the arrival ceremony. (*Table 42*) These included the commander of troops and his staff, the Army Band, and the right-hand platoon of each of the five companies from the active Army, Marine Corps, Navy, Air Force, and Coast Guard. All

CASKET IS TRANSFERRED TO THE CAISSON FOR PROCESSION TO THE CAPITOL

other escort units continued along Constitution Avenue, turned left onto 1st Street and then onto D Street, and proceeded to a designated dispersal area on Louisiana Avenue.

The escort commander meanwhile turned right off Constitution Avenue onto a Capitol grounds access road opposite New Jersey Avenue, where he waited for the cortege. When the head of the cortege reached the access road, the special honor guard, national color detail, clergy, caisson and body bearers, personal flag bearer, groom and caparisoned horse, and the car carrying President Nixon turned onto the road and halted. The remaining vehicles turned at Delaware Avenue and proceeded to the East Plaza. All these cars except those bearing the honorary pallbearers stopped at the east steps to discharge their passengers, who then entered the rotunda to take positions for the arrival ceremony. A reception committee consisting of members of Congress and of the diplomatic corps, the Deputy Secretary of Defense, and the three service secretaries was already present in the rotunda. The honorary pallbearers were driven to the Law Library entrance, where escort officers waited to guide them to ceremonial positions at the top of the steps just outside the rotunda. (*Diagram 121*)

TABLE 42—TROOP LIST, ARRIVAL CEREMONY AT THE U.S. CAPITOL FOR
FORMER PRESIDENT DWIGHT D. EISENHOWER

Duty	U.S. Army		U.S. Marine Corps		U.S. Navy		U.S. Air Force		U.S. Coast Guard		Total	
	Officers	Enlisted Men	Officers	Enlisted Men	Officers	Enlisted Men	Officers	Enlisted Men	Officers	Enlisted Men	Officers	Enlisted Men
Escort commander and staff	1	....	....	....	....	....	....	....	....	....	1	....
Special honor guard	2	....	1	....	1	....	1	....	1	....	6	....
Commander of troops and staff	2	....	1	....	1	....	1	....	1	....	6	....
Honor cordon	1	12	....	12	....	12	....	12	....	12	1	60
National color detail	....	1	....	1	....	1	....	....	....	....	....	3
Clergy	1	....	....	....	....	....	....	....	....	....	1	....
Body bearers	1	2	....	2	....	2	....	1	....	1	1	8
Personal flag bearer	....	1	....	....	....	....	....	....	....	....	....	1
Band	1	91	....	....	....	....	....	....	....	....	1	91
Military escort, active	1	28	1	28	1	28	1	28	1	28	5	140
Guard of honor	2	11	1	11	1	11	1	11	1	11	6	55
Saluting battery	1	13	....	....	....	....	....	....	....	....	1	13
Site control	4	8	....	....	....	....	....	....	....	....	4	8
Security cordon	1	84	....	....	....	....	....	....	....	....	1	84
Ushers	....	12	....	....	....	....	....	....	....	....	....	12
Guides	....	8	....	....	....	....	....	....	....	....	....	8
Floral detail	1	4	....	....	....	....	....	....	....	....	1	4
Traffic guides	....	13	....	....	....	....	....	....	....	....	....	13
Parking detail	3	15	....	....	....	....	....	....	....	....	3	15
Total	22	303	4	54	4	54	4	52	4	52	38	515

Already in position for the arrival ceremony was a joint honor cordon of one officer and sixty men lining the steps that led to the rotunda. When the participating escort units reached the plaza, they countermarched to their ceremonial positions facing the Capitol, with the Army Band at the right of the formation and the platoons on line to the left, in order of seniority of their respective services. The escort commander and elements of the cortege on the access road then moved to positions on the plaza for the arrival ceremony. (*Diagram 122*)

After all participants were in position the commander of troops, Col. Robert M. Daugherty, Commanding Officer, 3d Infantry, brought the escort units and honor cordon to present arms. The Army Band then sounded ruffles and flourishes and played "Hail to the Chief." At the first note of music, the saluting battery from the 3d Infantry, located on the grounds across Constitution Avenue from the Capitol, delivered a 21-gun salute, firing the rounds at five-second intervals. Following the salute, the Army Band played a hymn, "The Palms."

As the hymn began, the body bearer team lifted the casket from the caisson. The procession, which would take General Eisenhower's body up the east steps of

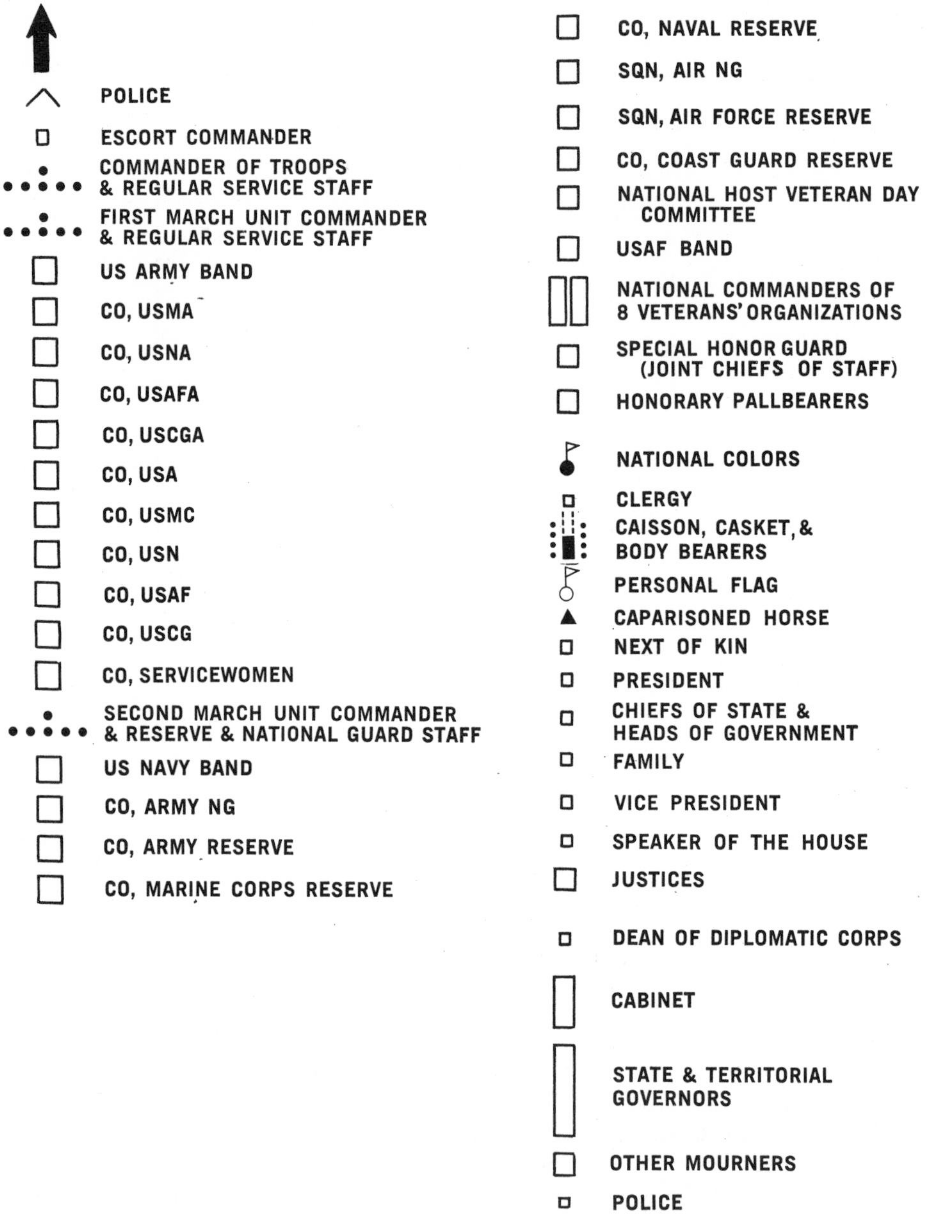

POLICE

ESCORT COMMANDER

COMMANDER OF TROOPS
& REGULAR SERVICE STAFF

FIRST MARCH UNIT COMMANDER
& REGULAR SERVICE STAFF

US ARMY BAND

CO, USMA

CO, USNA

CO, USAFA

CO, USCGA

CO, USA

CO, USMC

CO, USN

CO, USAF

CO, USCG

CO, SERVICEWOMEN

SECOND MARCH UNIT COMMANDER
& RESERVE & NATIONAL GUARD STAFF

US NAVY BAND

CO, ARMY NG

CO, ARMY RESERVE

CO, MARINE CORPS RESERVE

CO, NAVAL RESERVE

SQN, AIR NG

SQN, AIR FORCE RESERVE

CO, COAST GUARD RESERVE

NATIONAL HOST VETERAN DAY
COMMITTEE

USAF BAND

NATIONAL COMMANDERS OF
8 VETERANS' ORGANIZATIONS

SPECIAL HONOR GUARD
(JOINT CHIEFS OF STAFF)

HONORARY PALLBEARERS

NATIONAL COLORS

CLERGY

CAISSON, CASKET, &
BODY BEARERS

PERSONAL FLAG

CAPARISONED HORSE

NEXT OF KIN

PRESIDENT

CHIEFS OF STATE &
HEADS OF GOVERNMENT

FAMILY

VICE PRESIDENT

SPEAKER OF THE HOUSE

JUSTICES

DEAN OF DIPLOMATIC CORPS

CABINET

STATE & TERRITORIAL
GOVERNORS

OTHER MOURNERS

POLICE

Diagram 120.   Order of march, main procession.

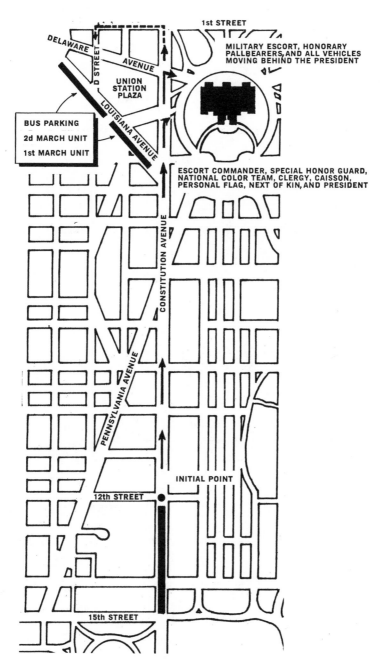

Diagram 121.   Route of march, main procession.

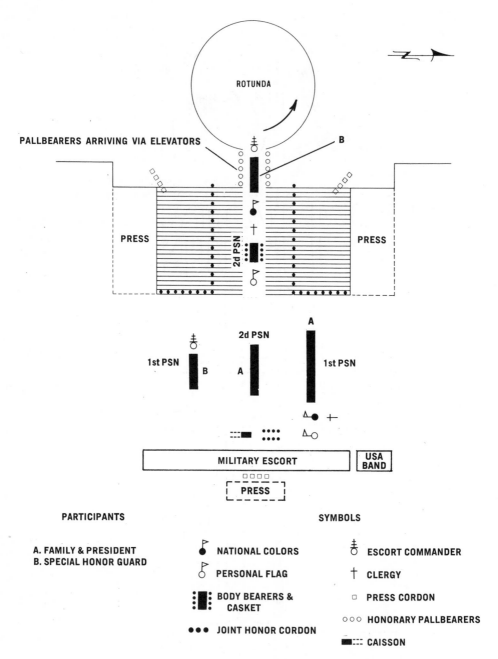

Diagram 122.   Arrival ceremony at the Capitol.

CAISSON ARRIVES AT THE CAPITOL

the Capitol and into the rotunda, formed with General O'Malley in the lead followed by the special honor guard, the national color detail, the clergy, the body bearers with the casket, the personal flag bearer, the Eisenhower family, and President Nixon and his party. The honorary pallbearers, who were standing at the top of the steps, fell in at the rear of the procession.

The clergy stopped at the foot of the Lincoln catafalque, which had been set up in the center of the rotunda. The national color detail, the body bearers with the casket, and the personal flag bearer moved to the right in a semicircle, then marched to the catafalque. Meanwhile, the Eisenhower family and others in the procession were guided to positions along the circumference of the room. (*Diagram 123*) The body bearers then placed the casket on the catafalque and removed a clear plastic cover which had protected the casket and the flag draping it from a light rain that had fallen during the main funeral procession. The first relief of a joint guard of honor, one officer and four enlisted men, was posted at the bier, and the body bearers were dismissed.

At this point President Nixon delivered a eulogy. When he finished, an Army enlisted man entered the rotunda with a wreath which the President, assisted by the wreath bearer, placed at the bier. After the clergy delivered the final benediction, the Eisenhower family left the hall by the east entrance. President Nixon then led the remaining mourners out of the room.

At 1800 the rotunda was opened to the public and from then until midnight some 2,000 people passed by General Eisenhower's bier each hour. In the early

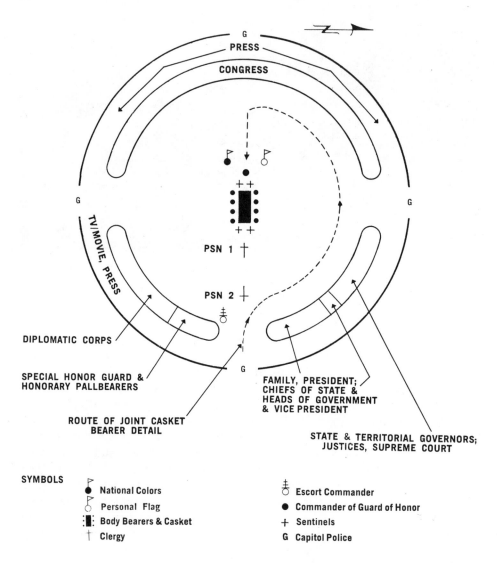

Diagram 123.   Formation in the rotunda.

PRESIDENT NIXON DELIVERS A EULOGY IN THE ROTUNDA

hours of 31 March the crowd dwindled to about a hundred an hour, but at dawn it increased and continued to grow until the doors were closed at 1330.

Ceremonies scheduled for 31 March were to begin at 1600 with the movement of General Eisenhower's casket from the Capitol to the Washington National Cathedral for the funeral service at 1640. Following this service, the body was to be taken to Union Station and placed aboard a special funeral train for transportation to Abilene, Kansas.

A half hour before the departure ceremony was scheduled to start, participating troops took their positions at the Capitol. (*Table 43*) Inside, a national color detail, personal flag bearer, chaplain, and joint body bearer team were preparing to form the procession that would take General Eisenhower's casket from the rotunda to a hearse on the East Plaza. Outside the U.S. Coast Guard Band, one officer and forty-five musicians, formed on the south side of the plaza at the foot of the east steps. A joint honor cordon, one officer and sixty enlisted men, lined the steps. In line with the northern rank of the honor cordon on the plaza beside the east steps were members of the Joint Chiefs of Staff and the commandant of

HONOR GUARD STANDS WATCH WHILE BODY
OF THE GENERAL LIES IN STATE

the Coast Guard, in position to serve again as the special honor guard. Standing with these officials was General O'Malley, the escort commander. Other officials and the Eisenhower family, scheduled to arrive a few minutes before the departure ceremony began, would stand on the plaza opposite the special honor guard. The honorary pallbearers were in two ranks next to the family group. Farther out on the plaza, across from the center of the steps, was the hearse. To its front and rear were the remaining cars that would make up the cortege. (*Diagram 124*)

At 1600, after the Eisenhower family and the remaining dignitaries had arrived and taken their places on the plaza, the joint guard of honor was dismissed from its vigil at the bier. The body bearers lifted the casket from the catafalque and placed it on a movable bier. The national color detail then led the way out the east entrance of the rotunda, followed by the chaplain, the body bearers with the casket, and the personal flag bearer. (General Andrew J. Goodpaster took the place of Dr. Milton S. Eisenhower as honorary pallbearer. Just before the afternoon ceremonies Dr. Eisenhower became ill and was taken to Walter Reed Army Medical Center.)

As the national color detail appeared outside the east entrance of the Capitol, the honor cordon presented arms. The procession halted when the body bearers with the casket reached the head of the steps. At that moment the Coast Guard Band sounded ruffles and flourishes and played "Hail to the Chief" and "Faith of Our Fathers." During the hymn the body bearers lifted the casket from the bier and the procession resumed, moving down the steps, through the honor cordon, and past the family and dignitaries on the plaza, to the hearse. After the casket was placed in the hearse, the band ceased playing and the honor cordon

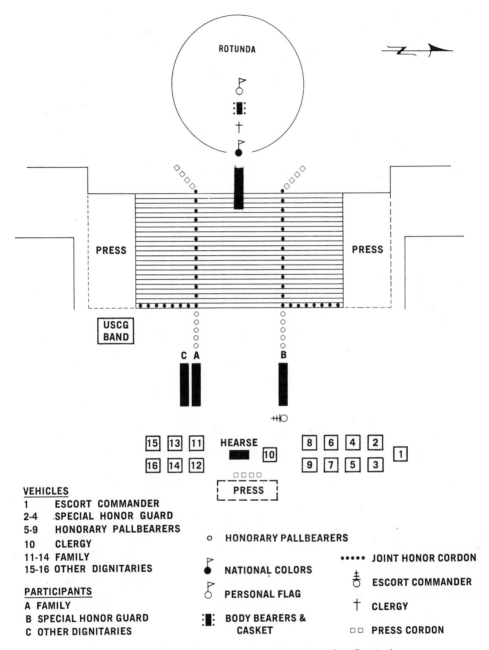

Diagram 124.   Departure ceremony at the Capitol.

TABLE 43—TROOP LIST, DEPARTURE CEREMONY AT THE U.S. CAPITOL
FOR FORMER PRESIDENT DWIGHT D. EISENHOWER

Duty	U.S. Army		U.S. Marine Corps		U.S. Navy		U.S. Air Force		U.S. Coast Guard		Total	
	Offi-cers	En-listed Men	Offi-cers	En-listed Men	Offi-cers	En-listed Men	Offi-cers	En-listed Men	Offi-cers	En-listed Men	Offi-cers	En-listed Men
Escort commander and staff.....	1	....	....	....	....	....	....	....	....	....	1	....
Special honor guard............	2	....	1	....	1	....	1	....	1	....	6	....
Honor cordon.................	1	12	....	12	....	12	....	12	....	12	1	60
National color detail............	....	1	....	1	....	1	....	....	....	....	....	3
Clergy......................	1	....	....	....	....	....	....	....	....	....	1	....
Body bearers.................	1	2	....	2	....	2	....	1	....	1	1	8
Personal flag bearer............	....	1	....	....	....	....	....	....	....	....	....	1
Band.......................	....	....	....	....	....	....	....	....	1	45	1	45
Site control.................	4	8	....	....	....	....	....	....	....	....	4	8
Security cordon...............	1	84	....	....	....	....	....	....	....	....	1	84
Guides......................	....	8	....	....	....	....	....	....	....	....	....	8
Floral detail.................	1	4	....	....	....	....	....	....	....	....	1	4
Traffic guides................	....	13	....	....	....	....	....	....	....	....	....	13
Parking detail................	3	15	....	....	....	....	....	....	....	....	3	15
Total....................	15	148	1	15	1	15	1	13	2	58	20	249

ordered arms. The Eisenhower family, escort commander, special honor guard, honorary pallbearers, clergy, and officials then went to their cars and, with a Metropolitan Police escort, departed for Washington National Cathedral.

Troops participating in the arrival ceremony at the cathedral meanwhile had taken up positions at the north transept entrance. (*Table 44*) The U.S. Marine Band stood in formation on the green across the driveway from the entrance. A joint honor cordon, one officer and twenty-two enlisted men, lined all but the top steps of the entrance; the top steps would later be cordoned by the honorary pallbearers. On the walk at the foot of the steps waited a national color detail, personal flag bearer, the clergy, and a joint body bearer team.

At the same time, persons attending the funeral service were entering the cathedral in order to be in their places before the cortege arrived. A joint service usher detail of 12 officers and 125 enlisted men seated them according to a predetermined plan. Among the dignitaries were the chiefs of state, heads of government, or other representatives of many nations. Former President and Mrs. Lyndon B. Johnson were also present; former President Harry S. Truman was unable to attend.

As the last of the guests were entering the cathedral, the cortege completed the journey from the Capitol, moving via Constitution Avenue, Virginia Avenue, Rock Creek Parkway, Massachusetts Avenue, 34th Street, and Woodley Road. When the motor column entered the cathedral grounds through the north tran-

CASKET IS CARRIED DOWN STEPS OF THE CAPITOL THROUGH THE HONOR CORDON

sept gate, the honor cordon came to attention. At the cathedral the procession stopped so that the hearse was opposite the entrance.

The Eisenhower family, and all others in the cortege except General O'Malley, the chaplain, and the honorary pallbearers, immediately entered the cathedral and were ushered to their seats. Afterward, the honorary pallbearers were guided to ceremonial positions at the top of the steps and General O'Malley and the chaplain took their places on the walk at the foot of the steps.

When everyone was in place, the site control officer signaled the body bearers, who moved to the rear of the hearse. The honor cordon then presented arms and the Marine Band sounded ruffles and flourishes and played "Hail to the Chief." As the hymn "A Mighty Fortress is Our God" was begun, the body bearers removed the casket from the hearse. General O'Malley led the way, the national color detail, the clergy, the body bearers with the casket, and the personal flag bearer followed, through the honor cordon and honorary pallbearers into the cathedral. The pallbearers joined the procession as the personal flag bearer passed them. (*Diagram 125*)

Inside the cathedral the casket was placed on a catafalque, and the national

TABLE 44—TROOP LIST, ARRIVAL CEREMONY AT WASHINGTON NATIONAL CATHEDRAL FOR FORMER PRESIDENT DWIGHT D. EISENHOWER

Duty	U.S. Army		U.S. Marine Corps		U.S. Navy		U.S. Air Force		U.S. Coast Guard		Total	
	Officers	Enlisted Men	Officers	Enlisted Men	Officers	Enlisted Men	Officers	Enlisted Men	Officers	Enlisted Men	Officers	Enlisted Men
Escort commander and staff	1										1	
Special honor guard	2		1		1		1		1		6	
Honor cordon	1	6		4		4		4		4	1	22
National color detail		1		1		1						3
Clergy	1										1	
Body bearers	1	2		2		2		1		1	1	8
Personal flag bearer		1										1
Band			1	54							1	54
Site control	2	3									2	3
Security cordon	1	37									1	37
Floral detail	1	4									1	4
Traffic guides	1	12									1	12
Parking detail	4	28									4	28
Total	15	94	2	61	1	7	1	5	1	5	20	172

colors and personal flag were posted nearby in holders. The color and flag bearers and the joint body bearer team then moved to the rear of the cathedral, while the escort commander and the honorary pallbearers took their seats.

The Very Reverend Francis B. Sayre, Jr., delivered the opening prayer. The Reverend Edward R. Elson, Chaplain of the Senate, then conducted a service based on Psalms 46 and 121, which were favorites of the former President. (Dr. Elson, while he was minister of the National Presbyterian Church, had baptized General Eisenhower in 1953.) The benediction was pronounced by the Right Reverend William F. Creighton, bishop of Washington.

At the conclusion of the service, General O'Malley, the special honor guard, and the honorary pallbearers were first to leave the cathedral, moving to the north transept entrance for the departure ceremony. (*Table 45*) The escort commander and the special honor guard occupied positions on the walk at the foot of the steps, while the honorary pallbearers lined both sides of the bottom section of steps. The joint honor cordon had shifted during the funeral service and now lined the remaining steps. The Marine Band had maintained its formation across the driveway from the entrance, and the cortege vehicles remained on the drive, with the hearse opposite the cathedral entrance.

After the escort commander and other participating officials had left the cathedral, the body bearer team, national color detail, and personal flag bearer

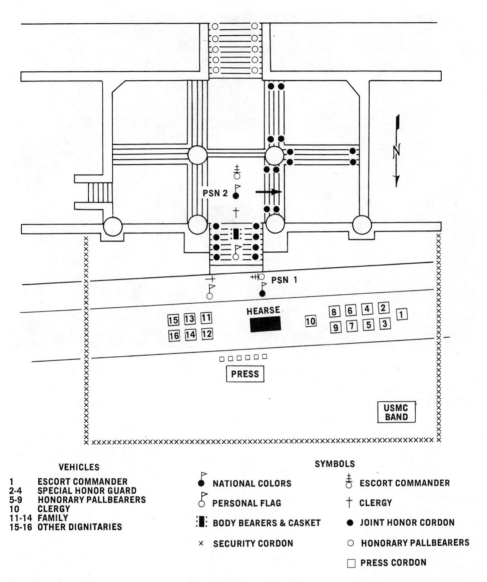

Diagram 125.   Arrival ceremony, Washington National Cathedral.

FUNERAL SERVICE IN WASHINGTON NATIONAL CATHEDRAL

TABLE 45—TROOP LIST, DEPARTURE CEREMONY AT WASHINGTON NATIONAL
CATHEDRAL FOR FORMER PRESIDENT DWIGHT D. EISENHOWER

Duty	U.S. Army		U.S. Marine Corps		U.S. Navy		U.S. Air Force		U.S. Coast Guard		Total	
	Officers	Enlisted Men	Officers	Enlisted Men	Officers	Enlisted Men	Officers	Enlisted Men	Officers	Enlisted Men	Officers	Enlisted Men
Escort commander and staff.....	1	....	....	....	....	....	....	....	....	....	1	....
Special honor guard.............	2	....	1	....	1	....	1	....	1	....	6	....
Honor cordon..................	1	6	....	4	....	4	....	4	....	4	1	22
National color detail...........	....	1	....	1	....	1					....	3
Clergy........................	1	....									1	....
Body bearers..................	1	2	....	2	....	2	....	1	....	1	1	8
Personal flag bearer............	....	1										1
Band.........................			1	54							1	54
Site control..................	1	....									1	....
Security cordon...............	1	37									1	37
Floral detail..................	1	4									1	4
Traffic guides.................	1	12									1	12
Parking detail.................	4	28									4	28
Total....................	14	91	2	61	1	7	1	5	1	5	19	169

came forward. The national color detail took up the colors and then led the way up the aisle to the entrance, followed by the clergy, the body bearers with the casket, and the personal flag bearer. Members of the Eisenhower family joined the procession as it moved up the aisle.

When the national color detail passed through the doorway the honor cordon presented arms. The body bearers with the casket halted at the door; the Marine Band sounded ruffles and flourishes and played "Hail to the Chief." As the hymn "Lead Kindly Light" was begun, the procession resumed, and the body bearers carried the casket to the hearse. The Eisenhower family and others who had come out of the cathedral observed the last movements of the procession from the bottom section of the entrance steps. After the body bearers placed the casket in the hearse, the band stopped playing and the honor cordon ordered arms. Members of the cortege then went to their cars, and the motor column left for Union Station. (*Diagram 126*)

In preparation for ceremonies at Union Station, a joint street honor cordon, composed of two officers and sixty-two enlisted men from each of the services, was stationed along Delaware Avenue from Constitution Avenue to the station's semicircular plaza. The cordon then stretched around the southeast arc of the plaza to the east entrance of the station. (*Table 46*) Each service manned a separate segment of the route. In a nearby parking lot the Army Band was in formation while

TABLE 46—TROOP LIST, ARRIVAL CEREMONY AT UNION STATION, WASHINGTON, D.C., FOR FORMER PRESIDENT DWIGHT D. EISENHOWER

Duty	U.S. Army		U.S. Marine Corps		U.S. Navy		U.S. Air Force		U.S. Coast Guard		Total	
	Officers	Enlisted Men	Officers	Enlisted Men	Officers	Enlisted Men	Officers	Enlisted Men	Officers	Enlisted Men	Officers	Enlisted Men
Escort commander and staff	1	....	....	....	....	....	....	....	....	....	1	....
Special honor guard	2	....	1	....	1	....	1	....	1	....	6	....
Honor cordon	1	27	....	27	....	27	....	27	....	27	1	135
National color detail	....	1	....	1	....	1	....	....	....	....	....	3
Clergy	1	....	....	....	....	....	....	....	....	....	1	....
Body bearers	1	2	....	2	....	2	....	1	....	1	1	8
Personal flag bearer	....	1	....	....	....	....	....	....	....	....	....	1
Band	1	54	....	....	....	....	....	....	....	....	1	54
Street cordon	2	62	2	62	2	62	2	62	....	....	8	248
Saluting battery	1	13	....	....	....	....	....	....	....	....	1	13
Site control	2	....	....	....	....	....	2	....	....	....	4	....
Security cordon	1	21	....	....	....	....	....	....	....	....	1	21
Guides	....	12	....	....	....	....	....	....	....	....	....	12
Parking detail	1	12	....	....	....	....	....	....	....	....	1	12
Total	14	205	3	92	3	92	5	90	1	28	26	507

PROCESSION LEAVES THE CATHEDRAL

the 3d Infantry saluting battery waited on grounds west of Delaware Avenue. (*Diagram 127*) At the east entrance a national color detail, personal flag bearer, and joint body bearer team were at hand to take General Eisenhower's casket to the train in procession. A joint honor cordon of 1 officer and 135 enlisted men lined both sides of the route that the procession would take to the funeral car on Track 17.

The cortege arrived at Union Station about 1800, via Constitution Avenue and turning left onto Delaware Avenue to pass through the joint street honor cordon. As the hearse entered Delaware Avenue, the 3d Infantry battery began firing a 21-gun salute, spacing the rounds so that the last was fired as the hearse stopped at the east entrance of the station. To assist in the timing of the salute, a vehicle carrying a representative of the battery escorted the cortege over Delaware Avenue and established the proper pace. As the procession moved through the street cordon, each cordon member presented arms when the hearse was within twelve steps of his position and ordered arms after the last vehicle had passed.

At the station, all cortege vehicles except the limousine carrying Mrs. Eisenhower were directed to parking places outside the east entrance. Her car was

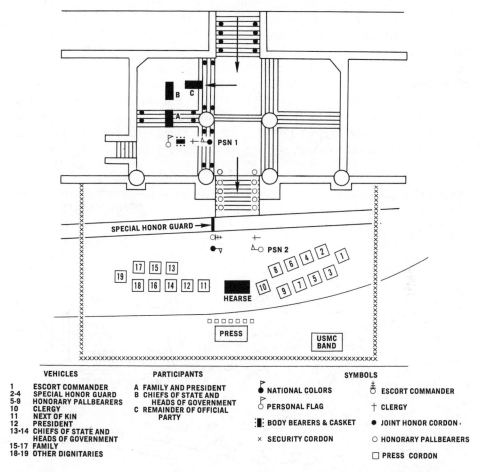

Diagram 126. Departure ceremony, Washington National Cathedral.

driven to the diplomat's entrance near the parking lot at the far east end of the station and proceeded through the concourse to Track 17. There Mrs. Eisenhower left the car to await the procession.

The other participants who had arrived with the cortege were guided from their vehicles to positions for the departure ceremony. The body bearer team, at the same time, marched to the rear of the hearse. The honor cordon lining the way to the train presented arms, and the band sounded ruffles and flourishes and played "Hail to the Chief" and "Army Blue." During the last selection, the body bearers removed the casket from the hearse and placed it on a movable bier. The procession then formed for the march to the train.

Leading the way was the escort commander, General O'Malley. Behind him were the special honor guard, national color detail, clergy, body bearers with the casket, personal flag bearer, honorary pallbearers, members of the Eisenhower family, President Nixon and his party, and other mourners. (*Diagram 128*) Arriving at Track 17, the procession stopped on the platform at the side entrance of the funeral car and the casket was lifted inside. (*Diagram 129*)

The funeral train was made up of a three-unit diesel locomotive and ten cars. The car that would carry the body of General Eisenhower to Kansas was a baggage car, specially prepared for the purpose. There were two crew cars, a car for ceremonial troops making the trip to Abilene, a business car, dining car,

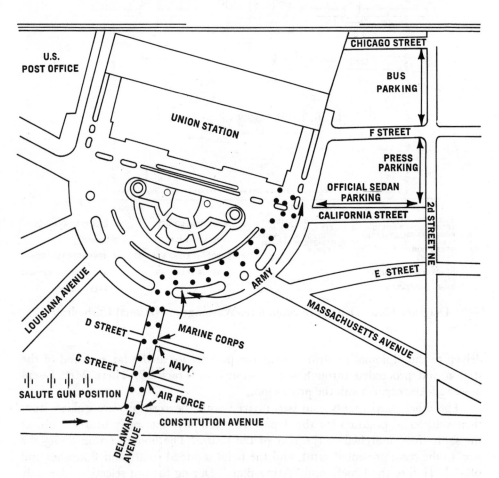

Diagram 127. Positions of street honor cordon and
saluting battery, Union Station.

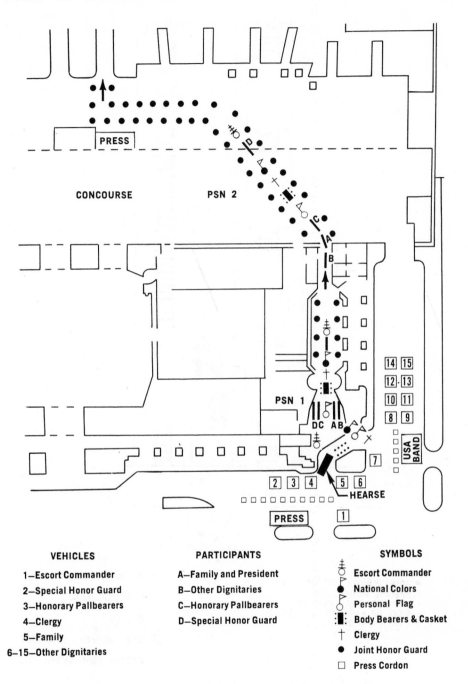

CONCOURSE

PSN 2

PSN 1

HEARSE

PRESS

PRESS

14 15
12 13
10 11
8   9

USA
BAND

7

2 3 4 5 6

1

VEHICLES	PARTICIPANTS	SYMBOLS
1—Escort Commander	A—Family and President	‡ Escort Commander
2—Special Honor Guard	B—Other Dignitaries	● National Colors
3—Honorary Pallbearers	C—Honorary Pallbearers	⚲ Personal Flag
4—Clergy	D—Special Honor Guard	▮ Body Bearers & Casket
5—Family		† Clergy
6—15—Other Dignitaries		● Joint Honor Guard
		□ Press Cordon

Diagram 128.   Departure ceremony, Union Station.

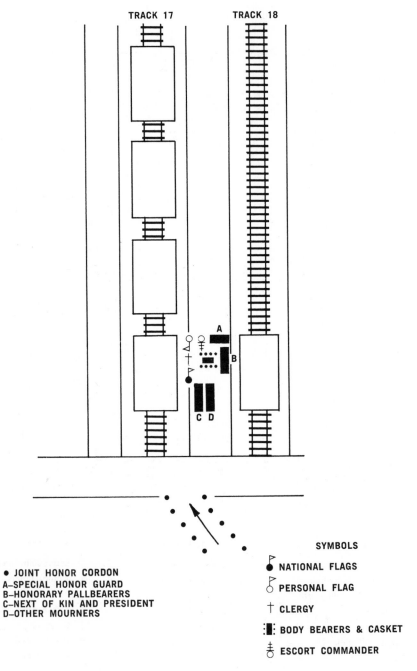

Diagram 129.   Trainside formation, Union Station.

lounge car, and three cars for the Eisenhower family and friends. Mrs. Eisenhower rode in the last car, the Santa Fe, which had often been used by General Eisenhower when he was President. Besides the Eisenhower family and close friends, some two dozen persons boarded the train to accompany the general's body to Abilene: railway officials, secret service men, and military officials from the Military District of Washington and the Fifth Army. Ceremonial troops consisted of one officer, eight body bearers, a national color detail of three, and a personal flag bearer; during the journey these troops would act as a guard of honor at the casket.

All passengers were aboard by 1840 and the train left Washington a few minutes later. Using Chesapeake and Ohio, Baltimore and Ohio, Norfolk and Western, and Union Pacific tracks, the funeral train passed through seven states—Virginia, West Virginia, Kentucky, Ohio, Indiana, Illinois, and Missouri—to reach its destination in Kansas. The governor of each of these states was advised beforehand of the points and scheduled times at which the train would enter and leave his state, and his help in expediting passage of the train was requested. He was also asked in behalf of the Eisenhower family not to inform the public of the train's route in order to prevent such accidents as had occurred when crowds gathered along the tracks during the movement of Senator Robert F. Kennedy's funeral train from New York to Washington the previous year.

The route of the train nevertheless became known, at least partly as the result of disclosures by train company officials. Either equipped with this knowledge or able to anticipate the progress of the train once it was on its way, people gathered along the track at many points. Stops ranging from ten minutes to an hour were made at several stations for crew changes and train service; the longest were at Cincinnati, St. Louis, and Kansas City. At Mrs. Eisenhower's request, while in Cincinnati the funeral car was marked on the outside with black bunting and flags so that it would be easily identifiable to those watching the train's passage. Around 0645 on 2 April, after more than thirty hours, the funeral train pulled into a siding near the Union Pacific Station in Abilene.

A little more than a month before General Eisenhower's death, Headquarters, Fifth U.S. Army, located at Fort Sheridan, Illinois, had published a final version of OPLAN KANSAS under which the funeral ceremonies for the former President would be carried out in Abilene. In accordance with this plan, a provisional detachment, commanded by the deputy commanding general of the Fifth Army and manned by troops from various units and installations within the Fifth Army

Area, was set up on 29 March to complete arrangements and then to conduct the ceremonies scheduled for 2 April in Abilene. Joining this Fifth Army group on 1 April to fulfill the responsibility of the Commanding General, Military District of Washington, for co-ordinating all funeral arrangements were Paul C. Miller, Chief of Ceremonies and Special Events, Military District of Washington, and a small staff. Also arriving from Washington by air on the same day were a joint body bearer team, national color detail, and personal flag bearer, who would replace their respective groups traveling with the funeral train, and about fifty officers and men from all the uniformed services who would serve as the joint honor guard, firing party, and bugler.

As originally planned, the total troop requirement for the Abilene ceremonies —administrative, support, and ceremonial—stood at 2,419. This number later increased when the need for more escort officers arose. In addition, eleven civilians had active administrative roles.

The Army troops to be used accounted for most of the total, numbering some 2,049. Active Army forces were supplied by Headquarters, Fifth Army; Fort Riley, Kansas; Fort Leavenworth, Kansas; Fort Leonard Wood, Missouri; the Military District of Washington; and the Army Photographic Agency in Washington. Other Army troops were from the 89th Division (U.S. Army Reserve) and the Kansas National Guard. The 9th Marine District supplied 114 marines; the Ninth Naval District, 116 Navy men; and Forbes Air Force Base, 116 airmen. The 24 Coast Guardsmen who participated were from Washington, although they were under the direction of the Second Coast Guard District. All troops from Washington were billeted in Abilene. Active forces from within the Fifth Army Area, which arrived on 31 March, were billeted at Fort Riley while the Reserve forces stayed in their own quarters.

The opening ceremony at Abilene was to take place at 1000 on 2 April, when General Eisenhower's casket was to be removed from the funeral train. The casket was then to be taken in procession through Abilene to the Dwight D. Eisenhower Library over a route about twelve blocks long. The funeral service was to be held on the steps of the library (inside in a small auditorium if the weather was bad) and conducted jointly by the former Army Chief of Chaplains, the Reverend Luther D. Miller of Washington National Cathedral; the Reverend Robert H. MacAskill of the First Presbyterian Church in Gettysburg, Pennsylvania; and the Reverend Dean Miller of the Palm Desert Community Church in Palm Desert, California. Following the service, General Eisenhower's casket was to be carried to the nearby Place of Meditation where Canon Miller was to conduct the burial rites. The Abilene ceremonies were scheduled to end around noon.

On the morning of 2 April, before the funeral train reached Abilene, an Army cordon of three officers and sixty-six men surrounded the railroad siding where the train would stop. The joint guard of honor also reported to the site before the train's arrival in order to be ready to take post in the funeral car, where General Eisenhower's body would lie until 1000. (*Table 47*)

When the train arrived, the Fifth Army mortuary officer inspected the funeral car to insure that everything was in order. The new guard of honor took post immediately afterward, relieving the troops who had stood watch during the journey. Admission to the funeral car was restricted to persons invited by the Eisenhower family.

The troops participating in the opening ceremony at the funeral car assembled at 0900. (*Table 48*) Among them were Lt. Gen. Vernon P. Mock, the Fifth

TABLE 47—TROOP LIST, PERIOD OF REPOSE, ABILENE, KANSAS, CEREMONY FOR FORMER PRESIDENT DWIGHT D. EISENHOWER

Duty	U.S. Army		U.S. Marine Corps		U.S. Navy		U.S. Air Force		U.S. Coast Guard		Total	
	Officers	Enlisted Men	Officers	Enlisted Men	Officers	Enlisted Men	Officers	Enlisted Men	Officers	Enlisted Men	Officers	Enlisted Men
Guard of honor	2	5	1	5	1	5	1	5	1	5	6	25
Site control	2	1									2	1
Security cordon	3	66									3	66
Floral detail	1	6									1	6
Mortuary officer	1										1	
Total	9	78	1	5	1	5	1	5	1	5	13	98

TABLE 48—TROOP LIST, DEPARTURE CEREMONY AT UNION PACIFIC STATION, ABILENE, FOR FORMER PRESIDENT DWIGHT D. EISENHOWER

Duty	U.S. Army		U.S. Marine Corps		U.S. Navy		U.S. Air Force		U.S. Coast Guard		Total	
	Officers	Enlisted Men	Officers	Enlisted Men	Officers	Enlisted Men	Officers	Enlisted Men	Officers	Enlisted Men	Officers	Enlisted Men
Escort commander and staff	1										1	
Special honor guard	1		1		1		1		1		5	
National color detail		1		1		1						3
Body bearers	1	2		2		2		1		1	1	8
Personal flag bearer		1										1
Band	1	28									1	28
Site control	3	2									3	2
Security cordon	3	66									3	66
Guides	1	12									1	12
Total	11	112	1	3	1	3	1	1	1	1	15	120

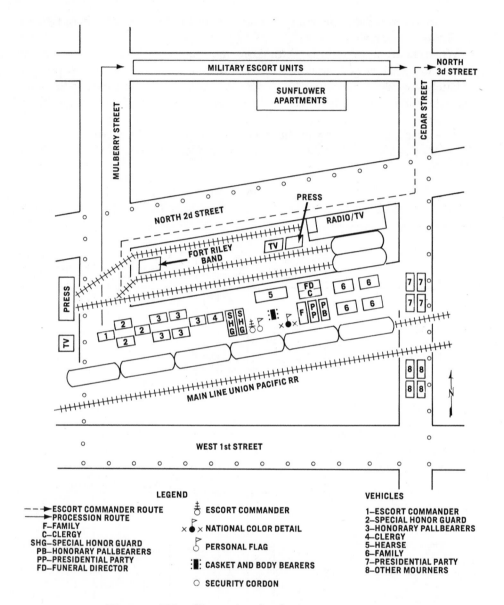

Diagram 130. Formation for departure ceremony,
Union Pacific Station, Abilene, Kansas.

Army commander, who would act as escort commander throughout the day; the special honor guard composed of five general or flag officers from all the uniformed services; the Fort Riley Band; and the body bearer team, national color detail, and personal flag bearer who had been flown in from Washington to relieve their respective counterparts on the train.

On Abilene's North 3d Street, a block and a half north of where the train stood, the military escort units assembled in march order facing east, the first direction the procession would take. These units included the commander of troops and his staff of five; the Fifth Army Band; a company each of the active Army, Marine Corps, Navy, and Air Force; and a company each of Army Reserve and National Guard troops. (*Diagram 130*)

During the last half hour before 1000, the honorary pallbearers who had participated in the Washington ceremonies assumed positions at the door of the funeral car; just before the beginning of the ceremony, the members of the Eisenhower family took their places. President Nixon, Mrs. Nixon, and their daughter Tricia had arrived from Washington at the airport in Salina, west of Abilene, traveled to Abilene by helicopter, and to the train by car.

Promptly at 1000, with all participants in position, the body bearers that had traveled in the train from Washington brought General Eisenhower's casket to the door of the funeral car, where they halted.

TABLE 49—TROOP LIST, FUNERAL PROCESSION, ABILENE, FOR FORMER PRESIDENT DWIGHT D. EISENHOWER

Duty	U.S. Army		U.S. Marine Corps		U.S. Navy		U.S. Air Force		U.S. Coast Guard		Total	
	Officers	Enlisted Men	Officers	Enlisted Men	Officers	Enlisted Men	Officers	Enlisted Men	Officers	Enlisted Men	Officers	Enlisted Men
Escort commander and staff.....	1	.....	.....	.....	.....	.....	.....	.....	.....	.....	1	....
Special honor guard............	1	.....	1	.....	1	.....	1	.....	1	.....	5	.....
Commander of troops and staff...	3	.....	1	.....	1	.....	1	.....	.....	.....	6	.....
National color detail............	.....	1	.....	1	.....	1	.....	.....	.....	.....	.....	3
Body bearers.................	1	2	.....	2	.....	2	.....	1	.....	1	1	8
Personal flag bearer.............	.....	1	.....	.....	.....	.....	.....	.....	.....	.....	.....	1
Band......................	1	75	.....	.....	.....	.....	.....	.....	.....	.....	1	75
Military escort												
Active.....................	4	85	4	85	4	85	4	85	.....	.....	16	340
National Guard.............	4	85	.....	.....	.....	.....	.....	.....	.....	.....	4	85
Reserve....................	4	85	.....	.....	.....	.....	.....	.....	.....	.....	4	85
Street cordon.................	10	720	.....	.....	.....	.....	.....	.....	.....	.....	10	720
Site control.................	5	5	.....	.....	.....	.....	.....	.....	.....	.....	5	5
Total.................	34	1,059	6	88	6	88	6	86	1	1	53	1,322

CASKET IS CARRIED FROM THE FUNERAL TRAIN, ABILENE, KANSAS

The Fort Riley Band played ruffles and flourishes and "Hail to the Chief."
When the band began the hymn "God of Our Fathers," the casket was handed
to the body bearers on the platform, who carried it to a hearse. After the casket
was in the hearse, the Eisenhower family, Presidential party, honorary pallbearers,
special honor guard, and other mourners entered automobiles which were already
in procession. At the same time, the escort commander, General Mock, the national color detail, the body bearer team, and the personal flag bearer took their
marching positions. The cortege then moved north on Mulberry Street to join the
military escort. (*Table 49*) General Mock led the cortege for a short distance,
then turned off and proceeded by a separate route to his position at the head of
the escort. (*See Diagram 130.*)

The procession followed North 3d Street for three blocks eastward, turned
south on Buckeye Avenue as far as South 4th Street, and then turned east again
on South 4th to enter the Dwight D. Eisenhower Library grounds. (*Diagram
131*) The route was lined on both sides by an Army street honor cordon of 10
officers and 720 enlisted men.

As the procession formed and moved to the library grounds, a toll was played

PROCESSION LEAVES UNION PACIFIC STATION, ABILENE, KANSAS

on the carillon in the Place of Meditation, the bell sounding at five-second intervals. When the military escort reached the grounds, the escort commander, the commander of troops and his staff, the Fifth Army Band, each company commander and guidon bearer, and the left platoon of each company turned east on South 4th Street to proceed to the library building. The rest of the marching units continued south then made westward and northward turns to return to the railroad station, where the troops were released. (*See Diagram 131.*)

The escort units marched to positions on the Eisenhower Museum grounds opposite and facing the library steps. There the Fifth Army Band would play, and the troop units would render their salutes through the remainder of the ceremonies. (*Diagram 132*) The cortege halted on South 4th Street with the hearse at the walkway to the library. Already in seats on the library mall facing the steps were some 500 invited guests. Also in position before the arrival of the procession was a joint honor cordon, which lined the walkway from the street to the library steps and then continued west from the library to the Place of Meditation. (*Table 50*)

After the cortege arrived at the library, the Eisenhower family and other participants left their automobiles and took positions for the ceremony. The Fifth Army Band sounded ruffles and flourishes and played "Hail to the Chief." When the band began the hymn "A Mighty Fortress is Our God," the body bearers re-

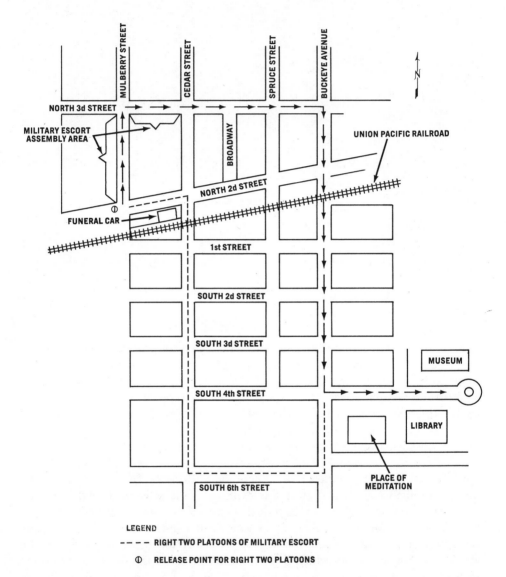

Diagram 131. Route of march, funeral procession, Abilene.

TABLE 50—TROOP LIST, FUNERAL SERVICE, ABILENE,
FOR FORMER PRESIDENT DWIGHT D. EISENHOWER

Duty	U.S. Army		U.S. Marine Corps		U.S. Navy		U.S. Air Force		U.S. Coast Guard		Total	
	Officers	Enlisted Men	Officers	Enlisted Men	Officers	Enlisted Men	Officers	Enlisted Men	Officers	Enlisted Men	Officers	Enlisted Men
Escort commander and staff	1	....	....	....	....	....	....	....	....	....	1	....
Special honor guard	1	....	1	....	1	....	1	....	1	....	5	....
Commander of troops and staff	3	....	1	....	1	....	1	....	....	....	6	....
Honor cordon	1	15	....	15	....	15	....	15	....	15	1	75
National color detail	....	1	....	1	....	1	....	....	....	....	....	3
Body bearers	1	2	....	2	....	2	....	1	....	1	1	8
Personal flag bearer	....	1	....	....	....	....	....	....	....	....	....	1
Band	1	75	....	....	....	....	....	....	....	....	1	75
Military escort												
Active	2	29	2	29	2	29	2	29	....	....	8	116
National Guard	2	29	....	....	....	....	....	....	....	....	2	29
Reserve	2	29	....	....	....	....	....	....	....	....	2	29
Site control	6	6	....	....	....	....	....	....	....	....	6	6
Security cordon	6	158	....	....	....	....	....	....	....	....	6	158
Ushers	5	30	....	....	....	....	....	....	....	....	5	30
Guides	2	24	....	....	....	....	....	....	....	....	2	24
Floral detail	1	6	....	....	....	....	....	....	....	....	1	6
Total	34	405	4	47	4	47	4	45	1	16	47	560

moved the casket from the hearse. The procession made its way to the library steps, with General Mock, the escort commander, leading the way, and followed by the special honor guard, national color detail, clergy, body bearers and casket, personal flag bearer, members of the Eisenhower family, the Presidential party, other mourners, and the honorary pallbearers in that order. Former President Johnson, who flew from Texas to Salina, had meanwhile joined the official party.

When the body bearers reached the top of the steps, they placed the casket on a locked movable bier and dressed the flag that draped the casket. The national color detail and personal flag bearer moved to either side of the casket, where they remained throughout the funeral service. After the Eisenhower family and others in the procession had been taken to seats behind the casket, the body bearers left the casket and went inside the library. (*Diagram 133*)

The three clergymen then conducted a religious service for the former President. During the service, a gust of wind characteristic of the Kansas plains blew the flag from the casket. It was quickly retrieved and put back by nearby military officers. Two body bearers then returned to hold the flag in place during the remainder of the service.

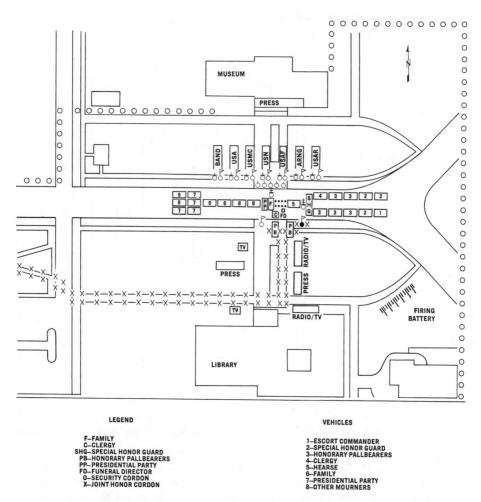

LEGEND

F–FAMILY
C–CLERGY
SHG–SPECIAL HONOR GUARD
PB–HONORARY PALLBEARERS
PP–PRESIDENTIAL PARTY
FD–FUNERAL DIRECTOR
O–SECURITY CORDON
X–JOINT HONOR CORDON

VEHICLES

1–ESCORT COMMANDER
2–SPECIAL HONOR GUARD
3–HONORARY PALLBEARERS
4–CLERGY
5–HEARSE
6–FAMILY
7–PRESIDENTIAL PARTY
8–OTHER MOURNERS

Diagram 132.   Formation, arrival ceremony, Eisenhower Library, Abilene.

At the conclusion of the funeral rites, the other body bearers returned to the library steps, and the team lifted the casket from the bier. At that point, the military escort troop units presented arms, and the Fifth Army Band sounded ruffles and flourishes and played the national anthem, "Army Blue," and the hymn "Lead Kindly Light." At the first note of "Army Blue," General Mock began the march to the Place of Meditation. The procession formed behind him in the same order that was followed when the casket was brought from the hearse to the library.

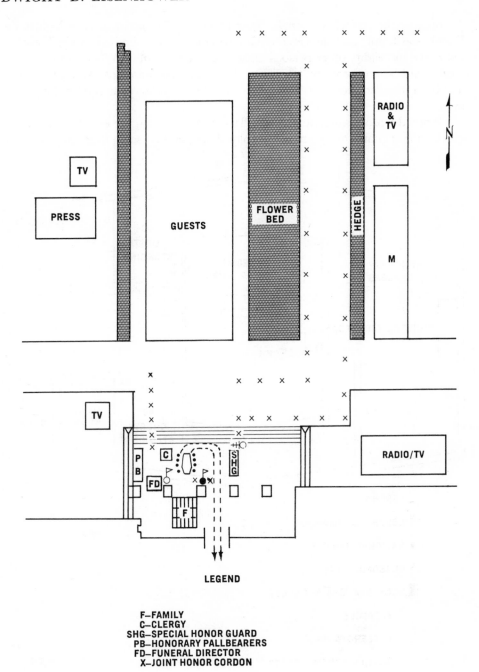

LEGEND

F—FAMILY
C—CLERGY
SHG—SPECIAL HONOR GUARD
PB—HONORARY PALLBEARERS
FD—FUNERAL DIRECTOR
X—JOINT HONOR CORDON

Diagram 133.   Funeral service, Eisenhower Library, Abilene.

Because the chapel was small, those attending the burial service, besides the Eisenhower family and the ceremonial participants, were limited to the Presidential party and eighty other persons designated by the family. Whereas the funeral service had been covered by television, the burial rites were not. An audio system had been installed, however, which allowed the public to hear the final proceedings.

When the procession reached the Place of Meditation, the escort commander, special honor guard, clergy, national color detail, and personal flag bearer entered

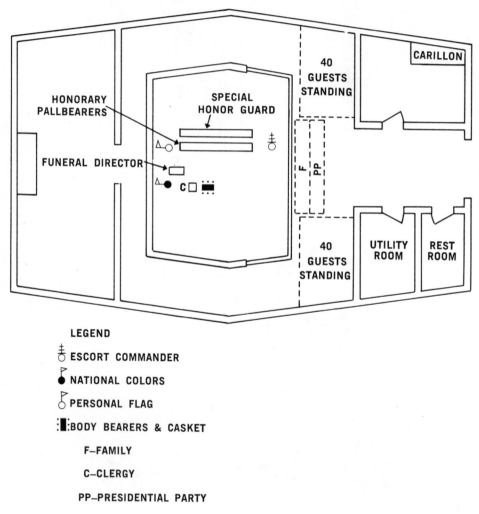

LEGEND

☦ ESCORT COMMANDER

● NATIONAL COLORS

⚑ PERSONAL FLAG

▪ BODY BEARERS & CASKET

F—FAMILY

C—CLERGY

PP—PRESIDENTIAL PARTY

Diagram 134.   Burial service, Place of Meditation, Abilene.

Body Bearers Take Up the Casket *after service in front of the Dwight D. Eisenhower Library, above. Procession moves to the Place of Meditation, below.*

TABLE 51—TROOP LIST, BURIAL SERVICE, ABILENE, FOR FORMER PRESIDENT DWIGHT D. EISENHOWER

Duty	U.S. Army		U.S. Marine Corps		U.S. Navy		U.S. Air Force		U.S. Coast Guard		Total	
	Officers	Enlisted Men	Officers	Enlisted Men	Officers	Enlisted Men	Officers	Enlisted Men	Officers	Enlisted Men	Officers	Enlisted Men
Escort commander and staff....	1	....	....	....	....	....	....	....	....	....	1	....
Special honor guard............	1	....	1	....	1	....	1	....	1	....	5	....
Commander of troops and staff...	3	....	1	....	1	....	1	....	....	....	6	....
National color detail.............	....	1	....	1	....	1	....	....	....	....	....	3
Clergy......................	1	....	....	....	....	....	....	....	....	....	1	....
Body bearers.................	1	2	....	2	....	2	....	1	....	1	1	8
Personal flag bearer.............	....	1	....	....	....	....	....	....	....	....	....	1
Band......................	1	75	....	....	....	....	....	....	....	....	1	75
Military escort												
Active....................	2	29	2	29	2	29	2	29	....	....	8	116
National Guard.............	2	29	....	....	....	....	....	....	....	....	2	29
Reserve...................	2	29	....	....	....	....	....	....	....	....	2	29
Saluting battery...............	2	36	....	....	....	....	....	....	....	....	2	36
Firing party..................	....	8	....	....	....	....	....	....	....	....	....	8
Bugler......................	....	1	....	....	....	....	....	....	....	....	....	1
Site control..................	4	3	....	....	....	....	....	....	....	....	4	3
Security cordon...............	6	158	....	....	....	....	....	....	....	....	6	158
Guides......................	2	24	....	....	....	....	....	....	....	....	2	24
Floral detail.................	1	6	....	....	....	....	....	....	....	....	1	6
Total..................	29	402	4	32	4	32	4	30	1	1	42	497

and moved directly to their ceremonial positions around the crypt. (*Table 51*) The body bearers followed next, placed the casket on a movable bier, and continued to the crypt, where the casket was put on the lowering device. The personal flag bearer, honorary pallbearers, the Eisenhower family, Presidential party, and invited guests then entered in that order for the burial service. (*Diagram 134*)

When everyone was in position, the former Army Chief of Chaplains, Canon Miller, read the burial rites; he paused, however, before pronouncing the benediction. At the pause, the site control officer for the chapel signaled the battery of six howitzers manned by two officers and thirty-six enlisted men from Fort Riley to deliver a 21-gun salute. The battery, in position just east of the library, fired the rounds at five-second intervals. (*See Diagram 132.*) The benediction was then pronounced. On the grounds just outside the chapel, the firing party discharged three volleys on a signal from the site control officer. Immediately after the last volley, the bugler blew taps. While the Fifth Army Band played "West Point Alma Mater," the body bearers folded the flag that had draped the casket of the former President. One of the bearers handed the flag to the escort commander,

BURIAL RITES AT THE CRYPT IN THE PLACE OF MEDITATION

General Mock. At that moment, on a signal relayed by the site control officer, the band stopped playing. General Mock then presented the flag to Mrs. Eisenhower, concluding the final rites for General Eisenhower. As the band played "America the Beautiful" and followed it by "The Old Rugged Cross," the Eisenhower family and the Presidential party were escorted from the chapel to their cars.

Bibliographical Note

These studies were written primarily from official records kept by the agencies of the Department of Defense involved in conducting funeral ceremonies. Documents providing background information included appropriate sections of United States Code, Title 24: Hospitals, Asylums, and Cemeteries; Army Regulations 600–25, Salutes, Honors, and Visits of Courtesy; and Army Regulations 600–30, Personnel: Honors to Persons. Further information of a general nature was obtained from War Department Pamphlet 21–39, Conduct of a Military Funeral, published in September 1947 and rescinded in 1960. Copies of these publications are in General Reference Branch, Office of the Chief of Military History, Department of the Army.

Of fundamental importance were contingency plans and official statements of policy which defined the types of funerals to be conducted, specified the civil and military officials entitled to each type, assigned responsibility for making funeral arrangements, and described in text and diagram the composition and procedure of the ceremonies. Letter, ANWGT 293, Headquarters, Military District of Washington, 17 June 1952, subject: Military Funerals, provided a summary of policies and plans that were placed in effect in 1949 and remained in force until 1958. Succeeding plans and policies were published in a document entitled State, Official, and Special Military Funeral Policies and Plans, prepared for the Department of Defense by Headquarters, Military District of Washington, in September 1958. Revisions of these plans and policies, which were still in force in 1970, were set out in Department of the Army Pamphlet 1–1 (also OPNAV-INST 5360.1, AFM 143–2, and CG–390), State, Official, and Special Military Funerals, published jointly by the Departments of the Army, Navy, Air Force, and Treasury in December 1965. Copies of these documents are in Headquarters, Military District of Washington.

Of special significance in the preparation of these studies were plans developed for the funerals of certain individuals. Some of these plans, such as the one for the funeral of General of the Armies John J. Pershing, were drawn up long before the individuals died, and consequently were developed in considerable detail. Other individual plans, such as that for President John F. Kennedy, were prepared in a short time and in an atmosphere of crisis, and therefore were less fully or formally written.

In most cases, a basic individual funeral plan was prepared by the military agency assigned the responsibility for arranging and co-ordinating the ceremony; component plans were prepared by the military units scheduled to participate in or support the ceremony. Typical of basic individual plans were those developed by Headquarters, Military District of Washington; Headquarters, Potomac River Naval Command; and Headquarters Command, U.S. Air Force. Typical of component plans were those prepared by the 3d Infantry. Copies of the individual plans consulted were obtained from various agencies, including the National Archives in Washington; National Personnel Records Center in St. Louis, Missouri; Office of the Chief of Support Services, Department of the Army; Bureau of Naval Personnel, Department of the Navy; Headquarters, Military District of Washington; Headquarters Command, U.S. Air Force; and Headquarters, 1st Battalion, 3d Infantry.

After action reports prepared by the commands and staff agencies responsible for arranging and conducting the funeral ceremonies were basic sources for many of the studies. These reports varied in quality and content. The best of them included a narrative, supporting documents, and statements of problems encountered. As a rule, copies of after action reports are retained by the agencies that hold copies of the individual funeral plans.

The National Archives provided other pertinent information. Most useful were the file, Honors in Funeral Ceremonies, 1929–1931, which included material on the State Funeral for William Howard Taft, and the Mail and Records Branch File, Office of the Secretary of Defense, Volume I, March 1948 through June 1949, which contained information on the ceremony for former Secretary of Defense James V. Forrestal.

Considerable use was made of newspaper reports of the various funeral ceremonies. The *New York Times,* the *Washington Post,* and the *Evening Star* were most frequently consulted. Some clippings from local newspapers were available. Notable were accounts of the ceremony for Senator Styles Bridges printed in New Hampshire papers, which were provided by the Office of the Sergeant at Arms, U.S. Senate. Other newspaper accounts used came from the Biography and Miscellaneous files in the General Reference Branch, Office of the Chief of Military History.

Periodicals and published works provided little information. Useful for background material was John Vincent Hinkel, *Arlington: Monument to Heroes* (New Jersey: Prentice-Hall, 1965). The November 1968 issue of *Esquire* contained an article that was helpful on the ceremony for Senator Robert F. Kennedy. William Manchester, *Death of a President* (New York: Harper, 1967), included a detailed account of the funeral of John F. Kennedy.

Appendix A

Tables of Entitlement

Official	Funeral							
	State	Official	Special Military	Armed Forces Full Honor	Special Full Honor	Full Honor (Company)	Full Honor (Platoon)	Simple Honor
President of the United States ª	X							
Former President of the United States ª	X							
President-elect of the United States ª	X							
Other persons designated by the President ª	X							
Vice President of the United States ª		X						
Chief Justice of the United States ª		X						
Cabinet members ª		X						
Other government officials designated by the President of the United States ª		X						
Foreign civil dignitaries designated by the President of the United States ª		X						
Deputy Secretary of Defense ª			X					
Former Secretary of Defense ª			X					
Secretary of the Army, the Navy, and the Air Force ª			X					
Five-star generals and admirals			X					
Chief of Staff, U.S. Army			X					
Chief of Naval Operations			X					
Chief of Staff, U.S. Air Force			X					
Commandant, U.S. Marine Corps			X					
Commandant, U.S. Coast Guard			X					
Other persons designated by the Secretary of Defense ª			X					
Foreign military personnel designated by the President of the United States ª			X					
Assistant Secretary of Defense ª			X					
Under Secretary of the Army, the Navy, and the Air Force ª			X					

See footnote at end of table.

APPENDIX A–1—TABLE OF ENTITLEMENT, 1949 *(Continued)*

Official	Funeral							
	State	Official	Special Military	Com-bined Services Full Honor	Special Full Honor	Full Honor (Com-pany)	Full Honor (Pla-toon)	Simple Honor
Assistant Secretary of the Army, the Navy, and the Air Force ᵃ			X					
Former Deputy Secretary of Defense ᵃ				X				
Former Assistant Secretary of Defense ᵃ				X				
Former Secretary of the Army, the Navy, and the Air Force ᵃ				X				
Former Chief of Staff, U.S. Army and U.S. Air Force; Former Chief of Naval Operations				X				
Four-star generals and admirals					X			
Army commanders					X			
Lieutenant general, vice admiral, major general, rear admiral, brigadier general, colonel, and captain						X		
Officers below grade of colonel and captain							X	
All other military personnel								X

ᵃ Not entitled to burial in any national cemetery by virtue of this position alone.

Appendix A–2—Table of Entitlement, 1958

Official	Funeral							
	State	Official	Special Military	Armed Forces Full Honor	Special Full Honor	Full Honor (Company)	Full Honor (Platoon)	Simple Honor
President of the United States [a]	X							
Former President of the United States [a]	X							
President-elect of the United States [a]	X							
Other persons designated by the President [a]	X							
Vice President of the United States [a]		X						
Chief Justice of the United States [a]		X						
Cabinet members [a]		X						
Other government officials designated by the President of the United States [a]		X						
Foreign civil dignitaries designated by the President of the United States [a]		X						
Deputy Secretary of Defense [a]			X					
Former Secretary of Defense [a]			X					
Secretary of the Army, the Navy, and the Air Force [a]			X					
Chairman, Joint Chiefs of Staff			X					
Five-star generals and admirals			X					
Chief of Staff, U.S. Army			X					
Chief of Naval Operations			X					
Chief of Staff, U.S. Air Force			X					
Commandant, U.S. Marine Corps			X					
Commandant, U.S. Coast Guard			X					
Other persons designated by the Secretary of Defense [a]			X					
Foreign military personnel designated by the President of the United States [a]			X					
Former Deputy Secretary of Defense [a]				X				
Former Chairman, Joint Chiefs of Staff (not five-star general or admiral)				X				
Assistant Secretary of Defense [a]				X				
Former Secretary of the Army, the Navy, and the Air Force [a]					X			
Former Chief of Staff, U.S. Army and U.S. Air Force; Former Chief of Naval Operations					X			

See footnote at end of table.

APPENDIX A–2—TABLE OF ENTITLEMENT, 1958 (*Continued*)

Official	Funeral							
	State	Official	Special Military	Joint Service Full Honor	Special Full Honor	Full Honor (Com-pany)	Full Honor (Pla-toon)	Simple Honor
Under Secretary of the Army, the Navy, and the Air Force ª......					X			
Four-star generals and admirals.....					X			
Assistant Secretary of the Army, the Navy, and the Air Force ª......					X			
Lieutenant general, vice admiral, major general, rear admiral, brigadier general, colonel, and captain......................						X		
Officers below grade of colonel and captain......................							X	
All other military personnel.........								X

ª Not entitled to burial in any national cemetery by virtue of this position alone.

Appendix A–3—Table of Entitlement, 1965

Official	Funeral							
	State	Official	Special Military	Armed Forces Full Honor	Special Full Honor	Full Honor (Company)	Full Honor (Platoon)	Simple Honor
President of the United States......	X							
Former President of the United States	X							
President-elect of the United States ª	X							
Other persons designated by the President ª..................	X							
Vice President of the United States ª		X						
Chief Justice of the United States ª..		X						
Cabinet members ª................		X						
Other government officials designated by the President of the United States ª................		X						
Foreign civil dignitaries designated by the President of the United States ª......................		X						
Deputy Secretary of Defense ª......			X					
Former Secretary of Defense ª......			X					
Secretary of the Army, the Navy, and the Air Force ª...........			X					
Chairman, Joint Chiefs of Staff.....			X					
Five-star generals and admirals.....			X					
Chief of Staff, U.S. Army..........			X					
Chief of Naval Operations.........			X					
Chief of Staff, U.S. Air Force.......			X					
Commandant, U.S. Marine Corps...			X					
Commandant, U.S. Coast Guard....			X					
Other persons designated by the Secretary of Defense ª.........			X					
Foreign military personnel designated by the President of the United States ª................			X					
Former Deputy Secretary of Defense ª				X				
Former Chairman, Joint Chiefs of Staff (not five-star general or admiral).......................				X				
Assistant Secretary of Defense ª.....				X				
Former Secretary of the Army, the Navy, and the Air Force ª......					X			
Former Chief of Staff, U.S. Army and U.S. Air Force; Former Chief of Naval Operations......					X			

See footnote at end of table.

APPENDIX A–3—TABLE OF ENTITLEMENT, 1965 (*Continued*)

Official	Funeral							
	State	Official	Special Military	Armed Forces Full Honor	Special Full Honor	Full Honor (Company)	Full Honor (Platoon)	Simple Honor
Under Secretary of the Army, the Navy, and the Air Force [a]					X			
Four-star generals and admirals					X			
Assistant Secretary of the Army, the Navy, and the Air Force [a]					X			
Lieutenant general, vice admiral, major general, rear admiral, brigadier general, colonel, and captain						X		
Officers below grade of colonel and captain							X	
All other military personnel								X

[a] Not entitled to burial in any national cemetery by virtue of this position alone.

Appendix B

Policies on Strength and Composition of Military Escorts, 1949, 1958, and 1965

APPENDIX B–1—STATE AND OFFICIAL FUNERALS

1949		1958		1965	
Total Units		**Total Units**		**Total Units**	
6 bands		3 bands		3 bands	
15 battalions		16 companies (enlisted men)		16 companies (enlisted men)	
		1 company (servicewomen)		1 company (servicewomen)	
Strength		**Strength**		**Strength**	
Not specified		Band	83–101	Band	92
		Company		Company	
		(enlisted men)	89	(enlisted men)	89
		Company		Company	
		(servicewomen)	102	(servicewomen)	74
Sources of Troop Units		**Sources of Troop Units**		**Sources of Troop Units**	
Military Academies		Military Academies		Military Academies	
(3 battalions)		(4 companies)		(4 companies)	
U.S. Military	1	U.S. Military	1	U.S. Military	1
U.S. Naval	1	U.S. Naval	1	U.S. Naval	1
U.S. Air Force	1	U.S. Air Force	1	U.S. Air Force	1
		U.S. Coast Guard	1	U.S. Coast Guard	1
Active Armed Forces		**Active Armed Forces**		**Active Armed Forces**	
(6 battalions)		(6 companies)		(6 companies)	
Army	3	Army	1	Army	1
Marine Corps	1	Marine Corps	1	Marine Corps	1
Navy	1	Navy	1	Navy	1
Air Force	1	Air Force	1	Air Force	1
		Coast Guard	1	Coast Guard	1
		Servicewomen		Servicewomen	
		(composite)	1	(composite)	1
Reserve Components		**Reserve Components**		**Reserve Components**	
(6 battalions)		(7 companies)		(7 companies)	
Army National Guard	1	Army National Guard	1	Army National Guard	1
Army Reserve	1	Army Reserve	1	Army Reserve	1
Marine Corps Reserve	1	Marine Corps Reserve	1	Marine Corps Reserve	1
Navy Reserve	1	Navy Reserve	1	Navy Reserve	1
Air National Guard	1	Air National Guard	1	Air National Guard	1
Air Force Reserve	1	Air Force Reserve	1	Air Force Reserve	1
		Coast Guard Reserve	1	Coast Guard Reserve	1

Appendix B–2—Special Military Funeral

1949	1958	1965
Total Units	Total Units	Total Units
2 bands	2 bands	2 bands
1 battalion	9 companies (enlisted men)	9 companies (enlisted men)
6 companies	1 company (servicewomen)	1 company (servicewomen)
Strength	Strength	Strength
Not specified	Band............. 83–101	Band.............. 92
	Company	Company
	(enlisted men). 89	(enlisted men).. 89
	Company	Company
	(servicewomen). 102	(servicewomen).. 74
Sources of Troop Units	Sources of Troop Units	Sources of Troop Units
Military Academies	Military Academies	Military Academies
(1 battalion)	(4 companies)	(4 companies)
(Furnished by the academy	U.S. Military......... 1	U.S. Military.......... 1
of the service to which the	U.S. Naval........... 1	U.S. Naval............ 1
individual had belonged.)	U.S. Air Force....... 1	U.S. Air Force........ 1
	U.S. Coast Guard..... 1	U.S. Coast Guard...... 1
Active Armed Forces	Active Armed Forces	Active Armed Forces
(6 companies)	(6 companies)	(6 companies)
Army.................. 3	Army.................. 1	Army.................. 1
Marine Corps........... 1	Marine Corps.......... 1	Marine Corps........... 1
Navy.................. 1	Navy.................. 1	Navy.................. 1
Air Force.............. 1	Air Force.............. 1	Air Force.............. 1
	Coast Guard........... 1	Coast Guard............ 1
	Servicewomen	Servicewomen
	(composite)......... 1	(composite)......... 1

Appendix B–3—Combined Services (Joint Service, Armed Forces) Full Honor Funeral

1949	1958	1965
Total Units	Total Units	Total Units
1 band	1 band	1 band
4 companies	4 companies	4 companies
Strength	Strength	Strength
Not specified	Band........ not specified	Band......... not specified
	Company..... 66	Company...... 66
Sources of Troop Units	Sources of Troop Units	Sources of Troop Units
Active Armed Forces	Active Armed Forces	Active Armed Forces
(4 companies)	(4 companies)	(4 companies)
Army................ 1	Army................ 1	Army................ 1
Marine Corps.......... 1	Marine Corps......... 1	Marine Corps.......... 1
Navy................ 1	Navy................ 1	Navy................ 1
Air Force.............. 1	Air Force............. 1	Air Force.............. 1

Appendix B–4—Special Full Honor Funeral

1949	1958	1965
Total Units [a]	Total Units [a]	Total Units [a]
1 band	1 band	1 band
1 battalion	4 companies	4 companies
Strength [a]	Strength [a]	Strength [a]
Not specified	Band........ not specified	Band........ not specified
	Company..... 66	Company...... 66
Sources of Troop Units	Sources of Troop Units	Sources of Troop Units
Active Armed Forces	Active Armed Forces	Active Armed Forces
Both the band and the troop units to come from the service of which the individual had been a member.	Both the band and the troop units to come from the service of which the individual had been a member.	Both the band and the troop units to come from the service of which the individual had been a member.

[a] The total numbers and sizes of units are those given in Army standing operating procedures at the time. Figures have varied depending upon the service conducting the ceremony.

Appendix B–5—Full Honor (Company) Funeral

1949	1958	1965
Total Units [a]	Total Units [a]	Total Units [a]
1 band	1 band	1 band
1 company	1 company	1 company
Strength [a]	Strength [a]	Strength [a]
Company to consist of two platoons only. Otherwise, strength not specified.	Band.............. 26 Company........... 64 (Company to consist of two platoons only.)	Band.............. 16–24 Company........... 40 (Company to consist of two platoons only.)
Sources of Troop Units	Sources of Troop Units	Sources of Troop Units
Active Armed Forces	Active Armed Forces	Active Armed Forces
Both the band and the troop units to come from the service of which the individual had been a member.	Both the band and the troop units to come from the service of which the individual had been a member.	Both the band and the troop units to come from the service of which the individual had been a member.

[a] The total numbers and sizes of units are those given in Army standing operating procedures at the time. Figures have varied depending upon the service conducting the ceremony.

APPENDIX B–6—FULL HONOR (PLATOON) FUNERAL

1949	1958	1965
Total Units *a*	Total Units *a*	Total Units *a*
1 band	1 band	1 band
1 platoon	1 platoon	1 platoon
Strength *a*	Strength *a*	Strength *a*
Not specified	Band.............. 26	Band.............. 16–24
	Platoon............ 32	Platoon............ 30
Sources of Troop Units	Sources of Troop Units	Sources of Troop Units
Active Armed Forces	Active Armed Forces	Active Armed Forces
Both the band and the troop units to come from the service of which the individual had been a member.	Both the band and the troop units to come from the service of which the individual had been a member.	Both the band and the troop units to come from the service of which the individual had been a member.

a The total numbers and sizes of units are those given in Army standing operating procedures at the time. Figures have varied depending upon the service conducting the ceremony.

Appendix B–7—Simple (Full) Honor Funeral

1949	1958	1965
No military escort	No military escort	No military escort

Appendix C

Summaries of State Funerals

APPENDIX C–1—STATE FUNERAL FOR FORMER PRESIDENT WILLIAM HOWARD TAFT
8–11 MARCH 1930

Primary responsibility for funeral arrangements
  Commanding General of the 16th Brigade, Fort Hunt, Virginia
Chronology of ceremonies
  8 March............ Date of death
  11 March............ Procession, Washington residence to U.S. Capitol
  11 March............ Arrival ceremony, U.S. Capitol
  11 March............ Lying in state, U.S. Capitol
  11 March............ Departure ceremony, U.S. Capitol
  11 March............ Main funeral procession
  11 March............ Arrival ceremony, All Souls' Unitarian Church, Washington
  11 March............ Funeral service, All Souls' Unitarian Church
  11 March............ Departure ceremony, All Souls' Unitarian Church
  11 March............ Procession to Arlington National Cemetery
  11 March............ Burial service, Arlington National Cemetery
Military escort units, main funeral procession
  Total: 2 bands, 3 battalions, 1 company
  Composition, active armed forces
    Army: 1 band, 1 infantry battalion, 1 artillery battalion
    Marine Corps: 1 band, 1 battalion
    Navy: 1 company

Appendix C–2—State Funeral for President John F. Kennedy 22–25 November 1963

Primary responsibility for funeral arrangements
  Commanding General of the Military District of Washington
Chronology of ceremonies
      22 November....... Date of death
      22 November....... Arrival ceremony, Andrews Air Force Base
      23 November....... Arrival ceremony, White House
      23 November....... Period of repose, White House
      24 November....... Departure ceremony, White House
      24 November....... Procession to U.S. Capitol
      24 November....... Arrival ceremony, U.S. Capitol
  24–25 November....... Lying in state, U.S. Capitol
      25 November....... Departure ceremony, U.S. Capitol
      25 November....... Main funeral procession (with halt at the White House)
      25 November....... Arrival ceremony, St. Matthew's Cathedral
      25 November....... Funeral service, St. Matthew's Cathedral
      25 November....... Departure ceremony, St. Matthew's Cathedral
      25 November....... Procession to Arlington National Cemetery
      25 November....... Burial service, Arlington National Cemetery

Military escort units, main funeral procession
  Total: 4 bands, 17 companies, 1 platoon
  Composition
    Active armed forces
      Army: 1 company, U.S. Military Academy (89); 1 company (89); 1 platoon, Special Forces (38)
      Marine Corps: 1 band (91), 1 company (89)
      Navy: 1 band (91); 1 company, U.S. Naval Academy (89); 1 company (89)
      Air Force: 1 band (91); 1 company, U.S. Air Force Academy (89); 1 squadron (89)
      Coast Guard: 1 company, U.S. Coast Guard Academy (89); 1 company (89)
      Servicewomen (composite): 1 company (82)
      Foreign unit: Black Watch Bagpipers (9)
    Reserve components
      Army: 1 company, National Guard (89); 1 company, Reserve (89)
      Marine Corps: 1 company, Reserve (79)
      Navy: 1 company, Reserve (89)
      Air Force: 1 squadron, National Guard (89); 1 squadron, Reserve (89)
      Coast Guard: 1 company, Reserve (89)

APPENDIX C–3—STATE FUNERAL FOR FORMER
PRESIDENT HERBERT C. HOOVER
20–25 OCTOBER 1964

Primary responsibility for funeral arrangements
   Commanding General of the Military District of Washington
     Ceremonies in New York: Commanding General of the First Army
     Ceremonies in Washington: Commanding General of the Military District of Washington
     Ceremonies in Iowa: Commanding General of the Fifth Army
Chronology of ceremonies

20 October........	Date of death
20–21 October........	Period of repose, Universal Funeral Chapel, New York
21 October........	Period of repose, St. Bartholomew's Episcopal Church, New York
22 October........	Funeral service, St. Bartholomew's Episcopal Church, New York
23 October........	Departure ceremony, St. Bartholomew's Episcopal Church, New York
23 October........	Procession to Pennsylvania Station, New York
23 October........	Departure ceremony, Pennsylvania Station, New York
23 October........	Arrival ceremony, Union Station, Washington
23 October........	Main funeral procession
23 October........	Arrival ceremony, U.S. Capitol
23–24 October........	Lying in state, U.S. Capitol
25 October........	Departure ceremony, U.S. Capitol
25 October........	Procession to Washington National Airport
25 October........	Departure ceremony, Washington National Airport
25 October........	Arrival ceremony, Municipal Airport, Cedar Rapids, Iowa
25 October........	Procession to Herbert Hoover Library, West Branch, Iowa
25 October........	Burial service, Herbert Hoover Library, West Branch, Iowa

Military escort units, main funeral procession
   Total: 1 band, 17 companies
   Composition
     Active armed forces
       Army: 1 band (56); 1 company, U.S. Military Academy (82); 1 company (82)
       Marine Corps: 1 company (82)
       Navy: 1 company, U.S. Naval Academy (82); 1 company (82)
       Air Force: 1 company, U.S. Air Force Academy (82); 1 company (82)
       Coast Guard: 1 company, U.S. Coast Guard Academy (82); 1 company (82)
       Servicewomen (composite): 1 company (82)
     Reserve components
       Army: 1 company, National Guard (82); 1 company, Reserve (82)
       Marine Corps: 1 company, Reserve (82)
       Navy: 1 company, Reserve (82)
       Air Force: 1 company, National Guard (82); 1 company, Reserve (82)
       Coast Guard: 1 company, Reserve (82)

Appendix C–4—State Funeral for General of the Armies John J. Pershing
15–19 July 1948

Primary responsibility for funeral arrangements
  Commanding General of the Military District of Washington
Chronology of ceremonies
  15 July............ Date of death
  17–18 July............ Period of repose, Walter Reed General Hospital Chapel, Washington
  18 July............ Departure ceremony, Walter Reed General Hospital Chapel
  18 July............ Procession to U.S. Capitol
  18 July............ Arrival ceremony, U.S. Capitol
  18–19 July............ Lying in state, U.S. Capitol
  19 July............ Departure ceremony, U.S. Capitol
  19 July............ Main funeral procession
  19 July............ Honors at Tomb of the Unknown Soldier, Arlington National Cemetery
  19 July............ Funeral service, Memorial Amphitheater, Arlington National Cemetery
  19 July............ Procession to gravesite, Arlington National Cemetery
  19 July............ Burial service, Arlington National Cemetery
Military escort units, main funeral procession
  Total: 2 bands, 6 battalions, 2 companies
  Composition, active armed forces
    Army: U.S. Army Band; the Army Ground Forces Band; 1 battalion, U.S. Military Academy (383);
      1 infantry battalion (488); 1 artillery battalion (280); 1 mechanized cavalry battalion (394);
      1 engineer battalion (488)
    Marine Corps: 1 company (121)
    Navy: 1 company (121)
    Air Force: 1 battalion (246)

APPENDIX C–5—STATE FUNERAL FOR GENERAL OF
THE ARMY DOUGLAS MACARTHUR
5–11 APRIL 1964

Primary responsibility for funeral arrangements

Commanding General of the Military District of Washington
Ceremonies in New York: Commanding General of the First Army
Ceremonies in Washington: Commanding General of the Military District of Washington
Ceremonies in Norfolk: Commanding General of the Continental Army Command

Chronology of ceremonies

5 April............	Date of death
6–7 April............	Period of private repose, Universal Funeral Parlor, New York
7 April............	Period of repose, 7th Regiment Armory, New York
7 April............	Private memorial service, 7th Regiment Armory, New York
8 April............	Departure ceremony, 7th Regiment Armory, New York
8 April............	Procession to Pennsylvania Station, New York
8 April............	Departure ceremony, Pennsylvania Station, New York
8 April............	Arrival ceremony, Union Station, Washington
8 April............	Main funeral procession
8 April............	Arrival ceremony, U.S. Capitol
8–9 April............	Lying in state, U.S. Capitol
9 April............	Departure ceremony, U.S. Capitol
9 April............	Procession to Washington National Airport
9 April............	Departure ceremony, Washington National Airport
9 April............	Arrival ceremony, Naval Air Station, Norfolk
9 April............	Procession to MacArthur Memorial, Norfolk
9 April............	Arrival ceremony, MacArthur Memorial, Norfolk
9–11 April............	Period of repose, MacArthur Memorial, Norfolk
11 April............	Departure ceremony, MacArthur Memorial, Norfolk
11 April............	Procession to St. Paul's Episcopal Church, Norfolk
11 April............	Arrival ceremony, St. Paul's Episcopal Church, Norfolk
11 April............	Funeral service, St. Paul's Episcopal Church, Norfolk
11 April............	Departure ceremony, St. Paul's Episcopal Church, Norfolk
11 April............	Procession to MacArthur Memorial, Norfolk
11 April............	Arrival ceremony, MacArthur Memorial, Norfolk
11 April............	Burial service, MacArthur Memorial, Norfolk

Military escort units, main funeral procession

Total: 3 bands, 17 companies

Composition

Active armed forces

Army: 1 band (83); 1 company, U.S. Military Academy (89); 1 company (89)

Marine Corps: 1 band (83), 1 company (89)

Navy: 1 company, U.S. Naval Academy (89); 1 company (89)

Air Force: 1 band (83); 1 company, U.S. Air Force Academy (89); 1 company (89)

Coast Guard: 1 company, U.S. Coast Guard Academy (89); 1 company (89)

Servicewomen (composite): 1 company (82)

APPENDIX C–5—STATE FUNERAL FOR GENERAL OF
THE ARMY DOUGLAS MACARTHUR
5–11 APRIL 1964 (*Continued*)

Reserve components
    Army: 1 company, National Guard (89); 1 company, Reserve (89)
    Marine Corps: 1 company, Reserve (89)
    Navy: 1 company, Reserve (89)
    Air Force: 1 company, National Guard (89); 1 company, Reserve (89)
    Coast Guard: 1 company, Reserve (89)

APPENDIX C–6—STATE FUNERAL FOR
THE UNKNOWN SOLDIER OF WORLD WAR I
24 OCTOBER–11 NOVEMBER 1921

Responsibility for funeral arrangements
  Ceremonies in France: Army Quartermaster General
  Ceremonies in the United States: Commanding General of the Military District of Washington
Chronology of ceremonies
  24 October............   Selection ceremony, Châlons-sur-Marne, France
  24 October............   Departure ceremony, Châlons-sur-Marne, France
  25 October............   Arrival ceremony, Le Havre, France
  25 October............   Procession to Pier d'Escale, Le Havre, France
  25 October............   Departure ceremony, Le Havre, France
   9 November..........   Arrival ceremony, Navy Yard, Washington, D.C.
   9 November..........   Procession to U.S. Capitol
   9 November..........   Arrival ceremony, U.S. Capitol
  10 November..........   Lying in state, U.S. Capitol
  11 November..........   Departure ceremony, U.S. Capitol
  11 November..........   Main funeral procession
  11 November..........   Arrival ceremony, Memorial Amphitheater, Arlington National Cemetery
  11 November..........   Funeral service, Memorial Amphitheater, Arlington National Cemetery
  11 November..........   Procession to tomb, Arlington National Cemetery
  11 November..........   Burial service, Arlington National Cemetery
Military escort units, main funeral procession
  Total: 2 bands, 1 drum corps, 5 battalions
  Composition
    Active armed forces
      Army: 1 band, the Army Drum Corps, 1 infantry battalion, 1 mounted artillery battalion,
        1 cavalry squadron
      Marine Corps: 1 band
      Composites: 1 combined battalion, marines and bluejackets
    Reserve components
      Army National Guard: 1 engineer battalion

Appendix C-7—State Funeral for the Unknown Soldiers of World War II and the Korean War 12–30 May 1958

Primary responsibility for funeral arrangements
    Project co-ordinator: Army Quartermaster General
        Selection of a soldier from the transatlantic phase of World War II: Commander in Chief, U.S. Army, Europe
        Selection of a soldier from the transpacific phase of World War II: Commanding General of the Far East Air Forces
        Selection of unknown soldier of the Korean War: Commanding General, U.S. Army, Pacific
        Selection of unknown soldier of World War II: Chief of Naval Operations
        Ceremonies in Washington: Commanding General of the Military District of Washington
Chronology of ceremonies

12 May	Selection ceremony, World War II soldier from the transatlantic phase, France
15 May	Selection ceremony, unknown soldier of Korean War, Hawaii
16 May	Selection ceremony, World War II soldier from the transpacific phase, Hawaii
26 May	Selection ceremony, unknown soldier of World War II, at sea, off Virginia Capes
28 May	Arrival ceremony, Naval Gun Factory, Washington
28 May	Procession to U.S. Capitol
28 May	Arrival ceremony, U.S. Capitol
28–30 May	Lying in state, U.S. Capitol
30 May	Departure ceremony, U.S. Capitol
30 May	Main funeral procession
30 May	Arrival ceremony, Memorial Amphitheater, Arlington National Cemetery
30 May	Funeral service, Memorial Amphitheater, Arlington National Cemetery
30 May	Procession to tomb, Arlington National Cemetery
30 May	Burial service, Arlington National Cemetery

Military escort units, main funeral procession
    Total: 3 bands, 15 companies
    Composition
      Active armed forces
        Army: 1 band (100); 1 company, U.S. Military Academy (89); 1 company (89)
        Marine Corps: 1 company (89)
        Navy: 1 band (100); 1 company, U.S. Naval Academy (89); 1 company (89)
        Air Force: 1 band (100), 1 squadron (89)
        Coast Guard: 1 company (89)
        Servicewomen (composite): 1 company (80)
      Reserve components
        Army: 1 company, National Guard (89); 1 company, Reserve (89)
        Marine Corps: 1 company, Reserve (89)
        Navy: 1 company, Reserve (89)
        Air Force: 1 company, National Guard (89); 1 company, Reserve (89)
        Coast Guard: 1 company, Reserve (89)

APPENDIX C–8—STATE FUNERAL FOR FORMER
PRESIDENT DWIGHT D. EISENHOWER
28 MARCH–2 APRIL 1969

Primary responsibility for funeral arrangements
  Commanding General of the Military District of Washington
    Ceremonies in Washington: Commanding General of the Military District of Washington
    Ceremonies in Abilene, Kansas: Commanding General, Fifth U.S. Army
Chronology of ceremonies

28 March	Date of death
28–29 March	Period of private repose, Gawler's funeral establishment, Washington
29 March	Arrival ceremony, Washington National Cathedral
29–30 March	Period of repose, Bethlehem Chapel, Washington National Cathedral
30 March	Departure ceremony, Washington National Cathedral
30 March	Main funeral procession to U.S. Capitol
30 March	Arrival ceremony, U.S. Capitol
30–31 March	Lying in state, U.S. Capitol
31 March	Departure ceremony, U.S. Capitol
31 March	Arrival ceremony, Washington National Cathedral
31 March	Funeral service, Washington National Cathedral
31 March	Departure ceremony, Washington National Cathedral
31 March	Departure ceremony, Union Station, Washington
2 April	Arrival ceremony, Abilene, Kansas
2 April	Procession to Dwight D. Eisenhower Library, Abilene
2 April	Arrival ceremony, Dwight D. Eisenhower Library
2 April	Funeral service, Dwight D. Eisenhower Library
2 April	Departure ceremony, Dwight D. Eisenhower Library
2 April	Procession to Place of Meditation, Dwight D. Eisenhower Library grounds
2 April	Burial service, Place of Meditation

Military escort units, main funeral procession
  Total: 3 bands, 17 companies
  Composition
    Active armed forces
      Army: 1 band (92); 1 company, U.S. Military Academy (89); 1 company (89)
      Marine Corps: 1 company (89)
      Navy: 1 band (92); 1 company, U.S. Naval Academy (89); 1 company (89)
      Air Force: 1 band (92); 1 company, U.S. Air Force Academy (89); 1 company (89)
      Coast Guard: 1 company, U.S. Coast Guard Academy (89); 1 company (89)
      Servicewomen (composite): 1 company (81)
    Reserve components
      Army: 1 company, National Guard (89); 1 company, Reserve (89)
      Marine Corps: 1 company, Reserve (89)
      Navy: 1 company, Reserve (89)
      Air Force: 1 company, National Guard (89); 1 company, Reserve (89)
      Coast Guard: 1 company, Reserve (89)

Appendix D

Summaries of Official Funerals

APPENDIX D–1—OFFICIAL FUNERAL FOR FORMER
SECRETARY OF DEFENSE JAMES V. FORRESTAL
22–25 MAY 1949

Primary responsibility for funeral arrangements
  Commanding General of the Military District of Washington
Chronology of ceremonies
  22 May............... Date of death
  25 May............... Main funeral procession
  25 May............... Arrival ceremony, Memorial Amphitheater, Arlington National Cemetery
  25 May............... Funeral service, Memorial Amphitheater, Arlington National Cemetery
  25 May............... Departure ceremony, Memorial Amphitheater, Arlington National Cemetery
  25 May............... Procession to gravesite, Arlington National Cemetery
  25 May............... Burial service, Arlington National Cemetery
Military escort units, main funeral procession
  Total: 1 band, 1 battalion, 4 companies
  Composition, active armed forces
    Army: 1 company
    Marine Corps: 1 company
    Navy: U.S. Naval Academy Band; 1 battalion, U.S. Naval Academy; 1 company
    Air Force: 1 company

APPENDIX D–2—OFFICIAL FUNERAL FOR FORMER
SECRETARY OF STATE JOHN FOSTER DULLES
24–27 MAY 1959

Primary responsibility for funeral arrangements
    Department of State
Chronology of ceremonies
        24 May............ Date of death
    25–26 May........... Period of repose, Dulles residence, Washington
        26 May........... Procession to Washington National Cathedral
        26 May........... Arrival ceremony, Washington National Cathedral
    26–27 May........... Period of repose, Bethlehem Chapel, Washington National Cathedral
        27 May........... Funeral service, Washington National Cathedral
        27 May........... Departure ceremony, Washington National Cathedral
        27 May........... Main funeral procession
        27 May........... Burial service, Arlington National Cemetery
Military escort units, main funeral procession
    Total: 1 band, 6 companies
    Composition, active armed forces
        Army: 1 band, 1 company (89)
        Marine Corps: 1 company (89)
        Navy: 1 company (89)
        Air Force: 1 company (89)
        Coast Guard: 1 company (89)
        Servicewomen (composite): 1 company (102)

Appendix D–3—Official Funeral for U.S. Representative to the United Nations Adlai E. Stevenson 14–19 July 1965

Primary responsibility for funeral arrangements
  Department of State
    Military ceremonies in Washington: Commanding General of the Military District of Washington
    Co-ordination in Illinois: Governor of Illinois
    Military ceremonies in Illinois: Commanding General of the Fifth Army
Chronology of ceremonies [a]

14 July............	Date of death
14–15 July............	Period of repose, U.S. Embassy, London
15 July............	Departure ceremony, London
15 July............	Arrival ceremony, Andrews Air Force Base
15 July............	Procession to Washington National Cathedral
15 July............	Arrival ceremony, Washington National Cathedral
15–16 July............	Period of repose, Bethlehem Chapel, Washington National Cathedral
16 July............	Funeral service, Washington National Cathedral
16 July............	Departure ceremony, Washington National Cathedral
16 July............	Procession to Andrews Air Force Base
16 July............	Departure ceremony, Andrews Air Force Base
16 July............	Arrival ceremony, Capitol Airport, Springfield, Illinois
16 July............	Procession to state capitol, Springfield, Illinois
16 July............	Arrival ceremony, state capitol, Springfield, Illinois
16–18 July............	Period of repose, state capitol, Springfield, Illinois
18 July............	Departure ceremony, state capitol, Springfield, Illinois
18 July............	Procession to Bloomington, Illinois
18–19 July............	Period of repose, Unitarian Church, Bloomington, Illinois
19 July............	Funeral service, Unitarian Church, Bloomington, Illinois
19 July............	Procession to Evergreen Memorial Cemetery, Bloomington, Illinois
19 July............	Burial service, Evergreen Memorial Cemetery, Bloomington, Illinois

[a] Contrary to custom, the ceremonies for Mr. Stevenson did not include a main funeral procession.

Appendix E

Summaries of Special Military Funerals

APPENDIX E–1—SPECIAL MILITARY FUNERAL FOR CHIEF OF NAVAL OPERATIONS ADMIRAL FORREST P. SHERMAN 22–27 JULY 1951

Primary responsibility for funeral arrangements
  Commandant of the Potomac River Naval Command
Chronology of ceremonies

22 July............	Date of death
24 July............	Funeral service aboard *Mount Olympus*, Naples, Italy
24 July............	Departure ceremony, Capodichino Airport, Naples, Italy
25 July............	Arrival ceremony, Washington National Airport
26–27 July............	Period of repose, Bethlehem Chapel, Washington National Cathedral
27 July............	Main funeral procession
27 July............	Funeral service, Memorial Amphitheater, Arlington National Cemetery
27 July............	Burial service, Arlington National Cemetery

Military escort units, main funeral procession
  Total: 3 bands, 2 battalions, 7 companies
  Composition, active armed forces
    Army: 1 band; 1 battalion, U.S. Military Academy (240); 1 infantry company (100); 1 artillery
      battery; 1 armored car detachment
    Marine Corps: 1 company (100)
    Navy: 1 band; 1 battalion, U.S. Naval Academy (240); 1 company (100)
    Air Force: Andrews Air Force Base Band, 1 company (100)
    Servicewomen (composite): 1 company (120)

Appendix E–2—Special Military Funeral for Former Air Force Chief of Staff General Hoyt S. Vandenberg 2–5 April 1954

Primary responsibility for funeral arrangements
  Commanding General, Headquarters Command, U.S. Air Force
Chronology of ceremonies
    2 April............... Date of death
    3 April............... Procession, Rinaldi Funeral Home to Washington National Cathedral
    3 April............... Arrival ceremony, Washington National Cathedral
  3–5 April............. Period of repose, St. Joseph's Chapel, Washington National Cathedral
    5 April............... Funeral service, Washington National Cathedral
    5 April............... Departure ceremony, Washington National Cathedral
    5 April............... Main funeral procession
    5 April............... Burial service, Arlington National Cemetery
Military escort units, main funeral procession
  Total: 2 bands, 3 battalions, 4 companies
  Composition, active armed forces
    Army: 1 band; 1 battalion, U.S. Military Academy (400); 1 company (42)
    Marine Corps: 1 company (42)
    Navy: 1 battalion, U.S. Naval Academy (400); 1 company (42)
    Air Force: 1 band, 1 air cadet battalion (400), 1 company (42)

APPENDIX E–3—SPECIAL MILITARY FUNERAL FOR FORMER
ARMY CHIEF OF STAFF GENERAL PEYTON C. MARCH
13–18 APRIL 1955

Primary responsibility for funeral arrangements
  Commanding General of the Military District of Washington
Chronology of ceremonies
  13 April.............. Date of death
  18 April.............. Main funeral procession
  18 April.............. Burial service, Arlington National Cemetery
Military escort units, main funeral procession
  Total: 2 bands, 1 battalion, 7 companies
  Composition, active armed forces
    Army: 1 band; 1 battalion, U.S. Military Academy; 1 infantry company; 1 artillery battery; 1
      armored company
    Marine Corps: 1 band, 1 company
    Navy: 1 company
    Air Force: 1 squadron
    Servicewomen (composite): 1 company

APPENDIX E–4—SPECIAL MILITARY FUNERAL FOR
DEPUTY SECRETARY OF DEFENSE DONALD A. QUARLES
8–12 MAY 1959

Primary responsibility for funeral arrangements
  Commanding General of the Military District of Washington
Chronology of ceremonies
        8 May............ Date of death
    11–12 May............ Period of repose, Bethlehem Chapel, Washington National Cathedral
       12 May............ Funeral service, Washington National Cathedral
       12 May............ Departure ceremony, Washington National Cathedral
       12 May............ Main funeral procession
       12 May............ Burial service, Arlington National Cemetery
Military escort units, main funeral procession
  Total: 1 band, 5 platoons
  Composition, active armed forces
    Army: 1 platoon (26)
    Marine Corps: 1 platoon (26)
    Navy: 1 platoon (26)
    Air Force: 1 band, 1 platoon (26)
    Coast Guard: 1 platoon (26)

APPENDIX E–5—SPECIAL MILITARY FUNERAL FOR FORMER
CHIEF OF NAVAL OPERATIONS FLEET ADMIRAL WILLIAM D. LEAHY
20–23 JULY 1959

Primary responsibility for funeral arrangements
    Commandant of the Potomac River Naval Command
Chronology of ceremonies
        20 July . . . .   Date of death
        22 July . . . .   Arrival ceremony, Washington National Cathedral
    22–23 July . . . .   Period of repose, Bethlehem Chapel, Washington National Cathedral
        23 July . . . .   Funeral service, Washington National Cathedral
        23 July . . . .   Departure ceremony, Washington National Cathedral
        23 July . . . .   Main funeral procession
        23 July . . . .   Burial service, Arlington National Cemetery
Military escort units, main funeral procession
    Total: 1 band, 5 companies
    Composition, active armed forces
        Army: 1 company (89)
        Marine Corps: 1 company (89)
        Navy: 1 band, 1 company (89)
        Air Force: 1 company (89)
        Coast Guard: 1 company (89)

APPENDIX E–6—SPECIAL MILITARY FUNERAL FOR
FLEET ADMIRAL WILLIAM F. HALSEY, JR.
16–20 AUGUST 1959

Primary responsibility for funeral arrangements
  Commandant of the Potomac River Naval Command
Chronology of ceremonies
        16 August.......... Date of death
        19 August.......... Arrival ceremony, Naval Air Station, Washington
        19 August.......... Procession to Washington National Cathedral
        19 August.......... Arrival ceremony, Washington National Cathedral
     19–20 August.......... Period of repose, Bethlehem Chapel, Washington National Cathedral
        20 August.......... Departure ceremony, Washington National Cathedral
        20 August.......... Main funeral procession
        20 August.......... Burial service, Arlington National Cemetery
Military escort units, main funeral procession
  Total: 1 band, 5 companies
  Composition, active armed forces
    Army: 1 company (89)
    Marine Corps: 1 company (89)
    Navy: 1 band, 1 company (89)
    Air Force: 1 company (89)
    Coast Guard: 1 company (89)

APPENDIX E–7—SPECIAL MILITARY FUNERAL FOR
GENERAL OF THE ARMY GEORGE C. MARSHALL
16–20 OCTOBER 1959

Primary responsibility for funeral arrangements
  Commanding General of the Military District of Washington
Chronology of ceremonies
    16 October......... Date of death
    19 October......... Procession from S. H. Hines Funeral Home to Washington National
                        Cathedral
    19 October......... Arrival ceremony, Washington National Cathedral
 19–20 October......... Period of repose, Bethlehem Chapel, Washington National Cathedral
    20 October......... Departure ceremony, Washington National Cathedral
    20 October......... Procession to Fort Myer Chapel
    20 October......... Arrival ceremony, Fort Myer Chapel
    20 October......... Funeral service, Fort Myer Chapel
    20 October......... Departure ceremony, Fort Myer Chapel
    20 October......... Procession to gravesite, Arlington National Cemetery
    20 October......... Private burial service, Arlington National Cemetery
Honor guard units, Fort Myer Chapel ª
  Total: 1 band, 1 platoon
  Composition, active armed forces
    Army: 1 band
    Composites: 1 joint service platoon (31)

ª Ceremonies did not include a main funeral procession with a military escort.

APPENDIX E-8—SPECIAL MILITARY FUNERAL FOR SECRETARY OF
THE NAVY-DESIGNATE JOHN T. MCNAUGHTON,
SARAH MCNAUGHTON, AND THEODORE MCNAUGHTON
19–25 JULY 1967

Primary responsibility for funeral arrangements
  Commanding General of the Military District of Washington (at the request of the Commandant,
    Naval District of Washington, who was responsible under current funeral policies)
Chronology of Ceremonies
  19 July . . . .   Date of death
  24 July . . . .   Arrival ceremony, Andrews Air Force Base
  25 July . . . .   Arrival ceremony, Washington National Cathedral
  25 July . . . .   Funeral service, Washington National Cathedral
  25 July . . . .   Departure ceremony, Washington National Cathedral
  25 July . . . .   Main funeral procession
  25 July . . . .   Burial service, Arlington National Cemetery
Military escort units, main funeral procession
  Total: 1 band, 5 companies
  Composition, active armed forces
    Army: 1 company (66)
    Marine Corps: 1 company (66)
    Navy: 1 band, 1 company (66)
    Air Force: 1 company (66)
    Coast Guard: 1 company (66)

Appendix F

Summaries of Combined Services
Full Honor Funerals

APPENDIX F–1—COMBINED SERVICES FULL HONOR FUNERAL FOR
FORMER DEPUTY SECRETARY OF DEFENSE STEPHEN T. EARLY
11–14 AUGUST 1951

Primary responsibility for funeral arrangements
  Commanding General of the Military District of Washington
Chronology of ceremonies
      11 August.......... Date of death
    11–14 August.......... Period of repose, Gawler's funeral establishment, Washington
      14 August.......... Funeral service, Washington National Cathedral
      14 August.......... Main funeral procession
      14 August.......... Burial service, Arlington National Cemetery
Military escort units, main funeral procession
  Total: 1 band, 4 companies
  Composition, active armed forces
    Army: 1 band, 1 company (90)
    Marine Corps: 1 company (90)
    Navy: 1 company (90)
    Air Force: 1 company (90)

Appendix F–2—Combined Services Full Honor Funeral for Former Secretary of War Robert P. Patterson 22–25 January 1952

Primary responsibility for funeral arrangements
  Commanding General of the Military District of Washington
    Ceremonies in New York: Commanding General of the First Army
    Ceremonies in Washington: Commanding General of the Military District of Washington
Chronology of ceremonies
  22 January............ Date of death
  24 January............ Period of repose, 7th Regiment Armory, New York
  25 January............ Funeral service, Washington National Cathedral
  25 January............ Main funeral procession
  25 January............ Burial service, Arlington National Cemetery
Military escort units, main funeral procession
  Total: 1 band, 4 companies
  Composition, active armed forces
    Army: 1 band, 1 company
    Marine Corps: 1 company
    Navy: 1 company
    Air Force: 1 company

APPENDIX F–3—COMBINED SERVICES FULL HONOR FUNERAL FOR
FORMER ARMY CHIEF OF STAFF GENERAL CHARLES P. SUMMERALL
14–17 MAY 1955

Primary responsibility for funeral arrangements
  Commanding General of the Military District of Washington
Chronology of ceremonies
    14 May............... Date of death
    17 May............... Funeral service, chapel, Fort Myer, Virginia
    17 May............... Main funeral procession
    17 May............... Burial service, Arlington National Cemetery
Military escort units, main funeral procession
  Total: 1 band; 4 companies; 1 detachment of cadets, The Citadel
  Composition
    Active armed forces
      Army: 1 band, 1 company
      Marine Corps: 1 company
      Navy: 1 company
      Air Force: 1 company
    Other
      The Citadel: 1 detachment (10)

Appendix G

Summary of Special Full Honor Funeral for General Walter Bedell Smith
9-14 August 1961

Primary responsibility for funeral arrangements
  Commanding General of the Military District of Washington
Chronology of ceremonies
    9 August............ Date of death
    14 August............ Procession from Gawler's funeral establishment to Fort Myer Chapel
    14 August............ Arrival ceremony, Fort Myer Chapel
    14 August............ Funeral service, Fort Myer Chapel
    14 August............ Departure ceremony, Fort Myer Chapel
    14 August............ Procession to gravesite, Arlington National Cemetery
    14 August............ Private burial service, Arlington National Cemetery
Honor guard units, Fort Myer Chapel [a]
  Total: 1 band, 1 platoon
  Composition, active armed forces
    Army: 1 band (32)
    Composites: 1 joint service platoon (32)

---

[a] Ceremonies did not include a main funeral procession with a military escort.

Appendix H

Summary of Full Honor (Company) Funeral for Rear Admiral Richard E. Byrd
11-14 March 1957

Primary responsibility for funeral arrangements
  Bureau of Naval Personnel, Department of the Navy
Chronology of ceremonies
  11 March . . . . Date of death
  14 March . . . . Arrival ceremony, Union Station, Washington
  14 March . . . . Procession to Fort Myer Chapel
  14 March . . . . Arrival ceremony, Fort Myer Chapel
  14 March . . . . Funeral service, Fort Myer Chapel
  14 March . . . . Departure ceremony, Fort Myer Chapel
  14 March . . . . Main funeral procession
  14 March . . . . Burial service, Arlington National Cemetery
Military escort units, main funeral procession
  Total: 1 band, 1 company
  Composition, active armed forces
    Navy: 1 band
    Composites: 1 company, bluejackets and marines

Appendix I

Summaries of Funerals Without Formal Classification

APPENDIX I-1—FUNERAL FOR FORMER ARMY CHIEF OF STAFF
GENERAL MALIN CRAIG
25–30 JULY 1945

Primary responsibility for funeral arrangements
   Funeral was private. Support needed by the family was supplied by the War Department.
Chronology of ceremonies [a]
25 July.	Date of death
30 July.	Private funeral service, chapel, Fort Myer, Virginia
30 July.	Private burial service, Arlington National Cemetery

[a] The ceremonies for General Craig did not include a main funeral procession with a military escort.

APPENDIX I–2—FUNERAL FOR SENATOR ROBERT A. TAFT
31 JULY–4 AUGUST 1953[a]

Primary responsibility for funeral arrangements
   U.S. Senate officials
Chronology of ceremonies [b]
   31 July............... Date of death
    2 August............ Arrival ceremony, Washington National Airport
    2 August............ Procession to U.S. Capitol
    2 August............ Lying in state, U.S. Capitol
    3 August............ Memorial service, U.S. Capitol
    3 August............ Procession to Washington National Airport
    4 August............ Private funeral service, Indian Hill Church, Cincinnati, Ohio
    4 August............ Private burial service, Indian Hill Church Cemetery, Cincinnati, Ohio

---

[a] Referred to as a State Funeral by Senate officials but not so designated by the President, the single authority for ordering a state ceremony.
[b] The ceremonies for Senator Taft did not include a main funeral procession with military escort.

Appendix I–3—Funeral for Senator Styles Bridges
26–29 November 1961[a]

Primary responsibility for funeral arrangements
  Adjutant General, state of New Hampshire (for the public funeral service)
Chronology of ceremonies
          26 November....... Date of death
          28 November....... Private funeral service, East Concord, New Hampshire
          28 November....... Main funeral procession
          28 November....... Arrival ceremony, state capitol, Concord, New Hampshire
      28–29 November....... Period of repose, state capitol, Concord, New Hampshire
          29 November....... Public funeral service, state capitol, Concord, New Hampshire
          29 November....... Departure ceremony, state capitol, Concord, New Hampshire
          29 November....... Procession to Pine Grove Cemetery, East Concord, New Hampshire
          29 November....... Burial service, Pine Grove Cemetery, East Concord, New Hampshire
Military escort units, main funeral procession
  Total: 1 band, 1 platoon
  Composition, active armed forces
    Army: 18th Army Band (27), 1 platoon (approximately 30)

[a] Referred to as a State Funeral because of ceremonies held in the New Hampshire state capitol.

APPENDIX I–4—FUNERAL FOR SENATOR ROBERT F. KENNEDY
6–8 JUNE 1968

Primary responsibility for funeral arrangements
   Members and representatives of the Kennedy family. Also involved were the Assistant Secretary of
   Defense (Manpower and Reserve Affairs), the Under Secretary of State, and the Commanding
   General of the Military District of Washington.
Chronology of ceremonies *
      6 June.............   Date of death
   6–8 June.............   Period of repose, St. Patrick's Cathedral, New York
      8 June.............   Funeral service, St. Patrick's Cathedral, New York
      8 June.............   Procession to Pennsylvania Station, New York
      8 June.............   Arrival ceremony, Union Station, Washington
      8 June.............   Procession to Arlington National Cemetery
      8 June.............   Burial service, Arlington National Cemetery

* The ceremonies for Senator Kennedy did not include a main funeral procession with military escort.

U.S. GOVERNMENT PRINTING OFFICE: 1972 O—424-140